Fintech and Cryptocurrency

Scrivener Publishing
100 Cummings Center, Suite 541J
Beverly, MA 01915-6106

Publishers at Scrivener
Martin Scrivener (martin@scrivenerpublishing.com)
Phillip Carmical (pcarmical@scrivenerpublishing.com)

Fintech and Cryptocurrency

Edited by
Mohd Naved
V. Ajantha Devi
and
Aditya Kumar Gupta

WILEY

This edition first published 2023 by John Wiley & Sons, Inc., 111 River Street, Hoboken, NJ 07030, USA and Scrivener Publishing LLC, 100 Cummings Center, Suite 541J, Beverly, MA 01915, USA
© 2023 Scrivener Publishing LLC
For more information about Scrivener publications please visit www.scrivenerpublishing.com.

Wiley Global Headquarters
111 River Street, Hoboken, NJ 07030, USA

For details of our global editorial offices, customer services, and more information about Wiley products visit us at www.wiley.com.

Limit of Liability/Disclaimer of Warranty
While the publisher and authors have used their best efforts in preparing this work, they make no representations or warranties with respect to the accuracy or completeness of the contents of this work and specifically disclaim all warranties, including without limitation any implied warranties of merchantability or fitness for a particular purpose. No warranty may be created or extended by sales representatives, written sales materials, or promotional statements for this work. The fact that an organization, website, or product is referred to in this work as a citation and/or potential source of further information does not mean that the publisher and authors endorse the information or services the organization, website, or product may provide or recommendations it may make. This work is sold with the understanding that the publisher is not engaged in rendering professional services. The advice and strategies contained herein may not be suitable for your situation. You should consult with a specialist where appropriate. Neither the publisher nor authors shall be liable for any loss of profit or any other commercial damages, including but not limited to special, incidental, consequential, or other damages. Further, readers should be aware that websites listed in this work may have changed or disappeared between when this work was written and when it is read.

Library of Congress Cataloging-in-Publication Data

ISBN 978-1-119-90481-6

Front cover images supplied by Pixabay.com
Cover design by Russell Richardson

Set in size of 11pt and Minion Pro by Manila Typesetting Company, Makati, Philippines

Printed in the USA

10 9 8 7 6 5 4 3 2 1

Contents

4 Adoption of Fintech: A Paradigm Shift Among Millennials as a Next Normal Behaviour 59

Pushpa A., Jaheer Mukthar K. P., Ramya U., Edwin Hernan Ramirez Asis and William Rene Dextre Martinez

Preface

The rise of cryptocurrency and financial technology (fintech) has drastically changed the way people think and use money. This new type of innovation involves the use of software and other technologies to improve and automate the financial services industry. Some of these include online lending platforms and financial software.

Unlike traditional financial transactions, which are usually controlled by a central bank or government, cryptocurrencies use cryptography to ensure that all transactions are secure. This type of digital currency is decentralized. The rise of cryptocurrency and fintech has been attributed to the technological advancements that have occurred in the financial industry over the past decade. These changes have led to the emergence of numerous startups that have disrupted the traditional financial sector. The rise of cryptocurrencies has raised various questions about the role of central bank and the traditional currency.

Despite the various advantages of cryptocurrencies and fintech, they still have a number of risks that they can potentially affect. For instance, due to the lack of regulation, the lack of proper supervision has led to the emergence and manipulation of market prices and fraud. In addition, the rapid pace of innovation in the financial industry has raised concerns that these technologies could potentially displace thousands of jobs. Due to the rapid emergence and evolution of cryptocurrencies and fintech, policy-makers and the public have become more aware of the potential impact of these innovations on the financial industry. This book explores the history and development of these technologies. It also aims to provide an overview of the multiple potential uses of these innovations.

In this book, we have investigated the various players in the financial industry and examine the potential impacts of these innovations on the economy and consumers. We will also talk about the challenges and risks that have emerged in the space. This book aims to provide a comprehensive understanding of the various aspects of cryptocurrency and financial technology. It will also help financial professionals and technology enthusiasts understand the potential of these innovations. Digital currencies, decentralization of money, and the growth of new technologies like blockchain, the Internet of Things, and machine learning have produced new opportunities and difficulties for banking and finance, as well as users of these services in electronic commerce. New banking and finance technologies may improve operational efficiency, risk management, compliance, and client pleasure, but they can decrease barriers and introduce new concerns, such as cybersecurity risk.

Cryptocurrencies with smart contracts for payments and trading, as well as AI systems with adaptive algorithms that allow picture and speech recognition, expert judgement, group categorization, and forecasting in a variety of fields, are instances of increased automation. Simultaneously, the potentials pose risks and raise regulatory concerns. The rise of blockchain technology and its widespread use have had a significant impact on the operation and management of digital systems. At the same time, researchers and practitioners have paid close attention to digital finance. Blockchain's first applications were limited to the production of digital currency, but it has now been expanded to include financial and commercial applications. Innovative digital finance has had a huge impact on business and society since it has been extensively adopted by businesses and consumers (e.g., digital payment, crowdfunding, digital lending, supply chain finance, and robotic consulting).

The Chapter 1 "**Evolution of Fintech in Financial Era**" discuss FinTech enables the individual to take appropriate decisions regarding financial services during a reasonable period of time and can be used by individuals as well as businesses for tracking and managing the financial needs. The aim of the paper is to study the various related concepts of FinTech as well as how it works in financial era. The focus is also given to analyze various tools and techniques which can be used in this innovative financial technique. The estimation of future framework regarding FinTech is also incorporated in the study along with its evolution in financial era. The study will provide deep insight into FinTech as it is a U-Turn for the banking mechanism and will play a major role transforming the financial world digitally.

The evolution of financial technology, or fintech, has had a significant impact on the financial industry in recent years. From mobile banking to cryptocurrency, fintech has revolutionized the way we access and use financial services. In this chapter, we will explore the history and development of fintech, as well as its current and future role in the financial industry.

We will also delve into the potential challenges and opportunities that fintech presents for traditional financial institutions, as well as for consumers and businesses. This chapter aims to provide a comprehensive overview of the evolution of fintech in the financial era, and to shed light on its potential to shape the future of finance.

Chapter 2 **"Digital Transformation of Financial Services in the Era of Fintech"** discuss a conceptual framework highlighting the growth of the financial technology sector. It starts with the concept of digital transformation and how it has impacted the various stakeholders. Our conceptual framework allows us to define FinTech- financial technology and then construct a taxonomy of the various FinTech domains. We apply the notion of digital transformation to the financial sector to better understand where the FinTech concept began and, where it is headed, how Digital transformation has acted as a significant change agent in the fintech sector. Fintech is one of the most critical developments in the financial sector with fast expansion, fueled mainly by favorable legislation, sharing economy and information technology which has created innovative value creation and appropriation pathways for the financial industry. In most countries worldwide, Fintech is rapidly becoming the go-to financial system.

Chapter 3 **"Reshaping Banking with Digital Technologies"** The banking sector has gone a long way to come into its present form. It is still undergoing changes due to the introduction of various technologies. The digitization in the year 2000 was a step hard to move but now the people are more open to changes and willing to adopt technologies for the sake of convenience. This chapter discusses the banking sector's adoption of Artificial Intelligence (AI), the evolution of fintech, the changes brought by fintech in banking industry and the challenges which the fintech is facing nowadays. The chapter discusses in-depth, the deployment of AI tools like automation RPA, iSaaS and bots. It focuses the areas in banking where AI applications are used and how. Though the changes have made traditional banking look more beautiful ad user friendly, the constant changes in the technology will ultimately define the future.

Chapter 4 **"Adoption of Fintech: A Paradigm Shift Among Millennials as a Next Normal Behaviour"** The pandemic has put the world into a global health crisis tipping to a paradigm shift in consumer's behaviour towards financial activities. People have adapted themselves to a new pattern in financial transactions like contactless payments, cashless transactions, online transactions and many more. There are greater chances for the end users to continue usage of fintech services during the next normal life (post Covid-19) as they have become familiar with the usage and convenience of fintech services. There is a need for examining the characteristics that control the user's adoption intention of fintech payments apps during and post covid-19. Review of literature indicates that earlier experiments did not measured influence of Covid-19 (pandemic) on the behaviour of the clients. Past studies indicate lack of literature in this topic of study. The study implies to provide insightful hindsight to the existing literature and business community to tap the rural markets that accounts to only 22-28% of India population having access to internet and frame strategies to improve financial infrastructure with financial literacy.

Chapter 5 "**A Comprehensive Study of Cryptocurrencies as a Financial Asset: Major Topics and Market Trends**" The article comprises a set of theoretical and methodological approaches to studying the concept of "cryptocurrencies as a financial asset and market trends." and identifies some trends of development of the real sector in the project financing market. This paper provides a systematic review of the empirical literature based on the major topics that have been associated with the market for cryptocurrencies since their development as a financial asset. It also presents an overview of the advantages of current trends in the market. Each influences the perception of the role of cryptocurrencies as a credible investment asset class and legitimate value. We posit that cryptocurrencies may perform some useful functions and add economic value, but there are reasons to favor the regulation of the market. While this would go against the original libertarian rationale behind cryptocurrencies, it appears a necessary step to improve social welfare.

Chapter 6 "**Customers' Satisfaction and Continuance Intention to Adopt Fintech Services: Developing Countries' Perspective**" Finance Technology (Fintech) has emerged as the current trend in the financial world. Fintech services gain popularity from the increasing adoption by organizations and consumers. By applying empirical research, this chapter aims to explore the important factors influencing consumer satisfaction and continuance intention to adopt Fintech services. As previous studies on customers' behavioral intention to adopt Fintech were mostly conducted in the context of developed countries, there is a paucity of research in the developing countries' perspective. To address the research gap, this study focused on five selected developing countries, namely Malaysia, Indonesia, India, Nigeria and Philippines. Drawing on the extended Technology Acceptance Model (TAM) for the proposed research model, customer innovativeness, hedonic motivation, perceived usefulness, perceived ease of use, system quality and technology selfefficacy have positive effect on customer satisfaction and subsequently, continuance intention to adopt Fintech. The findings recommend that Fintech service providers to develop effective strategic frameworks to build consumer satisfaction and encourage their continuance intention to adopt Fintech.

Chapter 7 "**Fintech Apps: An Integral Tool in Titivating Banking Operations**" Inception of fin-tech companies like Google pay, Paytm,

Phone pe, Bharat pe, BHIM, amazon pay, mobikwik, paytm money, upstox, grow and payment banks like Airtel, Vodafone idea, Jio. The services offered by these fin-tech companies are endless. It has become essential for everyone who's carrying out online transactions like buying and selling financial products, investing in IPO, starting SIP in mutual funds, exchanging currency, opening new international bank accounts, and receiving financial advice are forced to use the possible apps of fin tech companies. The study examines the influence of fin-tech apps on the revenue system of the Indian banks through the expansion of the customer base and the frequency of usage. Every transaction done through the fin tech apps generates revenue to the bank indirectly. This study tries to identify key high influenced fin tech app that contributes to the operational revenue of the bank. The frequently and most widely used fin-tech app by the customers are considered to conduct the study. The primary data is used for the study and sample considered for the study is around 390 respondents. In addition we also identify the factors that makes the customer to use the app frequently which is taken from the previous studies like network speed, security factors, ease of handling, additional freebies and services, support system, etc. Here we also measure the usage of non-banking services through these apps. The tools used here are basic statistical analysis like correlation between the factors and the frequency of usage and Multiple Linear regression and SEM to identify the high impact factors on the increased frequency of usage. The result of the study would deliver which of the Indian banks has used the fin-tech companies to the maximum extent

Chapter 8 "**Analytical Study of Fin-Tech in Banking: A Utility Model**" India is the 5th largest growing developing country among the globe, and undoubtedly it is fastest growing itself into the Fin-tech market in recent years too. Paperless loaning, portable banking, secure installment passages, versatile wallets, and different ideas are now being taken on in India. The ongoing paper is focusing on understanding the purpose of Fin-tech for the banking sector in India. The author analyses the developments of Fin-tech trends, especially in Indian banking sectors. The authors additionally attempted to figure out the quantity of variables influencing clients' aims to utilize these services with the goal that the Indian financial area will further develop its Fin-tech framework. To realize this, the information gathered through an overview of clients of banks in Chandigarh,, which ranks first or top performer in SDG Index among union territories. The Index for Sustainable Development Goals (SDGs) evaluates the progress on three key parameters viz social, economic and environmental. The information is gathered from the time period of January 2022 to February 2022 through survey questionnaire. The Sample size is 400 customers of banks located in Tricity-a good economic sector of India. To analyze the information, the author utilized multivariate regression to appraise the model which is used in this research. The outcomes show that Fin-tech service is vital for the Indian financial area specially banking sectors. The study has found the success factors that positively and significantly impact the Willingness of clients to use Fin-tech services through banks with the help of multivariate regression. The study has found the success factors that positively and significantly impact the Willingness of clients to use Fin-tech services with the help of multivariate regression. The factors which identified are Perceived Utility (PU), Sensible Usability (SU), Customer Belief (CU), and social implications (SOI). With the help offactors identified banks need to pay attention to these elements more so that they can work on the convenience of Fin-tech benefits more. Based on discoveries, banks might have a premise to revise the nature of Fin-tech services. Moreover, the outcomes are additionally significant for policymakers and researchers.

Chapter 9 "**Is Digital Currency a Payment Disruption Mechanism?**" Digital economies are omnipresent, evident, and inhabit every sphere of human existence. Blockchain technology has changed how private currencies such as bitcoin and Ethereum are traded in open markets. To strengthen and protect the economic & financial system against such private currencies, the central banks around the world have leaped to introduce their own Central Bank Digital Currency (CBDC) for phasing out with high technology transformations. The present paper will be a first of its kind attempt to capture the perceptions and real-time issues of common people in the implementation of CBDC in a large country like India. As CBDC is still in its pilot phase of implementation, researchers have used the bottom-up approach to capture the requisite information from the common man view and the thematic analysis method was used to finalize the variables - financial literacy & inclusion, infrastructure, technical know-how, trust & belief in the system, and acceptance level for further discussion. The result analysis highlights, that government and implementing agencies of CBDC should ensure to reach the unreached population, especially in Tier-2 & 3 cities with proper technology infrastructure, and frequently hold awareness/orientation campaigns to realize the benefits of financial inclusion and easy adaptation of digital currency.

Chapter 10 "**Investor Sentiment Driving Crypto-Trade in India**" describe the key factors driving the investor sentiments towards trading in the highly volatile cryptocurrencies. It attempts to gain insight into the reasoning behind the investor decision to trade in them. Extensive review of literature sheds light on the factors driving investment in cryptocurrencies.

It is evident that the awareness levels for crypto, the future of crypto investments and the potential returns that they are offering have created a huge interest among the general public. The reasoning behind trading and investing in cryptocurrencies are also unique in their nature. The adoption of taxation policies by the government although may seem like a deterrent however, the 'Fear-of-Missing-Out' or 'FOMO' seems to have caught hold of the investors in pushing such investment decisions. The sample consists of the retail investor and the investment advisors in India using the structured questionnaire. Stratified Sampling Technique was utilized for the purposes of this study. The Independent Samples t-test was used to analyse the data and final results were interpreted from them. The results showcase certain parameters such as awareness, promotion, global acceptance, future of investment, 'Fear-of-Missing-Out' or 'FOMO' etc. as some of the factors driving trade and investment in cryptocurrencies. There are significant differences in sentiments of Retail Investors and Investment Advisors. Gender also plays a role in sentiments driving these investment decisions and finally education levels of individuals are also critical as well.

Chapter 11 "**Applications of Digital Technologies and Artificial Intelligence in Cryptocurrency - A Multi-Dimensional Perspective**" enlighten the basic idea behind cryptocurrency is that it is a network-based, totally virtual exchange medium that utilizes cryptographic algorithms such as Secure Hash Algorithm 2 (SHA-2) and Message Digest 5 (MD5) to secure the data. Transactions within the blockchain era are secure, transparent, traceable, and irreversible. Cryptocurrencies have gained a reputation in practically all sectors, including the monetary sector, due to these properties. The uncertainty and dynamism of their expenses, however, hazard investments substantially despite cryptocurrencies' growing popularity amongst approval bodies. Studying cryptocurrency charge prediction is fast becoming a trending subject matter in the global research community. Several device mastering and deep mastering algorithms, like Gated Recurrence Units (GRUs), Neural nets (NNs), and nearly short-term memory, were employed by the scientists to analyze and forecast cryptocurrency prices. As a part of this chapter, we discuss numerous aspects of cryptographic protection and their related issues. Specifically, the research addresses the state-of-the-art by examining the underlying consensus mechanism, cryptocurrency, attack style, and applications of cryptocurrencies from a unique perspective. Secondly, we investigate the usability of blockchain generation by examining the behavioral factors that influence customers' decision to use blockchain-based technology. To identify the best crypto mining strategy, the research employs an Analytic Hierarchy Process (AHP) and Fuzzy-TOPSIS hybrid analytics framework.

Furthermore, it identifies the top-quality mining methods by evaluating providers' overall performance during cryptocurrency mining.

Chapter 12 "**A Study on the Influence of Personality on Savings and Investment in Cryptos**" explains the paradigm shift requires spreading the light of decentralized ledger technology, extraordinarily implementing cryptocurrencies, and being visible as a game-changer. Blockchain technology, along with cryptocurrencies like Bitcoin, Ethereum, and Litecoin, is a tool for global economic transformation that is rapidly gaining traction in the finance industry. However, these technologies have had low popularity in the consumer market. Many platforms have been misunderstood and ignored when there is an obvious hole in among them.

Within the past few years, international stakeholders, governments, and regulators have been diversifying options for investing in cryptocurrencies. No matter what cryptocurrency device shape is used, the device can be viewed as a component of a specific Blockchain class and the functions it can perform within an economic ecosystem can be customized. The perception of cryptocurrencies has been influenced by the prominent technology underlying them. This has led to many challenges, such as security threats, economic instability, and a lack of standardized practices. Additionally, consumers do not seem to be familiar with those technologies. On many platforms, there is a clean hole in among that is no longer being considered and is being misunderstood.

The basic idea behind cryptocurrency is that it is a network-based, totally virtual exchange medium that utilizes cryptographic algorithms such as Secure Hash Algorithm 2 (SHA-2) and Message Digest 5 (MD5) to secure the data. Transactions within the blockchain era are secure, transparent, traceable, and irreversible. Cryptocurrencies have gained a reputation in practically all sectors, including the monetary sector, due to these properties. The uncertainty and dynamism of their expenses, however, hazard investments substantially despite cryptocurrencies' growing popularity amongst approval bodies. Studying cryptocurrency charge prediction is fast becoming a trending subject matter in the global research community. Several device mastering and deep mastering algorithms, like Gated Recurrence Units (GRUs), Neural nets (NNs), and nearly short-term memory, were employed by the scientists to analyze and forecast cryptocurrency prices. As a part of this chapter, we discuss numerous aspects of cryptographic protection and their related issues. Specifically, the research addresses the state-of-the-art by examining the underlying consensus mechanism, cryptocurrency, attack style, and applications of cryptocurrencies from a unique perspective. Secondly, we investigate the usability of blockchain generation by examining the behavioral factors that influence customers' decision to use blockchain-based technology. To identify the best crypto mining strategy, the research employs an Analytic Hierarchy Process (AHP) and Fuzzy-TOPSIS hybrid analytics framework. Furthermore, it identifies the top-quality mining methods by evaluating providers' overall performance during cryptocurrency mining.

Crypto currency is a digital currency that can be usedin the same way-like traditional currencyas a second hand. It uses encryption to secure its transactions, control the growth of a single form of coin, and track every transaction across the whole network. A survey of 434 Indian investors was conducted. In addition to socio-demographic characteristics study related to the human populations gender, income, age, and education, financial behavior (savings, investment) were collected and analyzed. The purpose to invest in crypto currencies is impervious by socio-demographic characteristics or financial literacy. This study looks into the impact of behavioral and socio-demographic characteristics on investors' intentions to invest in crypto currencies. This article creates an attempt to scan the impact of investors' personalities on their investment behaviour. Financial advisors would benefit from studying the elements that control the behaviour of investors belonging to an assortment of personality groups in order to edify individual investors found on their personality type and create investor programs for them.

Chapter 13 "**Deep Neural Network in Security: A Novel Robust CAPTCHA Model**" The CAPTCHA verifies that the user is a human by using a password to strengthen personal identification security on the web services. Web services can be made vulnerable by automated attacks on websites. CAPTCHA is a well-known security method for protecting websites from being attacked by automated attack tools. When a CAPTCHA is given a high level of distortion to make it resistant to automated attacks, it becomes difficult for humans to recognise it. The problem can be addressed in a variety of ways using a neural network. Deep learning models Dense net, Mobile Net, and VGG were used to test the security in the presented research work. To assess the model's fitness, the models performed batch normalisation using the required additional layer. With loss and accuracy, the best model is visualised. The experimental findings confirmed the neural network's superiority over the current state-of-the-art technique for captcha recognition.

Chapter 14 "**Customer's Perception of Voice Bot Assistance in the Banking Industry in Malaysia**" the purpose of the chapter is to investigate customer's perception of implementing voice bot technology in the banking industry. The ongoing pandemic environment has led to limited face-to-face interaction with customers and reduced instances of going to ATMs for withdrawals. Some of the challenges that customers face is the unavailability of bank officers to attend to them, the long waiting time for services or banks are not open when they need it the most. Customer perception of the banking industry is reliant on the customer satisfaction provided. The banks should ensure to cater personalized and 24/7 multi-lingual service to their customers to retain their customers. To meet these demands, many banks in Malaysia, are now on the verge of introducing voice bots to engage their customers 24/7. The study has adopted a mixed method. The study revealed that convenience, time-saving, and perceived enjoyment are factors that drive the adoption of voice bot's assistance in the banking industry. The study also adds value to academic literature for future researchers. The study contributes insights into customer perception of voice bot assistance, and it provides practical recommendations to implement voice bots smoothly and efficiently in the banking industry.

Chapter 15 "**Application of Technology Acceptance Model (TAM) in Fintech Mobile Applications for Banking**" The rising prominence of Fintech payment services has a great impact on banking. It is increasingly becoming a global trend. Mobile payment applications and gateways are a well-liked use of Fintech services for banking. Of course, contactless payments are much more appreciated in today's world. This research paper aims to study the factors that influence customers' usage of Fintech services for banking. A descriptive and analytical study was conducted through a structured Questionnaire. The Technology Acceptance Model is used to examine the extent to the perceived usefulness, brand image, and perceived risk influence the usage of Fintech. The data have been analyzed and hypotheses have been tested by using statistical measures and quantitative methods. This study identified three factors Perceived usefulness, Brand image, and Perceived risk which influence the usage of Fintech services for banking. Perceived usefulness is the most enabling influencing factor on the usage of Fintech services. The results show that perceived usefulness and brand image have a significant positive influence on the usage of Fintech services, while perceived risks do not significantly affect the usage of Fintech services. It is expected that the findings of this empirical study would have enabled adding to the present contributions on the subject.

Chapter 16 "**Upsurge of Robo Advisors: Integrating Customer Acceptance**" discuss the rise of fintech in the digital community opens the door for companies to introduce robo advisors. Robo Advisors have emerged as a result of technological advances, and it is important to use Robo Advisors to manage and direct projects in the financial industry. Robo Advisors are automated online investment services available to both private and institutional investors. The portfolio management service is critical for the efficient distribution and use of the surplus of economic activity in large markets. These robots are programmed to eliminate the dangers of prejudice and human error. This research article is about exploring the strengths and weaknesses of robo advisers, and as opportunities and threats, especially when compared to traditional financial advisors. The current research provides a research framework to understand the acceptance of robo-advisors by investors. To evaluate the intention of customers to use the equation model of the technical structure was used to test ideas. The effects of ease of use and perceived usability are therefore important aspects of the purpose of using the service of robo advisors. The marketing strategies used should take into account the client's level of familiarity with the robots. It contributes to a better understanding of customer attitudes towards robo advisor use in FinTech. The findings of this study provide relevant research on financial institutions, banks, policy makers, asset managers, FinTech developers and financial staff/advisors to increase the acquisition of Robo Advisors through the adoption of sustainable services.

Chapter 17 "**Super Apps: The Natural Progression in Fin-Tech**" provides insights into the evolution of the concept of Super Apps, the market, key players, their business models, and their role in financial inclusion. The chapter also details the risks inherent to Super Apps and the measures to mitigate the same. Super Apps refer to an ecosystem that includes within itself a full suite of solutions such as banking, marketplace, and lifestyle services to satisfy various needs of a user. They provide a seamless and integrated experience and save them from switching between multiple individual apps. The market space for Super Apps is highly competitive, with fin-tech giants, banking companies, and big tech rivalling each other to acquire and retain consumers. The concept of a "Super App" seems to be a natural progression from the various offerings of the fin-tech sector.

Evolution of Fintech in Financial Era

Tanya Kumar and Satveer Kaur*

PCJ School of Management, Maharaja Agrasen University, Baddi (HP), India

Abstract

FinTech is one of the automated and innovative approaches which play a major role in digitalization of financial services through advancement in financial world. FinTech has wider access and can be used in various spheres of life. FinTech will also affect the financial decisions of the people which require financial as well as digital literary. FinTech enables the individual to take appropriate decisions regarding financial services during a reasonable period of time and can be used by individuals as well as businesses for tracking and managing the financial needs. The aim of the paper is to study the various related concepts of FinTech as well as how it works in financial era. The focus is also given to analyze various tools and techniques which can be used in this innovative financial technique. The estimation of future framework regarding FinTech is also incorporated in the study along with its evolution in financial era. The study will provide deep insight into FinTech as it is a u-turn for the banking mechanism and will play a major role transforming the financial world digitally.

Keywords: Artificial intelligence, blockchain technology, digitalization, financial era, financial world, FinTech

1.1 Introduction

Innovative technology which is the merger of finance and information technology is commonly known as 'FinTech.' The concept is gaining its relevance since the past five years. There is a regulated financial framework which leads to financial innovation in terms of technological advancements and tracking of needs and requirements of the individuals over a period of

---

Corresponding author: drsatveerkaur@mau.edu.in

Mohd Naved, V. Ajantha Devi, and Aditya Kumar Gupta (eds.) Fintech and Cryptocurrency, (1–12)

time [1]. FinTech is one of the automated and innovative approaches which play a major role in digitalization of financial services through advancement in financial world. It provides the win-win situation to the early adopters as it is gaining its important in modern world which is providing various opportunities to the new comers in the market. It provides the opportunities to optimize the portfolios of financial securities along with mitigation of risks over a period of time [2].

FinTech has wider access and can be used in various spheres of life. FinTech will also affect the financial decisions of the people which require financial as well as digital literary. FinTech enables the individual to take appropriate decisions regarding financial services during a reasonable period of time and can be used by individuals as well as businesses for tracking and managing the financial needs. There are numerous platforms which regulate the working of financial services and with FinTech, it would be appropriate to track them effectively. FinTech is reshaping the landscape of financial services. It offers better outcomes to the customers using the mechanism of tailoring the services using advice of the investors on the basis of customized needs of the customers at better returns in minimum inputs in terms of money as well as efforts [3].

1.2   Review of Literature

Gnanmote (2018) [4] carried an analytical study to evaluate the FinTech in Indian economy in pre as well as post Covid-19 pandemic. The study was empirical in nature and adopted quantitative method to achieve the objective. Both primary as well as secondary data was used for collection of data. Interview method using semi-structured questionnaire was the method adopted for collection of primary data from experts to have the insight towards their knowledge towards financial services using Fintech approach. It was determined that the systematic approach has gaining wider reach among the customers post-Covid which is forcing them to move towards the adoption of new technology which managing their financial mechanisms.

Kavuri & Milne (2019) [5] discussed about the related concepts of FinTech by identification of future working and growth of FinTech. Authors also tried to identify the related gaps in previous literatures as which could further help the policy makers as well as government regulators to manage the working of financial services in the economy. There were total six gaps identified by the authors in their research paper such as, dynamic organisational structure of financial services, different variants in financial intermediation, encouragement of cashless mechanism of making payments, reach of vulnerable customers in both developing as well as developed countries, introduction of artificial intelligence in data processing, emerging new financial regulations as well as technologies.

Legowo *et al.* (2020) [6] described the role and importance of FinTech mechanism in enhancing the technological framework. The study adopted descriptive as well as qualitative approach to achieve the objectives. The study employed primary as well as secondary data which provides deep-insight to the authors about the detailed scenario of FinTech and its technological framework. The primary data was collected using questionnaires which were filled by 154 respondents which were selected using convenience sampling method. The data was analysed using descriptive statistics. The theoretical framework was developed by considering three types of theory such as grand theory, middle theory and applied theory.

Philippon (2017) [7] highlighted in her research paper about issues as well as challenges faced by FinTech in India with the objective to fill the research gap among the present literatures in the area along with studying the conceptual overview of the FinTech along with its adoption among customers using digital mechanisms. The stress was also given to identify various motivators in adoption of financial technologies along with the barriers in adoption of this technological advancement in the country. It was analysed that FinTech are required to be groomed using acceptable means of regulating them using systematic approach which provides them the reasonable opportunity to grow and expand in the future horizons.

Subanidja *et al.* (2020) [8] studied the impact of FinTech on the performance of banking and financial institutions. The research study was empirical in nature which implied convenience sampling technique to draw the sample out of target population of the study. The questionnaires were used for collection of primary data. The sample size of the study was 100 respondents and the results were derived on the basis of responses gathered from them. SEM was the tool used for testing the model fit for the study using Smart PLS software. It was determined that there must be collaboration between banking system as well as financial sector to regulate the FinTech in desired manner and through which the economic growth can be initiated in the economy leading to the sustainable growth of the economy as a whole.

Zavolokina *et al.* (2016) [9] reviewed related literatures on FinTech as how it leads to financial innovation with the perspective of press media.

The study was conceptual in nature. The study implied exploratory as well as descriptive research design. The study used 829 articles which were collected from 46 different newspapers to achieve the objectives of the research study which provided the insight to the authors to gain the familiarity with the concept of FinTech and to derive the conclusions accordingly. The study was one of the first study which was being conducted to find the impact of FinTech on press media as it is one of the concepts which can be considered by using the technological aspects as well as various other practical applications of the technology in managing the financial services

1.3   Objectives and Research Methodology

The study is being conducted to achieve the following objectives such as:

1. To study the concepts and working of FinTech.
2. To analyze the tools and techniques used in FinTech.
3. To estimate the future framework of FinTech.
4. To study the evolution of FinTech in financial world.

The study is conceptual in nature and the analytical research design is followed in the study with the aim to achieve the predetermined objectives and deriving the conclusion on that basis. Secondary data is used in the study which is derived from secondary sources such as websites, blogs, journal articles, research papers and so on.

1.4   Working of FinTech

Financial markets play a major role in stabilising the Indian economy as well as regulating the economic growth by offering wide number of financial services to the people using value authentication as well as providing them the opportunity to invest their money using fair and transparent approach of FinTech as it is enabled by Artificial Intelligence. One of the commonly known adoptions of FinTech is Blockchain technology which is providing abundant services to the individuals in terms of financial innovation. There are various patents which are taking place these days in financial innovation due to new as well as existing players in the financial world [10].

There are various regulatory changes which are taking place day-by day as per the provisions of financial services. These technologies run on algorithms of automatic programs. There are various financial solutions which are the reasons behind the stability and encouragement of FinTech in modern world [11]. The collaborative practice among public as well as private stakeholders made it possible to manage the market at reasonable costs with desired level of efficiency as well as effectiveness. It is the process of managing the financial operations as well as for enabling the new financial ventures by exploring the context of FinTech in the digital world [12].

1.5   Tools and Techniques used in FinTech

FinTech can be used in making payments from one person to another or may be by one business to the next which make use of data transmission technologies, handling the user experiences and employment of data analytical techniques as well as handling the security issues among the people to make them rely on the financial services provided using FinTech. FinTech also offers advisory services using Internet of Things, advanced algorithms, automations using advanced sensors as well as artificial intelligence [13]. These are virtual trading platforms which regulate the exchange of payments in order to handle the financial aid of the individuals. There are wide number of apps which are developing day-by-day such as wealthtech and investtech which are the sub-divisions of FinTech which not require any geographical existence but are virtually registered and listed which offers the regulatory medium of exchange among the people [14].

The financing opportunities of the FinTech can be enabled using smart phones, artificial intelligence, big data, CSCW (Computer-supported cooperative work) and machine learning etc. The compliance mechanism of FinTech can be handled using robotics, drones, artificial intelligence, algorithms and so on. FinTech make use of crow funding which is one of the sources of raising the funds and management of the financial needs. There are various factoring services which can be handled using FinTech operations offering credit facilities to its clients when the need occurs. The assets can also be managed using FinTech such as social trading, robo-advice, personal financial management, investment and banking etc. These days search engine comparison can also be regulated using FinTech due to management of technological architecture using information technology is another regulator of FinTech [15].

The framework of Fintech and Cryptocurrency is presented in Figure 1.1. It has been clearly highlighted that there are different participants of Fintech platforms as well as different types of Fintech platforms. The Figure 1.1 also provides insight towards the factors that can influence the development of Fintech platforms in long run. The participants of Fintech platforms are inclusive of Fintech startups, regulators, banks, international payment system, associations of bankers as well as financiers, incubators, accelerators, vendors and so on. The types of platforms related to Fintech include mobile phone services, social media and other informational sources contributing towards financial services, cryptography, market place lending, startups and new business models, artificial intelligence, digital identification, biometrics, application programming interface, applications and other different sources. The factors on which this framework is dependent

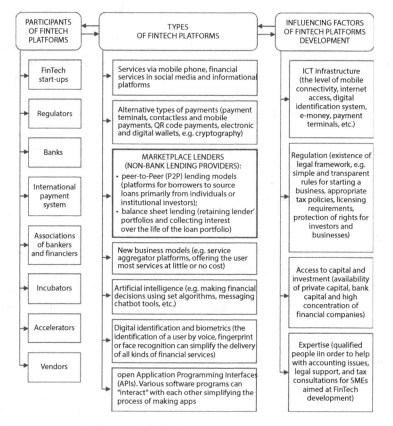

Figure 1.1 Framework of FinTech. Source: https://www.researchgate.net/figure/Theoretical-approaches-to-Fintech-platform https://www.researchgate.net/figure/Theoretical-approaches-to-Fintech-platform-basics_fig6_326468708basics_fig6_326468708.

consists of ICT infrastructure, regulatory framework related to licensing and transparency, capital access as well as investment, expertise and so on.

1.6   Future Framework of FinTech

FinTech is one of the deep-rooted deliberate actions which are changing the structure of financial services as how they are developed, perceived, promoted as well as delivered in the market and along with it how it is consumed in the market [16]. The consumers must be aware about all these practices which could help to reap the effective returns from the same. It manages the business models related to financial services which aim to deliver better as well as innovative services to their clients and making their efforts to attract the new customers in the market. It has the global reach which is emerging not only in India but in the whole world. It is the approach which is modernising the financial architecture by reorganising it as per the dynamic trends in digital era [17].

The banking functions can be regulated which handle the monetary system of the economy and the policies are regulated and managed as per the needs of the technological improvement in the field [18]. It is one of the competitive regimes which can be used by the start-ups to lead the market by tapping the less tapped area which could help them to grow as well as expand their business operations and would further benefit the economy as a whole. FinTech has very wide future which could lead to the improvements in the field of banking system as well as financial markets of India. It is one of the doors opening opportunity which is knocking the doors of the success are to be adopted at the right time to succeed and rule the market. The related norms and procedures are under development which would be based upon the related research as well as providing convenience and security to the customers.

1.7   Evolution of FinTech in Financial World

FinTech is evolving in various fields such as finance, technology, consumer behaviour ecosystem and so on [19]. The support of FinTech is based upon techno-enabled systems which help to increase their level of efficiency using customer-centric approach [20]. FinTech is the impression which is offering unique as well as transparent opportunity to the banking population by providing them the financial services without considering the intermediary at minimal cost. The non-financial players are also finding it one of the best opportunities to secure their future in the longer period of time. With the technological improvements in all the areas, the efforts are being made in the area of banking as well as finance as their various components combined to it such as financial innovation as well as financial inclusion [21].

The risks can be minimised while dealing with these transparent mechanisms which offer the required level of transparency as well as security among the investors. Financial inclusion is also gaining the due importance in the developing countries like India which helps in managing the required level of risks and cost associated while dealing with those financial services [22]. It was determined that the systematic approach has gaining wider reach among the customers post-Covid which is forcing them to move towards the adoption of new technology which managing their financial mechanisms. FinTech is providing better customer experience in the form of secured personalisation, better service speed, significant functionality, convenient to be used and uses interactive mechanism [23]. FinTech is evolving to provide attractive services to the customers ensuring effective service quality as well as functionality. It offers the 24x7 access to the financial market. There are wide number of innovative products and financial services offered by financial institutions using appropriate use of financial mechanism which also offers the easy opportunity to set up as well as register the user interface [24].

As discussed in Figure 1.2, the evolution of Fintech can be traced from 1950s because at that time, Diner's Club introduced the first universal credit card. In 1960s to 1970s, the first ATM of the world was installed by Barclays in Enfield in London. As we move to the next year in 1980s, e-trade launched their first online brokerage services and along with that at the end of same year, online tele-banking was introduced in Britain by the Nottingham Building Society. After 1990s, it was found that Standard Federal Credit

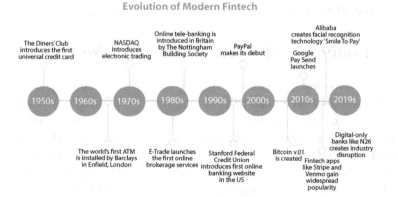

Figure 1.2 Evolution of FinTech. Source: https://financesonline.com/uploads/2019/10/ Evolution-of-Modern-Fintech-1.jpg.

Union introduced their first online banking website in the US and PayPal made its debut in the market. In the beginning of 2010, Bitcoin was created and by mid of the year Google Pay Send was launched. It was also analysed that during 2010 to 2019, Fintech has gained a due relevance in the market which is inclusive of introduction of different applications, face recognition technology by Alibaba, digitalised banking mechanism and so on.

1.8   Discussion and Conclusion

FinTech is one of the innovative approaches introduced in the field of banking system as well as financial world. There are wide number of FinTech start-ups which are taking place today which are offering numerous opportunities to the investors as it would lead to their empowerment, transparency in tracking their investments, efficiency as well as effectiveness, removal of intermediaries, accessibility to required information etc [25]. Transformation can be felt in the field of finance as well as information technology which is one of the innovative approaches which are customised according to the needs as well as requirements of the society. The study contributes to various areas of research such as finance, information technology, social sciences. The study also provides deep insights to explore in the area of FinTech to various educationists, practitioners, investors, government regulators and so on [26].

There are three generations of FinTech which can be traced in the Indian economy as ATMs were the first generation of the FinTech. While, Internet as well as Internet of Things is the second generation of FinTech and on the other hand, data enabling technologies are the third generation of FinTech in the digital world [27]. FinTech is one of the revolutionised concepts in the traditional financial services providers as they hold the money, lend the money and move the money [28]. But the legacy in the financial markets can be enabled using FinTech and its working can be traced from cryptocurrencies which are regulated using blockchain technology which is one of the parts of FinTech revolution offering countless opportunities such as buy-now-pay-later along with various peer-to-peer lending platforms to enable the automated working of FinTech platforms without any intermediary which provides them opportunity to directly meet their consistent needs over a period of time [29].

References

1. Zavolokina, L., Schwabe, G., & Dolata, M. (2016, December 14). FinTech-What's in a Name? *Zurich Open Repository and Archive*.

2. Barefoot, J. A. (2020, June). Digital Technology Risks for Finance: Dangers Embedded in Fintech and Regtech. *Harvard Kennedy School: Mossavar-Rahmani Center for Business and Government.*

3. Yuen, M. (2022, April 15). *Overview of the fintech industry: stats, trends, and companies in the ecosystem market research report.* Retrieved from https://www.insiderintelligence.com/insights/fintech-ecosystem-report/

4. Gnanmote, A. K. (2018). *FinTech Revolution in Banking: Leading the Way to Digital.* Retrieved from Infosys.

5. Kavuri, A., & Milne, A. (2019, February 09). Fintech and the Future of Financial Services: What Are the Research Gaps? *SSRN Electronic Journal.*

6. Legowo, M. B., Subanidja, S., & Sorongan, F. A. (2020, May). Role of FinTech Mechanism to Technological Innovation: A Conceptual Framework. *International Journal of Innovative Science and Research Technology, 5*(5), 35-41.

7. Philippon, T. (2017, August). *The FinTech Opportunity.* Retrieved from Monetary and Economic Development.

8. Subanidja, S., Legowo, M. B., & Sorongan, F. A. (2020, October 01). The Impact of FinTech on the Financial and Banking Sustainable Performance: Disruption or Collaboration. *ICEBE,* 01-08.

9. Zavolokina, L., Dolata, M., & Schwabe, G. (2016). The FinTech phenomenon: antecedents of financial innovation perceived by the popular press. *Financial Open,* 1-16.

10. Myzyka, B. (2022, January 17). *FinTech and Banks Future: How Financial Technology Affects the Banking Industry.* Retrieved from Tech Magic: https://www.techmagic.co/blog/fintech-and-banking/

11. Artha, B., & Jufri, A. (2020, December). Fintech: A Literature Review. *Journal Proaksi, 7*(2), 59-65.

12. Almomani, A. A., & Alomari, K. F. (2021, August 25). Financial Technology (FinTech) and its Role in Supporting the Financial and Banking Services Sector. *International Journal of Academic Research in Business and Social Sciences, 11*(8), 1793-1802.

13. Harasim, J. (2021, December 14). FinTechs, BigTechs and Banks - When Cooperation and When Competition? *Journal of Risk and Financial Management,* 1-16.

14. Walden, S. (2020, August 03). *What Is Fintech and How Does It Affect How I Bank?* Retrieved from Forbes Advisor: https://www.forbes.com/advisor/banking/what-is-fintech/

15. Nazariy, H. (2021, September 29). *The Impact of FinTech on the future of banks and financial services.* Retrieved from Geniusee: https://geniusee.com/single-blog/fintechshttps://geniusee.com/single-blog/fintechs-impact-on-the-future-of-banking-and-financial-servicesimpact-on-the-future-of-banking-and-financial-services

16. Sanmath, P. A. (2018, October). FinTech Banking - The Revolutionised Digital Banking. *International Journal of Trend in Scientific Research and Development (IJTSRD),* 172-180.

17. Sahni, T. (2022, January 11). Fintech Industry of India: A New Vogue in The Market. *International Journal of Engineering Research & Technology (IJERT)*, *10*(01).
18. Mention, A.-L. (2020, June 30). The Age of FinTech: Implications for Research, Policy and Practice. *The Journal of FinTech*, 1-25.
19. Iman, N. (2020, February 06). The rise and rise of financial technology: The good, the bad, and the verdict. *Cogent Business and Management, 7*(1).
20. Gupta, S., & Agrawal, A. (2021, December). Analytical Study of FinTech in India: Pre and Post Pandemic Covid-19. *Indian Journal of Economics and Business, 20*(3), 33-71.
21. Sahay, R., Allem, U. E., Lahreche, A., Khera, P., Ogawa, S., Bazarbash, M., *et al.* (2020). The Promise of Fintech: Financial Inclusion in the Post COVID-19 Era. *International Monetary Fund: Monetary and Capital Markets Development, 20(01)*.
22. Beck, T. (2020, July). FinTech and Financial Inclusion: Opportunities and Pitfalls. *Asian Development Bank Institute.*
23. Kiilu, N. (2018). Effect of FinTech Firms on Financial Performance of the Banking Sector in Kenya.
24. P. Krishna Priya, K. A. (2019, September). Fintech Issues and Challenges in India. *International Journal of Recent Technology and Engineering (IJRTE), 8*(3), 904-908.
25. Kagan, J. (2020, August 27). *Financial Technology – Fintech.* Retrieved from Investopedia: https://www.investopedia.com/terms/f/fintech.asp
26. Chang, V., Baudier, P., Zhang, H., Xu, Q., Zhang, J., & Arami, M. (2020, June 21). How Blockchain can impact financial services – The overview, challenges and recommendations from expert interviewees. *PubMed Central.*
27. Graham, A. (n.d.). *Fintech and Banks: How Can the Banking Industry Respond to the Threat of Disruption?* Retrieved from Finance: https://www.toptal.com/finance/investmenthttps://www.toptal.com/finance/investment-banking-freelancer/fintech-and-banksbanking-freelancer/fintech-and-banks
28. Rupeika-Apoga, R., & Thalassinos, E. I. (2020, April 02). Ideas for a Regulatory Definition of FinTech. *International Journal of Economics and Business Administration, VIII* (2), 136-154.
29. Sen, S. (2017). *Report of the Working Group on FinTech and Digital Banking.* Reserve Bank of India Central Office Mumbai.

Webliography

Fintech. (2022). *CFA Institute*: https://www.cfainstitute.org/en/research/fintech. Retrieved on 10th April, 2022 at 10:20 P.M.

FinTech and Market Structure in the COVID-19 Pandemic. (2022, March 21). *Financial Stability Board*: 1-26. Retrieved on 12th April, 2022 at 06:45 P.M.

How fintech is changing the future of traditional banking. (2020). *University of Bath*: https://online.bath.ac.uk/articles/impact-of-fintech-on-banking. Retrieved on 15th April, 2022 at 09:15 P.M.

What is Financial Technology (FinTech)? A Beginner's Guide for 2022. (n.d.). *Columbia Engineering Boot Camps*: https://bootcamp.cvn.columbia.edu/blog/what-is-fintech/ Retrieved on 14th April, 2022 at 07:55 P.M.

Fintech Framework https://www.researchgate.net/figure/Theoretical-approaches-to-Fintechhttps://www.researchgate.net/figure/Theoretical-approaches-to-Fintech-platform-basics_fig6_326468708platform-basics_fig6_326468708 Retrieved on 25th April, 2022 at 06:15 P.M.

Evolution of Fintech https://financesonline.com/uploads/2019/10/Evolution-of-Modern https://financesonline.com/uploads/2019/10/Evolution-of-Modern-Fintech-1.jpgFintech-1.jpg Retrieved on 20th April, 2022 at 08:10 P.M.

Fintech (Financial Technology). (n.d.). Retrieved from https://corporatefinance institute.com/resources/knowledge/finance/fintech-financialtechnology/

Digital Transformation of Financial Services in the Era of Fintech

Ayesha Siddiqui[1], Arti Yadav[2] and Najib H.S. Farhan[3*]

[1]Department of General Management, Universal Business School, Karjat, Maharashtra, India
[2]Department of Commerce, Ramanujan College, University of Delhi, New Delhi, India
[3]Department of Finance, Universal Business School, Karjat, Maharashtra, India

Abstract

The present chapter analyses a conceptual framework highlighting the growth of the financial technology sector. It starts with the concept of digital transformation and how it has impacted the various stakeholders. Our conceptual framework allows us to define FinTech-financial technology and then construct a taxonomy of the various FinTech domains. We apply the notion of digital transformation to the financial sector to better understand where the FinTech concept began and, where it is headed, how Digital transformation has acted as a significant change agent in the fintech sector. Fintech is one of the most critical developments in the financial sector with fast expansion, fueled mainly by favorable legislation, sharing economy and information technology which has created innovative value creation and appropriation pathways for the financial industry. In most countries worldwide, Fintech is rapidly becoming the go-to financial system.

Keywords: FinTech, digital transformation, financial services

2.1 Introduction

Innovation in finance can not only have a significant impact on financial services, but it can have an affirmative impact on the entire nation [1].

*Corresponding author: najib720000@gmail.com; Najib.farhan@ubs.org.in

Mohd Naved, V. Ajantha Devi, and Aditya Kumar Gupta (eds.) Fintech and Cryptocurrency, (13–34)
© 2023 Scrivener Publishing LLC

Finance and technological innovations are not new, and innovation in digital transformation has led to progress in terms of enhanced system connectivity, cost and power efficiency, and the creation of new and usable data [2]. Digital transformation in finance is known as Digital Financial Services and mainly depends on digital technologies for their usage and delivery to consumers. The latest advancement or innovation in digital financial services is Fintech which is highly influenced by the developments like machine learning, smart mobile phones, big data and artificial intelligence [3]. [4] has elucidated Fintech as a "technologically enabled financial innovation that could result in new business models, applications, processes, or products with an associated material effect on financial markets and institutions and the provision of financial services". The difference in scope of Fintech and traditional digital transactions is somewhat arbitrary as Fintech primarily excludes using internet banking and credit cards [5]. Still, Fintech helps overcome the impediments to utilizing traditional financial services like information asymmetry, geographical barriers, and cost [6].

In most countries worldwide, Fintech is rapidly becoming the go-to financial system. Almost all financial institutions in developed countries like the United Kingdom and the United States have adopted Fintech [7]. In developing countries, Fintech fuels growth by offering economic freedom. India, China, some African countries, Mexico and the United States, have shown the most positive effects of adopting financial services [8]. Focusing more on digital banking solutions in the Fintech industry, the annual economic growth is boosted by up to 2.2 percent [9]. In addition, nearly 300 countries worldwide have seen rapid expansion in mobile payment services along with the increase in certain developing nations; the number of individuals having payment accounts has risen to 80%, indicating a real financial revolution on par with industrialized economies [10–12].

The rapid advancements in the escalating supremacy of information and communication technologies, mobile technology, predictive analytics, mobile technology, big data, cloud infrastructure, personalization and self-learning are the Fintech movement's driving force [13]. Some analysts argue that technology and financial innovation are closely intertwined, and that economic development will eventually slow if financiers do not innovate [14]. Because information technology (IT) has made it possible to create economies of scale, the conflict between financial innovation and technology has grown [15]. In the services and manufacturing sectors, the pace of the digital transformation and the scientific conversation around business and IS research have been defined by the extent and speed of technological innovation [16]. While handling the organizational barriers and structural changes that affect the digital process's positive and negative effects, the digital transformation process comes into the picture where digital technologies lead to distractions triggering responses in strategic form from organizations that search to modify their value creation paths [17].

Therefore, the present study's core idea is to add to the literature by synthesizing the role of digital transformation and Fintech concerning financial services. This chapter provides a conceptual framework that may be utilized by investors seeking value in the FinTech sector's development. It started by defining the term FinTech-financial technology and then continued to create a taxonomy of the various FinTech areas. Investors looking to diversify their alternative investment portfolio may utilize this conceptual framework to find FinTech businesses with the most promising sectors and technology. Hence, investors might devise a strategy similar to allocating across sectors. The notion of digital transformation is applied to the financial services sector to understand better where the FinTech Revolution began and where it is headed. As we use it, digital change requires a catalyst. The Global Financial Crisis was the trigger that catapulted FinTech technologies into the spotlight. The COVID-19 pandemic is the trigger that will guarantee that the most successful FinTech technologies are broadly embraced, while those that do not offer a solution to consumers and companies will go away. Therefore, the concept of digital transformation enables us to emphasize FinTech's sensitive risk-reward balance. While money was available and values were inflated in recent years, the market shift that began in the first half of 2020 had put in motion a similar economic development to when the Dot-Com bubble crashed. Some may argue that the society didn't get the benefit from the exponential growth of e-commerce and technology, but the bubble burst has guaranteed that smart money flowed to the most promising concepts, which is expected to happen in FinTech in the coming future. Unlike earlier book chapters, this one focus only on the subject of Digital Transformation. Several ideas have been proposed. We decided that defining multiple concepts in such a short document would be inappropriate, yet there was a requirement to draw attention to Digital Transformation since few literature evaluations were undertaken when matched up to, say, the term Digital transformation. Thus, this work presents a concept of Digital Transformation depending on the review of literature, provides a basic summary of the literature, and makes some recommendations for further research.

The study is divided into various sections, starting with a brief introduction, followed by a review of literature on the concerned theme. In the third and fourth sections, an overview of the concept of digital transformation and Fintech has been given, followed by an assessment of the role of digital transformation and Fintech on the development of services in the financial aspect and the conclusion of the study.

2.2   Review of Literature

As quite a lot of banks are now shifting to the cashless, paperless and digitization processes as part of FinTech, it is swiftly changing the appearance of the banking sector. As FinTech use grows in the financial industry, academicians and research scholars are researching the opportunities and challenges FinTech is creating for the service sector. Thus, this chapter will review previous research on FinTech in two sections. The first section demonstrates the studies related to FinTech, and the second section analyses the studies related to digital transformation.

2.2.1   Studies on FinTech

Fintech is the interaction of information technology with financial services; however, the concept has been heavily explored for some time. For instance, the influence of information technology, productivity, and consumer welfare on the banking business has been discussed during the previous few decades [18]. According to [19], the financial services sector is currently undergoing consolidation, which will likely be followed by specialization-driven fragmentation. According to [20], technical progress that results in banking financial advances has implications for developments in Fintech. Since Fintech does not use conventional intermediaries while providing financial services, its interest has grown over time.

In addition, [21] distinguished between innovations in information and communication and analysed the impact on financial intermediation of technological change. Various studies compared provision associated with credit by banks and nonbanks and documented the rise of Fintech lending across countries [22]. [23] Provided a synopsis highlighting the competition faced from big technology organizations and their influence on strategies adopted by businesses. Some other studies discussed how banking got impacted by Fintech and Bigtech [24, 25]. To make certain an efficient and effective distribution of resources in the economy, ICT (Information and Communication Technology) in financial intermediation plays a key role in the financial system by transforming savings into investment. This is done by financial intermediaries through screening and monitoring of uncertain investments on behalf of the savers who cannot do so [26, 27].

Therefore, customers and the economy gain from financial institutions' forward-thinking attitudes.

Financial institutions are trying to fulfil customers' expectations by adopting advanced technologies like machine learning, artificial intelligence, and Fintech [28]. In order to have a competitive and long-term stay in the market for financial services, digital industry transformation is imperative [29].

In terms of borrowers with low risk, extra time-sensitive and less sensitive to price, Fintech organizations can charge higher rates due to the convenience of online origination [30]. Financial inclusion is also one of the considerable aspects of Fintech for undeveloped countries as well as unserved or underserved sections of the population and enterprises with small and medium sizes, and it opens the door through changing consumption, provision, and structure of financial services [3].

However, FinTech firms still have not acquired a top place in the market in terms of building paths in corporate lending to medium and large organizations [31]. Still a tiny share of total credit despite its continuous growth, for instance, in China, where Fintech has the best share of total credit activity, it still has a share of only 3% in 2017 of total credit outstanding to the nonbank sector is represented by FinTech credit [32]. It has also been observed that countries with higher income per capita tend to be more critical for FinTech credit and a less competitive banking system, such as China, the United States, South Korea, and the United Kingdom [22, 33].

[34] found that recently the news platform was seen dominated by the financial technology aspect. Fintech, taken in its broadest sense, is the incorporation of technological advancements into financial services and procedures. Recent annual numbers reveal US$135.7 billion in global fintech investments [28]. In this expanding industry, startups, established technology companies, and banks have emerged as critical participants [34–36]. Regulators and policymakers view Fintech as a chance to make the financial system more efficient, effective, and robust [37]. Fintech technologies aim to make financial services like payments, savings, credit, and insurance more accessible to the underprivileged. The inability of 1.7 billion people globally, most of whom reside in developing nations, to access these essential financial services prevents them from escaping poverty [12]. The fintech sector align with calls for creating a better world with ICTs and the innovations [38].

In addition, with changes in financial structure, the policy response is also becoming more challenging for financial services in the Fintech era. Most of the policy tools are generally aimed at objectives based on traditional financial regulation, privacy objectives concerning the data and level of competition [39]. Critical public infrastructure is mainly observed through a well-functioning financial system, and financial services providers take up an important place in that system through their role in credit intermediation and the payment system [40]. Therefore, financial services providers are legally subject to the regulations that also apply to the banking sector. The goal here is to limit the scope for regulatory arbitrage through shadow banking activities and to close the regulatory gaps between technology and services of financial nature.

Digitally including financial inclusion might offer a more thorough and perhaps quite different perspective of the development through time and across the nation. Some recent studies examine pertinent variables, such as financial transactions made on mobile devices and mobile money accounts, to determine digital financial inclusion [41, 42]. The amount of research on digital financial services (DFSs) and financial inclusion is fast expanding, with most of it concentrating on experiences in particular nations or regional advancements in Fintech activity. In their analyses of Kenya's fast adoption of mobile money and mobile phones [43] discover that mobile money significantly affects families' capacity to share risks. Most of the material now in circulation focuses on conventional financial inclusion, made possible by financial institutions like banks. This is determined by metrics that reflect the availability of and usage of conventional financial services, like the proportion of people with bank accounts and ATMs, or by combining various data into a composite index [44]. By examining pertinent indicators, such as financial transactions and mobile money accounts made on mobile phones, several recent research has evaluated the stage of digital financial inclusion [41, 45]. These metrics, however, only capture one component of digital financial inclusion at a given moment and do not provide a whole picture that combines several dimensions. Therefore, the further sections of the present chapter will try to add value to the present literature by highlighting the basic to advanced progress in the digital transformation of services related to finance, which led to the era of Fintech.

2.2.2   Studies on Digital Transformation

Over the last 20 years, data collection, transmission, and storing costs have declined due to the technological revolution. In recent times, customers' expectations for any service have changed significantly due to digital transformation [46]. In most cases, they want these services at anytime from anywhere, leading to the setting up of a high bar for various services industries [46]. Financial institutions have recognized this technology-focused shift, and wherever possible, they are trying to meet customers' demand for digital interaction [47]. Technology, transparency, and trust are the primary offerings of the Fintech companies as they can provide services more transparently, through easy-to-use interfaces, and that too at a lower cost. In addition, advancements in Fintech have the potential to capture a larger market share and wear away the brand equity of the existing players' costs [23, 48]. Further, it can overcome the information asymmetries by screening borrowers effectively based on big data via statistical models along with reduction for an extended branch network and the need for personnel [49].

Innovation has been accelerated by adopting technologies at a pace never previously thought possible [50]. In order to facilitate adaptable changes in information systems, operational processes, and society, businesses have been integrating digitalization [51]. The excellent adoption of digital transformation will significantly improve businesses' dynamic capabilities, resilience and flexibility, increasing their performance. Thus, digitalization should be a key component of business strategy in all organizations [52].

In the last two years, it has been noticed that several digital technologies have spurred the digitization or transformation of the service industry [53]. Cloud computing artificial intelligence (AI), big data, and the Internet of Things (IoT) are key digitalization technologies adopted by businesses [52]. Another recognized benefit of digitalization is that digitalization makes high-level consumer collaboration possible digitization, which can create new income streams [54].

Online commerce's most significant advantage is understanding and learning about clients over time without using extra channels to push goods or services to them. Further, it is argued that adopting technologies has aided businesses in creating and implementing creative business strategies [55]. The benefits are not limited only to businesses; society also benefits. Digitalization has drawn many knowledge workers to undertake cognitive activities [56]. It is believed that via the development of internal processes, digital transformation has made substantial changes in organizational structures [52]. Businesses have to formulate a strategy that promotes the digital transformation process in the era of services. Dematerialization, identification, and cooperation are the three shift facilitators proposed by [57].

Overall, digitalization makes all possible through advanced data analytics, connectedness across goods and services, and obfuscation of borders between suppliers, consumers, rivals, and even marketplaces [58]. In the quickly evolving marketplace, transformation in digital terms is quickly becoming a crucial motivator of competitive advantage [52].

2.3   Digital Transformation: A Conceptual Overview

The concept of Digital Transformation is adopting disruptive technology to improve productivity, creating value and programs that lead to prosperity. Many multilateral institutions, industry associations and governments have implemented long-term planning to ground their long-term strategies. Digitization and innovation are affecting and creating threats among stakeholders in the entire industry, specifically in the financial industry. Firms in almost all industry areas are implementing several plans to study and employ the perks of emerging digital technologies, for instance, social networks and big data [59, 60]. It involves the frequent transformation of the essential business operations and the effects on the functioning of products and processes. Hence, disrupting management processes [61]. The entire society is undergoing quick and profound transformations due to the maturation of digital technologies and their extensive penetration of all marketplaces [62]. In addition to the increased demands from the customer's end, the companies are also facing even tough competition due to the integration of global economies [63] and thus going an extra edge over the other companies to go digital before other companies go to attain the competitive advantages of other and survive [64]. As a product, "born digital" leaders (such as Google, Facebook, and Amazon) have grown into terrific powerhouses in the coming years, while those holding dominant industries for a long term have had their conventional value proposition threatened [59]. Despite the plethora of new technologies and methods for adopting them in industry and economy, genuine Digital Transformation is captivating much bigger and facing more problems than anticipated [65]. Unfortunately, there have been numerous latest examples of firms failing to keep up with the new reality of the digital world, such as Blockbuster's bankruptcy, which was caused mainly by those companies' inability to quickly create and execute new digitized business models [66]. Comprehensive Digital Transformation involves the evolution of various talents; the significance of the same will differ based on the industry's background and the organizations' exact demands. To remain competitive, digital technology should become indispensable to how businesses run and must reorganize and perhaps re-invent their models.

The global expedite growth of digital finance is due to digital transformation. Financial services ratification has migrated from developed to emerging countries due to the rapid development of the internet and the subsequent financial revolution [67]. Traditional financial institutions' services were not generally found in many emerging economies until around a decade ago. The internet and smartphones both spread quickly in this atmosphere. Face-to-face banking contacts and visits to bank branches were not preferred by people in emerging economies who had never utilized traditional financial services. Although in emerging economies, the financial revolution is still essential compared to developed economies, it will encourage the digitization of financial services globally, both directly and indirectly, because of its fast-expanding size and rising influence on other industries through the usage of personal data. As a result of the changes in emerging markets, governments worldwide are promoting cashless payment policies [11].

The business world has been significantly altered by digital transformation. Researchers and practitioners are attempting to comprehend its structural evolution in various industries. Most players in the financial services industry recognize the importance of new technology in developing business performance and the happiness of consumers. Furthermore, the advancement of these advances has resulted in the entry of so-called FinTech's into the financial sector. These institutions have democratized access to financial services and influenced banking strategy significantly. The burning question is not how many services a system provides. The problem is determining which financial organizations (including banks and FinTech's) in the market can deliver the same service more efficiently, with higher quality, and with a more client-centered approach [68].

2.4   FinTech Ecosystem

FinTech has been the Buzzword in the area of Finance. According to Venture Scanner statistics, more than $165.5 billion was invested in FinTech startups from 2010 through the end of 2019—a time we assign to as the "FinTech Revolution." FinTech is still a barely known field, and investors seeking to diversify into non-traditional economic sectors may neglect it. The term "fintech" is complex, and its definition changes depending on who you ask. Let's have a look at its properties. First, fintech firms, not traditional financial institutions, provide it. Second, they are less expensive than traditional financial services since they use the internet. Third, by removing the established regulatory framework, disruptive innovation is encouraged. Personal financial management tools, corporate accounting services, online payments linked to AI-based management of assets, crowdfunding and financial transactions are just a few examples. Instead of delving into individual fintech services, the present study will address the interaction between fintech and traditional finance [11]. FinTech, in general aspect is the use of modern technologies to provide financial solutions to individuals and businesses. More explicitly, the emergence of a trend.

To boost financial activity, this new industry uses technology. [69] defined Fintech as "any new concepts that improve financial service operations by proposing technology solutions based on various business scenarios" [69]. Consecutive the GFC in 2008, advancements in mobile technologies and e-finance for financial organizations fueled innovation for Fintech. Internet, AI, integration in e-finance innovation, social networking and big data were all hallmarks of this growth [70]. Along with start-ups (the business related with financial service outside of banks), the term "fintech" can be defined as the application of information technology in the disciplines of finance, digital information innovation and financial innovation [71, 72]. Payment, Insurance, lending, crowdfunding, capital markets and wealth management, are the fintech models used in different business verticals [70]. With the establishment of cheques as a payment mode marked the beginning of technological advancement in the financial sector. Whereas, in 1958 the first credit card was issued by Bank of America, and ATMs began to aid process financial transactions, followed by the launch of a debit card as a transaction tool in 1968. Internet banking was introduced in the 1990s, aided by the expansion of the Internet. Fintech innovations such as mobile payments and crowdsourcing were introduced in the 2000s.

The various subdivisions of the FinTech Industry are as follows:

- Crowdfunding is a type of fundraising in which many contributors (known as "backers") commit financial resources to accomplish a common aim. The platform provides as a middleman in place of a traditional bank [73]. Based on the type of attention given to investors for the fund invested by them, crowdfunding websites can be split into four subsegments. Whereas, Donation-based crowdfunding investors are not compensated financially for their offerings (although they may obtain indirect personal advantages from the act of gift [74], they do receive some sort of non-monetary compensation in reward-based crowdfunding.

- FinTech's that provide direction, aggregated indicators and asset disposal management of individuals comes under the asset management segment. It is divided further into sub-sections. Investors (or "followers") can discuss, observe, and replicate the investment strategies or portfolios of other associates of a social network through social trading [75]. The combined judgment of a huge number of traders is expected to help individual investors. Based on the trade plan of a social trading platform, participants may be charged for order charges, or percentages, and spreads of their investment. Portfolio management systems that give algorithm-based and totally automated investing advise as well as making investment choices are referred to as robo-advice [76]. The algorithms used by robo advisors are typically based on diversification strategies passive investment [15].
- The personal financial management (PFM) that offers software services for the management and display of financial data and offer personalized financial planning, in particular fall within the segment of FinTech companies. Clients can use PFMs to see their assets. With one application, numerous financial institutions as well as loans collected from diverse lenders.
- The payments segment is a catch-all term for FinTech's whose apps and services deal with domestic and international payment transactions. The blockchain and cryptocurrency sub-segment falls under this banner and includes FinTech's that offer cryptocurrency (virtual currencies) as a substitute to traditional fiat currency. It is possible to save and exchange bitcoins, just as it is with legal cash [77]. Counterparties such as banks are unnecessary. One of the most popular cryptocurrencies is Bitcoin, which has had significant price volatility in the earlier period, has yet to set up itself as a reliable competitor to central bank-issued official currencies.
- The substitute payment methods sub-segment includes FinTechs that provide alternative payment options. This subsegment includes businesses that provide mobile payment solutions. The phrase "mobile payment" is used in the academic literature to refer to a variety of mobile phone-based functions [78]. It includes bank transfers or payments using a mobile phone. The substitute payment methods sub-segment includes companies that provide e-Wallets. It is a

storage mechanism for digital currencies as well as payment information for various payment systems.

- FinTech divisions which is not defined by the other three traditional bank operations, namely payment transactions, finance, and asset management are included in the other FinTech's division. The insurance subsegment includes FinTech services that provide or ease insurance acquisition. InsurTechs are another name for FinTechs, which provide peer-to-peer insurance, that permits a group of holders of policy to combine their resources and take joint risk in the event of a loss. If there is no loss happens within the group, the premium is partially reimbursed [79].

2.5   Role of Fintech and Digital Transformation with Respect to Financial Services

The financial services sector primarily consists of asset management, banking, and insurance operations, the first two of which are generally merged [50, 80]. The way of providing services to customers has changed rapidly due to digital transformation which is not just an innovative nice to have, but a necessity to adopt. As a result, recently, it has been noticed that digital transformation is accelerating. This acceleration has provided a huge potential for financial inclusion [6]. Research has provided empirical proof on the role of Fintech in increasing the access to financial services [43, 45, 81, 82]. Due to the easy access to technology and the increase of Fintech businesses, financial services found themselves compelled to change to keep up with growing digital population. Hence, financial service companies expanded their adoption of technology to articulate unique aspects of technology [83]. In the present scenario, financial services companies should be technologically innovative rather than adoptive in order to penetrate the market.

Fintech has significantly changed the financial sector by lowering the cost structure, improving the quality of financial service, and providing a more diverse and even financial environment [70, 84]. Fintech has made financial service firms be more agile, scalable and flexible. Following are some of the Fintech benefits:

- Cost reduction for financial business and customers: because of the absence of overhead costs connected with conventional organizations such as wages, rent and advertising, financial firms would save money on these expenses and use the money saved to invest in their customers. It has been shown that automation of many processes is more effective in things like predicting loan risk more precisely and that it also requires less human presence which lowers the cost of services that hey deliver to clients. Further, the drop in transaction cost has enabled consumers to increase their spending capacity with fosters business growth [84, 85]. Moreover, the reduction in transaction cost of financial services such as remittances has attracted a segment of population who could not enjoy such services before due to the high transaction cost [84].

- Speed and ease of use: these are the most prominent advantages of digital transformation in financial sector. Technological advancements in a wide range of enterprises and industries have resulted in faster transaction methods and systems. To improve the speed of the transfer operation in particular Fintech systems, a variety of delivery options are available, including an accelerated approach. The traditional method of sending money abroad used to be done by going to a bank office or using an internet banking program. Further, only few banks were doing such business. Fintech enabled payment systems, where transactions may be executed at any time and from any location, do not have these limitations [84, 86, 87]. Furthermore, digital transformation has enabled consumers to make transactions without having bank account, for instance mobile money [84].

- Faster approval rate. The approval rate is faster for online or digital lenders, Fintech innovations have made the application and approval procedure feasible within a day. There is a pressing need for services to be delivered quickly, and this may be accomplished with little information from the consumer. This need has been fulfilled by digital transformation which has reduced information asymmetries and other expenses associated with credit applications in order to make credit and other forms of fund raising more accessible and affordable [84]. As a results of automation and the usage of artificial intelligence, many customers prefer to engage with machines rather than people [88].

Despite the enormous advantages of financial technology for financial service sector, it is hampered by concerns about which is unfortunate.

Financial technology still has to show that it is safe and secure. In other words, Fintech services come with a variety of hazards, especially for consumers with less financial sophistication [84]. Following are some of the concern that would have some constrains on higher and faster digital transformation in the service sector:

- Cybersecurity threats: Data theft or penetration may bring a financial institution to its knees with only one security breach. When it comes to dealing with the consequences of a security breach, there are may be inadequate financial and human resources. Miss-selling, scams such as phishing, hacker attempts, illegal use of data, biased treatment as an outcome of artificial intelligence algorithms, and so on are all problems that Fintech might expose unsophisticated customers to. To make efficient use of Fintech goods and services and avoid these hazards, higher degrees of digital transformation are required [84, 89]. For that Fintech companies often invest a significant amount of money in their network and physical security. As a sequence, clients may be certain that their personal information is secure. Furthermore, central banks around the word launch several campaigns on cybersecurity and fraud prevention in financial technologies. These campaigns consist of numerous ideas to create awareness about online purchasing safety and personal data security [90].
- Excessive borrowing: Lower income and less educated families have less financial access in general, and they are also more likely to over borrow due to a lack of comprehension of loan rules and interest rates. Fintech may add to the over borrowing problem to the extent that it makes such borrowing easy and cheap [84]. Thus, financial service sector has to conduct campaigns that target Lower income and less educated families, especially in the rural areas in order to increase the financial literacy.

Digital transformation in services sector is promising of more innovations in the future. Regulatory authorities around the globe; more particularly in Asia have demonstrated a strong desire to promote the augmentation and development of Fintech, and a number of governments have created innovation offices and regulatory sandboxes. Thailand and Singapore make extensive use of regulatory sandboxes to test innovative Fintech models before allowing them to go live. Some nations, including Indonesia, Malaysia,

Vietnam, Lao PDR Thailand, and the Philippines have enacted favorable tax policies for Fintech enterprises, including lower corporate income tax rates and tax exemptions [84]. Hence, Fintech companies will not be pleased to stop their innovativeness at the current level; they will continue improving and expanding the scope of digital transformation even further.

2.6   Conclusion

Fintech is the application of modern technology to enhance the efficiency of services in financial sector and operations. Fintech or financial technology has created new value for financial industry. Recently Fintech is the most imperative developments in the financial sector, and it is growing rapidly, fueled mostly by the economy sharing, favorable legislation and information technology which has created innovative value creation and appropriation pathways for financial industry [91]. In most of countries worldwide, Fintech is rapidly starting to become the go-to financial system. Almost all of the financial institutions in developed economies like the United State or the United Kingdom have adopted FinTech. Fintech has significantly changed the financial sector by creating a more varied and stable financial environment, enhancing financial service quality and lowering costs. Digital transformation in financial sector is featured with Cost reduction for financial business and customers, Speed and ease of use, and faster approval rate.

Despite these features, there are some concerns such as Cybersecurity threats and Excessive borrowing which would hander fostering the digital transformation to higher level. Therefore, digital transformation in services sector is promising of more innovations in the future. Regulatory authorities around the globe; more particularly in Asia have demonstrated a strong desire to promote the growth and development of Fintech. For some financial services firms, the path to digital transformation might not be a straight line, it may even be a journey that teste the vision, resources, and leadership of firms. Therefore, firms have to deliver a deeply human experience that places the customers, employees, and partners' fist.

References

1. Anne-Laure Mention, "Digital Transformation in Financial Services: The Age of Fintech," 2020. https://researchoutreach.org/articles/digital-transformation-financial-services-age-fintech/

2. E. Feyen, J. Frost, L. Gambacorta, H. Natarajan, M. Saal, and others, "Fintech and the digital transformation of financial services: implications for market structure and public policy," *BIS Pap.*, 2021.
3. C. Pazarbasioglu, A. G. Mora, M. Uttamchandani, H. Natarajan, E. Feyen, and M. Saal, "Digital financial services," *World Bank*, p. 54, 2020.
4. F. S. Board, "Financial stability implications from FinTech," *Superv. Regul. Issues that Merit Authorities' Atten.*, vol. 27, 2017.
5. N. Nemoto, N. Yoshino, and others, "Fintech for Asian SMEs." Asian Development Bank Institute, 2019.
6. M. R. Sahay, M. S. Ogawa, P. Khera, M. S. Y. Ng, and others, "Is Digital Financial Inclusion Unlocking Growth?." 2021.
7. B. for International Settlements, "Sound Practices: Implications of fintech developments for banks and bank supervisors." Basel Committee on Banking Supervision (BCBS), 2018.
8. S. Ayriyan, "Fintech for Development: How Digital Financial Services Boost Economic Growth," *Payments Journal*, 2021. https://www.paymentsjournal.com/fintech-for-development-how-digital-financial-services-boost-economic-growth-2/
9. P. Khera, S. Ng, S. Ogawa, and R. Sahay, "Measuring digital financial inclusion in emerging market and developing economies: a new index," *Asian Econ. Policy Rev.*, 2022.
10. I. N. Machasio, "COVID-19 and Digital Financial Inclusion in Africa," 2020.
11. N. Iwashita, "Why fintech is not changing Japanese banking," *Asian Econ. Policy Rev.*, 2022.
12. A. Demirguc-Kunt, L. Klapper, D. Singer, and S. Ansar, *The Global Findex Database 2017: Measuring financial inclusion and the fintech revolution.* World Bank Publications, 2018.
13. W. E. Forum, "Digital Transformation: How Companies can win the race to meet customer expectations," 2022. https://reports.weforum.org/digital-transformation/the-race-to-meet-customer-expectations/
14. S. Michalopoulos, L. Laeven, and R. Levine, "Financial innovation and endogenous growth," 2009.
15. P. Sironi, *FinTech innovation: from robo-advisors to goal based investing and gamification.* John Wiley & Sons, 2016.
16. K. Kutzner, T. Schoormann, and R. Knackstedt, "Digital Transformation in Information Systems Research: a Taxonomy-based Approach to Structure the field.," in *ECIS*, 2018, p. 56.
17. G. Vial, "Understanding digital transformation: A review and a research agenda," *Manag. Digit. Transform.*, pp. 13–66, 2021.
18. A. N. Berger, "The Economic Effects of Technological Progress: Evidence from the Banking Industry," *J. Money. Credit. Bank.*, vol. 35, no. 2, pp. 141–176, 2003, doi:10.1353/mcb.2003.0009.
19. A. V Thakor, "Fintech and banking: What do we know?." *J. Financ. Intermediation*, vol. 41, p. 100833, 2020, doi: 10.1016/j.jfi.2019.100833.

20. W. S. Frame, L. Wall, and L. J. White, "Technological Change and Financial Innovation in Banking," in *The Oxford Handbook of Banking*, Oxford University Press, 2019, pp. 261–284. doi: 10.1093/oxfordhb/9780198824633.013.10.
21. A. Boot, P. Hoffmann, L. Laeven, and L. Ratnovski, "Fintech: what's old, what's new?." *J. Financ. Stab.*, vol. 53, p. 100836, 2021, doi: 10.1016/j.jfs.2020.100836.
22. S. Claessens, J. Frost, G. Turner, and F. Zhu, "Fintech credit markets around the world: size, drivers and policy issues," *BIS Q. Rev. Sept.*, 2018.
23. X. Vives, "Digital Disruption in Banking and its Impact on Competition." Paris: OECD, 2020.
24. R. M. Stulz, "FinTech, BigTech, and the Future of Banks," *J. Appl. Corp. Financ.*, vol. 31, no. 4, pp. 86–97, 2019, doi: 10.1111/jacf.12378.
25. K. Petralia, T. Philippon, T. N. Rice, and N. Veron, *Banking Disrupted?: Financial Intermediation in an Era of Transformational Technology*. ICMB International Center for Monetary and Banking Studies, 2019.
26. D. W. Diamond, "Financial Intermediation and Delegated Monitoring," *Rev. Econ. Stud.*, vol. 51, no. 3, p. 393, 1984, doi: 10.2307/2297430.
27. R. T. S. Ramakrishnan and A. V Thakor, "Information Reliability and a Theory of Financial Intermediation," *Rev. Econ. Stud.*, vol. 51, no. 3, p. 415, 1984, doi: 10.2307/2297431.
28. I. Pollari and M. Raisbeck, "Forging the Future: How financial institutions are embracing fintech to evolve and grow." Sydney, Australia: KPMG, 2017.
29. C. Scardovi and others, *Digital transformation in financial services*, vol. 236. Springer, 2017.
30. Y. Huang, L. Zhang, Z. Li, H. Qiu, T. Sun, and X. Wang, "Fintech credit risk assessment for SMEs: evidence from China," 2020.
31. F. S. Board, "FinTech and market structure in financial services: Market developments and potential financial stability implications," *Financ. Innov. Network, Financ. Stab. Board, Basel, Switz.*, 2019.
32. B. Lines, "How FinTech is Shaping Financial Services: PwC Global Fin-Tech Report," *Marketing*, vol. 34, no. 3, pp. 327–346, 2016.
33. J. Frost, L. Gambacorta, Y. Huang, H. S. Shin, and P. Zbinden, "BigTech and the changing structure of financial intermediation," *Econ. Policy*, vol. 34, no. 100, pp. 761–799, 2019.
34. A. Lagna and M. N. Ravishankar, "Making the world a better place with fintech research," *Inf. Syst. J.*, vol. 32, no. 1, pp. 61–102, 2021, doi: 10.1111/isj.12333.
35. D. Gozman, J. Liebenau, and J. Mangan, "The Innovation Mechanisms of Fintech Start-Ups: Insights from SWIFT's Innotribe Competition," *J. Manag. Inf. Syst.*, vol. 35, no. 1, pp. 145–179, 2018, doi: 10.1080/07421222.2018.1440768.
36. R. Hendrikse, D. Bassens, and M. Van Meeteren, "The Appleization of finance: Charting incumbent finance's embrace of FinTech," *Financ. Soc.*, vol. 4, no. 2, pp. 159–180, 2018, doi: 10.2218/finsoc.v4i2.2870.
37. M. Carney, "The promise of FinTech–something new under the sun," 2017.

38. G. Walsham, "Are We Making a Better World with Icts? Reflections on a Future Agenda for the IS Field," *J. Inf. Technol.*, vol. 27, no. 2, pp. 87–93, 2012, doi: 10.1057/jit.2012.4.
39. M. D. He *et al.*, *Fintech and financial services: Initial considerations.* International Monetary Fund, 2017.
40. D. Soumitra, B. Lanvin, S. Wunsch-Vincent, and others, *Global innovation index 2020: who will finance innovation?* WIPO, 2020.
41. M. E. Loukoianova *et al.*, *Financial Inclusion in Asia-Pacific.* International Monetary Fund, 2018.
42. N. Cámara and D. Tuesta, "Measuring financial inclusion: A muldimensional index," *BBVA Res. Pap.*, no. 14/26, 2014.
43. W. Jack and T. Suri, "Mobile money: The economics of M-PESA," 2011.
44. P. Honohan, "Cross-country variation in household access to financial services," *J. Bank. Financ.*, vol. 32, no. 11, pp. 2493–2500, 2008.
45. S. Davidovic, M. E. Loukoianova, C. Sullivan, and H. Tourpe, *Strategy for Fintech Applications in the Pacific Island Countries.* International Monetary Fund, 2019.
46. M. & Company, "The Next Normal The recovery will be digital," 2020. [Online]. Available: https://www.mckinsey.com/~/media/mckinsey/business functions/mckinsey digital/our insights/how six companies are using technology and data to transform themselves/the-next-normal-the-recovery-will-be-digital.pdf
47. S. T. Mnuchin and C. S. Phillips, "A Financial System That Creates Economic Opportunities–Nonbank Financials, Fintech, and Innovation," *Rep. to Pres. Donald J. Trump, Exec. Order 13772 core Princ. Regul. United States Financ. Syst. Gov. Print. Off.*, 2018.
48. M. Dietz, S. Khanna, T. Olanrewaju, and K. Rajgopal, "Cutting through the noise around financial technology," *McKinsey Company, Febr.*, 2016.
49. M. Bazarbash, *Fintech in financial inclusion: machine learning applications in assessing credit risk.* International Monetary Fund, 2019.
50. G.-C. Liu and C.-C. Lee, "The relationship between insurance and banking sectors: does financial structure matter?" *Geneva Pap. Risk Insur. Pract.*, vol. 44, no. 4, pp. 569–594, 2019.
51. P. Parviainen, M. Tihinen, J. Kääriäinen, and S. Teppola, "Tackling the digitalization challenge: how to benefit from digitalization in practice," *Int. J. Inf. Syst. Proj. Manag.*, vol. 5, no. 1, pp. 63–77, 2017.
52. T. Kretschmer and P. Khashabi, "Digital transformation and organization design: An integrated approach," *Calif. Manage. Rev.*, vol. 62, no. 4, pp. 86–104, 2020.
53. M. Paiola and H. Gebauer, "Internet of things technologies, digital servitization and business model innovation in BtoB manufacturing firms," *Ind. Mark. Manag.*, vol. 89, pp. 245–264, 2020.
54. R. Scherer, A. Rohatgi, and O. E. Hatlevik, "Students' profiles of ICT use: Identification, determinants, and relations to achievement in a computer

and information literacy test," *Comput. Human Behav.*, vol. 70, pp. 486–499, 2017.

55. H. Hokkanen, C. Walker, and A. Donnelly, "Business model opportunities in brick and mortar retailing through digitalization," *J. Bus. Model.*, vol. 8, no. 3, pp. 33–61, 2020.

56. C. Loebbecke and A. Picot, "Reflections on societal and business model transformation arising from digitization and big data analytics: A research agenda," *J. Strateg. Inf. Syst.*, vol. 24, no. 3, pp. 149–157, 2015.

57. B. Tronvoll, A. Sklyar, D. Sörhammar, and C. Kowalkowski, "Transformational shifts through digital servitization," *Ind. Mark. Manag.*, vol. 89, pp. 293–305, 2020.

58. K. Porter, R. Simons, and J. Harris, "Comparison of three techniques for scour depth measurement: photogrammetry, echosounder profiling and a calibrated pile," *Coast. Eng. Proc.*, no. 34, p. 64, 2014.

59. J. Ross *et al.*, "Designing digital organizations," *Work. Pap. Inf. Syst. Res.*, no. 406, pp. 1– 19, 2016.

60. M. Fitzgerald, N. Kruschwitz, D. Bonnet, and M. Welch, "Embracing digital technology: A new strategic imperative," *MIT sloan Manag. Rev.*, vol. 55, no. 2, p. 1, 2014.

61. C. Matt, T. Hess, and A. Benlian, "Digital transformation strategies," *Bus. Inf. Syst. Eng.*, vol. 57, no. 5, pp. 339–343, 2015.

62. C. Ebert and C. H. C. Duarte, "Requirements engineering for the digital transformation: Industry panel," in *2016 IEEE 24th International Requirements Engineering Conference (RE)*, 2016, pp. 4–5.

63. G. Westerman, C. Calméjane, D. Bonnet, P. Ferraris, A. McAfee, and others, "Digital Transformation: A roadmap for billion-dollar organizations," *MIT Cent. Digit. Bus. capgemini Consult.*, vol. 1, pp. 1–68, 2011.

64. A. S. Bharadwaj, "A resource-based perspective on information technology capability and firm performance: an empirical investigation," *MIS Q.*, pp. 169–196, 2000.

65. E. Zinder and I. Yunatova, "Synergy for digital transformation: Person's multiple roles and subject domains integration," in *International Conference on Digital Transformation and Global Society*, 2016, pp. 155–168.

66. T. Hess, C. Matt, A. Benlian, and F. Wiesböck, "Options for formulating a digital transformation strategy.," *MIS Q. Exec.*, vol. 15, no. 2, 2016.

67. PwC, "What lies ahead in digital payments trends for 2021," 2021. https://www.pwc.in/industries/financial-services/fintech/dp/what-lies-ahead-in-digital-payments-trends-for-2021.html

68. E. Paulet and H. Mavoori, "Conventional banks and Fintechs: how digitization has transformed both models," *J. Bus. Strategy*, 2019.

69. K. Leong and A. Sung, "FinTech (Financial Technology): what is it and how to use technologies to create business value in fintech way?." *Int. J. Innov. Manag. Technol.*, vol. 9, no. 2, pp. 74–78, 2018.

70. I. Lee and Y. J. Shin, "Fintech: Ecosystem, business models, investment decisions, and challenges," *Bus. Horiz.*, vol. 61, no. 1, pp. 35–46, 2018.
71. G. Zavolokina, L. Dolata, and M. Schwabe, "FinTech—What's in a name?," in *Thirty Seventh International Conference on Information Systems, Dublin, Ireland*, 2016, pp. 469–490.
72. R. R. Suryono, I. Budi, and B. Purwandari, "Challenges and trends of financial technology (Fintech): a systematic literature review," *Information*, vol. 11, no. 12, p. 590, 2020.
73. P. Belleflamme, T. Lambert, and A. Schwienbacher, "Crowdfunding: Tapping the right crowd," *J. Bus. Ventur.*, vol. 29, no. 5, pp. 585–609, 2014.
74. J. Andreoni, "Giving with impure altruism: Applications to charity and Ricardian equivalence," *J. Polit. Econ.*, vol. 97, no. 6, pp. 1447–1458, 1989.
75. Y.-Y. Liu, J. C. Nacher, T. Ochiai, M. Martino, and Y. Altshuler, "Prospect theory for online financial trading," *PLoS One*, vol. 9, no. 10, p. e109458, 2014.
76. ESA, "Discussion Paper on Automation in Financial Advice," 2015. [Online]. Available: https://www.eba.europa.eu/sites/default/documents/files/documents/10180/1299866/b7e305c8-9383-4c46-a800-b0deb1e5b2a2/JC2015080 Discussion Paper on automation in financial advice.pdf?retry=1
77. BaFin, "Virtuelle Wahrungen/Virtual currency (VC)," *BaFin*, 2017. https://www.bafin.de/DE/Aufsicht/FinTech/VirtualCurrency/virtual_currency_node. html
78. N. Mallat, "Exploring consumer adoption of mobile payments–A qualitative study," *J. Strateg. Inf. Syst.*, vol. 16, no. 4, pp. 413–432, 2007.
79. V. Wolff-Marting, "Peer-to-Peer-und Friend-to-Friend-Versicherungsmodelle und die Herausforderungen aus IT-Sicht," *Vom*, vol. 11, 2014.
80. O. Werth, C. Schwarzbach, D. Rodríguez Cardona, M. H. Breitner, and J.-M. von der Schulenburg, "Influencing factors for the digital transformation in the financial services sector," *Zeitschrift für die gesamte Versicherungswiss.*, vol. 109, no. 2, pp. 155–179, 2020.
81. M. A. N. Sy, M. R. Maino, M. A. Massara, H. P. Saiz, and P. Sharma, *FinTech in Sub-Saharan African Countries: A Game Changer?* International Monetary Fund, 2019.
82. M. N. R. Blancher *et al.*, *Financial inclusion of small and medium-sized enterprises in the Middle East and Central Asia*. International Monetary Fund, 2019.
83. S. Nambisan, K. Lyytinen, A. Majchrzak, and M. Song, "Digital Innovation Management: Reinventing innovation management research in a digital world.," *MIS Q.*, vol. 41, no. 1, 2017.
84. P. J. Morgan, "Fintech and financial inclusion in Southeast Asia and India," *Asian Econ. Policy Rev.*, 2022.
85. S. Agarwal, W. Qian, Y. Ren, H.-T. Tsai, and B. Y. Yeung, "The real impact of FinTech: Evidence from mobile payment technology," *Available SSRN 3556340*, 2020.

86. H.-S. Ryu and K. S. Ko, "Sustainable development of Fintech: Focused on uncertainty and perceived quality issues," *Sustainability*, vol. 12, no. 18, p. 7669, 2020.
87. S. Agarwal and J. Zhang, "FinTech, lending and payment innovation: A review," *Asia-Pacific J. Financ. Stud.*, vol. 49, no. 3, pp. 353–367, 2020.
88. T. Truong, "How FinTech industry is changing the world," 2016.
89. P. J. Morgan, B. Huang, and L. Q. Trinh, "The need to promote digital financial literacy for the digital age," *Digit. AGE*, 2019.
90. OECD, "Supporting financial resilience and transformation through digital financial literacy," 2021. [Online]. Available: www.oecd.org/finance/supporting-financial-resilience-and-transformation-through-digitalfinancial-literacy.htm
91. K. Boratyńska, "Impact of digital transformation on value creation in Fintech services: an innovative approach," *J. Promot. Manag.*, vol. 25, no. 5, pp. 631–639, 2019.

3

Reshaping Banking with Digital Technologies

Ankita Srivastava[1] and Aishwarya Kumar[2*]

*[1]School of Management Studies, National Forensic Sciences University,
Gandhinagar, Gujarat, India*
[2]ICFAI Business School, The ICFAI University, Dehradun, India

Abstract

The banking sector has gone a long way to come into its present form. It is still undergoing changes due to the introduction of various technologies. The digitization in the year 2000 was a step hard to move but now the people are more open to changes and willing to adopt technologies for the sake of convenience. This chapter discusses the banking sector's adoption of Artificial Intelligence (AI), the evolution of financial technology (fintech), the changes brought by fintech in banking industry and the challenges which the technology in finance is facing nowadays. The chapter discusses in-depth, the deployment of Artificial intelligence tools like Robotic Process Automation, iSaaS and bots. It focuses the areas in banking where AI and machine learning applications are used and how. Though the changes have made traditional banking look more beautiful ad user friendly, the constant changes in the technology will ultimately define the future.

Keywords: Banking, AI, fintech, digitization, etc.

3.1 Banking and Artificial Intelligence (AI)

Banking sector is a developing area which seeing quick acceptance of AI. The artificial intelligence guarantees balanced interface with the clients using the assistance of the computer-generated helpers and their administrations, accessible to the clients ceaselessly. Nowadays, we need everything mechanized from residence to workplace to simplify our tasks. Computer based intelligence turns into a fundamental portion of our lives. To utilize greatest benefit, it is essential to embrace newfangled technologies.

---

*Corresponding author: aishwarya.kumar60@gmail.com

Mohd Naved, V. Ajantha Devi, and Aditya Kumar Gupta (eds.) Fintech and Cryptocurrency, (35–58)

The components of artificial intelligence exemplified by mechanized automated practice with data analytics to upgrade the client services, around which business rotates and various bots and simulated helps will aid the clients in the monetary decision-making process [1].

To comprehend in what way new advancements and their implementations are altering the future of the banking industry, we sincerely must understand the reference of AI and ML in banking. AI or artificial intelligence and ML or machine learning include forms of algorithms, which permit dives into cognitive conception for machines with the utilization of vast data handling and computing power. For instance, Goldman Sachs[1] and UBS[2] apply multifaceted calculations that copy the work of a human stock trader, the basic machine intellect is deployed with humanoid comparable decision-making ability for doing a particular chore. One more instance of the technology deployment by UBS and Deloitte, they made a straightforward, robotized program for managing their clients' post stock trade allocation demands [2]. The framework (shown in Illustration 1) does a computerized audit of messages directed by customers itemizing in what way they need to designate huge block trade across funds, then processes and implements expected exchanges. Illustration 1 shows the framework of a computerized audit of customer messages.

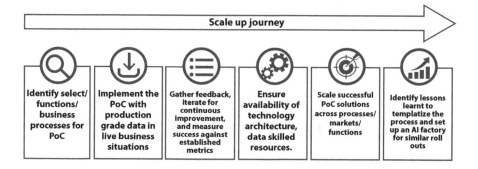

AI builds algorithms, databases, and learning engines which notices behavior, and learn to act accordingly when the data is fed to it. AI evolves through distinct phases when deployed. These phases include:

---

[1] https://www.goldmansachs.com/what-we-do/global-markets/gset-equities.html

[2] https://www.ubs.com/global/en/careers/meet-us/2018/work-in-robotics-at-ubs.html

3.1.1   Basic Algorithms and Machine Intellect

Simple machine intellect or algorithm-based reasoning that replaces a few components of human perception or judgment ability for particular jobs. Neural networks or calculations that can settle on human-comparable choices for quite certain capacities, and perform better compared to humans on a benchmark premise [3]. In this phase, the brainpower of machine learning or discernment abilities can learn new assignments or interact with new data beyond its underlying programming. As o f now, many machine intellects devise this competence.

3.1.2   Artificial Common Intelligence

A humanoid alike smart machine intellect and learning framework that not just excel in the Turing assessment and answers as a human would, but also can impersonate human judgment constructs. It also processes non-rational or triggering signs like sentiments, manner of speaking, facial expressions, and subtleties that presently a living being knowledge would be able to detect [4]. Such an AI would be able to effectively execute any cerebral task that a person would be able. Models include Sophia (Hanson Robotics) and Singularity.io5.

3.1.3   Ultra Smart AI

A machine intelligence or assortment of robust machine intelligence that have outperformed human knowledge of an individual or on an aggregate base to the degree that they can comprehend and handle ideas that human brains are unable to comprehend [5]. The scope of impact of artificial intelligence is extensive. Terminologies like cognitive computing, machine intelligence, and artificial intelligence are not substitutable, however they do come under the umbrella of the extensive expansions in AI that mature today.

To simplify the impact of AI, it is divided into two broad areas. The first is the interactive AI layer amid consumer and the organization. The second is internal one i.e. from the perspective of process.

Illustration 2 shows the deployment of AI in the banking industry.

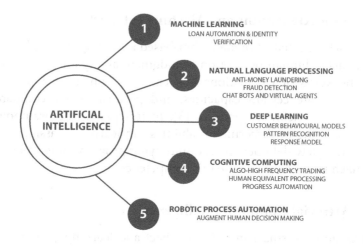

3.2   Fintech Evolution

Fast innovative progressions are empowering new ways to deal with a scope of monetary activities, from onboarding bank clients to sending super rapid trading techniques. Whereas fiscal organizations stood amongst the absolute initial private space to create huge interests in data innovation, and keeping in mind that technological innovation stays at the center of their business, most enormous organizations have gained critical inheritance of technical debt. This implies that these organizations are profoundly capitalized into unyielding frameworks that are timeworn. Withdrawing from these frameworks would be very difficult and exorbitant for these organizations, and ensuing the financial crisis, ventures of this nature verged are unimaginable [6].

These heritage frameworks caused it challenging for banks to hasten up with a portion of the thrilling novel prospects introduced by means of the speedy development of technology. Although a few monetary foundations perceived the capability of interacting with clients through innovative platforms like cell phones, utilizing cloud computing, or in any event, investigating new trading procedures empowered by man-made consciousness (AI), genuine execution was incredibly troublesome inside a working model obliged by old centralized computer frameworks [7].

Although banks attempted to focus on assets for development and fight their inheritance frameworks, nonfinancial advanced contributions were evolving quickly. Computerized locals like WeChat, WhatsApp, Uber, Facebook and Airbnb were altering their separate businesses as well as clients' assumptions for digital encounters in all cases. These innovative technologybased organizations habituated shoppers to anticipate that digital services should be well-timed, customized, and on request [8].

When contrasted with these assistances, a developing amount of buyers started to perceive financial institutions as obsolete and impervious to transformation. More youthful clients have demonstrated to be especially disappointed with the financial encounters presented by banks. As a matter of fact, the millennial disturbance index saw that as 71% of millennials would prefer to go to a dental specialist than pay attention to their bank [9]. This situation, especially when aggravated by the dissatisfaction sensed in regards to banks by a larger number of people soon after the worldwide financial crisis and the covid pandemic has likely extended the pool of people able to explore newfangled financial technology contributions. The conjunction of the following three impetuses has constrained banks- insurance specialists, asset supervisors, and a large group of other personnel in monetary organizations to reconsider the cutthroat dangers they face. It has additionally constrained them to start reconsidering the manners by means where technology might help in conveying their worth to the clients. This alteration made many consider a statement made by Bill Gates (technology idealist), the organizer behind Microsoft, who proposed in 1994 that "banking is necessary, banks are not"[3]. Another declaration after right around 10 years after the fact repeats this feeling. In 2013, Jack Ma, the pioneer behind Alibaba, contended, "Two major opportunities are coming down the line for the monetary business. One is online banking, every one of the monetary establishments goes on the web; the second is cyberspace finance, driven by outsiders."[4] It is an assurance that the fate of monetary administrations would be described via fast transformation by means of technological innovation because the focal operator of fresh client contributions and cutthroat procedures.

With the known acceptance of technology in the financial ecosystem, a few amazing open doors grew up leading to the word "fintech". The term "Fintech" is a combination of "financial technology." It is a buzzword meant for any innovation that is utilized to increase, smooth out, digitize, or distraught customary monetary administrations [10].

---

[3] https://techwireasia.com/2019/11/fintech-companies-prove-gates-point-banking-is-necessary-banks-arenot/

[4] https://www.ft.com/content/0cae83c4-c936-367c-9bf8-d5a082c9597e

3.3   AI Opportunities in Fintech

Coronavirus has altered the manner in which each industry works; the Financial Industry is no exemption. With work-groups as of now not ready to operate in organization buildings, the requirement intended on integrating automated innovation in Finance business has not been persuasive. Banks and Financial Institutions have taken on arising advances to adapt to the vulnerabilities that Covid has introduced to them [11]. Fresher technology has assisted them in tackling the changing workplaces and bringing dexterity and adaptability into a business arrangement. Organizations in the monetary area might use artificial intelligence to investigate and oversee information from different sources to give important insights. These pioneering outcomes assist banks in defeating the challenges they face on an ordinary premise while offering everyday types of assistance, for example, credit the board or installment handling. Here are some instances of FinTech development driven by AI, and the primary advantages FinTech organizations can acquire from artificial intelligence (AI).

3.3.1   Automation

Fintech mechanization is characterized by the reception of robotized devices to smooth out end-to-end monetary tasks. To mechanize their procedures, Fintech organizations require an enterprise mechanization platform that operates and manage the commercial junctures and conveys continuous real-time results. The mechanization necessities of FinTech organizations shift from conventional banks to other monetary establishments [12]. FinTech is known for quicker and minimal expense administration contrasted with the assistance presented by customary monetary organizations, and robotization can assist them with conveying simply that. For Fintech, there are different IT requirements for mechanization and reconciliation. The developing tech scene, computerization, and incorporation empower FinTechs to speed up and smooth out their administrations. There are various automation devices accessible to browse. FinTech organizations can pick the right tool in view of their particular business prerequisites. It requires a formal procedure that addresses the organization's needs for joining and robotization. Here are a few popular automation tools for the fintech industry.

3.3.1.1   *Robotic Process Automation (RPA)*

Robotic Process Automation is considered to be the most useful automation strategy in FinTech. It is a UI-based computerization device that is important for certain chores. Explicit assignments like separating data from a heritage framework or a centralized computer can be performed by using RPA [13, 14]. RPA works best in situations when the user interface stays the same. It is possible to apply RPA's API to cloud-based venture mechanization in order to automate business activities.

3.3.1.2   iPaaS

Integration Platform as a Service (iPaaS) is a stage that normalizes how applications are incorporated into an organization, making it simpler to mechanize business cycles and offer information across applications [15]. iPaaS is proposed to organizations on a membership premise. Most iPaaS arrangements need on-premise deployment i.e. when data is stored on your own servers, and you install and manage the software.

3.3.1.3   iSaaS

Integration Software as a Service (iSaaS) package is a cloud-based incorporation instrument that gives either prepackaged or effectively configurable coordination streams that are pointed toward aiding non-IT business clients and even purchasers to address straightforward application and information combination issues [16]. This incorporation programming is presented on a membership premise that is alluded to iSaaS services. These agreements do not provide the security components or combination capabilities that iPaaS agreements do.

Individual employees can automate tasks like routing incoming emails to a spreadsheet or a Slack channel.

3.3.1.4   Bots

An Internet bot, web robot, robot, or just bot, is a product application that runs computerized errands over the Internet, normally with the aim to imitate human action on the Internet, like messaging, for a huge scope of programming that performs mechanized assignments by running content is alluded to as Bots [17]. They can organize work in informing stages like Slack, answer demands, and work with the finishing of processes, or collaborations.

3.3.1.5   Enterprise Automation

Cloud-native enterprise robotized solutions that make use of API relationships can be used to integrate enterprise applications, automate data, and computerize work processes for SaaS apps. Solutions for commercial automation consolidate strong combination capacities with computerization [18]. The IT division can plan business capacity mechanization through largescale business automation in collaboration with non-IT divisions. These arrangements include a user-friendly interface that is centralized in control. All of the fundamental use cases for digital transformation were created to support automation. Additionally, it provides a powerful combination with client-driven computerization, giving Fintech companies a comprehensive solution for every scenario. Automation was worked to help all the center use-cases for advanced change. It similarly offers areas of strength for client-driven computerization so Fintech associations have a united response for all cases.

3.3.2   Improved Decision Making

The critical distinction among banking institutions and fintech is the magnitude of fast one makes decision. In a standard commercial bank, to adopt a new monetary service, you first need to agree to the venture, then begin gathering a genuine, specific credentials, and settle for the last resolution with various departments. This process could expect nearby six to eight months. Though, in majority fintech associations, these decisions are significantly more simplified as these decisions can be made rapidly at the investor's level with a singular call allowing the venture to start quickly. This advantage licenses fintech to be more serious, creative, and speedier than standard banks [19].

In decision-making through AI, the data is handed over to an AI platform, and tasks like information crunching, pattern spotting, inconsistency location, and complex examination are possible by AI [20]. An ultimate choice is then made by an individual or AI completely.

Virtual simulation intelligence is valuable for companies since it has the remarkable ability to constantly demonstrate itself - the more data focused decisions it makes, the more it learns. Computer based acumen educate itself and deploy data collections to assemble models which develops staggeringly perfect at making forecasts over this data [21]. These identical models can then be used on live data logically to make assumptions, arrangements, and ideas constantly, allowing associations to go with unprecedented business decisions.

For instance, at Peak, client exchange information is used - taken from heaps of buys - to realize what items certain portions of clients are purchasing together. This model is then used to suggest correlative items on a site. Assuming that appears to be natural, this is on the grounds that different organizations like Amazon adopt a similar strategy to improve proposals to their clients to increment buys.

3.3.3 Customization

One method for making an interpretation of the data into worth maybe through AI instruments, which couldn't just further develop client encounters but additionally set aside the bank's profit. As per a Business Insider Intelligence report from last year, front-office utilizations of AI could save the financial business an expected \$199 billion by 2023[5]. Artificial intelligence-based approaches, as per creator Eleni Digalaki, could assist with improving on client communications through the sharing of customized experiences with clients, by giving over easier client associations to bots or voice collaborators, and by facilitating confirmation processes. She writes, "Certain AI use cases have proactively acquired unmistakable quality across banks' tasks, with chatbots in the front office and anti-payments fraud in the central office"[6].

Personalization, obviously, isn't restricted to the proposed product or exciting cash-saving tips while surfing the web. It can likewise prevent theft. By catching strange charges through fraud deception capacities, banks can help consumers hugely. Simulated intelligence-based apparatuses can assist with limiting the effect of banking services that can be computerized while carrying extra worth to the in-person association when it's required [22].

Yet, past working with more straightforward communications, the utilization of AI offers the potential to grow client bases. One late focal point of the Consumer Financial Protection Bureau includes utilizing AI models as an elective way to deal with passing judgment on reliability for individuals without customary records. This information can assist moneylenders with settling on better-informed choices that can extend the bank's range to new client bases [23].

By joining the force of customized advanced components using innovation with the individual touch that a retail branch can bring, banks can stay aware of shoppers in numerous settings while offering something that an online-just choice essentially can't.

---

[5] https://www.businessinsider.in/finance/news/the-impact-of-artificial-intelligence-in-the-banking-sectorhow-ai-is-being-used-in-2020/articleshow/72860899.cms

[6] https://www.businessinsider.in/finance/news/the-impact-of-artificial-intelligence-in-the-banking-sectorhow-ai-is-being-used-in-2020/articleshow/72860899.cms

3.4   Reshaping the Banking

3.4.1   Payments

The effect of technology on payments is promptly clear. We have made considerable progress from the times of manual credit card imprinter and to paper-based handling of credit card slips. New payment structure factors including QR codes, cash-less cards, and versatile wallets are progressively coordinated into our day-to-day routines [24]. The developing presence of these computerized payment strategies is diminishing the utilization of money in both developed and developing economies. Worldwide noncash transactions are projected to develop at an annualized pace of around 18% from 2020 to 2025 and surpass the one and a half trillion mark.[7] An overview by Market Screener uncovers that the FinTech market will be valued at $26.5 trillion by 2022, developing at a CAGR of 6%. The genuine purpose for this development is the requirement for advances and protection and expanding revenue in ventures.

Illustration 3 shows Global Digital Payments Transactional value in USD billion – (2017-2024).

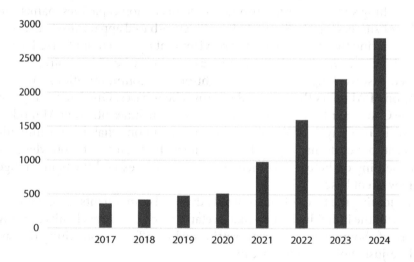

With advanced payment acknowledgment and volumes evolving quickly, it is nothing unexpected that payments are a key business. In 2019,

---

worldwide incomes from payments were US$1.9 trillion[8]. The new technologies are one of the major factors driving online payment volumes. The COVID-19 crisis essentially affected the worldwide payments industry, which has brought the banks to modernize further. COVID-19 has also brought a flood in the volume of transactions ahead by a few years. India had the biggest number of computerized web-based transactions of over 25.5 billion in 2020, trailed by the US (25.5 billion digital transactions) and China (15.7 billion online transactions). Additionally, with forced lockdowns, organizations had an opportunity to scale themselves carefully, bringing about customer expansion in digital spaces.

Payment transactions in banking are portrayed by an enormous number of processes, supporting countless client interactions for everyday banking, and creating huge volumes of data; that possibly make transactions in banking a great use case for AI [25]. Specifically, AI presents substantial prospects in regions like fraud detection and prevention, payments, and onboarding.

Artificial intelligence can assist with the detection and prevention of fraud by flagging up unusual payment transactions - for instance, where the sum included in the transaction is exceptionally enormous, or the payment transaction was started by somebody unexpected, or where the company/individual has never recently executed with the objective organization or country that is getting the payment [26, 27]. Moreover, AI instruments can identify and screen strange behavior in staff, for example, signing on to banking frameworks out of hours.

Artificial intelligence can be utilized to work on the speed and effectiveness of the payments process, by diminishing the degree to which people should be involved. For instance, today the most common way of paying a basic receipt can include critical human intercession both for the corporates and their bank, yet AI can work with straight-through handling of installments, via robotizing work processes, giving choice help, and applying picture acknowledgment to archives [28, 29]. Additionally, improvements in discourse acknowledgment innovation imply that banks can progressively deal with payments started through voice, where the initiator has utilized a PDA or savvy speaker.

Artificial intelligence frameworks can screen payment transactions from the point the payment message enters the bank till it leaves the payment entryway by observing activities at an interaction level and proposing natural administrations and offers. With the admittance to takes care of

---

[8] https://www.mckinsey.com/industries/financial-services/our-insights/the-2021-mckinsey-global-paymentsreport

from monetary market on most recent patterns and process enhancements in different banks and so forth, AI frameworks can propose reasonable payment items for the client as far as handling time, payment charges, and payment use redid to client's movement design. For instance, assuming the client is sending subtlety exhortation data inside the payment message, the AI framework might suggest a payment item that offers counsel as a connection. Such brief tailor-made ideas go quite far in client maintenance and fulfillment.

3.4.2 Lending & AI-Based Credit Analysis

Machine learning and artificial intelligence are powering the future in the banking and financial industry. Though these new technologies are criticized for operating as a black box, their ability to analyze data without being limited to assumptions has helped the banks to classify and predict risk in a better way. The most recent use of technologies in managing credit risk in banks includes blockchain, artificial intelligence, mobile banking, text mining, cloud, and cyber-security techniques. The most commonly deployed machine learning algorithm in assessing bank credit risk is the Support Vector Machine. These new technologies have been largely used for classification problems in anticipating a potential client as "good" or "bad" to encourage a better credit choice. Hence it creates a predominance of classification-related algorithms. Numerous papers have explored the classification of the creditors and predicted the probability of default (PD), loss given default (LGD), and exposure at default (EAD).

Several studies over the years have assessed and differentiated the exhibitions of various modern and traditional ML models in bank credit risk. In spite of the negligible use of deep learning models in credit evaluation literature, deep learning models, for example, convolutional neural networks indicated better outcomes contrasted with measurable and customary AI and ML models.

When discussing Artificial Intelligence's dedication to credit examination, it really is difficult to distinguish between the advantages of calculating usage and that of huge data accessibility. For instance, logical criteria in the case of a loan include the type of loan, the borrower's characteristics (age, pay, marital status), and their financial history. Given these elements, a typical example of a rating is the FICO score that is widely used in the United States monetary sector to evaluate the dependability of commercial clients. These rating variables installment history, unsettled obligations, duration of credit, and the latest opened accounts, among others. Large data, on the other hand, come from a far wider variety of sources, perhaps as a result of the digitalization of client relationships (digital footprints) or the use of brandnew categories of client data, such as informal community activities. Huge data analysis of quite diverse data sources is fully expected, even when there is no obvious relation to the dependability of the clients. Fintech companies as well as traditional financial institutions (banks) can make use of these kinds of data. Depending on the type of commercial bank one considers, it is almost guaranteed that huge data undergo different types of management. FinTechs and comparable credit providers (such as lending platforms, online banks, neo-banks, and some seller sites) use huge data directly to create scores for internal purposes. These ratings are based on decisions on the expansion of credit, funding levels, and risk management of the advance portfolio. Credit counseling companies then make various attempts to make use of the vast amounts of data before creating credit risk scores that may be purchased by lending businesses. This re-appropriating of the assortment and examination of enormous data is thusly like the rethinking of customary scores, like FICO in the USA. Simultaneously, contingent upon the idea of the data gathered, it brings up unambiguous issues with regards to risk and administrative consistence.

Some FinTech offering FICO ratings in view of large data vow to coordinate data from the moneylender organization's and its directors on social media activity data, as well as information about the browsing behavior (such as an Internet address or a device used for browsing), of online credit applications. As an example, the initial Neo-Finance uses information on the type of job the advance applicant holds and his professional connections on the LinkedIn network. This financial tech hopes to increase financial awareness in developing countries by gathering forward-thinking data to provide both a credit score (Lenddo score) and a sort of personality assessment (Lenddo confirmation). According to its methodology, as many people as possible will be given access to credit while avoiding the need for a financial assessment (like FICO or a credit bureau). Their rating assembles various sources of data: client action on informal communities (e.g., Facebook, LinkedIn, Twitter), associations with individuals in danger, and route data from cell phones or PCs by the advance candidate. In a related vein, FinTech Zest Finance's ZAML (Zest Automated Machine Learning) invention is incredibly instructive. It creates a score using a variety of very different sources of information, including electronic fingerprints, the client's moving history, and the level of education indicated by the jargon used in writing and typing error detection, among others [30].

One more utilization of enormous data is embraced by business players, for a superior evaluation of the risk caused by their investors [31]. Another example is a huge online business organization situated in Germany, that only requires payment from customers after they receive their purchases within 14 days [32]. Each exchange is in this way understood as a momentary buyer advance, which expects that the organization can survey precisely the reliability of its clients. To do this, it depends on the advanced unique finger effect data had by clients' perusing action in the approach a web-based buy. The contemplations presented here are to draw an image of potential mixes between large data and the data based on artificial intelligence in inspecting strategies in the credit examination procedure. They don't yet report the more extensive financial effects (past the monetary establishments utilizing them straightforwardly) of AI use in association with reliability appraisals.

3.4.3 Wealth Management

The greatest of organizations and richest of people look for the administrations of trained financial advisors to deal with their wealth. Be that as it may, monetary guides, in spite of their experience, mastery, or devotion, are human toward the day's end. And you never want human mistakes in the administration of your money or other assets. Likewise, depending a lot on your monetary consultant may likewise leave you helpless against possible misrepresentation. Your financial advisor has generally your private monetary data, all things considered.

Artificial intelligence isn't a curiosity in the monetary area and has a few applications in this domain. Applications powered by artificial intelligence can either augment human abilities by handling vile tasks or proactively take on new crucial tasks for businesses. In either case, AI in asset management ensures a high level of gauge accuracy by looking at billions of different circumstances and relevant data [33].

The assets incorporate an individual's all monetary property in general. The handling of explicit investments, such as securities, mutual funds, bonds, and other analogous assets in your portfolio, is the subject of asset management. The most well-known uses of AI in asset the executives incorporate is portfolio-related decision making, compliance management, and monetary guidance [34].

3.4.3.1 Portfolio Management

Machine learning and AI's apophenia capabilities are efficiently used to determine which stocks should stay and leave in one's portfolio. AI determines the relationship between risks and returns connected to every stock by weighing a massive number of variables, including the organization's financial health, its appetite for risk, and the historical or sporadic performance of stocks in a particular class [35]. These ideas continue working on sufficiency by persistent learning and assessment of financial stock exchange patterns.

Aside from quantitative patterns, AI-based assets management tools likewise utilize subjective information from the web, for example, monetary estimates, newscasts, and online societal media. AI in asset management evaluates the types of stocks that can decrease absolutely with no likelihood of rising again while keeping the risk variable elements, such as losing mortgage property, bankruptcy, and the other subjective factors. For instance, a company's stock will plummet if it receives negative press for some reason in the securities exchange according to the perception, a reality AI decides ahead of time with the assistance of predictive analysis [36].

3.4.3.2 Compliance Management

Computer-based intelligence empowers a business to oversee risks such that administrative compliance is accomplished. Artificial intelligence calculations can be used to separate administrative data from public notice and then use the data to produce a report. Businesses can also utilize AI to track changes to speculative laws using reliable internet sources such investment strategy statements, IMAs, exemptive rulings, and related documents. From the perspective of consistency, one of the main goals of AI in asset management is to reduce the number of false alarms that are generated by conventional, rule-based compliance frameworks. As late as 2021, almost 95% of all warnings for inheritance compliance-ready frameworks at some banks[9] were "misleading positive" alerts. In order to identify money laundering schemes and produce alerts, banks have spent decades and significant sums of money developing automated transaction monitoring systems.

Artificial intelligence and AI catch, clean and investigate numerous information components to smooth out compliance-ready frameworks. Along these lines, a company can avoid spending needless time and money on researching enormous alarm lines to track down insights concerning caution. Costs are saved in alternate ways as well, for example, the mechanization of complicated administration processes that actually rely upon manual work and paper-based documentation in a couple of affiliations [37]. According to an analysis, administrative and compliance expenditures account for about 15% to 20% of an organization's daily costs[10].

In addition to these, AI in asset management regularly enables organizations to direct their HR for the tasks that require "human" contact,

---

[9] https://thestack.technology/transaction-monitoring-banking/
[10] https://nexusfrontier.tech/5-ways-ai-improves-compliance-programs-in-asset-management/

effectively manage assets and investments, robotize management change at the time of administrative changes (thereby sparing significant fines), and moderate human error in asset management. AI integration in asset management operates just as you would expect it to in a financial context.

3.4.3.3 Robo-Advisory

One of the main subsets of AI, machine learning technology, exhibits a guarantee in the area of abundance management. Currently, there are over 100 robot financial advisors spread across 15 countries. Financial indicators project that roughly US$16 trillion will be in assets that Robo-guides will be in charge of managing [38]. Before presenting the finest financial options available, robo-guides use client input and take into account factors like risk appetite, liquidity, and others. This is done before making an interest in the offers, bonds, or other financial assets [39].

Robo-counselors have gone through four primary advancements. The primary stage included client-financial backers getting single-item recommendations based on a web-based survey that clients would fill to take care of data about their speculation inclinations. No delegate API was intricated. The ensuing improvement consolidated the usage of risk-based portfolio tasks and the possibility of resources. The third advancement accomplished the usage of estimations for rebalancing recommendation. The last improvement automates money related speculations with self-learning and uses AI and high level mechanics to robotize assets shift. Artificial intelligence will keep on being intensely engaged with robot monetary counselors [40].

Wealth management encompasses a much wider range of concepts than asset management, which only includes a small number of things. Before making recommendations to increase someone's wealth, it looks at the numerous factors that affect their overall finances. Advances in wealth management also make use of some of AI's asset management capabilities, such as cost reduction and improved navigation.

The main applications of artificial intelligence in business and privately managed money management are as follows:

a) Tax Planning
A tax planning helper by the name of Odele[11] is an illustration of AI-based automated tax planning. The tool could be a valuable asset for businesses, entrepreneurs, wealthy families, and similar clients. Odele, an AI-based tax

---

[11] https://www.linkedin.com/pulse/help-us-create-odele-tax-operating-system-disrupt-services-pollock/

organizer, assesses tax hypotheses, forecasts, and designs autonomously. Also, such a framework breaks down information from past records and other monetary sources to work out sums, for example, lost pay because of duty and other comparative figures. In view of the examination of earlier years, the device suggests ideal tax planning and design for clients. Factors, for example, individual way of life may likewise be thought of. Lastly, the framework improves and keeps up with new information from organizations like the IRS to help you build and modify tax assessment approach. For the most part, tax assessment in any nation accompanies ways of absolving oneself from paying it in various ways. With AI-based tax management tools, people can fully understand the different ways to save money [41].

b) Estate Planning
Similar to the majority of conventional wealth management concepts, estate planning also operates by being buried in administrative tasks. Documentation would incorporate the actual duplicates of ID evidence records [42]. That method of domain arranging dials back the whole interaction. All things considered, AI can be effortlessly utilized to improve estate preparation. The innovation can give bits of knowledge into arranging your domain while remaining on the right half of government or state regulations.

Artificial intelligence is adequately progressed to break down an individual's perplexing circumstance and give an ideal result in regards to their estate. Moreover, AI could make legal documents for such people. Factors, for example, decision making in regards to the exchange of estates can be robotized with AI and ML [43].

In addition to these, wealth management has a few other areas that can be improved with AI's help. Giving clients individualized commitment and customer service is one such area. As of now, devices, for example, chatbots are being utilized for further developing the client support chief point of interaction. Chatbots work with independently to resolve client questions in regards to privately invested money management [44].

Artificial intelligence in wealth management studies various factors with the aim of allowing companies to choose the best stocks or different assets in the currency market. On the financial side, wealth management is broader and covers topics such as tax planning, estate preparation, and various elements. AI may be costly to implement and operate, but the level of convenience it brings to the money market is unparalleled.

3.5   Insurance

The insurance business has just started its introduction to AI, and organizations are now exploring different avenues regarding better approaches to integrate it into their everyday tasks fully expecting the further innovative turn of events. Pogreb, an underwritwer at Argo Group sees much more potential for smoothing out the endorsing system. She expects that the quantity of utilizations a human guarantor is expected to deal with will fundamentally drop as AI tracks down its spot in the insurance business. "We accept with innovation and AI, a ton of human underwriting should be possible away with," Pogreb said. "The level of insurance applications that require human touch will go down decisively, perhaps 80% to 90%, and even to low single digits." While AI reception has come in simple ways, it's as of now definitely changing the lay of the land. Insurance agencies that need to remain serious ought to try things out of AI, Wolanow said, "Organizations can plan and remain cutthroat by beginning to evaluate the effect of AI on their business by prototyping their own calculations," he said. "A singular AI calculation that plays out its examination on an independent premise is very reasonable, and as a rule, an independent investigation device is more than fit for reason."[12] Insurers exist to deal with cases and assist clients with covering them, however, evaluation of claim is difficult. Agents should audit several policies and go over everything about deciding how much amount of claim the client will get for their case. That can be a cautious process - and AI can help [45]. AI devices can quickly figure out what's associated with a case and gauge the potential expenses included. They might investigate pictures, sensors, and the safety net provider's authentic information. A insurers plan can then investigate the AI's outcomes to confirm them and settle the case. The outcome benefits both the guarantor and the client. Boundless industry reception of a specific innovation frequently mirrors the advantages it offers to organizations in the area, in some cases with no conspicuous impacts on the client.

That isn't true with the insurance industry AI, which enjoys clear benefits for the client. Artificial intelligence helped risk appraisal and can assist insurers with better tweaking plans so clients pay just for what they really need [46]. It can likewise limit human errors in the application cycle, so clients are bound to get plans that appropriately met their requirements.

---

[12] https://www.businessnewsdaily.com/10203-artificial-intelligence-insurance-industry.html

It can likewise grow a insurers plan's client care choices and smooth out the case endorsement process. The outcome is clients get what they need.

3.6 Challenges Faced by Fintech in Banking

3.6.1 Regulatory Compliance

The regulatory compliance is one of the prevalent hurdle which the fintech enterprises face as the financial sector is one of the most regulated sectors. The traditional fintech softwares do not work on blockchain and other crucial technologies so the government interference will be always there. It's better to go for legal consultants to avoid any discrepancy.

3.6.2 Customer Trust

As indicated by Accenture, 79 percent of brokers and 82 percent of US investors concur that AI will change how banks accumulate data and communicate with purchasers. Enormous data and AI have had their effect in each financial institution. Utilizing large data, banks can gather personal data about clients, economic wellbeing of clients, monetary behavior, propensities, and in-application movement. Banks need this information in order to provide additional highrisk financial services and calculate credit scores. AI automates the entire interaction to distinguish misrepresentation, perform risk investigation, and manage transactions successfully with the help of enormous amounts of data.

3.6.3 Blockchain Integration

One can find numerous applications for financial technology that integrate blockchain innovation. While some of these firms don't think a blockchain is a workable option, others see it as a way to improve data exchange. By implementing a blockchain, one may increase the trustworthiness of the Fintech industry because it allows one to look into and follow each stage of a transaction, stop any changes to it, and keep track of it continuously. In any case, coordinating a blockchain is a difficult undertaking for majority of financial institutions.

Up to this point, banks and other monetary foundations have been delayed to get on the blockchain pattern. However, fintech startups are attempting to distraught the Fintech area. Be that as it may, they ought to think about the conventional banks and state run administrations into account, as these foundations are as yet dubious of new innovations.

3.7   Conclusion

In spite of the fact that, it's difficult for customary banking to embrace recent fads and technological advances. It is said with confidence that in time, versatile technologies will turn out to be much more normal in the monetary landscapes, since these help banks operate more effectively while being advantageous and practical for people. In a sense, fintech companies are modernizing their operations and setting a benchmark for the banking sector. The processes and administrations in institutions are being improved and mechanized by monetary innovation in technology. Nonetheless, these difficulties push our creative mind in new ways and support unrivaled development, yet there's opportunity to get better.

References

1. A. V Thakor, "Fintech and banking: What do we know?," *J. Financ. Intermediation*, 2020.
2. Deloitte Report, "Artificial intelligence in post-trade processing," 2021.
3. G. Teles, J. J. P. C. Rodrigues, R. A. L. Rabê, and S. A. Kozlov, "Artificial neural network and Bayesian network models for credit risk prediction," *J. Artif. Intell. Syst.*, vol. 2, no. 1, pp. 118–132, 2020, doi: 10.33969/ais.2020.21008.
4. M. Andrejevic and N. Selwyn, "Facial recognition technology in schools: Critical questions and concerns," *Learn. Media Technol.*, 2020.
5. B. C. Stahl, A. Andreou, P. Brey, T. Hatzakis, and ..., "Artificial intelligence for human flourishing–Beyond principles for machine learning," *J. Bus. ...*, 2021.
6. M. Palmié, J. Wincent, V. Parida, and U. Caglar, "The evolution of the financial technology ecosystem: An introduction and agenda for future research on disruptive innovations in ecosystems," *Technol. Forecast. ...*, 2020.
7. H. Pallathadka, E. H. Ramirez-Asis, T. P. Loli-Poma, and ..., "Applications of artificial intelligence in business management, e-commerce and finance," *Mater. Today ...*, 2021.
8. S. Ma, J. Murfin, and R. Pratt, "Young firms, old capital," *J. financ. econ.*, 2021.
9. Scratch, "The Millennial Disruption Index," US, 2013.
10. D. W. Arner, J. N. Barberis, and R. P. Buckley, "The Evolution of Fintech: A New Post-Crisis Paradigm?," *SSRN Electron. J.*, 2015, doi: 10.2139/ssrn.2676553.

11. Z. Bao and D. Huang, "Shadow banking in a crisis: Evidence from FinTech during COVID-19," *J. Financ. Quant. Anal.*, 2021.

12. P. S. Perumal, M. Sujasree, S. Chavhan, D. Gupta, and ..., "An insight into crash avoidance and overtaking advice systems for Autonomous Vehicles: A review, challenges and solutions," ... *Artif. Intell.*, 2021.

13. K. Kelley, *RPA in banking gives fintech a competitive edge.* ... /feature/ RPAinbanking-gives-fintech ..., 2019.

14. M. A. Unal and O. Bolukbas, "The Acquirements of Digitalization with RPA (Robotic Process Automation) Technology in the Vakif Participation Bank," *2021 4th Int. Conf. ...*, 2021, doi: 10.1145/3459955.3460602.

15. M. Marian, "iPaaS: Different Ways of Thinking," *Procedia Econ. Financ.*, vol. 3, no. December 2012, pp. 1093–1098, 2012, doi: 10.1016/s2212-5671(12)00279-1.

16. W. Sun, K. Zhang, S. K. Chen, X. Zhang, and H. Liang, "Software as a service: An integration perspective," *Lect. Notes Comput. Sci. (including Subser. Lect. Notes Artif. Intell. Lect. Notes Bioinformatics)*, vol. 4749 LNCS, pp. 558–569, 2007, doi: 10.1007/978-3-540-74974-5_52.

17. M. Wessel *et al.*, "The power of bots: Understanding bots in OSS projects," *Proc. ACM Human-Computer Interact.*, vol. 2, no. CSCW, 2018, doi: 10.1145/3274451.

18. A. Kintonova *et al.*, "Automation of Business Processes At the Enterprise During a Brand Formation," *J. Interdiscip. Res.*, pp. 107–113, 2019.

19. A. Agarwal, C. Singhal, and R. Thomas, "AI-powered decision making for the bank of the future," *McKinsey Co.*, no. March, 2021.

20. M. Abuhusain, "The role of artificial intelligence and big data on loan decisions," *Accounting*, vol. 6, no. 7, pp. 1291–1296, 2020, doi: 10.5267/j.ac.2020.8.022.

21. S. Fallahpour, E. N. Lakvan, and M. H. Zadeh, "Using an ensemble classifier based on sequential floating forward selection for financial distress prediction problem," *J. Retail. Consum. ...*, 2017.

22. S. Carta, G. Fenu, D. R. Recupero, and R. Saia, "Fraud detection for E-commerce transactions by employing a prudential Multiple Consensus model," *J. Inf. Secur. ...*, 2019.

23. S. Rahi, N. M. Yasin, and F. M. Alnaser, "Measuring the role of website design, assurance, customer service and brand image towards customer loyalty and intention to adopt internet banking," *J. Internet Bank. ...*, 2017.

24. S. Agarwal and J. Zhang, "FinTech, Lending and Payment Innovation: A Review," *Asia-Pacific J. Financ. Stud.*, vol. 49, no. 3, pp. 353–367, 2020, doi: 10.1111/ajfs.12294.

25. I. R. de Luna, F. Liébana-Cabanillas, and ..., "Mobile payment is not all the same: The adoption of mobile payment systems depending on the technology applied," ... *Forecast. Soc. ...*, 2019.

26. S. C. Valverde, D. B. Humphrey, and R. L. Del Paso, "Electronic payments and ATMs: changing technology and cost efficiency in banking," *25th SUERF Colloq. Vol.*, 2004.

27. D. Humphrey, M. Willesson, G. Bergendahl, and ..., "Benefits from a changing payment technology in European banking," *J. Bank. ...*, 2006.
28. P. K. Senyo, J. Effah, and E. L. C. Osabutey, "Digital platformisation as public sector transformation strategy: A case of Ghana's paperless port," *Technol. Forecast. Soc. ...*, 2021.
29. H. Choi, J. Park, J. Kim, and Y. Jung, "Consumer preferences of attributes of mobile payment services in South Korea," *Telemat. Informatics*, 2020.
30. J. Jagtiani and C. Lemieux, "The roles of alternative data and machine learning in fintech lending: evidence from the LendingClub consumer platform," *Financ. Manag.*, 2019.
31. N. Bussmann, P. Giudici, D. Marinelli, and J. Papenbrock, "Explainable Machine Learning in Credit Risk Management," *Comput. Econ.*, vol. 57, no. 1, pp. 203–216, 2021, doi: 10.1007/s10614-020-10042-0.
32. T. Balyuk, A. N. Berger, and J. Hackney, "What is Fueling the FinTech Lending Revolution ? Local Banking Market Structure and FinTech Market Penetration The FinTech Revolution Is Upon Us ! FinTech → Derived from 'financial' and 'technology:' products and," in *2019 Community Banking in the 21st Century Conference*, 2019, pp. 1–21.
33. S. Chishti and T. Puschmann, *Using Artificial Intelligence in Wealth Management*, no. 1955. 2018.
34. D. Tammas-Hastings, "Artificial intelligence will play an increasing role in wealth management," *LSE Bus. Rep.*, pp. 1–2, 2020.
35. X. Zhang and Y. Chen, "An Artificial Intelligence Application in Portfolio Management," in *International Conference on Transformations and Innovations in Management (ICTIM-17)*, 2017, vol. 37, pp. 86–104, doi: 10.2991/ ictim-17.2017.60.
36. G. Vaia, W. DeLone, D. Arkhipova, and A. Moretti, *Achieving Trust, Relational Governance and Innovation in Information Technology Outsourcing Through Digital Collaboration*, vol. 38. 2020.
37. M. Camilli *et al.*, "Risk-Driven Compliance Assurance for Collaborative AI Systems: A Vision Paper," *Lect. Notes Comput. Sci. (including Subser. Lect. Notes Artif. Intell. Lect. Notes Bioinformatics)*, vol. 12685 LNCS, no. April, pp. 123–130, 2021, doi: 10.1007/978-3-030-73128-1_9.
38. D. Moulliet, J. Stolzenbach, A. Majonek, and T. Voelker, "The Expansion of Robo-Advisory in Wealth Management," *Deloitte*, pp. 1–5, 2016.
39. D. Jung, F. Glaser, and W. Köpplin, "Robo-advisory: Opportunities and risks for the future of financial advisory," *Contrib. to Manag. Sci.*, no. January, pp. 405–427, 2019, doi: 10.1007/978-3-319-95999-3_20.
40. V. Seiler and K. M. Fanenbruck, "Acceptance of digital investment solutions: The case of robo advisory in Germany," *Res. Int. Bus. Financ.*, 2021.
41. A. Faúndez-Ugalde, R. Mellado-Silva, and E. Aldunate-Lizana, "Use of artificial intelligence by tax administrations: An analysis regarding taxpayers' rights in Latin American countries," *Comput. Law Secur. Rev.*, vol. 38, 2020, doi: 10.1016/j.clsr.2020.105441.

42. N. Abd. Wahab, S. Maamor, Z. Zainol, S. Hashim, and K. A. Mustapha Kamal, "Developing best practices of Islamic estate planning: a construction based on the perspectives of individuals and estate planning providers," *ISRA Int. J. Islam. Financ.*, vol. 13, no. 2, pp. 211–228, 2021, doi: 10.1108/IJIF-03-2020-0052.

43. L. Munkhdalai, T. Munkhdalai, O. E. Namsrai, J. Y. Lee, and K. H. Ryu, "An empirical comparison of machine-learning methods on bank client credit assessments," *Sustain.*, vol. 11, no. 3, pp. 1–23, 2019, doi: 10.3390/su11030699.

44. S. Sarbabidya and T. Saha, "Role of Chatbot in Customer Service: A Study from the Perspectives of the Banking Industry of Bangladesh," *Int. Rev. Bus. ...*, 2020.

45. S. Cao, H. Lyu, and X. Xu, "InsurTech development: Evidence from Chinese media reports," *Technol. Forecast. Soc. Change*, 2020.

46. R. Fujii-Rajani, "FinTech developments in banking, insurance and FMIs," *Reserv. Bank New Zeal. Bull.*, 2018.

4

Adoption of Fintech: A Paradigm Shift Among Millennials as a Next Normal Behaviour

Pushpa A. [1*], Jaheer Mukthar K. P.[1], Ramya U.[2], Edwin Hernan Ramirez Asis[3] and William Rene Dextre Martinez[3]

[1]Kristu Jayanti College (Autonomous), Bengaluru, India
[2]Reva Business School, Bengaluru, India
[3]Universidad Nacional Santiago Antunez de Mayolo, Peru

Abstract

Any technology application embraced in finance is coined as financial technology otherwise known as Fintech. It describes the usage of any technology to assists delivery of financial services like online banking, mobile payment apps and cryptocurrency. The pandemic has put the world into a global health crisis tipping to a paradigm shift in consumer's behaviour towards financial activities. People have adapted themselves to a new pattern in financial transactions like contactless payments, cashless transactions, online transactions and many more. There are greater chances for the end users to continue usage of fintech services during the next normal life (post Covid-19) as they have become familiar with the usage and convenience of fintech services. The chapter aims at providing insights to the exiting literature on evolution and emergence from Indian and global perspective, dimensions of business models and ecosystem, prepositions of fintech adoption using TAM and theoretical framework and justifies the proposed model.

Keywords: Adoption of Fintech, Covid-19, loyalty, perceived ease of use, perceived usefulness, social norm

*Corresponding author: pushpa@kristujayanti.com

Mohd Naved, V. Ajantha Devi, and Aditya Kumar Gupta (eds.) Fintech and Cryptocurrency, (59–90)

4.1 Introduction

Innovation persists everywhere, enduring significant changes in all sectors. Technology changes are constant changes that have brought about unimaginable rapid changes. Technology advancements have made considerable changes in computer technology, telecommunication, production, etc. It has changed the world of finance as well. Any technology application embraced in finance is coined as financial technology otherwise known as FinTech. "Fintech" is the combination of two elements financial services and technology. It describes the usage of any technology improvement aimed at delivering financial services like online banking, mobile payment apps and cryptocurrency. Fintech includes a broad category of technologies that aims at changing the approach to handling financial transactions by customers and businesses. Fintech services notonly support as a backbone for companies and business houses to manage their operations and processes but also make consumer lives better by enabling them to use software/algorithms on computers and smartphones. Fintech a technological advancement intends novel product models and applications in financial services, widening the scope for improvement of the financial sector creating competition culture among the service suppliers, [1]. Financial know- how evolved after the credit and embraced several milestones in traditional financial institutions, startups, venture capitalists, crypto and regulators [2]. The Financial Stability Board (FSB) connotes FinTech" A technologically enabled financial innovation that could result in new products or business models, application, and procedures associating material effects on financial markets and institutions and the provisions of financial services". Research relating to fintech can be categorised as one stream of studies that mainly focus on the revolution and its effect on incumbent financial contributes to the growth of understanding of the setups of FinTech platforms. The other work-stream emphasis on exploring the factors that impact the platforms of Fintech adoption. The broader intention to adopt FinTech platforms relies on an individuals' reach to new technologies. Thus, behaviour towards adoption of fintech is regarded as financial technology adoption behaviour.

The chapter is structured into 4 sections. Section 4.1 presents the concepts of Fintech, the Evolution and emergence of Fintech, both global and Indian perspectives, Dimensions of fintech business models, the Fintech Ecosystem, and the prepositions of Fintech adoption. The Section 4.2 exhibits contextual backdrop of the study on FinTech and millennials. Section 4.3 exposes theoretical framework and justifies the proposed model. Section 4.4 uncovers the conclusion and implications for future empirical research.

4.1.1 Evolution of Fintech

Financial technology is an endeavour to craft financial products and services that assist people financially through/by using technology. Fintech is the blend of technology and finance to enhance traditional methods of providing financial services. This start of this journey can be traced back to several decades before the end users' individuals or institutions could download apps on their mobiles and make a transaction at the push of a button. The journey of evolution can be conceptualized in four stages from "Fintech 1.0 to Fintech 3.5", presented in Table 4.1 below:

Table 4.1 Conceptualisation of evolution of Fintech.

	Key concepts	Key players	Overview	Key advancements
Fintech 1.0 (1886-1967) Building infrastructure	Increased efficiency through IT	IT vendors	the focus of I.T. is to boost the efficiency of existing services	transatlantic cable (1866) Fedwire (1918) Diner's Card (1950) Credit Card by Amex in 1958
Fintech 2.0 (1967-2008) Development of traditional financial services	Analog to digital	fintech Startups	Application of new technology with API	ATM by Barclay's in 1967. Telex (1966)
Fintech 3.0 (2008-2014) Startup Era	API Ecosystem	Large startup companies	Advancements in API	API Blockchain A.I.
Fintech 3.5 (2014- Current) Emerging markets	nonlinear rise of the two most populous countries in Fintech;	API players	Rebundling of unbundled financial services	IoT

Fintech 1.0 (1886-1967): Building infrastructure
This era laid the foundation for the fintech revolution and aimed at increased efficiency and sophistication in finance functions. This phase was described as a stage of building the infrastructure to support the globalization of financial services in Fintech 2.0. The key event during this phase was the transatlantic cable in 1866, followed by Fedwire in 1918 in the USA, which facilitated the first automated fund transfer.

FinTech 2.0: (1967-2008) Disrupters unbundle financial business
This period began in 1967, indicating the move to digital from analog guided by traditional finance institutions. This phase marks the unveiling of the ATM usage at Barclays bank and the first ever handheld calculator indicates the onset of contemporary epoch of FinTech. Many significant progresses took shape in early 1970s, like the digital stock exchange, NASDAQ, and Society for worldwide interbank (SWIFT) in 1973. During 1980s there was shift to mainframe computers in banks introducing them to online banking advancing to 1990s, the advent of internet and e-commerce business simulations. In the beginning of 21st century, the banks were fully digitalized in processes and interactions with clients and customers. The era ended in 2008 due to the Global Financial crisis.

Fintech 3.0: (2008-2014) Start up Era
The global financial crisis during 2008 led to the distrust of the traditional banking system by the public, paving the way for a new fintech era. This paved the way for the inception of the first digital decentralized currency, the Bitcoin (2009). Also, digital wallets like Google wallet (2011) and Apple Pay (2014) came into existence. During this phase of evolution, new technology innovations came into the application, key technologies include A.I. (Artificial Intelligence), and blockchain technology bring about APIs in finance.

Fintech 3.5: (2014-Current) Emerging markets
This phase of evolution signals the move away from the developed world toward developing countries. The emerging countries are not burdened with complex physical banking infrastructure as they are the early adopters of fintech solutions. As of date, the two emerging countries inclining to the usage of Fintech are China and India. The fintech 3.5 era symbolizes combining financial institutions and other businesses with new financial services.

4.1.2   Technology Innovation in the Financial Sector - Building a Digital Future

Fintech refers to innovations in financial services backed by innovations in information and communication technology (ICT). The epoch of Industry 4.0, indicates the evolution of Fintech, transforming the financial industry. Over the past few years, every aspect of the finance industry has been disrupted virtually by fintech companies. The chronicle of technical innovations in the financial sector instigated with the arrival of cheques to make payments (1945). The advent of Fintech can be traced back to the early 1950s when Bank of America supplied credit cards in 1958, ATM in 1967 emerged to manage the financial transaction, followed by the advent of transaction tool the debit cards. In the late 1990s, aided by the internet, Fintech revolutionized different markets, remarkably the banking and insurance sector when internet banking was unveiled.

Today, Fintech covers a broad category of technologies challenging the traditional financial infrastructure as more services transition to a new technology paradigm, most notably the payment apps on the mobile wallet, which intends to lessen the storing and handling of physical cash and augments online transactions. Fintech advancements of mobile payments and crowdfunding were initiated in the 2000s. The fintech industry is surging, ensuring secure, simple, and superior online banking services, [3]. In the 21st century, Fintech has provided opportunities like making payments online, checking balances, and executing account transactions, [4]. Over the years, Fintech advanced and introduced numerous signposts to the mass market like digitalized stock exchanges, online stock exchanges and bank mainframe computers. Each change brought a new milestone that we never thought about in the infrastructure of the banking sector.

Growth of Fintech - Global perspective
According to the report of Allied Market Research (AMR) report, global fintech market is anticipated to grow from $110.57 bn in 2020 to $698.48 bn by 2030, with a CAGR of 20.3% by 2030. Elements that drive the progress of the fintech global market in terms of improved focus on financial regulation, maintenance of transparency and convenience in terms of financial inclusions and assimilation of progressive technologies like Artificial intelligence (A.I.) and Machine learning (ML). The report also mentions that Regionwide, North America is and would retain the dominant share during the period and application wise, the banking segment ran the top market share in footings of revenue. Fintech, is a teamster in the digital financial sector in its advancement, has the resilience and capability to acclimatise to anomalous environmental

conditions. The outburst of the Covid-19 pandemic is an impetus to develop a product application for the fintech industry. The ultimatum for fintech know-hows all through the Covid-19 pandemic amplified with a upsurge in the usage and embracing of online and digitalized financial products among the customer across the world. New opportunities are awaited in the coming years in developing countries with promising expansion of offerings, rise in literacy rate, rapid urbanization and increase in the techno-savvy population. The below Figure 4.1 depicts the top 10 global fintech deals during 2021 and total value of Investments in fintech companies is shown in Figure 4.2.

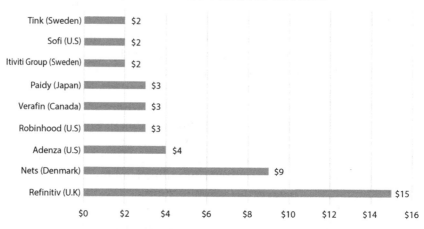

Figure 4.1 Top 10 global fintech deals in 2021(in U.S bn dollars). Source: statista.com.

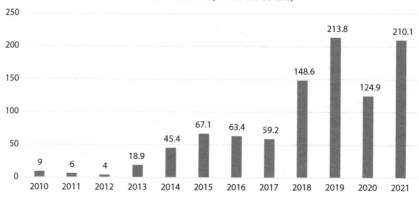

Figure 4.2 Total value of Investments in fintech companies worldwide (U.S bn dollars). Source: statista.com.

The total worth of funds into fintech establishments worldwide boosted significantly amid 2010 and 2019; it stretched to $213.8 billion. However, during 2020 the total value of investments saw a drop more than one third with a value of $124.9 bn, nonetheless in 2021 the outlay saw an upsurge up to $210.1 billion. The report registered that America is appealing the highest funds in the sector region-wise, reporting for roughly 80% of the total. Sector-wise analyses listed that the payment sector was the most popular sector that attracted the lion's share in the global funding with $51.7 billion.

The significant players in global fintech markets include Bankable, Blockstream Corporation Inc., Ant Group Co. Ltd., Paypal Holdings Inc., Tencent Holdings Ltd, Robinhood Markets Inc., Google Payment Corp., Circle Internet Financial Limited, Cisco Systems Inc., IBM Corporation, Goldman Sachs, Oracle, and TATA Consultancy Service Limited., and many more.

Growth of Fintech – Indian perspective

The KPMG report (2021), the Indian fintech sector invited over $2 bn in investment during the first half of 2021. According to the fintech market report 2021, the fintech market was appreciated at INR 2.30 Trn and is anticipated to reach INR 8.35 Trn by 2026, with a CAGR of 24.56% for the period 2021 to 2026. The report added that as of 2020, India stands as the biggest destination for investments worldwide with an utmost adoption rate of 87% than the global rate of 64%.

The Fintech sector in India has realised funding of $8.53 bn (in 278 deals) in FY-22. The Blinc Insights report added that the rapid pace of growth in the Indian fintech sector is backed by accelerated digitalization. The ecosystem of Indian Fintech industry consists of a broad category of sub segments, comprising Lending, Payments, Personal Finance Management, Wealth Management (WealthTech), Insurance Technology (InsurTech), Regulation Technology (RegTech), and many more. Below is the Figure 4.3 showing the trend of finTech funding in India.

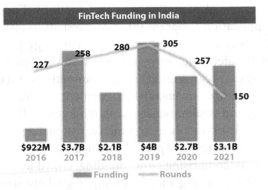

Figure 4.3 Total value of finTech funding and rounds. (Source: Blinc Insights).

During the AY 2020, Bengaluru based payments firm Navi Technologies attracted the highest investment of $397.59 million from the Angel funds, followed by Pine Labs, a Noida based company which attracted an amount of Rs.300 million from a private equity player, and Razor Pay with $100 million from GIC of Singapore, among few other firms making them a unicorn. The secret to the progress and market success of the Indian Fintech sector originates from the integrated ecosystem. A lucrative fintech ecosystem empowers the fintech market participants to get connect, engage, and share notions across vivid networks and groups adapts opportunities into industry. In the present era of a technology-driven society, no market participants can operate in silos. In the beginning of 2022, Indian Unified Payment interface (UPI) has grasped the involvement of 313 banks and has documented worth $5.4 bn monthly transactions over $128bn also 16 fintech companies have gained the "Unicorn status" with a estimate of over $1bn. The key player in the Indian fintech market include Paytm, Razorpay, Pine Labs, Groww, BharatPe, Policy Bazaar, CRED, Digital Insurance, CoinSwitch, Zeta, Acko, Vedhantu, etc.

4.1.3   Taxonomy of Fintech Business Model

There are plenteous forms of fintech platforms, different businesses like B2B, B2C, and P2P use fintech services to conduct business. Innovative models witness the growth of Fintech. FinTech companies fall into two distinct categories; they focus on consumers or businesses. Technology advancement is the crucial element that brings out software solutions to make business procedures and processes and everyday man life more tolerant. Fintech platforms first aim to provide customized services by understanding the future needs of end-users and to enrich the customers' experience by providing personalized/customized services. Secondly, it focuses on quickly rendering service faster by assisting businesses and customers with incomplete processes/financial operations and transactions. Fintech companies use the API (Application Program Interface) system to provide services in the best possible way with the assistance of technology providers. Thirdly, they ensure 100 % safety and convenience in dealing with multi-currencies and mobility. End users can complete their transactions at remote locations.

The financial innovations encompass payment services, digital lending, insurance, savings and wealth management, remittances, POS (point of sale), and RegTech. Mobile payments, e- commerce, risk management, customised consulting, virtual currencies, [5] portfolio management [6]. FinTech products encompass six areas, comprising crowd funding, crowd lending and peer-to-peer lending (digital financing, mobile trading (digital investment), electronic money and cryptocurrency (digital money), m-payment (digital payments), Robo-advisor (insurances and financial advice) [7]. [2, 8] together developed six business models in fintech, namely payment, wealth management, crowd-funding,Peer to Peer (P2P) lending, capital markets, and insurance services, personal financial consulting services, crowdfunding, virtual currencies, and cyber security. A comprehensive list of fintech models is widespread among individual clients or financial institutions. SMEs and corporates. Seven fintech business models, along with their operation mechanism, value prepositions, and significant companies in each fintech business model are shown in Figure 4.4 and discussed below.

Payment business models
It is the concept of digital banks through which an end-user can operate his current and savings accounts. The rise in cashless payments has enabled e-commerce players to roll out different business models. These models focus on improving the experience for end-users looking for a modernised pay-ments experience in terms of multichannel accessibility, speed, convenience. This model serves two markets, namely, customer and retail payment: whole-sale and corporate payments. Some widely used and popular applications included Apple Pay, Samsung Pay, Square Cash, Google Wallet and Venmo.

Wealth management model
An investment advisory platform that combines other financial services to address the need of affluent clients with cutting-edge technology such

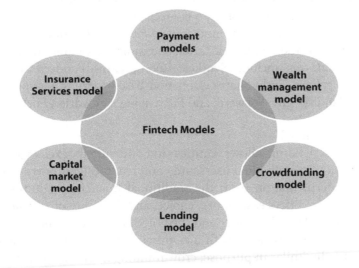

Figure 4.4 Dimensions of Fintech business models. (Source: Author compilation).

as Artificial intelligence and Machine learning to manage portfolios. It is an automated wealth management advisor (Robo-advisors), that provide holistic financial advice to the affluent client's wealth. These models aid from users shifting demographic and behaviour commending for computerized and unreceptive investment strategies for a delicate and straightforward fee structure. Some wealth management apps include Planto, Chloe, Gini, Mellow, Wealthfront, Motif and Folio, Supersplit, Moneyview, and Monefy.

Crowdfunding model

The digital era has enabled online platforms for fundraising for business ideas and non-profit causes for personal needs through the crowdfunding business model. Almost $73.93 billion in funds have been raised across in United States and Canada alone using online platforms in 2020. Crowdfunding is a method of arranging funds to create capital for entrepreneurship ventures/startups like artistic and creative projects or startups, rewards or ideas or donations from individual investors through online, social media or websites. It encompasses three parties, the project entrepreneur, contributor, and the moderator. The entrepreneur is a project initiator who need needs funds; the contributor is concerned in assisting the project, and the moderator is the institution that accelerates the engagement between the contributor and initiator. The moderating or regulating institutions facilitate the providers/contributors to use the information regarding the myriad of ventures and financing prospects. The most popular crowding business models are reward-based crowd funding, donation-based crowd funding, and donation-based crowd funding. The business rewards the project's supporters for funding them, and donation is a route to source money for charitable projects from the donors. Few models of reward crowdfunding platforms are Crowdfunder, RocketHub, Kickstarter, and Indiegogo. Equity-based crowdfunding platforms include SyndicateRoom, CrowdFunder, Crowdcube, Seedrs, AngelList, Early Shares. Donation-based funding platforms comprise GoFundMe, GiveForward, and FirstGiving. Crowdrise, Fuel a Dream.

P2P Lending model

Peer to Peer lending allows entities and individuals exchange finance directly amongst individual users and companies to lend/borrow without effective intermediation from the traditional financial institutions. This online platform offers ease of use, choice, and flexibility of advancing and borrowing funds to the lender and the borrower as they simply match the lender with the borrowers with a nominal fee. Crowdfunding and P2P lending are dissimilar in purpose; crowdfunding is with the drive of funding projects, whereas P2P lending's purpose is debt alliance and credit card refinancing, [9]. Lenders are enticed by access to the market, risk diversification, and lower transaction cost, but borrowers are enticed by information transparency (speed and availability). Some of the leading Fintech is Lending Club, Prosper, SoFi, Zopra, and RateSetter.

Capital market model

The financial technology innovations have disrupted and re-imaged the functioning of capital markets, both primary and secondary markets, including equity and bonds. The model holds across the broad spectrum of capital market spots like investment, trading, foreign exchange, and research. Among the spectrum of capital market areas, Fintech in trading is promising; trading fintech connects the investors and agents to deliberate and share information, buy and sell securities (commodities or stocks) and monitor the risk involved. Also, the foreign exchange transactions are covered by the fintech business solutions for capital markets. Individual clients and businesses widely accept it as it lowers the barriers and costs for the participants of capital market transactions. This model lets one view live pricing, send or receive funds in different exchanges firmly using mobile devices. The capital market fintech platforms include Robinhood, Estimize, eToro, Magna and Xoom.

Insurance services model

Fintech innovations have provided vital benefits like efficiency enhancements, cost cutbacks, risk evaluation, superior customer experience, and higher financial inclusion. The insurance fintech business model is the best adopted by the traditional insurance providers, enabling a more direct association between the insurer and the customer. It uses data analytics to assess and fit risk, and as the group of incumbent customers expands, they are offered products that meet their needs (insurance for car, life, healthcare, causality insurance. etc.). The disruptive innovations in the insurance sector supplement the traditional models of data collection and improvise risk analysis. Fintech innovations that have disrupted the insurance sector include platforms like Coverfox, Censio, Sureify, Ladder and The Zebra.

4.1.4   Fintech Ecosystem

Fintech has gained popularity due to the conducive fintech ecosystem. The fintech industry's growth hangs on exactly how the players within the ecosystem relate [10]. The financial ecosystem refers to the advancement and acceptance of new technologies to disrupt the traditional banking system. It comprises startups, artificial intelligence, blockchain, cloud computing, and many more, making financial services more accessible and practical.

The fintech ecosystem can be split into six main stakeholder groups: fintech startups, tech developers, financial consumers, incumbent financial institutions, and regulators. The participants of fintech ecosystem include entrepreneurs, financial and government institutions. The elements of the ecosystem contribute symbiotically to innovation, fuel the economy, encourage collaboration and enhance competition in the fintech industry, finally benefit the users. Figure 4.5 illustrates six components derived from the study.

The players in the fintech ecosystem in reshaping the financial services landscape are, firstly, the Investors like private equity houses, venture capitals, and angel investors etc., who consider the fintech providers as the next golden goose. Secondly, the traditional financial establishments like banking, insurance, stock brokerage companies, venture capitalists and financial service providers are a fragment of the fintech ecosystem, as they need ways to leverage technology advent and reduce the cost of business operations. Third, Government and financial regulators need to construct suitable laws to protect the end-users and guidelines for fintech service providers; the fintech industry needs to work with these parameters to build Trust among the end-users. Fourth, the universities and research institutions bridge the industry-academia gap by instructing curricula that focus on incubation and entrepreneurship skills that focus of fintech. Fifth, companies need to launch incubators for fintech experiments and the development of fintech services like- big data analytics, crypto, social media developers and cloud computing. Finally, end-users who are the most important for the existence of fintech companies; remain the

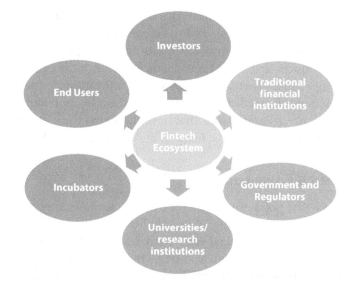

Figure 4.5 Players of Fintech ecosystem. (Source: Authors compilation).

imperative cogwheel of Fintech. The end-users represent both individuals and organizations. These elements symbiotically improve, accelerate the economy, and enable alliance and competition in the finance industry, eventually benefiting end-users. Interaction among the participants acts as crucial aspect in the development and permanence of the fintech sector.

Table 4.2 features the important drivers contributing to the growth of the fintech sector.

Table 4.2 Drivers of fintech growth.

Drivers	Facets
Talent	The surge in investments in tech-related disciplines (A.I.) like Oxford University and Harvard University and the Return of foreign-educated talents.
Era of Technology	Emerging know-hows like 5G, cloud computing, blockchain, augmented reality, IOT (Internet of Things) and AI (Artificial intelligence).
Funding	Seed capital and other forms of financing Start-ups.
Regulators	Strict regulatory and compliance laws by governments to regulate the services offered by the fintech units.
Financial service integration	Traditional financial institutions integrated and partnered with independent fintech suppliers.
End-user base shifts	Millennials and Gen Z, known as the generation of the digital world, form 30% of the world population as per Forbes. They are characterized as a techno-savvy generation as they are exposed to technology with a high preference for the cutting-edge automated, quicker, and more efficient technology and services than the legacy payment systems.
Increased security, less fear	End-users have a Lack of Trust in traditional banking as Fintech promises security and fearless transaction with Biometric authentication of a person with biological and structural characteristics, it includes fingerprint scanners, facial/iris recognition, vein mapping etc.
Borrowing & Lending money	Access to funds has become transparent and less centralized, shifting from traditional banking methods to services like crowdfunding and peer-to-peer lending.

(Source: Author compilation)

4.1.5   Prepositions for Fintech Adoption

According to EY insights on the fintech adoption index, the consumer segment tends towards fintech prepositions. The reports from EY insights reveal the global adoption rate as 64%, indicating that Fintech is taking over as a global mainstream. The consumer fintech adoption rate across 27 markets is shown in Figure 4.6.

This suggests that Fintech offers several benefits; the benefits are categorized as follows:

Choice
Traditional financial institutions provide as many financial services as possible under one roof; fintech providers provide advanced innovations. As such, customers have a wide choice of financial services from providers, meaning flexibility. Customers can choose any fintech solutions that best suit their needs, adding to their traditional banking habits.

Transparency
Over the past few years, the finance sector has seen an undoubted transformation from a simple mobile banking app to an insurtech platform. The fintech solutions have simplified the tedious financial activities and processes, stimulating the world that is reliant on technology. The usage of

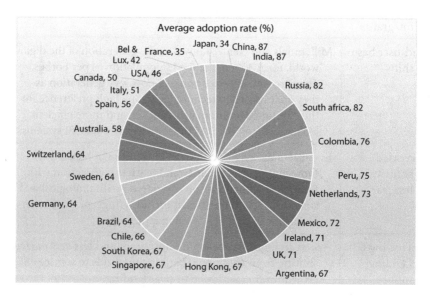

Figure 4.6 Consumer adoption rate. (Source: EY insights).

Fintech has seen a drastic increase for fintech solutions for payments and online money transfers among the fintech apps for insurance, investments, savings, financial planning, borrowings etc.,

A boon during Covid-19

Moreover, the adoption of Fintech has even more noticeable increased due to the Covid-19 pandemic, a situation that forced individuals across the globe to stay indoors and use digital solutions to manage their everyday financial transactions. With social distancing measures and staff reductions, the COVID-19 pandemic has contributed to the rapid rise of Fintech. Fintech solutions have offer both affordable and transparent ways to complete payments. The improved visibility in financial transactions because of innovative solutions like artificial intelligence, improved data analytics, blockchain, etc., has enhanced service delivery, enabling users to track their transactions.

Price

All fintech services usage include costs, whether conversion rates, processing fees or commission. Today's users are attentive to costs, so fintech solution providers must include as little cost as possible and be competitive. Most of the fintech solutions, compared to traditional banks, offer lower prices to their consumers and businesses.

Speed

Financial institutions relying on traditional means and age-old processes do not confirm speedy services. However, fintech solutions guarantee speedy services as they use artificial intelligence, automation, or work algorithms to speed up digital payments and online payments. Today's fast-paced digital world expects and enjoys speed and agility to adapt; it also means accessibility. The encroachments of Fintech have made it possible for traditional financial institutions to fasten their processing and approval of applications resulting in a better and more satisfying user experience. Literature shows substantial improvement in the fintech infrastructure, specifically the launch of new payment mechanisms and interfaces like IMPS (Immediate Payment Services), UPI (unified payment interface), and other mechanisms speed the financial transactions.

Convenience

Nowadays, customers anticipate convenience in all transactions in their lives, and fintech companies have assumed to meet their need for faster and quicker transactions with the disrupted technology advancements.

It is understood that fintech solutions depend on the internet and mobile connectivity. This accords the financial institutions reach wide customers or end-users and enables them to reach them back at the touch of a button. Fintech solutions are tailor-made as preferred by the customers. They are flexible in terms of time and location, providing convenience to the clients. Fintech has helped traditional banks adopt chatbots, enabling customers easily accessible in many languages, thus enabling financial intuitions to come out of their traditional means of relying on in-branch appointments that demand patience on the client's part.

4.1.6   Challenges of the Fintech Industry

Over the years, Fintech has drastically changed how people engage in their financial activities. Digital advances and trends in the fintech industry have improvised and automated the process and services within organisations, paving the way for growth and building reputation in the industry. This has transformed how people and financial institutions manage their money. However, there are challenges faced by the fintech industry, pushing them to imagine new ways and unparallel growth. Some of the challenges faced by the industry are:

Data Security and Privacy
There is always a question of risk in terms of security and privacy in the usage of fintech applications. Unlike traditional banking, the nature of the fintech business is that it stores enormous user data like credit card numbers, security codes, account statements, etc. The use of smartphones and online banking, mobile banking, payment apps etc., has put the information at risk of transit. However, on the other hand, data obstructing financial data seems easier.

Regulatory and compliance law
A safe fintech ecosystem demands a stringent regulatory framework to control and regulate the services provided by fintech entities to avoid fraud and data theft. However, these regulations and laws inevitably make it difficult for fintech startups/companies to complete a vast list of formalities before they begin their operations or enter new markets.

Focus on User Retention and Customer Experience
User retention and experience are significant concerns for the fintech sector. Fintech is complex, as the fintech app should manage to balance user experience and security. Though Fintech has changed swiftly, enabling

procedures to create an account simple and accessible, bots offer information to users' conversation UI to simulate speaking with a natural person. Fintech offers services that are neither easy to break nor too hard to access. Likewise, though they can access an app with two-factor authentication promising security, this could frustrate the user and lead to a bad experience. Hence, there is still much ground to be included in developing a seamless user experience that goes beyond the simple user interface.

Acquiring long-term users

In the contemporary scenario, where most people still use traditional banking services, understanding their niche, target audience, and strategies to acquire new and long-term users is a stunner challenge. Offering the best product is not what your users would expect in this competitive world. It is important for a fintech service provider to endorse himself informing the end users about the innovation. A solid and effective marketing strategy includes collaborations, advertising and many more boosting the popularity of the brand. It can thus be concluded that fintech start-ups or businesses need to frame strategies that augment competitive advantage for the business.

Finding a winning business model

Another critical challenge for a fintech industry is coping with the economic downtrend; most fintech businesses use cost-cutting tactics like employee reductions and wage cutbacks. There is a need to adapt or extend their resources and reconsider their revenue and expense strategies. They need to cope with the higher transaction volumes, contactless payments and many more and alter their business models. Startups should spend only on the necessary categories like hiring specialists necessary for business, avoid rapid expansion and expensive teams, reduce overspending on sales and marketing before establishing the market, present minimal viable products etc., Fintech face challenges in the way they earn money; they can cope with this by raising small-ticket loans because of low margins and high risks, offer Payment gateways acceptance and payment processing services at affordable rates for small businesses, partnerships with other businesses based on their customers demand and offer them suitable products from partners at special prices and many more.

4.2   Statement of the Problem and Research Questions

Fintech is a technology advancement that intends new product applications and models in financial services, widening the scope for advancement of the financial sector creating the culture of competition among the fintech service providers. The pandemic has put the world into a global health crisis, tipping to a paradigm shift in consumers' behaviour towards financial activities. People have adapted themselves to a new pattern in financial transactions like contactless payments, cashless transactions, online transactions, etc. The World Trade Organisation (WHO) urged end-users to utilize contactless payment methods as a substitute for the conventional mode of payment -cash transaction as it can be a carrier of the novel virus. This suspected risk of contracting the novel virus changed the end users' point of view toward day- to-day activities that need face to face contracts, banking, and payment systems. In this backdrop, the fintech industry and financial industry have sustained drastic growth during the pandemic. There are greater chances for the end-users to continue using fintech services during their next everyday life (post-Covid-19) as they have become familiar with the usage and convenience of fintech services. On the other side, it is a challenge for the service providers to retain the existing customers and attract new users.

Furthermore, Millennials are more receptive to Technology advancements as they have grown up with the internet. The Salesforce research claims that 37% of millennials relate to tech companies among the age groups. Millennials would be the primary users of both banking services and Fintech. ETBFSI (Sep 2021) posits that Fintech is enticing millennials, and fintech firms target the digitally techno-savvy millennials as their target of the new age. Consequently, there is a need to investigate the characteristics that induce the user's intend to embrace fintech payment apps post covid-19.

Past studies indicate a dearth of literature in this area of a study showing unanimity among researchers about the variables studied relating to the phenomena of adopting online business, including Fintech. This study implies providing insightful hindsight to the existing literature and business community to tap the rural markets where only 22-28% of the Indian population have an option to access internet facility and frame strategies to improve financial infrastructure with financial literacy.

4.3   Research Questions and Objectives

Contemplating the dearth of this area of study, some additional research questions need to be explored to increase the knowledge on fintech users' continuance of usage after the COVID 19. This study is based on the research questions outlined in this section. The fundamental questions trailed after in the study process precisely determine the study's objective. In this research, below mentioned questions are evaluated simultaneously; Fintech and Covid 19 implications. The main research questions concerning the study are:

> Q1: What are the precursors of FinTech that have transformed the landscape of the finance sector?
>
> Q2: Propose an acceptance model to foretell persistence of online transaction financial transactions post Covid-19.
>
> Q3: What is the role of Covid- 19 as a precursor to the adaptation of fintech services?

For the present study, two core objectives are deliberated: firstly, to explore the precursors for adoption and usage of FinTech during covid 19 and secondly, to study intention to adopt and use of FinTech services post-Covid 19, i.e., loyalty.

4.4   Conceptual Framework and Proposed Model

4.4.1   Conceptual Framework

Fintech, the evolving sector in the 21st century is defined as a tech-based business that collaborates with financial institutions. Few researchers explain Fintech as an interdisciplinary topic that is a blend of finance, and technology, and innovation management, [11]. Fintech as an industry consists of financial businesses that have transformed over decades; to expedite their service quality with innovative service delivery and enhance management effectiveness by exploiting the new cohort of information technology [12–14]. It has ensured the development of the finance sector, slashing the transaction cost, facilitating convenience using mobile phones [15–17] and promising security [18, 19]. Fintech is a technology advancement that intends new product applications and models in financial services, widening the scope for advancement of finance industry creating a society of competition amongst the fintech service providers

4.4.2   The TAM Model

There are numerous studies on users' behaviour toward information technology in areas of psychology, sociology, and information system research [20, 21]. The literature in past three decades exhibit that researcher have adopted various theoretical strategies to analyze technology adoption. Among the available theories of adoption, the oldest theories applied to envisage adoption behaviour, Theory of reasoned action (TRA), [22]; TAM (Technology Acceptance Model) by [23, 24]; UTAUT (unified theory of acceptance and use of technology) an extended TAM [25] is another grounded framework which is commonly used in various multidisciplinary studies. The extended TAM (UTAUT) used key constructs: namely., perceived ease of use, perceived usefulness, facilitating and social norms. The Innovation diffusion theory, proposed by [26] reveals how new innovations and ideas are accepted or adopted. TRA intends from the notion of behavioural science; it justifies that behavioural intention is impacted by social norms and attitudes, [27].

TAM is drawn from the defect of the Theory of reasoned action. The Theory applies psychological factors to study consumer adoption or acceptance. There are ample studies supporting the reliability and validity of perceived ease of use and perceived usefulness. [28–33], it has advanced as one of the widely accepted and applied models in the field of technology acceptance/adoption research. Though all the theories contribute to the research in acceptance or adoption of information technology, Researchers have seldom used the theories except TAM and UTAUT theories. Furthermore, each paradigm ignores the contribution made by the other model. Some of the studies have evaluated fintech acceptance from the contextual factors reminiscent of social influence, Trust, and risk [20, 34, 35]. Some of the studies have focused on technology factors and overlooked the social factors, [36, 37]. Prominent investigators have adopted TAM and UTUAT models and empirically tested and proved significantly in measuring the user's acceptance/adoption of technology, [20, 38–45].

The aspects of TAM have been adopted in numerous studies connecting COVID-19 as an influencer on acceptance of technology. [46] observed the association amongst utilitarian, hedonic, normative precursors that arouse intention among users to embrace online shopping during times of curfew. [46] experimental the influence of Trust on online purchase intention during Covid 19. [47] explored changes in users' patterns in digital banking services during demonetization [48] aimed to document the effects of the COVID–19 pandemic on digital finance app adoption. The study measures the Loyalty of end-users after the forced situation, the pandemic because if users are satisfied and contented with the services of Fintech, they tend to be loyal as they continue using them, [49]. There is very little literature, and hence, the study contributes theoretically to the extended model TAM by weaving PRC19 with the subconstructs of TAM2. Considering both behavioural and adoption attributes, the paper aims to propose a model for a future empirical study. The model is projected with Social Norm (S.N.), Trust (T.R.), perceived ease of use (PEOU), perceived usefulness (P.U.), intention to adopt, and Loyalty is proposed in the model for future empirical research to explore if these variables influence millennials adoption intention of fintech services during and post-pandemic as following normal behaviour.

4.4.3   Proposed Model and Hypothesis Framed

Using the extended TAM model, the study proposed a research model to analyze the paraphernalia of perceived Ease of use, Trust, and social norms, on adoption intention of Fintech mediated through perceived usefulness and its impact on the adoption of Fintech as a pre and post-adoption behaviour (Loyalty) of end-users of Fintech can be investigated. The proposed framework proposed is shown in Figure 4.7.

Perceived usefulness, and intention to adopt fintech services
Perceived usefulness is described as the assumption of a user that using a particular technology enhance the job efficacy, [50, 51]. The operational definition according to TAM describes P.U. as the degree to which the users find the usage of fintech services helpful; based on the scale developed by [23], the study adopted a list of attributes for P.U. Adoption of Fintech services assures rapid completion of the task, cutting the travel time, and lessen paperwork, [52, 53]. Past studies point out that P.U. has a significant influence on intention of users to adopt fintech applications like online purchases as they provide a quick shopping experience, [34, 54, 55] information technology, [52, 54, 56, 58–60]. The ubiquity of Fintech

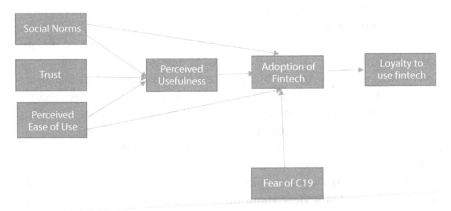

Figure 4.7 Proposed framework. (Source: Author compilation).

services paired with convenience exhibits a greater perceived usefulness, thus leading to a higher intention to adopt and use FinTech services. The millennials are tech-savvy individuals who are employed and consider costs and benefits in their daily decisions. Based on literature, study recommends the first hypothesis that P.U. of fintech services intensified during the pandemic positively influenced the adoption behaviour of millennials. Hence, perceived usefulness is proposed in the framework.

Perceived ease of use, perceived usefulness, and intention to adopt fintech
Perceived ease of use (PEOU) is regarded as one of the precursors in persuading the acceptance of new technology. It indicates to the end user's perception that using a particular technology is easy or effortless [23]. It is can also be defined as an individual's viewpoint on use of technology, that says users would be able to be free from mental stress and need not have to dedicate a lot of their effort and time to use it [50, 57, 61]. This impacts on individual's intention to use technology and envisages the perceived usefulness. There are a relatively few research experimented on users' PEOU and intention to adopt the technology, and most of the studies postulated that PEOU has an affirmative and direct impact on the user acceptance to adopt technology, [15, 62, 63]. Summarizing, the findings of past studies it isobserved that there is a theoretical correlation between POEU and adoptionof Fintech, it is the direct forecaster of user's intention to adopt technology. Thus, the study hypothesis that POEU of digital payments positively induce the millennial's intention to adopt digital payments and find them useful and helpful during the pandemic period.

Social norm, Perceived usefulness, and intention to adopt Fintech
The customer's perception of technical characteristics, the requirement to use and attitude toward it is influenced by social norms, statements and actions of significant family members, friends, and colleagues. Positive endorsements from the social groups (Friends, family members and Colleagues) persuade them to adopt new technology, [64]. It is assumed that an individual always consults his surroundings about new technology advancements and can be swayed. S.I. refers to the extent an individual is persuaded to use a particular technology. Studies hypothesize that Individuals are swayed by the beliefs and attitudes of people around them in the social media epoch, [65].

In the present study, social influence (S.I.) is identified as the social norm (S.N.), an individual's view about others (friends, family, colleagues, and relatives, who think that the individual ought to use fintech platforms, [66].

In addition, studies have suggested that individuals' inclination toward fintech services like mobile payment, online banking, online games, and mobile payments are positively associated with social influence. Opinions of social groups shared face to face on any means of social media plays a vital role in enticing adoption behaviour [20]. The social norm is studied as an essential precursor to behavioural intention in the two crucial theories TRA and TPB.

During medical emergencies, i.e., Covid-19, news updates, safety measures and concerns about the crises were propagated through traditional media across the globe; this led to severe changes in the way people performed their day-to-day activities. [67] found that S.N. had a significant effect on behaviour intention of using fintech services by Gen Y during Covid 19. Recent studies exhibit that expert reports/views in media have a direct influence on consumers behavioural intention of purchasing online during Covid 19 pandemic, [68] analysis of review suggest that it is reasonable to understand the influence of social norms on behaviour intention. This study hypothesizes that information shared in communication media and interest about the current situation represents S.N. an influencer of individual decisions on dealing their daily financial transactions. Precisely, we propose to forecast that SI influences millennials intention to adopt, motivating them to use adhere to the security measures of using mobile payments to avoid cash transaction. Hence, Social Norm is proposed in the framework.

Trust, perceived usefulness, and intention to adopt Fintech

Previous studies have presented a positive impact of trust on PU and adoption intention [69–71]. Trust (TR) indicates one's faith on an exchange activity, associated with reliability and integrity. Clients adopt a new technology advanced or a new service with ease only when it promises safety and fewer feeling of risk. Transparency in terms of security and privacy form the critical elements of fintech services that users think of and select the services, [52, 72]. The users are much concerned about leakage or theft of information both personal and official, they expect the service providers be more translucent in data collection for the online transactions and promise data security of the users, this eventually contributes to the repute of the service providers among its competitors. There is no doubt that if customers confidentiality is protected, they desire to use increases and will continue using the services, [14]. Thus, fintech firms offering high security and privacy attracts users trust and retain customers for a long term. It is of great sense to study how trust affects the attitude of potential users and their willingness to adapt.

But risk is the inherent characteristic of fintech, researchers have identified trust as a factor that is closely related to brand image and perceived risks and the more the users trust the service provider, the user parades more willingness to use the service, and it becomes easier for the service providers to frame strategies to attract customer. Hence, Trust is proposed in the framework.

Fear of Covid-19, adoption of Fintech and loyalty

Researchers have deliberated that Perceived risk (P.R.) significantly impacts the intent to use technology, [45]. The first to debate perceived risk (P.R.) as an instigator on consumer purchase decisions was Bauer, 1960. In the study of the adoption of fintech services like digital payments, online payments etc., "privacy and security" is identified as the primary risk factor influencing user intention [59]. Nevertheless, there are minimal studies that have concentrating on changing consumers adoption and usage intention of fintech services like digital payments. The outbreak of Covid-19 has negatively impacted the usage of physical money; contrary to this study [67] found that Perceived risk (P.R.) Covid 19 contributed to the use of digital payments. Using cash, and contact-based payment methods could be one of the causes for spread of COVID-19, also World Health organisation (WHO) encouraged consumers to use contactless payment ways for regular financial transactions. Cantered on the existing literature and article, the framework proposed included PRC19 impacted intention to adopt fintech service applications like digital banking, online payments, and e-wallets for their financial transactions.

Loyalty implies consumers intention to continue using a service or technology after a wow experience. User loyalty implies fintech users' online services or using apps for financial transactions after a good experience, exhibited by continuous usage and positive WOM (word of mouth). The conventional notion of brand loyalty extends to the online loyalty to customers' online behaviour [73]. Also stated as e-loyalty, it indicates to repeated usage behaviour and reuse intention of online services or apps in future, [74, 75]. The determinants of e-loyalty include service quality, [76, 77]; Trust in service, [32]. From the perspective of fintech adoption, the transparency in terms of security of data used for online services can enhance users' loyalty about Fintech. Fintech experience influences the user's Loyalty to the fintech services, [78]. Continuous usage of fintech services enables users to conclude the convenience and quality of the services. Hence this variable is included in the model.

4.5 Conclusion

Based on the TAM, a research framework model is constructed to understand the user adoption intention pre and post Covid 19 behaviour. The chapter presents a more refined and comprehensive view of the determinants of behavioural intention. An attempt is made to augment an understanding of the topic by distinguishing the determinants influencing the adoption of Fintech and comprehending the conflicting conclusions concerning the impact of the determinants. The researcher believes that the new theoretical framework with a future research agenda adds insights to the existing literature in the present area of study. This chapter aims to bring an extensive research base to employ Fintech in different ways and answer the research questions set earlier. It has tried to identify the growing number of surveys demonstrating the fintech transformation considering the oddities, complexities, and possibilities. The potential researcher can adopt this model and test for future research and compare the usage of Fintech among developed and developing countries and the usage of Fintech among the Women, Millennials and Gen Y. While the authors recognize that many voids can be found in this review and proposition, it optimistically turns out as an exciting fodder. It gives insights to business community to tap the rural markets that accounts to only 22-28% of India population having access to internet and frame strategies to improve financial infrastructure with financial literacy. A comprehensive and efficient measurement will improve a better investigation of the adoption model of Fintech services. Heeding the above suggestions, the study believes in strengthening and transforming what exists to be a user's status into empirical research and theorizing in management and business studies.

Acknowledgement

This work has not received any funding.

References

1. Thakor and Anjan V, "Fintech and banking: What do we know?" Journal of Financial Intermediation, vol. 41, no. 100833, 2020.
2. I. Lee and Yong Jae Shin, "Fintech: Ecosystem, business models, investment decisions, and challenges," Business Horizons, vol. 51, no. 1, pp. 35-46, 2018.

3. J. Kang, "Mobile payment in fintech environment: trends, security challenges, and services," Human- Centre. Comp. Inf. Sci, vol. 8, no. 1, pp. 1-16, 2018.

4. P. Tiwari and Kartika, "Impact of digitalization on empowerment and transformation of society," Res. J. Human. Soc. Sci., vol. 10, no. 2, pp. 305-310, 2019.

5. B. Nicoletti, "The future of FinTech: Integrating finance and technology in financial services., 2017.

6. T. Cham, SC Low, CS Lim, AA Khin and RLB Ling, "Preliminary Study on Consumer Attitude towards FinTech Products and Services in Malaysia," International Journal of Engineering & Technology, vol. 7, no. 2 29, pp. 166-169, 2018.

7. P. Gomber, Jascha-Alexander Koch and Michael Siering, "Digital Finance and FinTech: current researchand future research directions," J Bus Econ, vol. 87, p. 537–580, 2017.

8. C. Stern, Makinen, M and Qian, Z., "FinTechs in China – with a special focus on peer-to-peer lending," Journal of Chinese Economic and Foreign Trade Studies, vol. 10, no. 3, pp. 215-228, 2017.

9. D.-S. Zhu, T.-T. Lin and Y.-C. Hsu, "Using the technology acceptance model to evaluate user attitude and intention of use for online games.," Total Qual. Manag. Bus. Excell., vol. 23, p. 965–980., 2012.

10. D. Diemers, A. Lamaa, J. Salamat and T. Steffens, "Developing a Fintech Ecosystem in the GCC," 2015.

11. K. Leong and A. Sung, "FinTech (Financial Technology): What is It and How to Use Technologies to Create Business Value in Fintech," International Journal of Innovation, Management and Technology, vol. 9, no. 2, pp. 74-78, 2018.

12. D. McAuley, "What is FinTech. Retrieved from Wharton-Fintech," https://medium.com/whartonfintech/what-is-fintech-77d3d5a3e677.

13. D. Arner, J. Barberis and Rossbuckle, "The Evolution of Fintech: A New Post-Crisis Paradigm?" University of New South Wales Law Research Series, 2015.

14. Z. Hu, S. Ding, S. Li, L. Chen and S. Yang, "Adoption Intention of Fintech Services for BankUsers: An Empirical Examination with an ExtendedTechnology Acceptance Model," Symmetry, vol. 11, no. 3, p. 340, 2019.

15. Chen and Long, "From Fintech to Finlife: the case of Fintech Development in China," China economic journal, vol. 9, no. 3, pp. 225-239, 2016.

16. K. MN, M. S and S. MNI, "Mobile banking during COVID-19 pandemic in Bangladesh: a novel mechanism to change and accelerate people's financial access," Green Finance, vol. 3, no. 3, p. 253– 267, 2021.

17. B. AU, "Top Mobile Financial Services (MFS) in Bangladesh. Businesshaunt," https://www.businesshaunt.com/mobile-financial-services-mfs-in-bangladesh/., 2021.

18. C. L, "From Fintech to Finlife: the case of Fintech development in China.," China Econ J, vol. 9, no. 3, p. 225–239, 2016.

19. T. Puschmann, "Fintech," Business & Information Systems Engineering, vol. 59, no. 1, pp. 69-76, 2017.

20. J. Xie, Liying Ye, Wei Huang and Min Ye , "Understanding FinTech Platform Adoption: Impacts of Perceived Value and Perceived Risk," J. Theor. Appl. Electron. Commer., vol. 16, p. 1893–1911., 2021.

21. C. Yan, A. B. Siddik, N. Akter and Q. Dong, "Factors influencing the adoption intention of using mobile financial service during the COVID-19 pandemic: the role of FinTech," Environmental Science and Pollution Research, 2021.

22. I. Ajzen and M. Fishbein, "Attitude-behavior relations: A theoretical analysis and review of empirical research.," Psychological Bulletin, vol. 84, no. 5, p. 888–918, 1977.

23. F. D. Davis, "Perceived usefulness, perceived ease of use, and user acceptance of Information Technology," MIS Q. Manag., vol. 13, no. 3, p. 319–339, 1989.

24. D. FD, "A technology acceptance model for empirically testing new end-user information systems: theory and results," Massachusetts Institute of Technology, 1985.

25. V. Venkatesh and Fred D. Davis, "A Theoretical Extension of the Technology Acceptance Model: Four Longitudinal Field Studies," Management Science, vol. 46, no. 2, pp. 186-204, 2000.

26. R. E, Simon and Schuster, Difusion of Innovations, 2003.

27. G. Moore and I. Benbasat, "Development of an Instrument to Measure the Perceptions of Adopting and Information Technology Innovation," Information Systems Research, vol. 2, no. 3, pp. 192-222, 1991.

28. G. Bruner and A. Kumar, "Explaining consumer acceptance of handheld Internet devices," Journal of Business Research, vol. 58, no. 5, pp. 553-558, 2005.

29. P. A. Pavlou, H. Liang and Y. Xue, "Understanding and Mitigating Uncertainty in Online Exchange Relationships: A Principal–," MIS Quarterly, vol. 31, no. 1, pp. 105-136, 2007.

30. B. Hernandez, J. Jiménez-Martínez and M. J. M.-D. Hoyos, "Adoption vs acceptance of e-commerce: Two different decisions," European Journal of Marketing, vol. 43, no. 9/10, pp. 1232-1245, 2009.

31. P. Palvia, "The Role of Trust in e-Commerce Relational Exchange: A Unified Model.," Information & Management, vol. 46, pp. 213-220., 2009.

32. D. H. Shin, "An empirical investigation of a modified technology acceptance model of IPTV," Behaviour & Information Technology, vol. 28, no. 4, pp. 361-372, 2009.

33. G. Svendsen, J. Johnsen, L. Sorensen and Vitterso, "Personality and technology acceptance: The influence of," Behavior & Information Technology, vol. 32, no. 4, pp. 323-334., 2011.

34. H.-S. Ryu, "What makes users willing or hesitant to use Fintech? the moderating effect of user type," Industrial Management & Data Systems, vol. 118, no. 3, pp. 541-569, 2018.

35. M. K. A. nawayseh, "FinTech in COVID-19 and Beyond: What Factors Are Affecting Customers' Choice of FinTech Applications?" Journal of Open Innovation Technology Market and Complexity, 2020.

36. P. Senyo and Osabutey, Ellis L.C., "Unearthing antecedents to financial inclusion through FinTech innovations," Technovation, Elsevier, vol. 98, no. C, 2020.

37. I. M. Shaikh, Muhammad Asif Qureshi, Kamaruzaman Noordin, Junaid Shaikh, Arman Khan and Muhammad Saeed Shahbaz, "Acceptance of Islamic financial technology (FinTech) banking services by Malaysian users: an extension of technology acceptance model," Foresight, vol. 22, pp. 367-383, 2020.

38. C. Tiago Oliveira and Ales Popovic, "Understanding the Internet banking adoption: A unified theory of acceptance and use of technology and perceived risk application," International Journal of Information Management, vol. 34, no. 1, pp. 1-13, 2014.

39. A. A. Alalwan, Y. K. Dwivedi and N. P. Rana, "Factors influencing adoption of mobile banking by Jordanian bank customers: extending UTAUT2 with trust.," Int. J. Inf. Manage., vol. 37, p. 99–110, 2017.

40. "Internet of things – technology adoption model in India," Pertanika Journal of Science and Technology, vol. 25, no. 3, pp. 835-846, 2017.

41. F. Liébana-Cabanillas, V. Marinkovic, I. R. d. Luna and Z. Kalinic, "Predicting the determinants of mobile payment acceptance: A hybrid SEM-neural network approach," Technological Forecasting and Social Change, vol. 128, pp. 117-130, 2018.

42. R. Y. Khushbu Madan, "Understanding and predicting antecedents of mobile shopping adoption: A developing country perspective," Asia Pacific Journal of Marketing and Logistics, vol. 30, no. 1, pp. 139-162, 2018.

43. N. Singh, N. Sinha and F..Liébana-Cabanillas, "Determining factors in the adoption and recommendation of mobile wallet services in India: Analysis of the effect of innovativeness, stress to use and social influence," International Journal of Information Management, vol. 50, pp. 191-205, 2020.

44. S. Singh, M. M, Sahni and R. K. Kovid, "Exploring trust and responsiveness as antecedents for intention to use FinTech services," International Journal of Economics and Business Research, vol. 21, no. 2, pp. 254-268, 2021.

45. Z. Hu, S. Ding, S. Li, L. Chen and Shanlin Yang, "Adoption Intention of Fintech Services for Bank Users: An Empirical Examination with an Extended Technology Acceptance Model," Symmetry, vol. 11, p. 340, 2019.

46. M. K. Leong and Chaichi, K, "The Adoption of Technology Acceptance Model (Tam) And Trust In Influencing Online Purchase Intention During The Covid-19," International Journal Of Academic Research In Business And Social Sciences, vol. 11, no. 8, p. 468– 478, 2021.

47. S. Ahmed and S. Sur, "Change in the uses pattern of digital banking services by Indian rural MSMEs during demonetization and Covid-19 pandemic-related restrictions," Vilakshan - XIMB Journal of Management, 2021.

48. JonathanFu and MrinalMishra, "Fintech in the time of COVID–19: Technological adoption during crises," Journal of Financial Intermediation, vol. 50, p. 100945, 2022.
49. A. Kumar and Y. Arun Palanisamy, "Examining the consumers' preference towards adopting the mobile payment system," Int. J. Electron. Financ., vol. 9, p. 268–286, 2019.
50. S. A. Raza, A. Umer and N. S. Shah, "New determinants of ease of use and perceived usefulness for mobile banking adoption," International Journal of Electronic Customer Relationship Management, vol. 11, no. 1, p. 44, 2017.
51. P. Grover, A. K. Kar, M. Janssen and P. Vigneswara Ilavarasan, "Perceived usefulness, ease of use and user acceptance of blockchain technology for digital transactions – insights from user-generated content on Twitter," enterprise information systems, vol. 13, no. 6, pp. 771-800, 2019.
52. Y. Chang, Siew Fan Wong, Hwansoo Lee and Seon-phil J, "What motivates chinese consumers to adopt FinTech services: a regulatory focus theory," Proceedings of the 18th Annual International Conference on Electronic Commerce: e-Commerce in Smart connected World, pp. 17-19, 2016.
53. J. Lee, M H Ryu and D Lee, "A study on the reciprocal relationship between user perception and retailer perception on platform-based mobile payment service," J. Retailing Consum. Serv., vol. 48, pp. 7-15, 2019.
54. J. Wonglimpiyarat, "FinTech banking industry: a systemic approach," Foresight, , vol. 19, no. 6, pp. 590-603, 2017.
55. M. Moslehpour, Van Kien Pham, Wing-Keung Wong and Ismail Bilgiçli, "e-Purchase Intention of Taiwanese Consumers:Sustainable Mediation of Perceived Usefulness andPerceived Ease of Use," sustainability, vol. 10, no. 1, p. 234, 2018.
56. S. J. Hong, Thong J. Y. L and Tam, K. Y, "Understanding Continued Information Technology Usage Behaviour: A Comparison of Three Models in the Context of," Decision Support Systems, vol. 42, no. 3, pp. 1819-1834, 2006.
57. A. Ng and Kwok, B.K.B, "Emergence of Fintech and cybersecurity in a global financial centre: Strategic approach by a regulator," Journal of Financial Regulation and Compliance, vol. 25, no. 4, pp. 422-434, 2017.
58. V. Venkatesh, Michael G. Morris, Gordon B. Davis and Fred D. Dav, "User Acceptance of Information Technology: Toward a Unified View," MIS Quarterly, vol. 27, no. 3, pp. 425-478, 2003.
59. F. L. Cabanillas, A. Japutra and S. Molinillo, "Assessment of mobile technology use in the emerging market: Analyzing intention to use m-payment services in India," Telecommunications Policy, vol. 44, no. 9, p. 102009, 2020.
60. L. Vijayasarathy, "Predicting Consumer Intentions to Use On-Line Shopping: The Case for an Augmented Technology Acceptance Model.," Information & Management, vol. 41, pp. 747-762, 2004.
61. A. Tahar, H. A. Riyadh, H. Sofyani and W. E. Purnomo, "Perceived ease of use, perceived usefulness, perceived security and intention to use e-filing:

The role of technology readiness," Journal of Asian Finance, Economics and Business, , vol. 7, no. 9, p. 537–547, 2020.

62. V. Venkatesh and Fred D. Davis, "A Model of the Antecedents of Perceived Ease of Use: Development and Test," Decision Sciences, vol. 27, no. 3, pp. 451-481, 1996.

63. V. Venkatesh and Fred D. Davis, "A Theoretical Extension of the Technology Acceptance Model: Four LongitudinalField Studies," Management Science, vol. 46, no. 2, pp. 186-204, 2000.

64. A. D. Beldad and Sabrina M. Hegner, "Expanding the Technology Acceptance Model with the Inclusion of Trust, Social Influence, and Health Valuation to Determine the Predictors of German Users' Willingness to Continue using a Fitness App: A Structural Equation Modeling Approach," International Journal of Human–Computer Interaction, vol. 34, no. 9, pp. 882-893, 2017.

65. T. N. Grover, C. M.K.Cheung and J. B. Thatcher, "Inside out and outside in: How the COVID-19 pandemic affects self-disclosure on social media," International Journal of Information Management, vol. 55, p. 102188, 2020.

66. V. Venkatesh and J. Y. L. &. X. X. Thong, "Consumer acceptance and use of information technology: Extending the unified theory of acceptance and use of technology," MIS Quarterly, vol. 36, no. 1, p. 410–415., 2012.

67. A. Daragmeh, Csaba Lentner and Judit Sági, "FinTech payments in the era of COFinTech payments in the era of COVID-19: Factors influencing behavioral intentions of "Generation X" in Hungary to use mobile payment," Journal of Behavioral and Experimental Finance, vol. 32, p. 100574, 2021.

68. J. Koch, Britta Frommeyer and Gerhard Schewe, "Online Shopping Motives during the COVID-19 Pandemic—Lessons from the Crisis," sustainability, vol. 12, no. 24, p. 10247, 2020.

69. D. Chawla and H. Joshi, "Consumer attitude and intention to adopt mobile wallet in India – An empirical study," International Journal of Bank Marketing, 2019.

70. W. Alkhowaiter, "Digital payment and banking adoption research in Gulf countries: A systematic literature review," International Journal of Information Management, , vol. 53, p. 102102, 2020.

71. R. Alabdan[and S. M.M., "Understanding Proximity Mobile Payment Acceptance among Saudi Individuals: An Exploratory Study," International Journal of Advanced Computer Science and Applications, vol. 11, no. 4, pp. 264-270, 2020.

72. S. Barth, M. d. Jong, M. J. P. Hartel and J. Roppelt, "Putting the privacy paradox to the test: online privacy and security behaviors among users with technical knowledge, privacy awareness, and financial resources," Telemat. Inf., vol. 41, pp. 55-69, 2019.

73. M. Corstjens and R. Lal, "Building Store Loyalty through Store Brands," Journal of Marketing Research, vol. 37, pp. 281-291, 2000.

74. R. E. Anderson and S. S. Srinivasan, "E-satisfaction and e-loyalty: A contingency framework," Psychology & Marketing, vol. 20, no. 2, pp. 123-138, 2003.
75. A. Larsson, Responding to the FinTech Challenge: A study of Swedish bank managers' perception of FinTech's effects on digitalization and customer e-loyalty, Routledge, 2018.
76. D. Gefen, "Customer Loyalty in E-Commerce," Journal of the Association for Information Systems, vol. 3, pp. 27-51, 2002.
77. E. Toufaily, L. Ricard and J. Perrien, "Customer loyalty to a commercial website: Descriptive meta- analysis of the empirical literature and proposal of an integrative model," Journal of Business Research, vol. 66, no. 9, pp. 1436-1447, 2013.
78. M. Wang and Y. Chang, "Technology Leadership, Brand Equity, and Customer Loyalty towards Fintech Service Providers in China," AMCIS, 2018.

5

A Comprehensive Study of Cryptocurrencies as a Financial Asset: Major Topics and Market Trends

Gioia Arnone[1*] and Ajantha Devi Vairamani[2]

[1]*Department of Managerial and Quantitative Studies, University of Naples Parthenope, Napoli, Italy*
[2]*AP3 Solutions, Chennai, TN, India*

Abstract

The article comprises a set of theoretical and methodological approaches to studying the concept of "cryptocurrencies as a financial asset and market trends." and identifies some trends of development of the real sector in the project financing market. This paper provides a systematic review of the empirical literature based on the major topics that have been associated with the market for cryptocurrencies since their development as a financial asset. It also presents an overview of the advantages of current trends in the market. Each influences the perception of the role of cryptocurrencies as a credible investment asset class and legitimate value. We posit that cryptocurrencies may perform some useful functions and add economic value, but there are reasons to favor the regulation of the market. While this would go against the original libertarian rationale behind cryptocurrencies, it appears a necessary step to improve social welfare.

Keywords: Cryptocurrency, financial assets, market trends

5.1 Introduction

Cryptocurrency forms of money have stood out from financial backers, controllers, and the media since Bitcoin was first proposed by Nakamoto (Nakamoto & Bitcoin, 2008). Digital forms of money are distributed electronic money frameworks that permit online installments to be sent directly, starting

Corresponding author: gioia.arnone@studenti.uniparthenope.it; gioia.arnone@vub.be; https://orcid.org/0000-0002-6787-7283
Ajantha Devi Vairamani; https://orcid.org/0000-0002-9455-4826

Mohd Naved, V. Ajantha Devi, and Aditya Kumar Gupta (eds.) Fintech and Cryptocurrency, (91–104)
© 2023 Scrivener Publishing LLC

with one party and then the next, without a financial foundation. This way, unlike most other monetary resources accessible, they have no relationship with any more significant position, have no actual portrayal, and are vastly detachable. Additionally, unlike conventional monetary resources, the worth of digital forms of money does not depend on any unmistakable resource, a nation's economy or a firm, but rather depends on the security of a calculation that can follow all exchanges (Giudici *et al.*, 2020). The development of digital forms of money can be connected to their low exchange costs, distributed framework, and legislative free plan. This has prompted a flood in exchanging volume, instability, and cost of digital currencies, with cryptographic forms of money routinely in the standard news (Bariviera & Merediz-Solà, 2021).

Cryptocurrencies have experienced broad market acceptance and fast development despite their recent conception. Many hedge funds and asset managers have begun to include cryptocurrency-related assets in their portfolios and trading strategies (Jalal *et al.*, 2021). The academic community has similarly spent considerable efforts in researching cryptocurrency trading. This paper seeks to provide a comprehensive survey of the research on cryptocurrency trading, by which we mean any study aimed at facilitating and building strategies to trade cryptocurrencies (Zeng *et al.*, 2020).

Bitcoin is the main decentralized advanced cash and stays the cryptographic money market's chief. From October 2016 to October 2017, the market capitalization of Bitcoin expanded from $10.1 to $79.7 billion, while the cost bounced from $616 to $4800 (US dollars). This huge development introduced a valuable chance to acquire 680% of the profit from speculations each year, which some other resources can't present. In December 2017, the cost for each Bitcoin came to $19,500. As the blockchain space develops, Bitcoin will encounter an expanded contest in the closest future. Today, more than 1,000 cryptographic forms of money, including new items, for example, Ethereum, Ripple, Litecoin, and Dash, have added to an absolute market capitalization of nearly $190 billion (Mikhaylov *et al.*, 2021).

5.2   Literature Review

Numerous researchers endeavor to address normal examination questions taken from a wide finance exploration custom, such as market proficiency, resource valuing air pockets, virus and decoupling theories, instability bunching, and the effect of information declarations and media consideration give some examples. Many investigations are directed equal, using comparable datasets and comparative approaches, giving indistinguishable proof. In addition, because of the criticalness of these examination issues, many papers are distributed in short exploration notes, making it much more significant for monetary researchers to guarantee that their examination discoveries are particular. Along these lines, it is pivotal to survey the current papers in this examination field and distinguish a present edge of the scholarly nature of the investigations that consider the difficulties and potentially open doors encompassing cryptographic forms of money.

Nakamoto (2008) designed Bitcoin. It facilitated electronic payments between individuals without going through a third party. Since its introduction, Bitcoin has been the subject of challenges and opportunities for policymakers, consumers, entrepreneurs, and economists. Bitcoin is considered different from any other asset in the financial market. It creates new possibilities for stakeholders concerning portfolio analysis, risk management, and consumer sentiment analysis.

Thakkar & Chaudhari (2021) presented a normal air pocket model for Bitcoin and other digital forms of money that consolidates weighty tails and the likelihood of a total breakdown in resource costs, making this model a hypothetical refinement of the model by Cheah and Fry [2015]. Without any focal digital currency market guideline, the likelihood that the entire market can fall is higher for cryptographic forms of money than for different resources (Cheah & Fry, 2015; Thakkar & Chaudhari, 2021). The paper gives proof of an air pocket in Bitcoin and Ethereum, while there is no proof of an air pocket in Ripple. They dissected the value explosivity of the seven biggest digital forms of money by market capitalization utilizing day-to-day information. The outcomes show that all digital forms of money (Bitcoin, Ripple, Ethereum, Litecoin, Nem, Dash, and Stellar) experienced dangerous behavior. Besides, the review gives proof of multidirectional co-explosivity conduct, i.e., explosivity in one digital currency can prompt explosivity in other cryptographic forms of money. Simultaneously, this impact isn't guaranteed to rely upon the size of every cryptographic money (Celeste *et al.*, 2020).

The global practice of project funding has usually been utilized to execute enormous scope and capital-escalated projects for a long time. Organizations incorporating progressively into the world financial space face the need to carry out the tasks comparable in their intricacy and scale to the activities completed by their rivals on the planet markets. To that end, project funding turns out to be possibly increasingly famous and important in the market. The actual chance of full use of undertaking support is fundamental for the advancement of organizations and, over the long haul, for our country's monetary turn of events. Project funding as an apparatus for long-haul venture projects is planned to support long-haul interest in the genuine economy; however, because of the monetary approach sought after in Russia encounters a deficiency of obligation capital. Project funding development with its benefits will permit to take a critical quantum jump in Russia's change to another level (Peters *et al.*, 2015).

The year 2017 was the most un-unstable year starting around 1964, with simply 6.8% acknowledged unpredictability for the S&P 500 Index. Move of market instability. Bitcoin, nonetheless, was north of twelve times more unpredictable during a similar period. Simultaneously, many powers drive day-to-day variances and disparities. There was a steadiness in stocks that originated from a particularly solid agreement in late 2016 about the year ahead, further reflected in the moderately low Cboe Volatility Index (VIX) introduced (DeVries, 2016). Such changes in the assumptions for corporate income have the most effect. For Bitcoin and other digital currencies, this isn't true. There are no profit and agreement valuation structures for digital currencies aside from financial backers put on the item. The race to purchase digital forms of money pushes costs higher prompting a cost instability winding produced by the excited self-supporting force and theoretical way of behaving digital money financial backers saw between 2014 and late-2017 (Kristjanpoller *et al.*, 2020). Finance investor consideration is additionally seen as a critical determinant of potential market mispricing, as examined in (Charfeddine *et al.*, 2020) and (Sebastião *et al.*, 2021). Utilizing the VECM strategy, Mai *et al.* [2015] observed that online activity impacts are generally determined by the people who utilize web-based entertainment on rare occasions, also called the quiet larger part.

Further, messages on web discussions strongly affect Bitcoin returns more than tweets. Utilizing a critical information base spreading over 2010 through 2017, Urquhart (2018) observed that acknowledged unpredictability and the volume of Bitcoin exchanged, controlled for Bitcoin basics, are huge drivers of the following day's consideration for Bitcoin (Urquhart, 2018). Balcilar *et al.* (2017) show that volume can't assist with foreseeing the unpredictability of Bitcoin returns at any time of the contingent conveyance; however, it can anticipate returns aside from Bitcoin, bull, and bear market systems (Balcilar *et al.*, 2017). The study aims to summarize some theoretical and methodological positions concerning the formation of the mechanism of project financing with the participation of finance and an analysis of the current state of the project financing market and some trends of its development.

5.3   Methodology

Systematic analysis approaches can provide a more comprehensive understanding of the knowledge in the field, and the findings can change future directions of the research in this discipline by uncovering gaps in the literature. For new research areas such as those based on cryptocurrencies, a systematic analysis can be the most powerful tool to inform academics, professionals, and policy-makers about the current state of knowledge, consensuses, and ambiguities in the emerging discipline. Cryptocurrency finance research immediately adopted the same pattern. However, apart from the standard financial problems mentioned above in cryptocurrencies, several unique and specific issues cannot be addressed directly using quantitative research design and data mining. For example, regulatory disorientation, cybercriminal, and environmental sustainability are a few. This paper provides recommendations on how cryptocurrency research can be diversified to provide more meaningful contributions to knowledge.

This paper provides a systematic review of the empirical literature on the major topics that have attracted the attention of scholars. Our motivation to employ a systematic analysis in this study is threefold. First, this paper is motivated by the growing academic literature analyzing various issues associated with the rapid growth of cryptocurrency markets. Second, our study is motivated by a relative dearth of systematic literature reviews in finance. While systematic reviews have become very popular in medical science, psychology, neuroscience, economics, international business, and management, in finance, the preference was given to more narrative literature surveys. Thirdly, this review is motivated by the problem of paradigmatic unity in finance research. The majority of financial papers are conducted in broad traditions of positivist research. However, the important research questions for practitioners and policy-makers often rely on upon beyond this philosophical paradigm. The popularity of cryptocurrencies amongst users has attracted substantial media attention while becoming a popular topic in recent academic research. While new empirical evidence continues to emerge rapidly, there is a strong need to aggregate the existing knowledge in cryptocurrency research and identify the gaps in the existing literature.

It is important to generate research findings useful for policy-makers, businesses, and society and can be disseminated and replicated by scholars outside the financial community. Cryptocurrencies: an asset on a blockchain that can be exchanged or transferred between network participants and hence used as a means of payment but offers no other benefits. Within cryptocurrencies, it is then possible to distinguish those whose quantity is fixed and price market-determined (floating cryptocurrencies) and those where a supporting arrangement, software or institutional, alters the supply to maintain a fixed price against other assets (stable coins, for example, Tether or the planned Facebook Libra).

5.4   Findings

Cryptocurrencies are part of a larger class of financial assets known as "crypto-assets," which have similar peer-to-peer digital value transfers without the use of third-party organizations for transaction certification. What makes cryptocurrencies different from other crypto-assets? This depends on their intended use, i.e., whether they are given just for transfer or to serve other purposes. One can continue the differences highlighted in current governmental reports within the general category of crypto-assets, differentiating two additional sub-categories of crypto-assets on top of cryptocurrency (Pavlidis, 2020).

- Cryptocurrencies are a type of asset on a blockchain that can be transferred or moved between network members and therefore used as a form of payment—but with no additional features.
- Crypto securities are a type of blockchain asset that also has the potential for future payments, such as a portion of earnings.
- Crypto utility assets are blockchain assets that may be exchanged for or used to access pre-defined services or operations.

Within cryptocurrencies, it is feasible to differentiate between those whose source is rectified and the price is ascertained by the industry (floating cryptocurrencies) and those whose source is altered by a supplementary structure, such as software or financial, to sustain a defined price against other assets (fixed cryptocurrencies) (stable coins, for example, Tether or the planned Facebook Libra).

Crypto securities and crypto utility assets are further distinguished because they are offered by a public sale (initial coin offerings or ICOs). ICOs have been a significant form of investment for technology-oriented start-up enterprises adopting blockchain-based business models. These crypto-asset classifications are important for global regulators because they must decide if a crypto-asset should be regulated as an e-money, security, or another type of financial instrument, particularly in light of shareholder security issues in ICOs (Cumming *et al.*, 2019; Huang, 2021). The leading 12 crypto-assets by market capitalization are Tether, a stable coin, and Bitfinex's UNUS SED LEO, a utility coin; the remainder is floating cryptocurrencies.

5.5   Cryptocurrencies as a Major Financial Asset

Since the birth of Bitcoin almost a decade ago, scholars, politicians, and policymakers have been watching the rise of cryptocurrencies. Cryptocurrency proponents say there is an indication to back up the asset's steady development as a cashless means of payment that can transform the financial world as we know it.

Cryptocurrencies, particularly Bitcoin, are among the first and most well-known uses of the widely recognized blockchain concept, garnering far more interest than other blockchain use cases. Bitcoin had a market capitalization of $205.4 billion US dollars in the third quarter of 2019 (Cap, 2019). While Bitcoin is the most popular, other cryptocurrencies such as Ethereum, Ripple, and Litecoin have all grown in popularity in 2019 (TradingView, 2019). Many people predict that blockchain and cryptocurrency technologies will shift from conventional funds transfer to digital ones underpinned by secure ledgers in the future.

The number of decentralized node exchanges is likely to expand dramatically as a result of the underlying blockchain systems' absorption into our daily lives (Alphand *et al.*, 2018), putting more strain on the energy grid (De Vries, 2018), as well as infrastructure, peer-to-peer (P2P) networks, and storage volumes (Nakamoto, 2008). While the field of traditional infrastructure-like (cloud) communication analysis and prediction are well-studied, the influence of new networking paradigms, such as fog and edge (Busanelli *et al.*, 2019; Mäkitalo *et al.*, 2017), is projected to add a new degree of computational effort from both a telecommunications and computational standpoint. As a result, blockchains provide several distinct advantages over previous technologies. Redundant checking by several nodes ensures that a blockchain survives malfunctions and attacks. This resiliency goes much beyond replication because it occurs across the network without using a network hub or intermediary (Hyperledger, 2018). In general, the design of said distributed systems necessitates thorough management and operational analysis, but traditional methodologies may encounter several obstacles as the system's diversity grows.

Whereas the number of associated applications has been sharply rising (Lao *et al.*, 2020), there is still a shortage of standardized methods and techniques for performance assessment and behaviour observation block-chains. Without any preliminary operational review, the construction of blockchain-based, extremely complex, and dynamic systems could have a significant detrimental influence during the deployment phase. Most existing evaluation methods are based on emulation techniques, which copy and replicate the complete network's activity. It necessitates many computational, storage, and communication resources (Chen *et al.*, 2017; Dinh *et al.*, 2017). The deployment of true community-driven testnets receives less attention, although it necessitates major incentivization operations to entice people to participate (Ometov *et al.*, 2020; Zhidanov *et al.*, 2019). As a result, simulation creates a significant scaling issue for evaluating real-world deployments (Faria & Correia, 2019). Furthermore, such an evaluation necessitates significant technical work to adapt complex open-source solutions or production systems to test out rapidly growing systems. In this circumstance, modeling methodologies, such as analytical and simulation methods, might be used as an alternative to exchanging precision for assessment speed.

5.6   What is the Value of Cryptocurrencies? Current Market Trends

On the one hand, cryptocurrencies should be able to simplify financial transactions by removing intermediaries, lowering transaction costs, making them accessible to anyone with an Internet connection, and providing greater privacy and security (Böhme *et al.*, 2015; Richter *et al.*, 2015). Conversely, the actual financial value conveyed in operations of freely floating cryptocurrencies like Bitcoin's BTC and Ethereum's Ether is unknown. Despite the Bitcoin blockchain's thorough and unsubstantiated history of all prior operations, the knowledge only relates to notional quantities, i.e., the number of bitcoin units exchanged. Nevertheless, checking the exchange rates of cryptocurrencies versus existing fiat currencies might give you a sense of their market value. Cryptocurrency exchanges make this feasible, which keeps a near-constant price log for all actively traded coins. However, the resultant exchange rates are highly erratic; they show that cryptocurrencies have a non-zero value for individuals willing to buy them with fiat cash. What drives this worth without a sponsorship resource or a backer's responsibility? Some backer it is the expense of "mining" (energy and time spent on computational endeavors expected to finish the development of another square in the chain and compensated by a recently given digital money unit), but the expense borne by one individual from the organization doesn't legitimize the worth of the new digital money unit for different individuals from the organization (Dwyer, 2015). Others guarantee their fairly estimated worth is driven by the theoretical air pocket; yet, stringently talking, the fizz has appeared in vertical cost deviations from the basic worth (Siegel, 2003); subsequently, the fizz clarification is just fractional and brings up additional issues about what drives financial backers' convictions that feed their interest and, in this manner, support the fizz. If it is the ease and the speed of exchanges, new exchange innovations and asset move frameworks that enormously worked on in the new ten years (like TransferWise and comparative frameworks) ought to have cleared out a major piece of the digital money esteem, yet this doesn't appear to be the situation. A potential response might lie in the highlights that recognize digital forms of money from different resources and instalment frameworks.

Throughout most studies of cryptocurrencies, security, or indeed anonymity, is a key distinguishing trait. The worth of a cryptocurrency is essentially a measurement of how often users value transactional confidentiality. While confidentiality may be appealing for criminal activities (and some studies imply that cryptocurrencies are frequently used for these reasons), it's impossible to rule out the possibility that users want more privacy, avoiding the "Big Brother" effect of conventional money transfers. Additional considerations, such as trend (users need to utilize the technology that everyone else is discussing), hi-tech appeal (the want to use the most cutting-edge technology), or interest (the urge to try something different), may exist. Still, they appear to be more transient than the appeal of secrecy.

The introduction of crypto exchanges, where anybody can register profiles and trade crypto-assets versus each other and fiat currencies, has been a crucial step in the ascent of cryptocurrencies and other crypto-assets. The Euro and the British Pound are presently the most popular trading currencies against cryptocurrencies, whereas the Chinese Renminbi (CNY) has lost a lot of ground since the People's Bank of China tightened its regulations; roughly three-quarters of large exchanges offer trading assistance for two or more cryptocurrencies (Hileman & Rauchs, 2017). The featured crypto exchanges give substantial cryptocurrency price and trading statistics in the digital realm. The advent of these exchanges has spawned an extensive 'ecosystem' of services and players aimed at providing liquidity, profiting on price differences, and assisting both consumer and professional traders in their investments.

5.7   Conclusion

The need to escalate the support to cryptocurrency in the venture inter-action follows from the fruitful improvement of the financial framework and economy overall. Business banks are keen on a stable monetary climate essential for their exercises from one perspective. The present paper directs a precise investigation of cryptocurrency finance research's developing insights. We recognize that this examination field is youthful, and new observational and hypothetical proof keeps on arising consistently. Similarly, make sense of the principle restrictions and worries with digital currencies and the administrative issues facing legislatures and national banks. A restriction to our orderly investigation is the possible rejection of a few applicable examinations that will open up during the distribution interaction. We have incorporated the most applicable, peer-reviewed studies. Our principle discoveries exhibit that there are various holes in cryptocurrency-related writing. Even though there are numerous likely areas of interest regarding digital forms of money, we recognize ten significant holes in the writing, which, ideally, different specialists can use to add their insight around here. While digital currencies keep creating both an item and an exchanged market, we should direct our assumptions for their possible worth and advantages to society while being wary and considering the intrinsic perils they could produce inside our general public.

Then again, supportable finance improvement relies generally upon the level of unwavering quality of the financial framework and its successful working. At a similar time, the cooperation of credit organizations in the speculation of various areas of the economy happens just under good circumstances because the interests of the singular bank as a business foundation are centered around benefit amplification at an acceptable level of hazards. Because of the restricted admittance of the abroad business sectors under states of high vulnerability, the expansion in interests in the public economy goes down. Along these lines, the significance of drafting monetary instruments to make a proficient system for project funding, including credit banks, is clear. Hence considering the need to foster the creation area and forthcoming changes in the speculation strategy of Russia, we can expect with certainty that undertaking funding as a sort of financial assistance will be a viable device for commitment to the cutting edge economy.

References

Alphand, O., Amoretti, M., Claeys, T., Dall'Asta, S., Duda, A., Ferrari, G., Rousseau, F., Tourancheau, B., Veltri, L., & Zanichelli, F. (2018). IoTChain: A blockchain security architecture for the Internet of Things. *2018 IEEE Wireless Communications and Networking Conference (WCNC)*, 1–6.

Balcilar, M., Bouri, E., Gupta, R., & Roubaud, D. (2017). Can volume predict Bitcoin returns and volatility? A quantiles-based approach. *Economic Modelling, 64*, 74–81.

Bariviera, A. F., & Merediz-Solà, I. (2021). Where do we stand in cryptocurrencies economic research? A survey based on hybrid analysis. *Journal of Economic Surveys, 35*(2), 377–407.

Böhme, R., Christin, N., Edelman, B., & Moore, T. (2015). Bitcoin: Economics, technology, and governance. *Journal of Economic Perspectives, 29*(2), 213–238.

Busanelli, S., Cirani, S., Melegari, L., Picone, M., Rosa, M., & Veltri, L. (2019). A sidecar object for the optimized communication between edge and cloud in internet of things applications. *Future Internet, 11*(7), 145.

Cap, B. M. (2019). *Market Capitalization (USD) - Blockchain Explorer.*

Celeste, V., Corbet, S., & Gurdgiev, C. (2020). Fractal dynamics and wavelet analysis: Deep volatility and return properties of Bitcoin, Ethereum and Ripple. *The Quarterly Review of Economics and Finance, 76*, 310–324.

Charfeddine, L., Benlagha, N., & Maouchi, Y. (2020). Investigating the dynamic relationship between cryptocurrencies and conventional assets: Implications for financial investors. *Economic Modelling, 85*, 198–217.

Cheah, E.-T., & Fry, J. (2015). Speculative bubbles in Bitcoin markets? An empirical investigation into the fundamental value of Bitcoin. *Economics Letters, 130*, 32–36.

Chen, C., Qi, Z., Liu, Y., & Lei, K. (2017). Using virtualization for blockchain testing. *International Conference on Smart Computing and Communication*, 289–299.

Cumming, D. J., Johan, S., & Pant, A. (2019). Regulation of the crypto-economy: Managing risks, challenges, and regulatory uncertainty. *Journal of Risk and Financial Management, 12*(3), 126.

De Vries, A. (2018). Bitcoin's growing energy problem. *Joule, 2*(5), 801–805.

DeVries, P. D. (2016). An analysis of cryptocurrency, bitcoin, and the future. *International Journal of Business Management and Commerce, 1*(2), 1–9.

Dinh, T. T. A., Wang, J., Chen, G., Liu, R., Ooi, B. C., & Tan, K.-L. (2017). Blockbench: A framework for analyzing private blockchains. *Proceedings of the 2017 ACM International Conference on Management of Data*, 1085–1100.

Dwyer, G. P. (2015). The economics of Bitcoin and similar private digital currencies. *Journal of Financial Stability, 17*, 81–91.

Faria, C., & Correia, M. (2019). BlockSim: blockchain simulator. *2019 IEEE International Conference on Blockchain (Blockchain)*, 439–446.

Giudici, G., Milne, A., & Vinogradov, D. (2020). Cryptocurrencies: market analysis and perspectives. *Journal of Industrial and Business Economics, 47*(1), 1–18.

Hileman, G., & Rauchs, M. (2017). Global cryptocurrency benchmarking study. *Cambridge Centre for Alternative Finance, 33*, 33–113.

Huang, S. S. (2021). Crypto assets regulation in the UK: an assessment of the regulatory effectiveness and consistency. *Journal of Financial Regulation and Compliance.*

Hyperledger. (2018). *Hyperledger Blockchain Performance Metrics.*

Jalal, R. N.-U.-D., Alon, I., & Paltrinieri, A. (2021). A bibliometric review of cryptocurrencies as a financial asset. *Technology Analysis & Strategic Management,* 1–16.

Kristjanpoller, W., Bouri, E., & Takaishi, T. (2020). Cryptocurrencies and equity funds: Evidence from an asymmetric multifractal analysis. *Physica A: Statistical Mechanics and Its Applications, 545*, 123711.

Lao, L., Li, Z., Hou, S., Xiao, B., Guo, S., & Yang, Y. (2020). A survey of IoT applications in blockchain systems: Architecture, consensus, and traffic modeling. *ACM Computing Surveys (CSUR), 53*(1), 1–32.

Mäkitalo, N., Ometov, A., Kannisto, J., Andreev, S., Koucheryavy, Y., & Mikkonen, T. (2017). Safe, secure executions at the network edge: coordinating cloud, edge, and fog computing. *IEEE Software, 35*(1), 30–37.

Mikhaylov, A., Danish, M. S. S., & Senjyu, T. (2021). A New Stage in the Evolution of Cryptocurrency Markets: Analysis by Hurst Method. In *Strategic outlook in business and finance innovation: Multidimensional policies for emerging economies.* Emerald Publishing Limited.

Nakamoto, S. (2008). Bitcoin: A peer-to-peer electronic cash system. *Decentralized Business Review*, 21260.

Nakamoto, S., & Bitcoin, A. (2008). A peer-to-peer electronic cash system. *Bitcoin.–URL: Https://Bitcoin. Org/Bitcoin. Pdf, 4.*

Ometov, A., Bardinova, Y., Afanasyeva, A., Masek, P., Zhidanov, K., Vanurin, S., Sayfullin, M., Shubina, V., Komarov, M., & Bezzateev, S. (2020). An overview on blockchain for smartphones: State-of-the-art, consensus, implementation, challenges and future trends. *IEEE Access, 8*, 103994–104015.

Pavlidis, G. (2020). International regulation of virtual assets under FATF's new standards. *Journal of Investment Compliance.*

Peters, G., Panayi, E., & Chapelle, A. (2015). Trends in cryptocurrencies and blockchain technologies: A monetary theory and regulation perspective. *Journal of Financial Perspectives, 3*(3).

Richter, C., Kraus, S., & Bouncken, R. B. (2015). Virtual currencies like Bitcoin as a paradigm shift in the field of transactions. *International Business & Economics Research Journal (IBER), 14*(4), 575–586.

Sebastião, H. M. C. V., Cunha, P. J. O. R. Da, & Godinho, P. M. C. (2021). Cryptocurrencies and blockchain. Overview and future perspectives. *International Journal of Economics and Business Research, 21*(3), 305–342.

Siegel, J. J. (2003). What is an asset price bubble? An operational definition. *European Financial Management, 9*(1), 11–24.

Thakkar, A., & Chaudhari, K. (2021). A comprehensive survey on portfolio optimization, stock price and trend prediction using particle swarm optimization. *Archives of Computational Methods in Engineering, 28*(4), 2133–2164.

TradingView. (2019). *Cryptocurrency Market.*

Urquhart, A. (2018). What causes the attention of Bitcoin? *Economics Letters, 166,* 40–44.

Zeng, T., Yang, M., & Shen, Y. (2020). Fancy Bitcoin and conventional financial assets: Measuring market integration based on connectedness networks. *Economic Modelling, 90,* 209–220.

Zhidanov, K., Bezzateev, S., Afanasyeva, A., Sayfullin, M., Vanurin, S., Bardinova, Y., & Ometov, A. (2019). Blockchain technology for smartphones and constrained IoT devices: A future perspective and implementation. *2019 IEEE 21st Conference on Business Informatics (CBI), 2,* 20–27.

Customers' Satisfaction and Continuance Intention to Adopt Fintech Services: Developing Countries' Perspective

Song Bee Lian[1]* and Liew Chee Yoong[2]

[1]School of Marketing and Management, Asia Pacific University of Technology and Innovation, Kuala Lumpur, Malaysia
[2]Faculty of Business and Management, UCSI University, Kuala Lumpur, Malaysia

Abstract

Finance Technology (Fintech) has emerged as the current trend in the financial world. Fintech services gain popularity from the increasing adoption by organizations and consumers. By applying empirical research, this chapter aims to explore the important factors influencing consumer satisfaction and continuance intention to adopt Fintech services. As previous studies on customers' behavioral intention to adopt Fintech were mostly conducted in the context of developed countries, there is a paucity of research in the developing countries' perspective. To address the research gap, this study focused on five selected developing countries, namely Malaysia, Indonesia, India, Nigeria and Philippines. Drawing on the extended Technology Acceptance Model (TAM) for the proposed research model, customer innovativeness, hedonic motivation, perceived usefulness, perceived ease of use, system quality and technology self-efficacy have positive effect on customer satisfaction and subsequently, continuance intention to adopt Fintech. The findings recommend that Fintech service providers to develop effective strategic frameworks to build consumer satisfaction and encourage their continuance intention to adopt Fintech.

Keywords: Finance Technology, customer satisfaction, perceived usefulness, continuance intention to adopt, hedonic motivation, perceived ease of use, developing countries

*Corresponding author: song.beelian@apu.edu.my

Mohd Naved, V. Ajantha Devi, and Aditya Kumar Gupta (eds.) Fintech and Cryptocurrency, (105–136)

6.1   Introduction

Technological advancements and innovation have contributed to the increasing global adoption of Finance Technology (Fintech) services in the financial sector. Fintech services provide opportunities for organizations to innovate their business process through effective operational management, target cross-selling, personalize offers and improve service delivery to the customers in banking and finance industries [1, 2]. Customers utilized Fintech for purchases, investment and information search, which provide them benefits in the aspect of convenient, time and costs saving, and more options for purchases [3]. Fintech services can be categorized into traditional and emergent Fintech services [4]. Traditional Fintech services includes asset management and mobile backing leveraging on information technology to offer financial services, such as online banking [4]. Emergent Fintech services relates to innovative financial services supplemented by non-financial companies, examples include cryptocurrency, crowdfunding and mobile payment services [4]. Fintech has applied disruptive technologies such as Data Analytics and Blockchain improving existing business model and creating new service development in the financial services industry. Fintech involves the usage of mobile devices and other technology platforms to access bank account to perform transaction by going through various transaction notifications via SMS or APP [5]. Fintech has paved way for the usage of mobile application that created a seamless shopping experience to the customers. Through mobile service in Fintech, customers have more flexibility to make online purchases and payments. Retailers used various technology platforms to attract customers and promote usage of online channels for transaction.

Over the years, Fintech has grown rapidly and has been adopted worldwide. Fintech services have become essential to most businesses, consumers and suppliers. The global Fintech market was valued at USD7301.78 in 2020, and it is projected to grow at a CAGR of 23.58% from 2021 to 2025 [6]. Among the factors that will contribute to the continuous growth of Fintech are increasing innovations, higher adoption of e-commerce platforms and usage of mobile payment services [6]. The global Fintech market has achieved growth with a total of US$100 billion in funding secured in 2021, compared to US$48 billion in a year before 2020 [7]. Global consumer Fintech adoption has grown significantly with 75% of consumers used Fintech for payment services and/or money transfer in 2019 [8]. The top five leading countries for Fintech adoption in 2019 consists of the emerging and developed countries, namely China, United States, Mexico, South Africa and United Kingdom [9].

Nevertheless, Fintech is associated with various risks, such as operational, financial and legal risks, due to the technology influences and functionality [10]. Business transactions through online are subject to technical faults that have negatively affected customers' trust and satisfaction [10, 11]. Furthermore, these risks have resulted in increased uncertainty and barrier to adopt Fintech by consumers [5]. Data security issues and lack of mobile and technology expertise are among the factors that can hamper the growth of Fintech market [6]. Furthermore, consumers' complaints occurred in the system quality aspects such as server downtime or disruptions and error in barcode scans that have caused unable to perform transactions [12]. As the Fintech services are continuously evolving by leveraging on technology innovation, the challenges facing consumers are the requirement of adequate knowledge and skills, such as financial and digital literacy, to adopt Fintech [13]. The increasing competitiveness in Fintech services have contributed to greater differentiation between the service providers in improving service efficiency, managing operation costs and building risk control capabilities to attract consumers and encourage continuous adoption of Fintech [14]. Therefore, in the new era of competitive markets, the Fintech companies are facing various challenges to meet the changing consumers' demand and satisfaction [15].

Previous studies have to examined Fintech adoption in various context. Past research focused on customer satisfaction level in the Fintech services [12, 16–18], and specifically on mobile Fintech [19], mobile payment [20], mobile banking [21], mobile banking applications [22] and internet financial services [23]. Literature covered continuance intention to adopt Fintech services in specific areas, such as mobile payment [24–26], smartphone banking [27] and mobile banking [28]. Past studies investigated the influence of consumer satisfaction on continuance intention to adopt in specific Fintech services, such as mobile payment [24], mobile banking [29, 30] and banks' chatbot [31]. The determinants are used to examined its effect on customer satisfaction and intention to continue adoption in specific Fintech services, includes perceived usefulness [29], perceived ease of use [29], perceived privacy security [29], information quality [24, 31], system quality [24, 31], service quality [24, 31] and task technology fit [30]. However, there is limitation coverage on the predictor or antecedent factors on consumer satisfaction and continuance intention to adopt in the general context of Fintech. Yin and Lin [29] stressed that it is necessary for future research to explore on the important factors that influence customers' willingness to adopt Fintech. Furthermore, lack of studies found on Fintech adoption in developing countries [32].

Given the scarcity of empirical evidence and theoretical understanding on the antecedents influencing customer satisfaction and continuance intention to adopt Fintech services in the developing countries' perspective, the present study will apply the Technology Acceptance Model (TAM) as theoretical foundation to explore the relationships. Hence, the present study will address the research gap in the literature through empirical research in examining the factors affecting consumer satisfaction and continuance intention to adopt Fintech services in the developing countries context. The main research objectives are: (a) to examine the effect of customer innovativeness, hedonic motivation, perceived usefulness, perceived ease of use, system quality and technology self-efficacy on customer satisfaction in the Fintech services, (b) to examine the effect of customer satisfaction on continuance intention to adopt the Fintech services.

This chapter enhances to the existing literature through a proposed integrated research model to provide understanding on customer satisfaction and continuance intention to adopt Fintech services, extending the TAM. In the practical perspective, the findings would assist the Fintech companies to develop effective strategic frameworks to build consumers' satisfaction and encourage their continuance intention to adopt Fintech.

6.2   Understanding the Fintech Phenomenon in Developing Countries

Most developing countries are experiencing positive growth in the FinTech industry. The government in the developing countries has recognized the importance of FinTech towards the economic growth. Fintech industry in the developing countries has high potential investment capacity due to the development of mobile money [33]. Nevertheless, the different pace of economic development among the developing countries have affected the FinTech adoption level [34]. Developing countries with larger financial markets have more opportunities for Fintech innovation, adoption and growth compared to smaller financial market countries. Most businesses in the developing countries are dominated by the small and medium enterprises with constraints on financial and knowledge literacy to adopt Fintech [35].

India is the largest Fintech ecosystem in the world after United States and China, with Fintech market size worth USS31billion in 2021 [36]. The government in India has focused on policy and funding level to boost Fintech adoption and growth [37]. The FinTech adoption rate in India was

87 percent as compared to the global adoption rate of 64 percent as of 2021 [38]. In Indonesia, the largest segment of Fintech services came from digital payments with a total transaction value of US$72.91billion in 2022 [39]. Indonesia has funds constraint to improve its financial infrastructure and accessibility, adding to the fact that the country has large unbanked population, recorded at 95 million population in 2017 [40, 41].

Malaysia has achieved a remarkable growth of Fintech with transaction values of RM460 million recorded for mobile banking in 2020, increased by 125% compared to 2019 [42]. Various initiatives have been undertaken by the Malaysian government to boost Fintech adoption by the businesses and consumers. In November 2017, Malaysia has formed the Digital Free Trade Zone (DFTZTM) with the assistance of Malaysia Digital Economy Corporation (MDEC) and Alibaba Group. Therefore, the government in developing countries have given greater emphasis on the development of Fintech to facilitate the creation of new business areas and development of industries.

6.3   Literature Review

6.3.1   Technology Acceptance Model (TAM)

TAM conceptualizes that individuals decide to use a particular technology when performing a task [43]. TAM is significantly used in various studies for examining the usefulness of technology in different context of application [43]. TAM posited two main dimensions of perceived ease of use and perceived usefulness that influence user's behavioral intention, attitudes, and actual usage of technology [43]. Perceived usefulness refers to the level that individual believes in utilization of a particular technology build better performance [43]. Perceived ease of use relates to the individual's belief of information technology usage is effortless [43]. An individual will be more prone to adopt the technology when the technology is considered as useful and enhances their performance.

TAM has been applied extensively in research to analyze the consumer attitudes and behavioral intention to adopt Fintech [29, 38]. In many studies, additional variables were tested as antecedents to consumer attitudes and behavioral intention to adoption of Fintech. Research suggests to explore customer innovativeness [44], hedonic motivation [45], system quality [46] and technology self-efficacy [15] as factors that influence acceptance of technology. In this study, we proposed extension of the TAM model by adding variables related to customer innovativeness, hedonic motivation, system quality and technology self-efficacy. These additional variables are included in the extended TAM model to provide more holistic understanding and better insights on the important antecedent factors that influence customer satisfaction and continuance intention to adopt Fintech. The addition of the variables can bridge the existing theoretical gap that occurred in the TAM model. Drawing on TAM, the conceptual framework is developed to explain the critical factors influencing customer satisfaction and continuance intention to adopt Fintech in the developing countries.

6.3.2 Customer Satisfaction

Customer satisfaction relates to the customer overall assessment between the real experience they encountered from the performance of a product or service and customer's expectations [47]. In the service industry, customer satisfaction relates to the desired result of a service experience [48]. Customer satisfaction is an important driver to the development of customer intention to reuse services [49]. In Fintech services, customer satisfaction is applied as the key strategic tool to attract new customers, and sustain and develop existing customer relationships [50]. Fintech services that are innovative managed to create customer satisfaction due to customers' perceived usefulness and reliability of its services [17].

In a study conducted on mobile Fintech services, Zhang and Kim [19] concluded that the characteristics of security, benefits, flexibility and convenience, are the factors that contributed to customer satisfaction and use intentions. Therefore, it is crucial for Fintech services providers to prioritize on building and maintaining customers' satisfaction through the innovativeness, uniqueness and benefits of their services to achieve competitive advantages in the industry. Millennial consumers have strong buying interest on products or services when they are satisfied in using the Fintech services [51].

6.3.3 Customer Innovativeness

Customer innovativeness is conceptualized as "the degree to which an individual is relatively earlier in adopting an innovation than other members of his system" [52]. Highly innovative consumers, with creativeness and uniqueness characteristics, are the change agent for new information technology adoption [53]. In the evolving Fintech services that are associated with various risks effect, customer innovativeness is crucial to remove their anxiety feeling on the new technology and encourage their adoption [54].

As Fintech is a dynamic and innovative field, the Fintech adoption is highly associated with technology-driven consumers who prefer to experience new services [55].

In a study conduct on Fintech services in Brazil, Mainardes *et al.* [17] reported that customer innovativeness positively influence customer satisfaction, because customers who are open to innovation tend to perceived the services as reliable and useful. Therefore, Fintech innovation played an important role in stimulating and enhancing consumer innovation to adopt the services [56]. Consumer innovativeness affected by financial literacy and government support, was found as a significant predictor affect the adoption of Fintech in Indonesia [38].

6.3.4   Hedonic Motivation

Hedonic motivation involves the pleasure, amusement or cheerfulness obtained from the use of a technology [57]. Fintech services using mobile platform with the elements of entertainment, contributed to more willingness for consumers to use the technology. Hedonic motivation is an intrinsic value that influence consumers to achieve internal satisfaction. Hedonically motivated individuals are more willing to spend time engaging in activities that they would rather continue [58]. Bhatt and Nagar [20] posited that hedonic motivation dimensions for consumer's mobile banking services experiences were enjoyment, fun, pleasure and entertaining.

The pleasure and satisfaction obtained by consumers from the usage of mobile payment platforms are important elements that determined their Fintech adoption [59]. Empirical study conducted on customers of mobile banking in Jordan confirmed that hedonic motivation positively influenced behavioral intention and adoption of mobile banking [60]. Drawing on TAM, Salimon *et al.* [45] found that hedonic motivation significantly influenced consumers' smartphone banking usage in Nigeria. Young consumers feeling comfortable and satisfied in using existing mobile banking services will not have the intention to switch to other payment platforms [61]. For example, attractive and aesthetics design in Fintech contributed to consumers' pleasure and enjoyment in experiencing the services.

6.3.5   Perceived Usefulness

Perceived usefulness relates to the level that individual believes that using a technology build better performance [43, 62]. Fintech services created more efficiency for information searching, online purchase and transactions that have strengthened customers' perceived usefulness to adopt

Fintech [63, 64]. Perceived usefulness is the most effective predictor to customers' satisfaction due to benefits or values obtained from the usefulness of the Fintech system and services [23, 64]. In a study conducted on consumer behavioral intention to utilise mobile banking in Malaysia, Shanmugam *et al.* [62] concluded that positive perceived usefulness of Fintech was influenced by the perceptions of credibility and benefit.

In Fintech services, perceived usefulness has positive influence on customer satisfaction [17]. Supporting this claim, Yin and Lin [29] found that consumers believed in the interactive efficiency involving human, information and system characteristics of the mobile banking applications. Information interaction functions should have effective searching and browsing of information. High-quality information systems with security features contributes to higher utilization rate and consumers' satisfaction in using Fintech services [29, 66]. Perceived usefulness was influenced by perceived security, which created positive customer satisfaction in mobile Fintech payment services in Vietnam [26]. In an empirical research performed by Phuong *et al.* [25], they postulated that exist positive association between perceived usefulness and customer satisfaction in continuous intention to use an e-wallet. In contrast, perceived usefulness was identified to have no significant effect on young customers' satisfaction in e-wallet payment system context, as they are more concerned on perceived ease of use instead [15].

6.3.6   Perceived Ease of Use

Perceived ease of use is conceptualizes as the judgement of easy to learn and use to avoid the issue arising from the use of technology in financial transactions [67]. Perceived ease of use relates to the individual's belief of information technology usage is effortless [43] and not complicated [68]. In Fintech services, perceived ease of use was identified significantly influence customer satisfaction [17]. Fintech platforms with user-friendly interfaces and clear instructions enhanced the ease of use [12]. With that, ease of use is an advantage that contributed to customer satisfaction in Fintech adoption [22]. Fintech services that have the characteristics of expediency of access increases the consumers' adoption intention [65]. For example, digital payment used by customers for frequent purchases are referred to as ease of use and will increase customer satisfaction [21].

The problems associated with Fintech services, such as navigation problems and transaction issues, have caused difficulties in its usage and have negatively affected customer satisfaction [29]. As the extensiveness of Fintech services that linked to third-party platforms are important [69], but the lack of Fintech services' ability to link with third parties for transactions or other features may negatively influence customers' perception on ease of use and satisfaction. Hence, the service providers to prioritize on user-friendly and value features of Fintech to create consumer's perceived ease of use [56].

6.3.7 System Quality

The assessment for system quality involves usability, adaptability, reliability, availability and system response time [66]. Consumers' positive experience on the system quality of Fintech leads to their positive attitudes and behaviors, such as satisfaction [70]. The quality of the system of mobile banking increased consumer satisfaction due to the effective system's performance and trust in using the services [46]. Consumers obtained higher satisfaction when they experienced using better system performance, thus leads to continuous use intent [71].

Several studies reported that consumers are affected by the insecurity attitudes due to the unauthorized access to their personal information and financial data at the system with lack security protection [72]. The mobile phones usage for financial transactions connected or linked to the internet are exposed to the possibility of fraud [11]. The risks associated with Fintech services resulted from the financial, legal, security and operational issues shown that the Fintech systems are lacking in system quality result in the distrust and dissatisfaction of customers [73]. Therefore, lack of system quality in the Fintech services will negatively affect the customer satisfaction.

6.3.8 Technology Self-Efficacy

Technology self-efficacy relates to consumers' confidence in using the technology itself [74]. The dimension of technology self-efficacy has been extensively applied to explore consumers' acceptance on technology [75]. Consumers need to have knowledge, skill and ability to use the particular mobile technology so that it can facilitate their easy usage and adoption [76]. In a study conducted in Bangladesh, Karim *et al.* [15] reported that technology self-efficacy significantly influenced customer satisfaction due to the reasons of customers have strong ability, knowledge and confident in using the e-wallet payment technology.

Individual exhibits high level of technology self-efficacy, would have positive attitude and find it relatively less difficult in using new technology [77]. Women has lower self-efficacy in new technology which have negatively affected their attitudes and intention to adopt robo-advisors in Fintech services [78]. As Fintech is continuously evolving and innovating using new technologies, lacking of information technology knowledge and skills can be the barriers for consumers to adopt Fintech.

6.3.9   Continuance Intention to Adopt

Continuance intention to adopt Fintech services refers to individual's intention to continue using Fintech services [30]. Customers' continuance intention to adopt technology are influenced by their experience of usage and expectations on the future values of continuously using the technology [71]. Several previous studies have confirmed that customer satisfaction significantly influenced their continuance intention to adopt Fintech.

Susanto *et al.* [27] asserted that customers have positive satisfaction and continuance intention to adopt the smartphone banking services resulted from favourable perceived usefulness and trust. In the mobile banking applications usage perspective, Yin and Lin [29] asserted that user satisfaction exerts effect on users' continuance intention due to positive perceptions on usefulness, security and ease of use. Empirical research conducted on mobile payment in Africa, Franque *et al.* [24] posited that customer satisfaction is a significant factor that effect the continuance intention to adopt mobile payment.

6.3.10   Hypothesis Development

The review of literature from previous studies indicate that Fintech dimensions of customer innovativeness, hedonic motivation, perceived usefulness, perceived ease of use, system quality and technology self-efficacy have effect on customer satisfaction. Subsequently, customer satisfaction affects continuance intention to adopt Fintech. Referring to the above reviews, we formulated the hypotheses:

> H1: Customer innovativeness positively affects customer satisfaction.
> H2: Hedonic motivation has a significant positive influence on customer satisfaction.
> H3: There is a significant positive effect of perceived usefulness on customer satisfaction.
> H4: Perceived ease of use positively affects customer satisfaction.
> H5: System quality positively affects customer satisfaction.

H6: There is a significant positive effect of technology self-efficacy on customer satisfaction.

H7: Customer satisfaction positively affects continuance intention to adopt Fintech.

6.3.11   Conceptual Model

Drawing upon TAM, the conceptual model is formed as shown in Figure 6.1. Customer innovativeness, hedonic motivation, perceived usefulness, perceived ease of use, system quality and technology self-efficacy are correlated to customer satisfaction. Subsequently, customer satisfaction is correlated to their continuance intention to adopt Fintech services.

6.4   Research Methodology

6.4.1   Sample and Data Collection

The sample consisted users of Fintech in the developing countries and sample size of 422 was selected using convenience sampling method. Determination of sample size is based on 5 to 10 times the number of

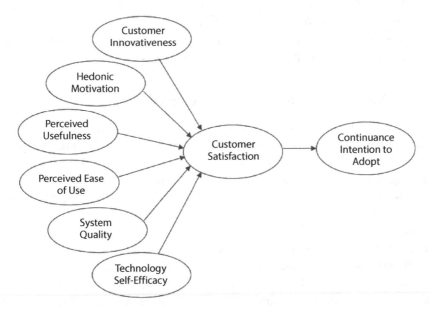

Figure 6.1 Conceptual model.

measuring items [79]. The measurement model has 8 constructs with a total of 33 measuring items, which justified the minimum sample size of 330 was required. By adopting quantitative approach, the survey questionnaire was used for data collection. Researchers have personally approached the potential respondents, who are users of Fintech and have experienced Fintech services for the past 3 months, from five developing countries, namely Malaysia, Indonesia, India, Nigeria and Philippines. Sample was drawn equally from the chosen five developing countries. Data were collected between February 2022 to April 2022. Response rate was 91% with a total 422 responses.

6.4.2   Measures of the Constructs

The 8 constructs of customer innovativeness, hedonic motivation, perceived usefulness, perceived ease of use, system quality, technology self-efficacy, customer satisfaction and continuance intention to adopt Fintech were measured by 33 items. Likert scale of 6-point from the range of 1 - strongly disagree to 6 - strongly agree were applied. The usage of 6-point scales provides more precised responses for the measurement items by eliminating the neutral point. The demographic covers the gender, age, income level and location details of the respondents.

In view that same source of measures used to gather the data, there is possibility of occurrence of common method variance (CMV) [80]. By running the Harman's single factor test for CMV [81], we can conclude that common method bias has cleared with the result of the single factor only account for 33.394% variance, which is below the threshold of 50%.

6.4.3   Validity and Reliability Assessment

We have conducted pilot study on 30 respondents to validate the survey questionnaires. The model was assessed through validity and reliability analysis. Table 6.1 present the constructs, measurement items, factor loading, Cronbach Alpha (CA), Average Variance Extracted (AVE) and Composite Reliability (CR) values. To evaluate the validity of the measures, Exploratory Factor Analysis (EFA) was performed to decide on items elimination for factor loading values of below 0.3. The results shown KMO value of 0.932. The factor loading results for the 33 items were between 0.598 and 0.902, which indicate the well construct validity and shall maintained for further analysis. The values for CA were above required limit of 0.7 [82], between 0.821 and 0.927. The AVE values were above cut-off

Table 6.1 Construct and measurement items.

Construct (Source)	Item	Statement	Factor loading	CA, AVE, CR
Customer Innovativeness [40]	CI1	When I hear about new Fintech service, I am usually interested to try it	0.756	0.880 (CA) 0.649 (AVE) 0.881 (CR)
	CI2	I like to experience the new Fintech service	0.832	
	CI3	I am always open to use new Fintech service	0.845	
	CI4	I always initiate to try the new Fintech service compared to my peers	0.787	
Hedonic Motivation [20]	HM1	Fintech service using mobile is fun	0.666	0.834 (CA) 0.509 (AVE) 0.837 (CR)
	HM2	Fintech service gives pleasurable experience	0.735	
	HM3	Fintech service is entertaining	0.802	
	HM4	Fintech service using mobile is enjoyable	0.749	
	HM5	Fintech service required little effort	0.598	
Perceived Usefulness [85]	PU1	Fintech service can meet my needs	0.688	0.821 (CA) 0.541 (AVE) 0.842 (CR)
	PU2	Fintech service enable effective transaction	0.797	
	PU3	Fintech service provide convenient to manage my financial activities	0.786	
	PU4	Overall, Fintech service is useful for me	0.662	

(Continued)

Table 6.1 Construct and measurement items. (*Continued*)

Construct (Source)	Item	Statement	Factor loading	CA, AVE, CR
Perceived Ease of Use [40]	PE1	Fintech service is easy to use	0.768	0.894 (CA) 0.681 (AVE) 0.895 (CR)
	PE2	The operation interface of Fintech is user-friendly	0.828	
	PE3	Fintech service can be easily used by using device (cellphone, APP, WIFI, etc)	0.892	
	PE4	Fintech service is easily understood	0.807	
System Quality [73]	SQ1	Fintech system is ease to use	0.754	0.903 (CA) 0.704 (AVE) 0.905 (CR)
	SQ2	Fintech system is highly reliable	0.848	
	SQ3	Fintech system enable me to accomplish my financial transaction	0.897	
	SQ4	Fintech system can be accessible well	0.851	
Technology Self-Efficacy [76, 77]	TE1	I am capable of using Fintech service	0.674	0.842 (CA) 0.583 (AVE) 0.847 (CR)
	TE2	I have the skills required to use Fintech service	0.846	
	TE3	I know how to link the connections of Fintech service with other related platforms	0.838	
	TE4	I can easily go through the steps in using Fintech service	0.678	

(*Continued*)

Table 6.1 Construct and measurement items. (*Continued*)

Construct (Source)	Item	Statement	Factor loading	CA, AVE, CR
Customer Satisfaction [86]	CS1	I have positive experience using Fintech service	0.843	0.927 (CA) 0.758 (AVE) 0.926 (CR)
	CS2	I have obtained good values from Fintech service	0.902	
	CS3	Fintech services fulfilled my needs and requirements	0.873	
	CS4	Overall, I am very satisfied using Fintech service	0.864	
Continuance Intention to Adopt [73]	CA1	I have intention to continue using Fintech service	0.783	0.873 (CA) 0.634 (AVE) 0.874 (CR)
	CA2	I would prefer Fintech	0.794	
	CA3	I will use Fintech service in future	0.817	
	CA4	I would positively consider Fintech service as my preferred choice	0.790	

values of 0.6 [83] between 0.509 0.758, and CR values were between 0.837 and 0.926, above threshold limit of 0.5 [84].

6.5   Results

6.5.1   Demographic Profile of the Respondent

From the total of 422 respondents, 45% are females and 55% are males. As for the age group, 8% respondents are 18-25 years, 22% respondents are 26-35 years, 28% respondents are 36-45 years, 22% respondents are 46-55 years and 20% belongs to age group 56 and above. The majority of respondents belong to the income category of RM 4,000 – RM 5,999 (40%), followed by RM 6,000 – RM 7,999 (30%), RM 2,000 – RM 3,999 (14%), above RM 8,000 (12%) and below RM 2,000 (4%). In frequency of using Fintech services, the majority of respondents 55% have experienced two to three times a month, 25% once a month and 20% above four times a month. As for their locations, the respondents are divided equally 20% at location Malaysia, Indonesia, India, Nigeria and Philippines respectively.

6.5.2   Structural Model Assessment

Structural Equation Modeling (SEM) analysis was applied to analyze the data using SPSS AMOS version 26. The structural model indices confirmed that the structural model has achieved a good fit. The probability level of the structural model was significant at p=0.000, with degree of freedom value of 369. RMSEA value was 0.053, below the acceptance level of 0.08 [87]. The chi-square and ratio of x2/df values were 1032.289 and 2.182 respectively. The incremental fit values, IFI of 0.935, CFI of 0.935 and TLI of 0.928, were all above 0.900.

The hypotheses results are presented in Table 6.2. Customer innovativeness (r = -0.032, p > 0.05) had no significant effect on customer satisfaction, was not supporting H1. The results concluded that customers were lacking in their characteristics of innovativeness to explore new Fintech services that can satisfy them. Hedonic motivation (r = 0.157, p > 0.05) shown no significant effect on customer satisfaction, was not supporting H2. Perceived usefulness (r = 0.282, p < 0.05) had a significant positive effect on customer satisfaction, supporting H3. This means that the respondents (customers) perceived Fintech services could fulfill their needs and requirements, and useful Fintech platforms. This finding was consistent

Table 6.2 Hypothesis testing.

Hypothesized relationships	Estimate	*p* Values	Result
H1 Customer Innovativeness → Customer Satisfaction	-0.032	0.726	Not Supported
H2 Hedonic Motivation → Customer Satisfaction	0.157	0.243	Not Supported
H3 Perceived Usefulness → Customer Satisfaction	0.282	0.011	Supported
H4 Perceived Ease of Use → Customer Satisfaction	0.415	***	Supported
H5 System Quality → Customer Satisfaction	0.299	***	Supported
H6 Technology Self-Efficacy → Customer Satisfaction	-0.017	0.906	Not Supported
H7 Customer Satisfaction → Continuance Intention to Adopt	0.510	***	Supported

Note: ***$p < 0.001$.

to the findings from previous studies conducted by Nguyen *et al.* [26] and Phuong *et al.* [25].

Perceived ease of use ($r = 0.415$, $p < 0.001$) shown a significant influence on customer satisfaction, supporting H4. Moreover, system quality ($r = 0.299$, $p < 0.001$) also achieved a significant positive influence on customer satisfaction, supporting H5. We can conclude that customers believe Fintech services have optimal level of system quality that contributed to their satisfaction to continue adoption. Therefore, respondents believe that Fintech has the required quality standard in its system. Technology self-efficacy ($r = -0.017$, $p > 0.05$) had no significant effect on customer satisfaction, was not supporting H6.

Finally, customer satisfaction ($r=0.510$, $p<0.001$) had a positive effect on continuance intention to adopt Fintech, supporting H7. This result was supported the findings of previous studies conducted by Yin and Lin [29], Franque *et al.* [24] and Susanto *et al.* [27]. Hence, our finding concluded that overall customers have achieved favorable satisfaction level in the Fintech services, which contributed to their intention to continue usage

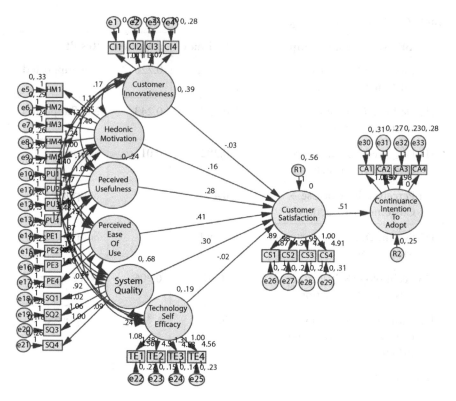

Figure 6.2 Structural model.

of the services. The squared multiple correlations for the endogenous variables were 0.385 for customer satisfaction and 0.482 for continuance intention to adopt Fintech constructs. Figure 6.2 shown the structural model.

6.6 Discussion

Fintech is an essential and important service in the development of finance and banking industries. The findings have provided better insights on the critical factors that affect customer satisfaction and their intention to continue adoption of Fintech services in the developing countries. Based on the hypothesis result, we concluded that customer innovativeness related to Fintech services in the developing countries have not reach a level which is convincing. Customers may have doubt or skepticism in using new Fintech services. Customers are depending on the Fintech companies to convince them on the benefits, processes and secure usage of their services. The reason for this is because Fintech firms are particularly vulnerable to various types of risk involving cybersecurity risk, credit default risk, regulatory uncertainty risk and compliance risk [88]. Cybersecurity risk include the risk of cyberattacks and these attacks are difficult to be detected due to the absence of regulatory monitoring [88, 89]. In addition, Fintech firms such as peer-to-peer (P2P) lending firms possess higher credit default risks as these firms do not adhere to any lending charters and they are also not responsible if the borrowers default [88]. Furthermore, Fintech firms also encounter regulatory requirement uncertainty risks whereby there is uncertainty with regards to whether approvals or licensing by the relevant authorities are needed for Fintech firms' activities [88, 90]. Even if regulations exist, Fintech firms particularly P2P firms encounter compliance risks as they encounter difficulties in adhering with the counter terrorism financing regulations and anti-money laundering in the countries in which they are located [89, 91].

The referral or electronic word-of mouth can play important influencing roles to build customer innovativeness in accepting and adopting the new Fintech services in the developing countries. For example, low financial literacy in the population of Indonesia was due to the lack of environment and information exposure are the factors causing lack of customer innovativeness to adopt Fintech services [40]. Hence, Fintech companies should leverage on more effective communication strategies with the potential and existing customers on their services. Through effective marketing communications campaign, newly enhanced positive features can be communicated using various channels to help build customer trust and satisfaction towards the new or existing services. Public awareness through public relation events focusing on the usage of Fintech service for convenience and efficiency transactions should be prioritized. Advertisements at media channels and social media platforms introducing the new Fintech services can attract customers to try out the services. For example, the Fintech payments in Indonesia, such as GoPay, OVO, Linkaja and Sakuku, have introduced the new services along with attractive advertisements and promotions for their customers.

To enhance the hedonic motivation of customers in the developing countries, Fintech firms should capitalize on the individual's intrinsic motivation in technological environment in order to increase the adoption and customer satisfaction of individuals using Fintech services [92]. Fintech firms can include gamification elements in its services to provide entertainment to the users, specifically to attract the young users. Smartphone financial applications with the application of game-playing elements that emphasize on social features enhanced consumers' motivation to adopt the services [93]. For example, game-like characteristics in Fintech, such as competition or contest with rewards and point-scoring (collecting money) provide more enjoyment and fun in the usage of the services. Integrated gamified elements in Fintech provide opportunities for the customers to be competent and self-determined in adopting the services. The creativity in gamification of Fintech services created revolutionizing finance for customers. All these are analogous to transforming bitter medicine into sweet ones so that patients can consume it in an easier manner [94]. However, as a caveat, practitioners such as Fintech firms should take precaution with respect to hedonic motivations as it is only effective on consumers or customers at the preliminary stage of the product or service life cycle [95]. Once customers begin to use the actual product or service and experience its usage, the product or service utility itself will be more important to them as compared to other product or service characteristics such as hedonic motivations, etc [96].

Customers place great importance to the usefulness of the Fintech services. The basic functions of Fintech, such as financial transactions, system stability and information sharing, provide meaningful evaluation on its usefulness. Mobile technologies integrating and enabling Fintech services are becoming more and more useful for the customers in the developing countries [25, 33]. Customer satisfaction and Fintech adoption can be improved through effective market targeting and improve service customization to meet customers' needs. To increase customer satisfaction for digital financial services such as Fintech, the Fintech firm needs to do more rather than just engaging with customers [97]. They should focus on how their activities, resources and experiences are related and they should also understand what drives customers, e.g. their goals, desires, visions and dreams. In order to achieve this, Fintech firms need to possess a thorough understanding of the ecosystem level value formation of customers which are enhanced by digitalization.

The findings concluded that perceived ease of use had the highest correlation value, and indicated this variable is the strongest factor influencing customer satisfaction in Fintech services in the developing countries. In Indonesia, consumers' perceived Fintech services have the characteristics of convenience, transaction suitability and security [98]. The ease of use of operating interfaces, flexibility using different devices, speed of information transmission and user-friendly features are among the important aspects that service providers must pay attention to. Fintech companies should provide easier navigation at the websites for users to understand and easily perform transactions or obtaining information. Daragmeh *et al.* [97] further suggested that Fintech services need to adopt electronic payment applications, which are generally easy to be utilized as well as compatible with the capabilities and technological savviness of Generation X consumers. They should also capitalize on the high financial literacy of Generation X consumers by providing easy to use services so that a huge segment of this market can be tapped.

It is important for Fintech companies to reassure their existing customers on the services are safe for financial transactions. The enhancement of security features, privacy protection and system quality of Fintech are crucial. Customers are highly demanded over the protection of transaction data and personal information. Barriers factors of Fintech adoption include security, financial, operational and legal risks [10], that require great attention by the companies to mitigate these risks. Companies should be dynamic in acquiring Fintech competence and drive continuous innovation through research and development, and technology investments. Additionally, consumers have expectations to adopt a technology if it offsets the risks and improve the benefits. Hence, it is crucial for Fintech companies to put in more efforts to mitigate the risks and to ensure that Fintech services can be used safety and confidently by the customers. Proper training on safe usage of Fintech services should be offered to the customers.

Preventive measures such as pre-testing on the Fintech system before launching and the stipulation of an antivirus software would help the mitigation and avoidance of Fintech impediments. With that, customer can feel more secure and confident in using Fintech services. Therefore, Fintech can built customer satisfaction and intention to continue adoption of the services. Moreover, to increase the safety of Fintech firms' financial transactions, suitable authentication mechanisms need to be designed to ensure that users' sensitive information are protected [99]. They suggest the usage of *RouteMap*, a map- and route-based graphical password scheme where users are able to generate a route on a Google Map as their credentials. Using this authentication mechanism, Meng *et al.* [99] further found that this mechanism not only enhance the safety of Fintech firms' financial transactions, they also found that the users are able to achieve more effective long-term and multiple password memory compared to other safety mechanisms.

Fintech system should focused to be more technology user-friendly by not only linking to users' all accounts and bank cards within the application, but also the link connections of Fintech services with other related third party platforms. Companies have to be more responsive to customers by providing necessary supports in the usage of Fintech. For example, various Fintech companies have dedicated customer service personnel to conduct live online chat to answer customers' queries immediately. In addition, social media sites can be utilized to engage effectively with the customers. In view that digital financial literacy is the major concern in customers' technology self-efficacy in the developing countries, training supports can be given to the customers to ease their usage of the new technology. By giving more digital finance exposure to the customers, addressing customers' problems and engaging customers well, Fintech companies could build customer satisfaction and loyalty towards their services.

Fintech companies can explore on strategic cooperation from supply chain to intermediaries levels to better manage Fintech system and service delivery. For example, to improve on the innovation of Fintech system, collaboration with the technology suppliers in the aspect of investment, knowledge sharing, resources sharing and research development are crucial. The successfulness of collaboration can bring valuable Fintech innovation into the markets to boost the customer satisfaction and adoption rate. More strategic cooperation between companies are needed particularly in the perspective of developing countries with issues in scarcity of resources, limited technology knowledge, and also the markets are mostly dominated by small and medium enterprises.

Moreover, firms should improve connectivity capacity with Fintech firms so that the liquidity of their supply chain finance (SCF) assets can be enhanced [100]. Due to firm is connected with many Fintech firms in its supply chain, the key performance indicators (KPIs) (e.g. fixed assets and the number of employees) can be assessed by the Fintech firms from various perspectives as well as increase the publicity of the firm. This will help enhance the tradability of the firm's supply chain finance (SCF) assets without increasing the assets' price volatility. Secondly, Li *et al.* [100] also argued that firms should improve their clarity capacity with Fintech firms in order to reduce the risk of their SCF assets. In a situation whereby a firm has the capacity to capitalize big data to visualize its environment and to make appropriate decisions during uncertainties. Ultimately, this reduce the risk of SCF assets. Thirdly, firms should also improve their continuity capacity by incorporating Environment, Social and Governance (ESG) into its supply chain activities consistent with the expectations from the various stakeholders such as the government, public, etc. This can improve the profitability of its SCF assets in the long run [100].

6.7 Theoretical and Practical Implications

This chapter findings concluded that perceived usefulness, system quality, perceived ease of use are important predictors that influenced customer satisfaction and continuance intention to adopt Fintech. These relationships were evidenced through the hypotheses acceptance. Hence, the conceptual model which was developed from TAM has validated the roles of existing variables of perceived ease of use and perceived usefulness in influencing customer attitude, represented by customer satisfaction and actual usage of technology. In addition, one additional variable of system quality was confirmed to have effect on customer satisfaction and continuance intention to adopt Fintech. As a conclusion, the TAM was validated and developed in its application in the Fintech adoption context in the developing countries.

The extended TAM can be applied by the Fintech companies to improve on strategies implementation to boost Fintech adoption. The proposed solutions given to enhance customer satisfaction and continuous adoption of Fintech would assist Fintech companies in the developing countries to better target the markets, build significant presence, achieve business growth and build competitive advantages. In view that customer satisfaction is the key strategic tool that build and enhance Fintech adoption [50], the companies could innovate their Fintech services to create more positive values or benefits to their existing customers and improve customers' seamless experiences. In addition, by leveraging on improved strategies for Fintech adoption, potential customers will be attracted to use and adopt the Fintech services. The findings are also useful for potential Fintech companies to better understand the influencing factors and consumer behavior in adoption Fintech services before deciding to venture into the developing countries.

6.8 Conclusion

The present study have several limitations which may contribute to future research. First, the present study has emphasized on customer innovativeness, hedonic motivation, perceived usefulness, perceived ease of use, system quality, technology self-efficacy, as the antecedent factors. Future studies can explore on other variables on adopter's external factors such as social influence, social cultural, environmental pressures, and policies and regulations. To provide more robust understanding on the factors related to adopter's internal factors, consumers' perceptions and characteristics can be investigated further. Consumers' perceptions such as perceived security, perceived risk, perceived safety, perceived enjoyment, perceived benefits, perceived privacy, perceived quality, perceived value, perceived task-technology fit, perceived relative advantage and superiority are critical factors.

Second, customer satisfaction was assessed as attitude in influencing the behavioral intention outcome. We suggest to examine different customer attitude variables such as customer belief, trust, motivation, experience and emotional reaction. Therefore, it can contribute to better understanding on the psychological process that affect customers' continuous intention to adoption Fintech. Third, our study emphasized on the customers' continuance intention to adopt Fintech services, and we proposed subsequent research to explore on other post-purchase consumer behavior of customer loyalty, customer regret, and customer continuous adoption. The coverage on more diverse areas of post-purchase consumer behavior will provide more targeted outcome strategies for the Fintech companies.

Fourth, the present study provided insights on Fintech adoption in the developing countries perspective, and comparative studies can be undertaken by exploring the emerging countries, developed countries or specific regions. In view that the economy development varies across continents or countries, more detailed research are required to provide holistic understanding on Fintech adoption progress and development. Fifth, we have selected samples of respondents from Malaysia, Indonesia, India, Nigeria and Philippines. Hence, subsequent studies can include more developing countries for samples collection to achieve generalization of the findings. Sixth, this research has generalized the Fintech services, but future research can apply the existing model to analyse in different specific or emerging Fintech areas, such as mobile payment, cryptocurrency, mobile banking applications and crowdfunding. Finally, TAM has been applied as the main model in this research to draw the relationships effect between the variables. It is recommended to integrate other models or theories into TAM to provide new insights and exploration on the improved theoretical model.

References

1. M. Ali, S. A., Raza, B. Khamis, C. H. Puah, and H. Amin, "How perceived risk, benefit and trust determine user Fintech adoption: a new dimension for Islamic finance," *Foresight*, vol. 23, no. 4, pp. 403-420, 2021.
2. A. L. Mention, "The Future of Fintech," *Res. Technol. Manag.*, vol. 26, no. 4, pp. 59-63, 2019.
3. R. Thakur and M. Srivastava, "Adoption readiness, personal innovativeness, perceived risk and usage intention across customer groups for mobile payment services in India," *Internet Res.*, vol. 24, no. 3, pp. 369-392, 2014.
4. N. F. Abdul Rahim, A. R. Jaaffar, M. N. Sarkawi, and J. b. Shamsuddin, "Fintech and Commercial Banks Development in Malaysia: Continuous Intention to

Use Fintech Services in IR 4.0 Environment," in *Modeling Economic Growth in Contemporary Malaysia (Entrepreneurship and Global Economic Growth)*, B. S. Sergi and A. R. Jaaffar, Eds.. Bingley: Emerald Publishing Limited, 2021, pp. 235-253.

5. H. Stewart and J. Jürjens, "Data security and consumer trust in FinTech innovation in Germany," *Inf. Comput. Secur.*," vol. 26, no. 1, pp. 109-128, 2018.

6. Research and Markets, "Global Fintech Market, by Technology (API; AI; Blockchain; Distributed Computing, Others), by Service (Payment; Fund Transfer; Personal Finance; Loans; Insurance; Others), by Application (Banking; Insurance; & Others), by Region, Competition, Forecast & Opportunities 2025," 2021. [Online]. Available: https://www.researchandmarkets.com/reports/ 5031390/global-fintech-market-by-technology-by-service

7. BDO, "Global Opportunities with Fintech," 2022. [Online]. Available: https://www.bdo.com.au/en-au/insights/financial-services/articles/global-opportunities-with-fintech

8. Statista, "Consumer fintech adoption rates globally from 2015 to 2019, by category," 2022. [Online]. Available: https://www.statista.com/statistics/1055356/fintech-adoption-rates-globally-selected-countries-by-category/

9. Statista, "Leading countries for fintech adoption 2019, by category," 2022. [Online]. Available: https://www.statista.com/statistics/942325/leading-countries-fintech-adoption-by-category/

10. H. S. Ryu, "Understanding Benefit and Risk Framework of Fintech Adoption: Comparison of Early Adopters and Late Adopters," in *Proc. 51st Hawaii International Conference on System Sciences*, 2018, pp. 3864-3873.

11. B. Shaw and A. Kesharwani, "Moderating Effect of Smartphone Addiction on Mobile Wallet Payment Adoption," *J. Internet Commer.*, vol. 18, no. 3, pp. 291–309, 2019.

12. R. S. Hutapea, "The Effect of Financial Technology (Fin-Tech) on Customer Satisfaction Level (A Case Study on SMEs)," *Adv. Eng. Res.*, vol. 198, pp. 668-674, 2020.

13. S. Ullah, U. S. Kiani., B. Raza, and A. Mustafa, "Consumers' Intention to Adopt m-payment/m-banking: The Role of Their Financial Skills and Digital Literacy," *Front. Psychol.*, vol. 13, no. 873708, 2022.

14. P. Dwivedi, J. I. Alabdooli, and R. Dwivedi, "Role of FinTech Adoption for Competitiveness and Performance of the Bank: A Study of Banking Industry in UAE," *Int. J. Glob. Bus. Compet.*, vol. 16, pp. 130–138, 2021.

15. M. W. Karim, M. A. M. Chowdhury, and A. K. Haque, "A Study of Customer Satisfaction Towards E-Wallet Payment System in Bangladesh," *Am. J. Econ. Bus. Inno.*, vol. 1, no. 1, pp. 1–10, 2022.

16. H. Khusnah, R. Putra, W. Husnaini, and K. Umami, "The Influence of Financial Technology (Fintech) Customer Satisfaction and Loyalty on the Buying Interest of Millenials in Surabaya during the Covid-19 Pandemic in 2020-2021 which in Mediated by Cashless Society," *J. Posit. Sch. Psychol.*, vol. 6, no. 4, pp. 1714-1727, 2020.

17. E. W. Mainardes, P. M. F. Costa, and S. N. Nossa, "Customers' satisfaction with fintech services: evidence from Brazil," *J. Financ. Serv. Mark.*, 2021 [Online]. Available: https://doi.org/10.1057/s41264-022-00156-x

18. R. Usman and H. K. Soo, "Factors Influencing Fintech's Customer Loyalty for Cross Border Payments: Mediating Customer Satisfaction," *Asia-Pacific J. Bus. Ventur. Entreneurship*, vol. 16, no. 6, pp. 287-297, 2021.

19. L. Zhang and H. Kim, "The Influence of Financial Service Characteristics on Use Intention through Customer Satisfaction with Mobile Fintech," *J. Syst. Manag. Sci.*, vol. 10, no. 2, pp. 82-94, 2020.

20. V. Bhatt and D. Nagar, "An empirical study to evaluate factors affecting customer satisfaction on the adoption of Mobile Banking Track: Financial Management," *Turk. J. Comput. Math. Educ.*, vol. 12, no. 10, pp. 5354-5373, 2021.

21. B. A. Fianto, C. K. Rahmawati, and I. Supriani, "Mobile banking services quality and its impact on customer satisfaction of Indonesian Islamic banks," *J. Ekon. Keuang. Islam*, vol. 7, no. 1, pp. 59-76, 2021.

22. C. H. Sampaio, W. J. Ladeira, and F. D. O. Santini, "Apps for mobile banking and customer satisfaction: A cross-cultural study," *Int. J. Bank Mark.*, vol. 35, no. 7, pp. 1133–1153, 2017.

23. M. Chen, S. Chen, H. Yeh, and W. Tsaur, "The key factors influencing internet finances services satisfaction: an empirical study in Taiwan," *Am. J. Ind. Bus. Manag.*, vol. 6, pp. 748-762, 2016.

24. F. B. Franque, T. Oliveira, and C. Tam, "Understanding the factors of mobile payment continuance intention: empirical test in an African context," *Heliyon*, vol. 7, no. 8, e07807, 2021.

25. N. D. Phuong, L. T. Luan, V. V. Dong, and N. N. Khanh, "Examining Customers' Continuance Intentions towards E-wallet Usage: The Emergence of Mobile Payment Acceptance in Vietnam," *J. Asian Finance Econ. Bus.*, vol. 7, no. 9, pp. 505-516, 2020.

26. D. D. Nguyen, T. D. Nguyen, T. D. Nguyen, and H. V. Nguyen, "Impacts of Perceived Security and Knowledge on Continuous Intention to Use Mobile Fintech Payment Services: An Empirical Study in Vietnam," *J. Asian Finance Econ. Bus.*, vol. 8, no. 8, pp. 287-296, 2021.

27. A. Susanto, Y. Chang, and Y. Ha, "Determinants of continuance intention to use the smartphone banking services: An extension to the expectation-confirmation model," *Ind. Manag. Data Syst.*, vol. 116, no. 3, pp. 508-525, 2016.

28. B. J. Slazus and G. Bick, "Factors that Influence FinTech Adoption in South Africa: A Study of Consumer Behaviour towards Branchless Mobile Banking," *Athens J. Bus. Econ.*, vol. 8, no. 1, pp. 43-64, 2022.

29. L. X. Yin and H. C. Lin, "Predictors of customers' continuance intention of mobile banking from the perspective of the interactivity theory." *ECON RES-EKON ISTRAZ*, 2022, to be published, doi:10.1080/1331677X.2022.2053782

30. Y. Y. Ling, W. C. Sng, C. M. Leong, and S. J. Ho, "Determinants of Mobile Banking Services Continuance Intention in Malaysia," *J. Mark. Adv. Pract.*, vol. 3, no. 1, pp. 20-40, 2021.

31. D. M. Nguyen, Y. T. H. Chiu, and H. D. Le, "Determinants of Continuance Intention towards Banks' Chatbot Services in Vietnam: A Necessity for Sustainable Development," *Sustainability*, vol. 13, no. 7625, 2021.

32. T. Tapanainen, "Toward Fintech Adoption Framework for Developing Countries -A Literature Review based on the Stakeholder Perspective," *Inf. Technol. Appl. Manag.*, vol. 27, no. 5, pp. 1-22, 2020.

33. C. Tidjani, "Readiness to the FinTech Industry in Developing Countries," in *Finance. International Handbooks in Business Ethics*, L. San-Jose, J. L. Retolaza, and L. van Liedekerke, Ed., Cham: Springer, 2021, pp. 1-32.

34. T. Imam, A. McInnes, S. Colombage, and R. Grose, "Opportunities and Barriers for FinTech in SAARC and ASEAN Countries, : *J. Risk Financ. Manag.*. vol. 15, no. 77, 2022.

35. M. Najib, W. J. Ermawati, F. Fahma, E. Endri, and D. Suhartanto, "FinTech in the Small Food Business and Its Relation with Open Innovation," *J. Open Innov. Technol. Mark. Complex.*, vol. 7, no. 88, 2021.

36. The Economic Times, "Traditional banks are using neobanks to reach out to tech-savvy customers: report," 2022. [Online]. Available: https://economic-times.indiatimes.com/tech/technology/traditional-banks-are-using-neo banks-to-reach-out-to-tech-savvy-customers-report/articleshow/91123864. cms?from=mdr

37. P. Rajeswari and C. Vijai, "Fintech Industry In India: The Revolutionized Finance Sector," *Eur. J. Mol. Clin. Med,*, vol. 8, no. 11, pp. 4300-4306, 2021.

38. A. Das and D. Das, "Perception, Adoption, and Pattern of Usage of FinTech Services by Bank Customers: Evidences from Hojai District of Assam," *Emerg. Econ. Stud.*, vol. 6, no. 1, pp. 7-22, 2020.

39. Statista, "Fintech: Indonesia," 2022. [Online]. Available: https://www.statista.com/outlook/dmo/fintech /indonesia #transaction-value

40. B. Setiawan, D. P. Nugraha, A. Irawan, R. J. Nathan, and Z. Zoltan, "User Innovativeness and Fintech Adoption in Indonesia," *J. Open Innov. Technol. Mark. Complex.*, vol. 7, no. 188, 2021.

41. The World Bank, "The Global Findex Database," 2017. [Online]. Available: https://globalfindex.worldbank.org/

42. The Edge Markets, "Fintech to help drive economic revival," 2021. [Online]. https://www.theedgemarkets.com/article/fintech-help-drive-economic-revival

43. F. D. Davis, "Perceived Usefulness, Perceived Ease of Use, and User Acceptance of Information Technology," *MIS Quarterly*, vol. 13, no. 3, pp. 319–40, 1989.

44. Z. Hu, S. Ding, S., S. Li, L. Chen, and S. Yang, "Adoption Intention of Fintech Services for Bank Users: An Empirical Examination with an Extended Technology Acceptance Model," *Symmetry*, vol. 11, no. 3, pp. 340, 2019.

45. M. G. Salimon, O. A. Aliyu, M. M. Yusr, and S. Perumal, "Smartphone banking usage in Nigeria: Gamification, technology acceptance and cultural factors empirical perspectives," *Electron. J. Inf. Syst. Dev. Ctries.*, vol. 87, e12174, 2021.

46. H. Nuhu, A. Y. Dutse, and T. Abubakar, "Understanding Quality, Satisfaction and Trust toward Intention to Use Mobile Banking," *Int. Acad. J. Manag. Mark. Entrep. Stud.*, vol. 9, no. 1, pp. 121-131, 2022.

47. P. Kotler and G. Armstrong, *Principles of Marketing*. 18th ed., Harlow: Pearson, 2021.

48. F. D. Orel, and A. Kara, "Supermarket self-checkout service quality, customer satisfaction, and loyalty: Empirical evidence from an emerging market," *J. Retail. Consum. Serv.*, vol. 21, pp. 118–129, 2014.

49. G. Daragahi, "The impact of innovation on customer satisfaction: A study of the cosmetics producer in Tehran," *Int. Rev.*, vol. 1-2, pp. 121-132, 2017.

50. K. Eriksson, C. Hermansson, and S. Jonsson, "The performance generating limitations of the relationship-banking model in the digital era – effects of customers' trust, satisfaction, and loyalty on client-level performance," *Int. J. Bank Mark.*, vol. 38, no. 4, pp. 889-916, 2020.

51. H. Khusnah, R. Putra, W. Husnaini, and K. Umami, "The Influence of Financial Technology (Fintech) Customer Satisfaction and Loyalty on the Buying Interest of Millenials in Surabaya during the Covid-19 Pandemic in 2020-2021 which in Mediated by Cashless Society," *J. Posit. Sch. Psychol.*, vol. 6, no. 4, pp. 1714-1727, 2020.

52. E. M. Rogers and F. Shoemaker, *Diffusion of Innovation: A Cross-Cultural Approach*. New York, NY: The Free Press, 1983.

53. F. Liébana-Cabanillas, V. Marinkovic, I. R. de Luna, and Z. Kalinic, "Predicting the determinants of mobile payment acceptance: a hybrid SEM-neural network approach," *Technol. Forecast Soc. Change,* vol. 129, no. C, pp. 117-130, 2018.

54. T. P. Chong, K. S. Choo, Y. S. Yip, P. Y. Chan, H. L. Teh, and S. S. Ng, "An Adoption of Fintech Services in Malaysia," *South East Asia J. Cont. Bus. Econ. Law*, vol. 18, no. 5, pp. 134-147, 2019.

55. C. M. Barbu, D. I., Florea, D. C. Dabija, and M. C. R. Barbu, "Customer Experience in Fintech," *J. Theor. Appl. Electron. Commer. Res.*, vol. 16, pp. 1415–1433, 2021.

56. A. F. Utami, I. A. Ekaputra, and A. Japutra, "Adoption of FinTech Products: A Systematic Literature Review. " *J. Creat. Commun.* vol. 16, no. 3, pp. 233–248, 2021.

57. V. Venkatesh, J. Y. L Thong, and X. Xu, "Consumer acceptance and use of information technology: extending the unified theory of acceptance and use of technology," *MIS Q*, vol. 36, no. 1, pp. 157–178, 2012.

58. D. Kahneman, "Objective Happiness," in: *Well-being: The foundations of hedonic psychology*, D. Kahneman, E. Diener, and N. Schwartz. Eds. New York: Russell Sage Foundation, pp. 2–25, 1999.

59. C. Morosan and A. DeFranco, "It's about time: revisiting UTAUT2 to examine consumers' intentions to use NFC mobile payments in hotels," *Int. J. Hosp. Manag.*, vol. 53, pp. 17–29, 2016.

60. A. A. Alalwan, Y. K. Dwivedi, and N. P. Rana, "Factors influencing adoption of mobile banking by Jordanian bank customers: extending UTAUT2 with trust," *Int. J. Inf. Manag.*, vol. 37, pp. 99–110, 2017.

61. H. Karjaluoto, N. Koenig-Lewis, A. Palmer, and A. Moll, "Predicting young consumers' take up of mobile banking services," *Int. J. Bank Mark.*, vol. 28, pp. 410–432, 2010.

62. A. Shanmugam, M. T. Savarimuthu, and T. C. Wen, "Factors Affecting Malaysian Behavioral Intention to Use Mobile Banking with Mediating Effects of Attitude," *Acad Res Int.*, vol. 5, no. 2, pp. 236-253, 2014.

63. M. Moslehpour, V. K. Pham, W. K. Wong, and İ. Bilgiçli, "E-purchase intention of Taiwanese consumers: sustainable mediation of perceived usefulness and perceived ease of use," *Sustainability*, vol. 10, no. 1, pp. 234, 2018.

64. S. Lee, "Evaluation of mobile application in user's perspective: case of P2P lending apps in fintech industry," *KSII T. Internet Info.*, vol. 11, no. 2, pp. 1105-1117, 2017.

65. L. Chen, "From Fintech to Finlife: The case of fintech development in China," *China Econ. J,,* vol. 9, no. 3, pp. 255-239, 2016.

66. W. H. Delone and E. R. Mclean, "The Delone and McLean of information systems success: a ten year update," *J. Manag. Inf. Syst.*, vol. 19, no. 4, pp. 9-30, 2003.

67. M. J. Alsamydai, "Adaptation of the Technology Acceptance Model (TAM) to the Use of Mobile Banking Services," *Int. Rev. Manag. Bus. Res.*, vol. 3, no. 4, pp. 2039-2051, 2014.

68. D. Suhartanto, D. Dean, T. A. T. Ismail, and R. Sundari, "Mobile banking adoption in Islamic banks: Integrating TAM model and religiosity-intention model," *J. Islam. Mark.*, vol. 11, no. 6, pp. 1405-1418, 2019.

69. J. Kang, "Mobile payment in Fintech environment: trends, security challenges, and services," *Hum. Cent. Comput. Inf. Sci.*, vol. 8, no. 32, pp. 1-16, 2018.

70. S. Nagaraju, "Mobile Banking- Perception of Customers and Bankers," *Int. J. Bus. Adm. Res. Revi.*, vol. 3, no. 9, pp. 236-241, 2015.

71. A. Bhattacherjee and A. Barfar, "Information technology continuance research: Current state and future directions," *Asia Pac. J. Inf. Syst.*, vol. 21, pp. 1–18, 2011.

72. A. G. Chin, M. A. Harris, and R. Brookshire, "A bidirectional perspective of trust and risk in determining factors that influence mobile app installation," *Int. J. Inf. Manag.*, vol. 39, pp. 49–59, 2018.

73. H. S. Ryu and K. S. Ko, "Sustainable Development of Fintech: Focused on Uncertainty and Perceived Quality Issues," *Sustainability*, vol. 12, 7669, 2020.

74. H. Holden and R. Rada, "Understanding the influence of perceived usability and technology self-efficacy on teachers' technology acceptance," *J. Res. Technol. Educ.*, vol. 43, no. 4, pp. 343-367, 2011.

75. H. Agourram, J. Alvarez, S. Sénécal, S. Lachize, J. Gagné, P. M. Léger, and M. Kurosu, "The Relationship Between Technology Self-Efficacy Beliefs and User Satisfaction – User Experience Perspective," in *Human-Computer Interaction. Design Practice in Contemporary Societies*, M. Kurosu, Eds., Cham: Springer, 2019, pp. 389-397.

76. S. Singh and R. K. Srivastava, "Predicting the intention to use mobile banking in India," *Int. J. Bank Mark.*, vol. 36, no. 2, pp. 357-378, 2018.

77. E. M. Rogers, "*Diffusion of Innovations*," Simon and Schuster, New York, 2010.

78. C. Flavián, A. Pérez-Rueda, D. Belanche, and L. V. Casaló, "Intention to use analytical Artificial Intelligence in services. The effect of technology readiness and awareness," *J. Serv. Manag.*, vol. 41, pp. 13-14, 2021.

79. J. F. Hair, G. T. M., Hult, C. M. Ringle, and M. Sarstedt, *A Primer on Partial Least Squares Structural Equation Modeling (PLS-SEM)*, 2nd ed., Thousand Oaks, CA: Sage Publications Inc., 2017.

80. S. J. Chang, A. V. Witteloostuijn, and L. Eden, "From the Editors: Common method variance in international business research," *J. Int. Bus. Stud.*, vol. 41, pp. 178–184, 2010.

81. P. M. Podsakof, S. B. MacKenzie, J. Y. Lee, and N. P. Podsakof, "Common method biases in behavioral research: a critical review of the literature and recommended remedies," *J. Appl. Psychol.*. vol. 88, no. 5, pp. 879–903, 2003.

82. M, Saunders, P. Lewis, and A. Thornhill. *Research Methods for Business Students*, 5th ed., Harlow: Prentice Hall, 2009.

83. R. Bagozzi, R. and Y. Yi, "On the evaluation of structural equation models," *J. Acad. Mark. Sci.*, vol. 16, no. 1, pp. 74-94, 1988.

84. C. Fornell and D. F. Larcker, "Evaluating structural equation models with unobservable variables and measurement error," *J. Mark. Res.*, vol. 18, no. 1, pp. 39-50, 1981.

85. D. Nurfadilah and S. Samidi, "How the Covid-19 Crisis is Affecting Customers' Intention to Use Islamic Fintech Services: Evidence from Indonesia," *J. Islamic Monetary Econ. Finance*, vol. 7, no. 1, pp. 83–114, 2021.

86. G. Biesok and J. Wyród-Wróbel, "Customer satisfaction - Meaning and methods of measuring," in: *Marketing and logistic problems in the management of organization*, H. Howaniec and W. Waszkielewicz, Ed., Bielsko-Biała: Wydawnictwo Naukowe Akademii Techniczno-Humanistycznej w Bielsku-Białej, 2021, pp. 23-41.

87. M. W. Browne, M.W., and Cudeck, R., "Alternative ways of assessing model fit," *Sociol. Methods Res.*, vol. 21, no. 2, pp. 230-258, 1993.

88. K. Najaf, C. Schinckus, and L. Chee Yoong, "VaR and market value of Fintech companies: An analysis and evidence from global data," *Manag. Finance*, vol. 47, no. 7, pp. 915-936, 2021.

89. B. K. B. Kwok. *Accounting irregularities in financial statements: A definitive guide for litigators, auditors and fraud investigators*, London: Routledge, 2017.

90. A. W. Ng and B. K. B. Kwok, "Emergence of Fintech and cybersecurity in a global financial centre," *J. Financ. Regul. Compliance,* vol. 25, no. 4, pp. 422-434, 2017.

91. BIS, "Introduction of guidelines on interaction and cooperation between prudential and AML/CFT supervision," 2019. [Online]. Available: https://www.bis.org/bcbs/publ/d483.pdf

92. K. Tamilmani, N. P. Rana, N. Prakasam, and Y. K. Dwivedi, "The battle of brain vs. heart: A literature review and meta-analysis of "hedonic motivation" use in UTAUT2," *Int. J. Inf. Manage.,* vol. 46, pp. 222-235, 2019.

93. J. Bayuk and S. A. Altobello, "Can gamification improve financial behavior? The moderating role of app expertise," *Int. J. Bank Mark.,* vol. 37, no. 4, pp. 951-975, 2019.

94. H. Van der Heijden, "User acceptance of hedonic information systems," *MIS Quarterly,* vol. 28, no. 4, pp. 695-704, 2004.

95. I. Lähteenmäki, S. Nätti, and S. Saraniemi, "Digitalization-enabled evolution of customer value creation: An executive view in financial services," *J. Bus. Res.,* vol. 146, pp. 504-517, 2022.

96. V. Venkatesh, J. Y. L. Thong, and X. Xu, "Consumer acceptance and use of information technology: Extending the unified theory of acceptance and use of technology," *MIS Quarterly,* vol. 36, no. 1, pp. 157-178, 2012.

97. A. Daragmeh, C. Lentner, and J. Sági, "FinTech payments in the era of COVID-19: Factors influencing behavioral intentions of "Generation X" in Hungary to use mobile payment," *J. Behav. Exp. Finance,* vol. 32, no. 4, 100574, 2021.

98. M. A. Nangin, I. R. G. Barus, and S. Wahyoedi, "The Effects of Perceived Ease of Use, Security, and Promotion on Trust and Its Implications on Fintech Adoption," *J. Consum. Sci.,* vol. 5, no. 2, pp. 124-138, 2020.

99. W. Meng, L. Zhu, W. Li, J. Han, and Y. Li, "Enhancing the security of FinTech applications with map-based graphical password authentication," *Future Gener. Comput. Syst.,* vol. 101, no. 12, pp. 1018-1027, 2019.

100. J. Li, Z. He, and S. Wang, "A survey of supply chain operation and finance with Fintech: Research framework and managerial insights," *Int. J. Prod. Econ.,* vol. 247, no. 1, 108431, 2022.

Fintech Apps: An Integral Tool in Titivating Banking Operations

Arun Prakash A.*, Leelavathi R., Rupashree R. and V.G. Jisha

Kristu Jayanti College, Bengaluru, India

Abstract

The present article aims to focus on fintech's contribution towards the Indian banking system and its revenue. The revenue stream of the banking system depends on the basic banking service including various deposit, loans and advance and locker facilities and non-banking services including credit cards, equity broking, commodity broking, FOREX, mutual fund and insurances. Fin-tech has changed the banking system drastically. The inception of fin-tech companies like Google pay, Paytm, Phone pe, Bharat pe, BHIM, amazon pay, MobiKwik, Paytm money, Upstox, grow and payment banks like Airtel, Vodafone idea, Jio. The services offered by these fin-tech companies are endless. It has become essential for everyone who's carrying out online transactions like buying and selling financial products, investing in IPO, starting SIP in mutual funds, exchanging currency, opening new international bank accounts, and receiving financial advice are forced to use the possible apps of fintech companies. The study examines the influence of fintech apps on the revenue system of Indian banks through the expansion of the customer base and the frequency of usage. Every transaction done through the fintech app generates revenue for the bank indirectly. This study tries to identify key highly influenced fintech app that contributes to the operational revenue of the bank. The frequently and most widely used fin-tech app by the customers are considered to conduct the study. The primary data used for the study and the sample considered for the study is around 390 respondents. In addition, we also identify the factors that make the customer use the app frequently which is taken from the previous studies like network speed, security factors, ease of handling, additional freebies and services, support system, etc. Here we also measure the usage of non-banking services through these apps. The tools used here are basic statistical analysis like the correlation between the factors and the frequency of usage and Multiple Linear regression and SEM to identify the high impact factors

*Corresponding author: arunprakash@kristujayanti.com

Mohd Naved, V. Ajantha Devi, and Aditya Kumar Gupta (eds.) Fintech and Cryptocurrency, (137–156)

on the increased frequency of usage. The result of the study would deliver which of the Indian banks has used the fin-tech companies to the maximum extent.

Keywords: Fintech, technological advancement, indian banking system, Fin-tech apps, banks revenue

7.1   Introduction

In recent decades India has witnessed a paradigm shift change in the banking and investment sector. The evolution of the banking and investment sector has been a disruptive change in terms of asset quality, information technology and regulatory norms. The banking system has lifted from the physical to the digital era which majorly includes a mobile wallet, online payment, scan and pay transactions etc. The growth of technology has enabled the system to come out with branchless banking, contactless communication, and a 24/7 virtual banking system. As a banking candidate hoping to work for the Reserve Bank of India at top management, you must be aware of the changes that are taking place in the banking sector, especially current and transitional changes. We'll take a look at the big picture of how the banking system has evolved over the years.

Another big component that the Indian banking sector is utilizing to improve productivity is technology. The implementation of CBS (Core Banking Solutions) in 2002, which allowed for the inclusion of advanced technical solutions, had been a significant step forward in the banking sector's use of technology. Core Banking Solutions has streamlined not only bank-to-customer transactions but also the computation of fines, maturity periods and interest, among other things. Following that, with the advent of the digital era in 2011, technical connectivity was taken to a new level, allowing for an extreme amount of client experience. The following is the list of the existing policy-sanctioned digitized banking platforms. The following are the list of Fintech apps considered for the study (Table 7.1).

Table 7.1 List of Fintech apps considered in the research.

Google pay	BHIM	upstox
Paytm	amazon pay	grow
Phone pe	mobikwik	Airtel, Vodafone idea, Jio.
Bharat pe	paytm money	

The key changes faced by the Indian banking sector following the tech transformation have had a significant impact on India's banking sector's development path, from offering exceptional customer engagement to guaranteeing remarkable productivity improvements.

Particularly in the post-demonetization period, the financial world has shown a substantial change towards digitalization, and its players are now better equipped to use the technologies available to them. The fin-tech industry has seen rapid growth in the last five years, with India accounting for 67 per cent of the more than 2100 fin-tech entities that have been established. The majority of fin-tech headquarters are in Mumbai and Bengaluru, which are considered India's financial and technological centres. India's fin-tech business is already worth US$31 billion and is expected to grow to US$84 billion by 2025. Fintech India's emergence and subsequent rise can be attributed to a variety of factors. Increased mobile and internet usage, technical innovation, government supervision and activities endurance to fin-tech and a favourable demographic in India have all been recognized as crucial key drivers. (Figure 7.1). Figure 7.2 clearly depicts the flow of application of loan process, since we have used certain

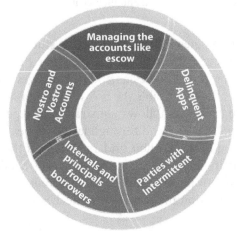

Figure 7.1 International operations involved in international lending.

Figure 7.2 Steps in loan processing.

Figure 7.3 Technologies serving Fintech and their challenges and opportunities.

loan apps and technologies in loan apps for the study. Storage and review of applications that can happen at the quicker time duration and gets the process done swiftly. Technologies as a key challenges and opportunities that could possible allow or disable the users from transacting (Figure 7.3).

The key challenges are as follows constraints in regulating the activities and transactions, issues faced through lack of appeal to investors, lack of education leading to the limited understanding of the investors, safety and breach of security. In addition to the above key challenges useage of internet facilities in rural areas and the acceptability of the information technology plays a predominent role in Fintech services with respect to global perspective.

Asia Pacific - Fintech deals:

Table 7.2 Table showing number of transactions quarter-wise based on technologies.

Technologies	Quarters	No. of transactions (approx in Mn)
ICMT	Q1'21	50
	Q2'21	60
	Q3'21	70
	Q4'21	80
	Q1'22	60
Dl	Q1'21	40
	Q2'21	40
	Q3'21	45
	Q4'21	45
	Q1'22	50
Payments	Q1'21	35
	Q2'21	40
	Q3'21	55
	Q4'21	40
	Q1'22	40
Banking technologies	Q1'21	10
	Q2'21	15
	Q3'21	25
	Q4'21	25
	Q1'22	25

(Continued)

Table 7.2 Table showing number of transactions quarter-wise based on technologies. (*Continued*)

Technologies	Quarters	No. of transactions (approx in Mn)
Financial media and data solutions	Q1'21	5
	Q2'21	10
	Q3'21	5
	Q4'21	10
	Q1'22	10
Insurance technology	Q1'21	15
	Q2'21	15
	Q3'21	15
	Q4'21	20
	Q1'22	10

The above Table 7.2 clearly depicts the number of transaction involved in the asia pacific zone across all the different fintech business verticles. International capital markets have witnessed the hioghest number of transactions, digital lending takes the second highest transactions and minmal transactions are registered in financial media and technologies Technologies and the total number of transactions that are made through the apps for all quarters of the year 21-22 and the values are in millions (Figure 7.4).

7.2 Objectives

- To study the contribution of fin-tech companies towards the revenue of the banking sector
- To identify the list of factors that influences the usage of fin-tech app
- To examine high influencing factor on the frequency of usage of the app

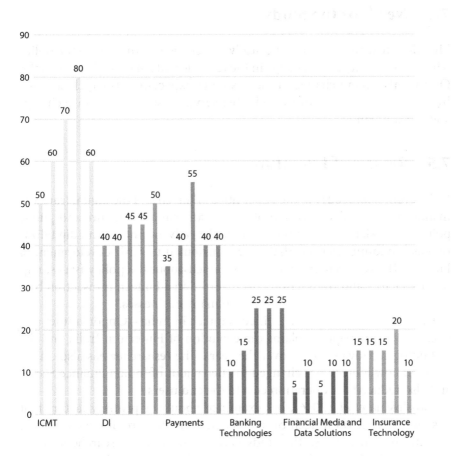

Figure 7.4 Asia Pacific - Fintech transactions quarter-wise based on technologies.

7.3   Statement of the Problem

The traditional banking system has evolved with the spread based operational revenue which is difference between the lending rate and deposit rate. But the modern banking system has evolved with various other income streams like, buying and selling financial products, investing in IPO, starting SIP in mutual funds, exchanging currency, opening new international bank accounts, and receiving financial advice are forced to use the possible apps of fin-tech companies. More over the customer expectation on the ease of usage, compatibility of the fin -tech app are leaping beyond the boundaries. This leads to the study that tries to identify key high influenced fin tech app that contributes to the operational revenue of the bank. The frequently and most widely used fin-tech app by the customers are considered to conduct the study.

7.4   Need for the Study

The identified the need for the study are change in the monetary policy which in turn affects the change in the revenue pattern of the Indian banks. On the other hand change in the customer expectation is largely affected by the compatibility, features, and other services aspect of the fin-tech apps and the companies.

7.5   Review of Literature

Erik Feyen, *et al.* (2021) in the paper titled "Fintech and the digital transformation of financial services: implications for market structure and public policy", have elaborated on the technological advancements and digitalization as economic frictions that have contributed towards development of Fintech. The researchers also have explained about the policy issues, regulatory factors and transaction cost involved in a Fintech transaction by a customer which has given a new rise to many businesses.

C. Vijai (2019), in the paper titled "Fintech in India – Opportunities and Challenges", the paper explains the evolution of Fintech in India and the technological advancement over the years. The researcher has also elaborated on how Fintech has changed the Behaviour of Indian Finance Sector and also reduced the operation cost to the end users.

Zavolokina *et al.* (2016), has examined about the primary factors that has an influence on fintech over time, Subjects that are discussed related to Fintech in the Press. The study carried out by the researchers in the paper focuses on inter disciplinary areas such as Information technology, Finance and Social sciences. The paper titled "The FinTech phenomenon: antecedents of financial innovation perceived by the popular press" on a whole has brought value to people who research in the area of FinTech.

Dr. Disha Mehta, Dr. Sweta Kumari (2021), in the paper titled "Drivers of FinTech in India - A Study of Customers' Attitude and Adoption" have analyzed the factors that drive a customer towards usage of Technological apps for Financial tranactions in their day to day life. The researchers have also made an attempt to understand the awareness and inclination of customers towards adoption of Fintech Products. The researchers concluded that this new technological advancement will be disruptive to payment and investment sector of the economy.

Sumeet Gupta, Adarsh Agrawal (2021), have attempted to analyze how Fintech has changed the traditional role of payments in India the study also analyses the influence of pandemic and its role in emphasing technological financial payments. The researchers in the paper "Analytical study of Fintech in India: Pre & Post Pandemic Covid-19" have found that the adoption of Fintech for transactions has drastically increased which is a positive sign for Financial Inclusion in the country.

Livea Rose Paul, Lipsa Sadath (2021), has explained the history of fintech, the several classifications of fin-tech apps and the systematic usage of fin-tech apps. The article found that technological innovations lead to a direct influence on global business strategy, profit generation, and resource optimization.

Dr. HimanshuMathur (2019) has examined about digital money and wallets in the paper titled "Digital Money & Wallet: A Conceptual Framework" the researcher has made an attempt in introducing the digital money and various types of digital wallets available in market. The paper emphasizes on various payment apps like Amazon pay, Google pay, phone pay, paytm etc.

7.6 Proposed Model

The predominant model that is adopted in the study and the classification of fintech apps and under different financial product categories are listed. The persuasion of users can happen through various factors that's the linking chain, which ends in the different banking verticals that possibly adapts the apps for the benefit of the banking operation (Figure 7.5).

7.7 Lending APPS

Lending apps that are successfully running in the stores which provides loan at different rate are listed. The study basically uses the respondent's opinion on these apps (Figure 7.6).

The lending apps are more appropriate for lenders in choosing the right customers to sell their financial products. It helps us do all transactions using smartphones. Most of the households becaming dual income families many donot find an appropriate time to visit financial institution physically and therefore these lending apps bridge the gap between lenders and borrowers by serving time and providing comfort.

7.8 Investment Apps

Investment apps have gained significant popularity in recent years, providing individuals with convenient and accessible ways to manage their

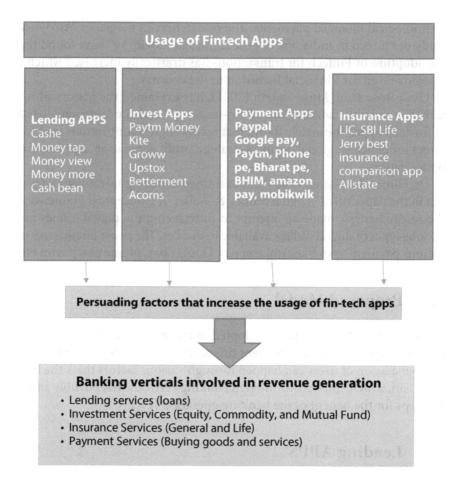

Figure 7.5 Model showing the usage of Fintech apps, persuading factors and revenue streams of banking verticals.

investments. There are several investment apps available that can help you manage your investments and make informed decisions. Here are some popular investment apps considered (Figure 7.7).

Investment apps help us to create a portfolio using different investment avenues. All these apps are used to create wealth and provide convenience to customers. Fintech investment apps also aid to revise a particular portfolio for an investor to revise and reconstruct the investment avenues depending upon the performance and the objectives and pupose of investment.

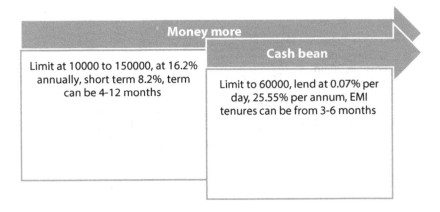

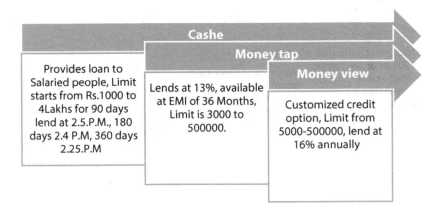

Figure 7.6 Lending APPS.

7.9 Payment Apps

Payment apps have revolutionized the way we handle financial transactions, offering convenient and secure alternatives to traditional payment methods. These apps allow individuals to send and receive money, make purchases, and manage their finances using their smartphones or other mobile devices (Figure 7.8).

The concept of digi wallet has evolved around the globle and has gained importance due to the above mentioned key payment apps. All payments are done through these apps are merchants are getting benefitted from these apps. And allows the customer to make a payment by tapping a smartphone. These apps allow to transfer a minimum of Rs.1 to the maximum limited as per the customization of apps developer.

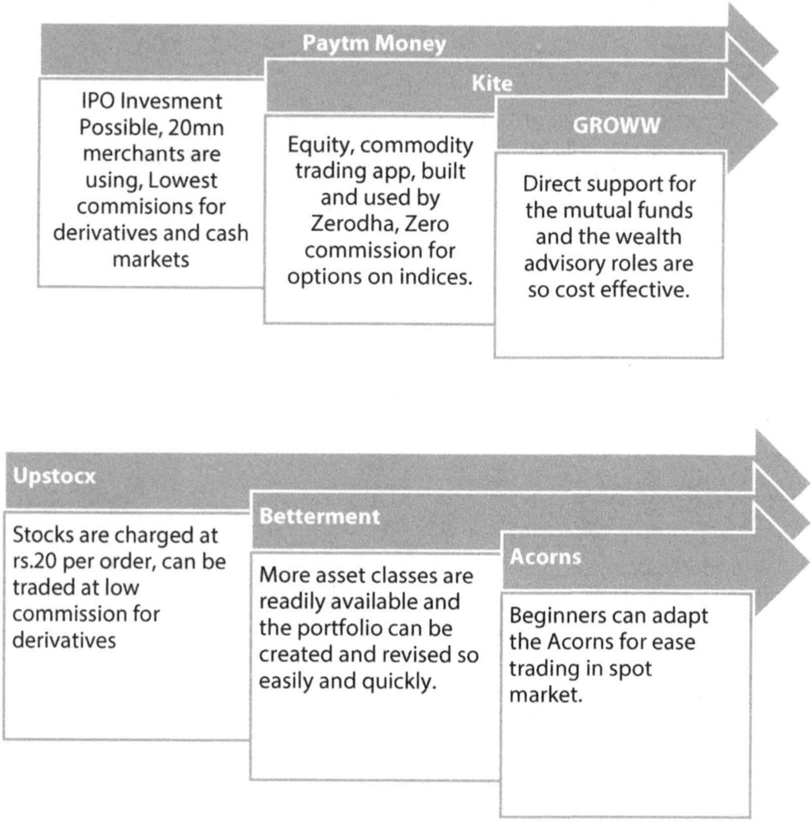

Paytm Money

IPO Invesment Possible, 20mn merchants are using, Lowest commisions for derivatives and cash markets

Kite

Equity, commodity trading app, built and used by Zerodha, Zero commission for options on indices.

GROWW

Direct support for the mutual funds and the wealth advisory roles are so cost effective.

Upstocx

Stocks are charged at rs.20 per order, can be traded at low commission for derivatives

Betterment

More asset classes are readily available and the portfolio can be created and revised so easily and quickly.

Acorns

Beginners can adapt the Acorns for ease trading in spot market.

Figure 7.7 Investment apps.

7.10   Insurance Apps

Insurance apps have become increasingly popular in recent years as more people seek convenient and efficient ways to manage their insurance policies and claims. These apps provide a range of features and benefits that streamline the insurance process, enhance customer experience, and offer peace of mind (FIgure 7.9).

Insurance apps have been noticed as the transition for the insurance sector. With the technological development and uninterruptedly growing client expectations, increase in smartphone usage. Additionally, it can help insurance companies to simplifly method and minimize the paperwork.

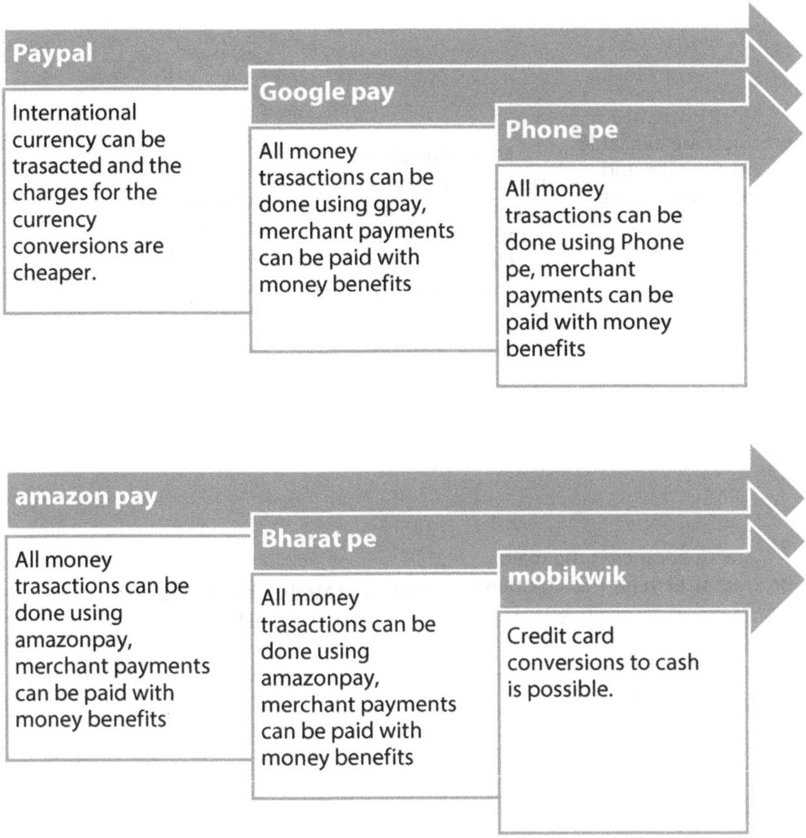

Paypal

International currency can be trasacted and the charges for the currency conversions are cheaper.

Google pay

All money trasactions can be done using gpay, merchant payments can be paid with money benefits

Phone pe

All money trasactions can be done using Phone pe, merchant payments can be paid with money benefits

amazon pay

All money trasactions can be done using amazonpay, merchant payments can be paid with money benefits

Bharat pe

All money trasactions can be done using amazonpay, merchant payments can be paid with money benefits

mobikwik

Credit card conversions to cash is possible.

Figure 7.8 Payment apps.

7.11 Persuading Factors that Increase the Usage of Fin-Tech Apps

The rise of fintech apps has transformed the way we manage our finances, offering numerous advantages that have persuaded millions of users to embrace these platforms. Here are some persuasive factors that contribute to the widespread adoption of fintech apps (Figure 7.10).

The mentioned Persuading factors are the key force behind driving customers to use various Fintech apps for availing different services related to investment, borrowing, payment and insurance. Day by day these apps are being upgraded due to increase in the number of users by the service providers.

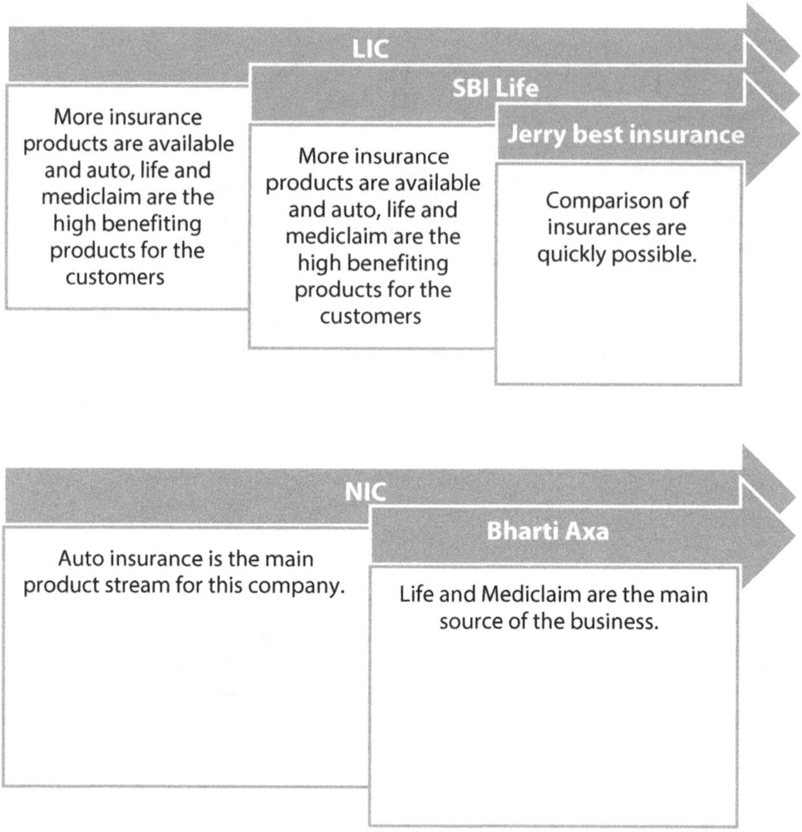

LIC

More insurance products are available and auto, life and mediclaim are the high benefiting products for the customers

SBI Life

More insurance products are available and auto, life and mediclaim are the high benefiting products for the customers

Jerry best insurance

Comparison of insurances are quickly possible.

NIC

Auto insurance is the main product stream for this company.

Bharti Axa

Life and Mediclaim are the main source of the business.

Figure 7.9 Insurance apps.

7.12 Methodology

The study requires both the involvement of primary and secondary data for the analysis. For Instance, to know about the compatibility of the fin-tech apps, we used the questionnaire to collect first-hand information from the users. Information like banking revenue and customer base are sourced through secondary resources.

The study includes demographical factors like age, gender, education profile, etc., and key variables such as Cash Back Offers, Product Discount Offers, Secured transactions, Flexibility to use, Shorter and Quicker transaction, Low borrowing interest rates and Free investment advisory services.

The research tools used for the study are Cronbach's Alpha Reliability test, Multiple Linear regression & Structural Equation Modelling.

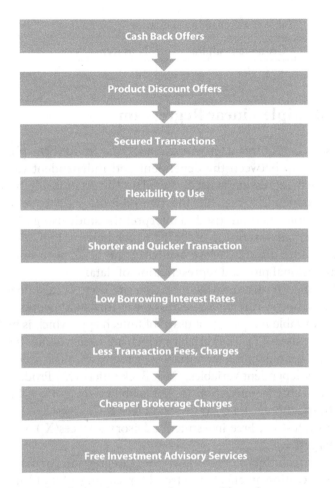

Figure 7.10 Persuading factors that increase the usage of fin-tech apps.

7.13   Results and Discussions

Cronbach's alpha is a mark of checking the trustworthiness and consistency of the data collected through the questionnaire. It refers to the proximity that exists between the variables that are used in the study. When the alpha remains high, it does not imply that the mark of factors is unidimensional. If additional evidence is required to prove the unidimensional nature of the scale taken in the research then it is advisable to go for further tools. Table 7.3 shows the Chronbach's Alpha, representing the reliability of data.

The alpha coefficient for the 18 items is .871, signifying the variables have fairly high internal uniformity.

Table 7.3 Reliability statistics.

Cronbach's alpha	N of items
.871	18

7.14   Multiple Linear Regression

Every research requires a prognostic analysis, to confirm the existence of a relationship between the dependent and independent variables, the multiple linear regression is used to explain the relationship between one continuous dependent variable and two or more independent variables. There are various methods used to interpret the study using MLR, and the scatter plot remains at the top of the list which helps us to plot the data and fit a straight line through. More explicitly, the MLR fits a line through a multi-dimensional plot and representation of data.

In MLR, the variable on which the tests are done is called endogenous/criterion/prognostic variable or regressand. This study works on the one dependent variable Frequency of usage of fintech apps which is highly compatible for the users (Y). The variables which are used to study the influence are called exogenous/predictor variables or regressors. This study considers the following dependent variables; Cash Back Offers (X_1) Product Discount Offers(X_2), Secured transactions(X_3), Flexibility to use(X_4), Shorter and Quicker transaction(X_5), Less transaction fees & Charges(X_6), Low borrowing interest rates(X_7), Free investment advisory services(X_8), Cheaper brokerage charges(X_9).

The Major techniques of Multiple Linear Regression Analysis are causal analysis, forecasting an effect, and trend forecasting. Out of this, we adopt the causal analysis for the study by using the intercept equation which is denoted at the bottom of Table 7.4.

The MLR considers the R-squared value as the major measure to identify the correctness of the equation and how far the dependent variable relies

Table 7.4 Regression statistics.

Multiple R	0.88107837
R Square	0.83006126
Adjusted R Square	0.8091067
Standard Error	33.738745
Observations	336

on the independent variables. This study's R-square value falls between 0 to 1, and it is at 0.83, which is more considerable to prove the relation between the exogenous and endogenous variables. Table 7.5 shows the factors witnessed in Fintech apps to increase the usage.

Dependent Variable $(Y) = 5.313162303 + 0.58884X_1 + 0.455878X_2 + 0.121994 X_3 + 0.451809X_4 + 0.809113X_5 + 0.16319X_6 + 0.558765X_7 + 0.561356X_8 + 0.13525X_9$

Y = Frequency of Usage of Fintech Apps
X_1 = Cash Back Offers, X_2 = Product discount Offers, X_3 = Secured transactions, X_4 = Flexibility to use, X_5 = Shorter and Quicker transaction, X_6 = Less transaction fees, Charges, X_7 = Low borrowing interest rates, X_8 = Free investment advisory services, X_9 = Cheaper brokerage charges

Table 7.5 Multiple linear regression.

Factors	Coefficients	Standard error	t stat	P-value
Intercept	5.313162303	0.134186	39.59549	2.1E-127
Cash back offers	0.58844743	0.057464	1.02402	0.306576
Product discount offers	0.45587864	0.015906	2.86608	0.004423
Secured transactions	0.121994065	0.063131	1.93241	0.054165
Flexibility to use	0.45180956	0.02388	1.89202	0.059364
Shorter and quicker transaction	0.809113453	0.09876	65535	2.1E-113
Less transaction fees, charges	0.16319691	0.089809	0.181716	0.004423
Low borrowing interest rates	0.5518765	0.45363	65535	0.00343
Free investment advisory services	0.561356	0.123265	65535	0.0023
Cheaper brokerage charges	0.4135254	0.43566	65535	0.001223

7.15   Structural Equation Modelling

The structured equation modelling clearly depicts the highest impacting variable that is considered for the study through the variance value across the dependent and independent variables. Quicker the transaction the most expected factor, followed by the flexibility and compatibility factors (Figure 7.11).

Absolute Model Fit:
   Computation of degrees of freedom (Default model)
   Minimum index value was achieved
      CMIN (Chi-square) = 14.746
      DF (Degrees of freedom) = 2
      PL (Probability level) = .000
      Degrees of freedom (9 - 7): 2

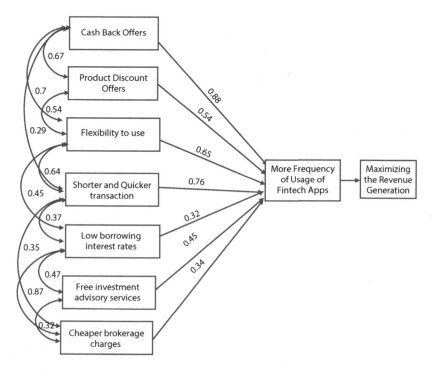

Figure 7.11 Structured equation modelling on the proposed model.

7.16   Conclusion

The study concludes that the revenue stream of the banking system depends on banking and non-banking services. In this digital era, technological progressions propel growth in all fields and especially the banking system. The invention of the fintech apps led the banks to maximize their revenue stream by building more customer base and increasing the total number of transactions. People have started using fintech apps and they become part of the bank's revenue directly and indirectly. More usage of the fintech apps by customers for the services like lending, investing and payment. The factors like Cash Back Offers, Product Discount Offers, Secured transactions, Flexibility to use, Shorter and Quicker transaction, Low borrowing interest rates and Free investment advisory services creates notable influence on the frequent usage of apps that leads to an increase in banking transactions. This act is the driving force for democratizing digital financing and fueling national development.

References

Agarwal, S. – Hauswald, R. (2010): Distance and private information in lending. The Review of Financial Studies, 23(7), p. 2757-2788.

Beck, T. – Demirgüç-Kunt, A. – Levine, R. (2000): A new database on the structure and development of the financial sector. The World Bank Economic Review, 14(3), p. 597-605.

Bhandari, M. (2016): India and the Pyramid of Opportunity. In: The FinTech Book: The Financial Tech-nology Handbook for Investors, Entrepreneurs and Visionaries, p. 81-83.

Dr. Disha Mehta, D. S. K. January 2021. Drivers of FinTech in India - A Study of Customers Attitude and Adoption. ZENITH International Journal of Multidisciplinary Research , 11(1).

Erik Feyen, J. F. L. G. H. N. M. S., July 2021. Fintech and the digital transformation of financial services: implications for market structure and public policy. Bank for International Settlements, Issue ISSN 1682 - 7651, p. Online.

Liudmila Zavolokina, M. D. a. G. S., 2016. The FinTech phenomenon: antecedents of financial innovation perceived by the popular press. Financial Innovation, Springer Open.

Sumeet Gupta, A. A., December 2021. Analytical study of Fintech in India: Pre & Post Pandemic Covid-19. Indian Journal of Economics and Business, 20(3).

Vijai, C., January 2019. Fintech in India - Opportunities and Challenges. SAARJ Journal on Banking and Insurance Research (SJBIR), 8(1).

8

Analytical Study of Fin-Tech in Banking: A Utility Model

Neha Kamboj[1]* and Mamta Sharma[2]

[1]IILM School of Management, IILM University Gurugram, Haryana, India
[2]IKGPTU Kapurthala, Jalandhar, Punjab and CBSA, Landran, Mohali Punjab, India

Abstract

India is the 5th largest growing developing country among the globe, and undoubtedly it is fastest growing itself into the Fin-tech market in recent years too. Paperless loaning, portable banking, secure installment passages, versatile wallets, and different ideas are now being taken on in India. The ongoing paper is focusing on understanding the purpose of Fin-tech for the banking sector in India. The author analyses the developments of Fin-tech trends, especially in Indian banking sectors. The authors additionally attempted to figure out the quantity of variables influencing clients' aims to utilize these services with the goal that the Indian financial area will further develop its Fin-tech framework. To realize this, the information gathered through an overview of clients of banks in Chandigarh,, which ranks first or top performer in SDG Index among union territories. The Index for Sustainable Development Goals (SDGs) evaluates the progress on three key parameters viz social, economic and environmental. The information is gathered from the time period of January 2022 to February 2022 through survey questionnaire. The Sample size is 400 customers of banks located in Tricity- a good economic sector of India. To analyze the information, the author utilized multivariate regression to appraise the model which is used in this research. The outcomes show that Fin-tech service is vital for the Indian financial area specially banking sectors. The study has found the success factors that positively and significantly impact the Willingness of clients to use Fin-tech services through banks with the help of multivariate regression. The study has found the success factors that positively and significantly impact the Willingness of clients to use Fin-tech services with the help of multivariate regression. The factors which identified are

*Corresponding author: nehakamboj2000@gmail.com

Mohd Naved, V. Ajantha Devi, and Aditya Kumar Gupta (eds.) Fintech and Cryptocurrency, (157–172)
© 2023 Scrivener Publishing LLC

Perceived Utility(PU), Sensible Usability (SU), Customer Belief (CU), and social implications (SOI). With the help of factors identified banks need to pay attention to these elements more so that they can work on the convenience of Fin-tech benefits more. Based on discoveries, banks might have a premise to revise the nature of Fin-tech services. Moreover, the outcomes are additionally significant for policymakers and researchers.

Keywords: Fin-tech, customers, multivariate regression, factors, indian banking, trends

8.1 Introduction

Fin-tech, as the name suggests, is the blend of finance and technology. Technology hasalways played a predominant role in every field. As far as financial sector is concerned, itinfluenced it tremendously, Consider, for illustration, Introduction of credit card i.e. Centralbank of India introduced the first credit card in 1980s in India [13]. HSBC bank introduced the first ATM in India in the year of 1987 [20]. Consequently, the step at which new technologies are demonstrated and brought into finance is more quickly than any other time. Eventually, considerably more generally, this Fin-tech change is undeniable in that outstanding change is happening from outside the financial business, as energetic starting up firms and immense overall creative firms are attempting to upset the tenants, presenting new things and advance technologies and giving a critical new extent of challenge. Simply step into a specialist situated Fin-tech gathering: with its crowd made generally of people in their twenties from Silicon Valley and Silicon Alley, there is obviously a new thing in the air [2, 8, 31].

Born in context to economic needs, the arena of finance has been driven by an integral stimulus to absorb valuable elements, containing technological innovation, tobenefititsgrowth. The developmentof India's financial sector has been complemented by endlesstechnological progress. After financial informatization and electronation, Internet Finance arose to grow rapidly in India and gained wide spread recognition since 2017. In India we have seen a drastic increase in the Fin-tech market. Walmart Inc's PhonePe application accounts for 47% of online cash exchanges in India, while homegrown Paytm represents 10%. Alphabet Inc's, Google Pay, which controls 37% of the market, is utilizing its hunt mastery to impact clients' decision of bank deposits [32]. In the present scenario Fin-tech is the requirement of many developing economies such as China, India, Korea, UK [3, 15].

In India, the Fin-tech market is developing and having a promising future (Table 8.1). The Fin-tech market of India has gainedmuch attention from the bankingindustry, policy makers and researchers.soitis the subjecton which it requires more discussion in conferences and business forums. In any case, not much exact examination has been led in this setting to learn Fin-tech and its application in financial areas connected with the ongoing Indian economy situation.

Table 8.1 Fin-tech trends in India.

Particulars	By	Year	Source
Introduction of Credit card	Central bank of India	1980	www.rbi.com
Introduction of ATM	HSBC	1987	www.rbi.com
Introduction of Banking website	ICICIBank	1998	www.rbi.com
Introduction of Electronic Trading-Geojit Securities was the first to go online	National Stock Exchange (NSE)	2000	www.sebi.com
Paypal Makes its debut	PayPal Payments PrivateLimited	2017	www.paypal.com
Introduction of Google Pay- Google sent off an application for payment in India known as Tez, using the Unified Payments Interface (UPI).	Google	2017	wwwgoogle.com
Introduction of Crypto currency-Central Bank Digital Currency(CBDC)	CentralBank	2021	www.rbi.com

Compiled by Author

India's urban advanced foundation, explicitly UPI has effectively shown how to challenge customary officeholders. As brought up in the initial segment, UPI exchanges estimated have outperformed Rs 4 trillion in value (April, 2021). Aadhaar approvals have passed 55 trillion (April, 2021). At last, India is at the highest point of operationalizing its own digitized stage. These indices exhibit India has the technology heap to fully facilitate technology [16, 32]. There are more than 2100 Fin-tech firms in India, out of which more than 67 percent have been commenced in the last five years. India's Fin-tech segment has also grasped exponential development in funding; investments worth more than US$8 billion we perceived across various stages of investment in 2021. According to Amitabh Kant (CEO, NITI Aayog), the Indian Fin-tech sector has accumulative funding of over US$27.6 billion and is anticipated to be valued at over US$150 billion by 2025. Currently, worldwide, there are 187 Fin-tech unicorns of which 18 Unicorns arein India. These are Policy Bazaar, Pay tm Razor Pay, Bill Desk, Zoho, Zerodha, Cred, Chargebee, Digit, Groww, Pine Labs, Zeta, BharatPe, CoinDCX, Of Business, Upstox, Acko and Slice. Slice was thelatest entry in the Fin-tech unicorn list, hovering US$220 million in a series-B round [33].

So, this is a worthy topic for conducting research as there is still little scope to explore Fin-tech and its application towards banking in India in the present economic scenario. After identifying, this author has conducted this analysis. The authors have taken various factors that impacted the customer decision regarding the use of Fin-tech Services. The data regarding this research has been collected through surveys conducted among bank customers. The research showed very fascinating results which are very helpful to formulate policies for policymakers, bankers, researchers who are doing well in the field of banking industry in India.

8.2　Literature Analysis and Development of Hypothesis

Utilizing Fin-tech, the range of services available at banks will raise to their end clients [31]. thus, Fin-tech is certainly not a plain mix of monetary services and IT, yet an innovation requesting for customary services to broaden the extension [17] for clients, Fin-tech makes many new revel in open doors and works with clients more prominent helpful to execute [5]. Obviously, Fin-tech can uphold banking services on cell phones and tablets. Hence, buyers can custom financial services all over, as a swap for going to the standard counter [28]. Subsequently, it tends to be accepted that Fin-tech services assume an exceptionally critical part in the banking sector and all together bring several customer benefits, It is essential to take into account elements that influence consumers' desire to use Fin-tech services in order to thrive at Fin-tech services towards the banking industry [5, 6, 28]. As a result, banks will enlarge market share and advance operational efficiency. With respect to influencing clients' goal to utilize Fin-tech services, zeroing in on four elements: Perceived Utility (PU), customer belief (CU), Sensible Usability (SU), and Social Implications (SI).

8.2.1 Perceived Utility (PU) and Willingness to Adopt Fin-Tech (WUF) Services

The utility of the service can extensively effect the client's goal towards utilize Fin-tech services in Baking industry. Fin-tech services provide consumers with several pros, primarily reduced cost, and time andeffort to realize financial transactions [24, 25]. Furthermore, Fin Tech service can offer an added remarkable experience for clients, so conquering the restrictions of standard banking services. Thus, it tends to be expected that the impression of convenience can decidedly impact clients' goal to reuse Fin-tech services again and again. This consequence is also found in various experiential studies, via [6, 19, 23] On the grounds of this, the following hypothesis is put forth:

> H1: Perceived Utility (PU) has a positive impact on the Willingness to use Fin-tech (WUF) services.

8.2.2 Sensible Usability (SU) and Willingness to Use Fin-Tech (WUF) Services

The awareness of convenience can be perceived as how many clients feel good and satisfied. Fin-tech services, whenever utilized easily, can offer exceptional encounters for shoppers, in like that, the singular necessities of every client can meet. Going against the norm, if the utilization of Fin-tech service is perplexing, buyers will be exceptionally inclined to chance upon mistakes while utilizing, then it could be the reason for financial misfortunes for clients. Consequently, the sensitivity of usability is one of the fundamental factors that lead to clients' aim to utilize these services [4],

[22, 29]. In this way, the usability can emphatically influence the shopper's plan to utilize Fin-tech services. This result is likewise tracked down in experimental investigations of [1, 17, 26]. In this way, the accompanying research hypothesis is proposed by the authors.

> H2: Sensible Usability (SU) has a positive impact on the Willingness to use Fin-tech (WUF) services.

8.2.3   Customer Belief (CU) and Willingness to Use Fin-Tech (WUF) Services

Belief is considered as definitive component for innovation reception, especially those advances planned for monetary exchanges [15]. In a very cutthroat financial industry, there is a prominence on trust to shape strong relationships with customers [29]. Trust in Fin-tech services are like customers have optimism in the belief, reliability and munificence of these applications [15, 20, 21]. In contrast, since the substituting cost tocustomary financial systems are high, trust is regarded crucial for financial transactions [20, 25]. Certainly, the consequence of trust in such indeterminate and precarious situations is reduced risk and thus positive aims toward using new technologies [9, 10]. Consequently, the following hypothesis is proposed:

> H3: Customer Belief (CU) has a positive impact on the Willingness to use Fin-tech (WUF) services.

8.2.4   Social Implications (SI) and Willingness to Use Fin-Tech (WUF) Services

Customers' choices to use first hand technology are swayed by the opinions of others in their immediate vicinity, especially in the social media age, Family, relatives and coworkers have all been sources of positive feedback about new technology that might inspire users to use them [28, 30]. When regulars observe that individuals in society use Fin-tech services, they are have a tendency to employ it [31]. Social Implications have favorable and considerable effect on the adoption of Fin-tech services like smart phone payment service providers [7, 12]. But this depends on factors like prior experience. The following theories are put out in light of Indian society's collectivistic philosophy:

> H4: Social implications (SI) have a positive impact on the Willingness to use Fin-tech (WUF) services.

8.3   Research Design

The paper accentuates on realizing Fin-tech in the Banking area in India. To unwind this exploration level headed, the researchers dissect Fin-tech development patterns in the financial area (banking) in India. To survey the prominence of Fin-tech services in banking industry, the authors led thought of components influencing clients' expectation or willingness to utilize Fin-tech services. To understand this, the researchers gathered information through a review of clients of banks in Chandigarh area; this ranks first or topper former in SDG Index among union territories. The Index for Sustainable Development Goals (SDGs) evaluates the progress on three key parameters viz. social, economic and environmental [32]. The study time frame is from January 2022 to February 2022 as indicated by the pre-planned overview survey. The number of Samples included for this study is 400 clients using banks facilities. For the determination of number of samples slovin's formula has identified. The absolute populace of Chandigarh is 1191000. The sample size came out 399.54 roughly 400. For examination, the researcher utilized test called multivariate regression the exploration model. Prior to continuing regression examination, the analysts led Cronbach's Alpha test and Exploratory Factor Analysis (EFA) to restrict the suitable elements to lay into the exploration model.

The research model is developed in view of the outcomes of going before studies and the examination speculations that the researchers have proposed. Thusly, the reliant variables are given in Figure 8.1. The variables used in this exploration model and their description is mentioned in Table 8.2.

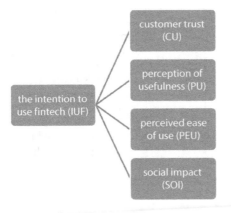

Figure 8.1 Proposed model for research.

Table 8.2 Variables depiction in the exploration model.

Variables		Description	Inferences by
Perceived Usefulness (PU)	PU1	Fin-tech service can address the requirements of clients	[21, 24]
	PU2	Clients save a great deal of time while utilizing Fin-tech services	[20, 23, 28]
	PU3	Utilizing Fin-tech services increments client Work proficiency.	
	PU4	Clients can get to numerous utilities connected while utilizing Fin-tech service.	
Perceived Ease of Use (PEU)	PEU1	The tasks acted in Fin-tech services are very basic for clients.	[1, 4, 12, 17, 26]
	PEU2	Directions on the Fin-tech services framework are clear and straightforward.	
	PEU3	Clients can associate with Fin-tech services framework all over.	
Customer Trust (CU)	CU1	Fin-tech service has good data Security capacity.	[9, 10, 14, 15, 21, 22]
	CU2	Fin-tech services are given by trustworthy units.	
	CU3	Clients feel sure while utilizing Fin-tech services.	

(*Continued*)

Table 8.2 Variables depiction in the exploration model. (*Continued*)

Variables		Description	Inferences by
Social Impact (SOI)	SOI1	Neighbors (such as relatives, companions, Colleagues.) are often using Fin-tech services.	[7, 12, 27, 30]
	SOI2	Client's work/study on environment upholds Fin-tech services.	
	SOI3	Fin-tech service is in line with the high level example of society.	

Compiled by authors

8.4 Empirical Results

By and large, Fin Tech in India has grown rapidly lately. Fin-tech associations also assist with banks to offer inventive consumables by applying high technology and innovation. Thereby, banks have promising circumstances to further develop service quality, upswing functional productivity. In unambiguous, Fin-tech firms themselves are not monetary organizations, so money exchanges actually need to go through banks. All in all, Fin-tech organizations require working with banks to advance together. For clients, they will have more courses while getting to banking administrations and they will save a great deal of time and upswing effectiveness while utilizing banking services. To confirm the appropriate factors that should be remembered for the current examination model, Cronbach's alpha test (which is expected to actually take a look at the inner consistency) and exploratory element investigation (which is expected to follow the general elements among the chose variable) have been inferred. The outcome of the results is shown in the Table 8.3.

In the Table 8.3, The Test results of Cronbach's alpha and EFA have been concluded. The outcome of cronbach's alpha is more than its like value i.e. 0.7, which means scale here using is un-dimensional and reliable. For finding out the contribution and finding out the structure of factors, EFA Model has been used. These variables are Perceived Usefulness, Customer Belief, Perceived Ease of Use, and Social implications and Willingness to use Fin-tech services. Based on the EFA, the factor loading values indicates the correlation of the given variables with factor in Table 8.3.

Table 8.3 Outcome of EFA.

Variables		Cronbach's Alpha	Factor loading			
			1	2	3	4
Perceived Usefulness (PU)	PU1	0.901	0.881			
	PU2		0.778			
	PU3		0.651			
	PU4		0.566			
Perceived Ease of Use (PEU)	PEU1	0.894		0.886		
	PEU2			0.782		
	PEU3			0.712		
Customer Trust (CU)	CU1	0.843			0.895	
	CU2				0.678	
	CU3				0.621	
Social Impact (SOI)	SOI1	0.791				0.821
	SOI2					0.798
	SOI3					0.671

Compiled by author

It has seen that the attributes are highly loaded to Perceived Utility (PU), with values 0.566 and above. Similarly the set of attributes with other factors namely Customer Belief, Perceived Ease of Use, and Social implications are also having a value greater than 0.566.

After testing reliability of the data Multiple Linear Regression test has been applied to check the impact and design a research Model. In Multiple Linear Regression test, Independent and dependent variables are calculated by the average observed variables of each factor extracted with the help of EFA. The total variation is calculated 60.2 percent. From this analysis it has been found that the hypothesis where the attributes suggested as the Willingness to use fin-tech services and interdependent factors related with them is accepted. The value of R square is 85% that shows 85% of variation in Willingness of customers to use Fin Tech services are due to the selected independent variables.

The ANOVA variance analysis shows F = 41.759 that is statistical significant (0.0004) at 5% level of significant. This implies the regression model used for this analysis is consistent with the data and variables taken for the study.

Table 8.4 Estimation of regression coefficients.

Dependent Variable (Willingness of customers to use the Fin-tech services) (ICUF)		
Variables	**Beta**	**Sig.**
Perceived Usefulness (PU)	0.457***	0.0004
Perceived Ease of Use (PEU)	0.459***	0.0034
Customer Trust (CU)	0.558***	0.0487
Social Impact (SOI)	0.398***	0.0084
N		400
Anova		0.0004***
RSquare		85%

***indicates significant at 5% level of significance

By the consequence of above Table 8.4, the accompanying equation can be derived. A model could be drawn that has been displayed in the Figure 8.2.

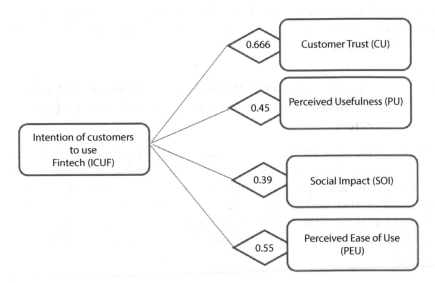

Figure 8.2 Estimation of outcomes of the regression coefficients.

8.4.1 Effect of Perceived Utility of Fin-Tech Services (PU) on the Willingness of Customers to Use Fin-Tech (ICUF) Services

The result of the examination portrays that the impression of value of Fin-tech benefits decidedly influences the aim of clients to utilize Fin-tech Services. The results are also steady with the earlier studies of [5, 18, 24, 30]. It shows that Simple usage of Fin-tech services gives a sign that an innovation is planned not to make it hard for the wearer, however, the utilization of innovation makes it simpler for somebody to complete their work. All in all, somebody who utilizes innovation will work simpler than somebody who utilizes a manual framework [28].

8.4.2 Effect of Perceived Ease of Use of Fin-Tech Services (PEU) on the Willingness of Customers to Use Fin-Tech (ICUF) Services

The Study uncovered that positive effect of Perceived Ease of Use of Fin-tech Services on the goal of clients to utilize Fin-tech services. This is additionally very reliable with the attributes of moderately new innovations in financial markets, for example, Fin-tech. Since, while planning to utilize the assistance, clients frequently pose the inquiry like "Is it simple to utilize or not?" In like manner, if the Fin-tech administration is agreeable and simple to utilize, clients won't hold back while making a goal to utilize this help. The positive effect of the apparent convenience on Fin-tech aims is additionally steady with past perceptions of [1, 17, 26].

8.4.3 Effect of Customer Belief in Fin-Tech Services (CU) on the Willingness of Customers to Utilize Fin-Tech (ICUF) Services

The study has also shown the positive influence of Customer Belief on the expectation to use Fin tech services. This variable's outcome is likewise steady with the prior investigations as [11, 14, 15, 20, 21]. In Indian Financial market we have seen many banks providing Fin-tech services to their customers. The banks that are which are providing many services as Fin-tech services creates the trust among the customers to utilize these services.

8.4.4 Social Influence (SI) Impact on the Willingness of Customers to Utilize Fin-Tech (ICUF) Services

The variable Social Influence decidedly affects the expectation of clients to utilize Fin-tech (ICUF) services, since when an individual see others to utilize Fin-tech, it builds the delicacy among the clients to utilize these services. In the earlier studies [7, 12, 14, 15, 24] same tenderness has been seen which shows the greater impact on using Fin-tech services.

8.5 Conclusion

The Results indicates that the Fin Tech services are vital for Indian banking sector as a developing country. The study has found the success factors that positively and significantly impact the Willingness of customers to use Fin Tech services with the help of multivariate regression. The factors which identified are Perceived Utility (PU), Sensible Usability (SU), Customer Belief (CU), and social implications (SOI). With the help of factors identified banks need to pay attention to these elements more so that they can improve the usability of Fin-tech services more. Indiangovernment and Banking sectors together formed some policies to increase the usability of Fin Tech services.

The author offers the accompanying arrangement suggestions in light of the discoveries of this review to encourage the improvement of Fin Tech services in the banking area in India:

✓ Banks must continue to develop the characteristics of Fin Tech services, which are largely focused on boosting the service's usefulness for all consumer segments. At the same time, users should be able to complete transactions quickly and easily using Fin Tech services.

✓ Banks must have a strategy in place to improve their image and reputation in the market. Simultaneously, banks should effectively advance and spread information about items and their services that are provided overall population to improve its brand value and decrease transactional risks.

✓ Banks should extend their associations with Fin Tech firms to benefit from the last's innovative benefits, determined to work on the nature of super advanced application benefits and giving better client encounters. Banks will actually want to differentiate their items and services by using state of the art innovation, supporting client access for a minimal price, because of this coordinated effort, simultaneously, and banks ought to contribute more, upgrade their specialized framework and further develop framework security.

✓ Banks should further develop their training programs for excellent HRs. This human asset should be capable in unambiguous information, yet in addition in monetary administrations applications in view of current innovation.

✓ In addition, the authorities must complete and supplement the legal structure, process, and regulations governing Fintech activity. Building Fin Tech advancement arrangements, on the other hand, must be connected to money related and financial strategies.

Albeit the exploration objective was met, it was in any case restricted on the grounds that it didn't address various different perspectives that could impact Fin Tech client support, like the data innovation stage, buyer monetary capacity, and dangers related with utilizing the services.

References

1. Abbasi, G. A., Sandran, T., Ganesan, Y., & Iranmanesh, M. (2022). Go cashless! Determinants of continuance intention to use E-wallet apps: A hybrid approach using PLS-SEM and fsQCA. *Technology in Society*, 101937.
2. Al Nawayseh, M. K. (2020). Fintech in COVID-19 and beyond: what factors are affecting customers' choice of fintech applications?. *Journal of Open Innovation: Technology, Market, and Complexity*, 6(4), 153.
3. Alam, N., Gupta, L., & Zameni, A. (2019). *Fintech and Islamic finance*. sl: Springer International Publishing.
4. Bartlett, R., Morse, A., Stanton, R., & Wallace, N. (2022). Consumer-lending discrimination in the FinTech era. *Journal of Financial Economics*, 143(1), 30-56.
5. Chen, X., You, X., & Chang, V. (2021). FinTech and commercial banks' performance in China: A leap forward or survival of the fittest?. *Technological Forecasting and Social Change*, 166, 120645.
6. Chen, Y., & Sivakumar, V. (2021). Invesitigation of finance industry on risk awareness model and digital economic growth. *Annals of Operations Research*, 1-22.

7. Darmansyah, D., Fianto, B. A., Hendratmi, A., & Aziz, P. F. (2020). Factors determining behavioral intentions to use Islamic financial technology: Three competing models. *Journal of Islamic Marketing, 12*(4), 794-812.
8. Demertzis, M., Merler, S., & Wolff, G. B. (2018). Capital Markets Union and the fintech opportunity. *Journal of financial regulation, 4*(1), 157-165.
9. Dinev, T., & Hu, Q. (2007). The centrality of awareness in the formation of user behavioral intention toward protective information technologies. *Journal of the Association for Information Systems, 8*(7), 23.
10. Garrouch, K. (2021). Does the reputation of the provider matter? A model explaining the continuance intention of mobile wallet applications. *Journal of Decision Systems, 30*(2-3), 150-171.
11. Hu, Z., Ding, S., Li, S., Chen, L., & Yang, S. (2019). Adoption intention of fintech services for bank users: An empirical examination with an extended technology acceptance model. *Symmetry, 11*(3), 340.
12. Isaac, O., Abdullah, Z., Aldholay, A. H., & Ameen, A. A. (2019). Antecedents and outcomes of internet usage within organisations in Yemen: An extension of the Unified Theory of Acceptance and Use of Technology (UTAUT) model. *Asia Pacific Management Review, 24*(4), 335-354.
13. Jadhav, N. 2003 "Central Bank Strategies, Credibility and Independence: Global Evolution and Indian Experience." *RBI Occasional Papers..*24(1 and 2)..2005. *Monetary Policy, Financial Stability and Central Banking in India.* Macmillan India Ltd., New Delhi.
14. Kaushik, A. K., Agrawal, A. K., & Rahman, Z. (2015). Tourist behaviour towards self-service hotel technology adoption: Trust and subjective norm as key antecedents. *Tourism Management Perspectives, 16*, 278-289.
15. Kewell, B., & Michael Ward, P. (2017). Blockchain futures: With or without Bitcoin?. *Strategic Change, 26*(5), 491-498.
16. Kulviwat, S., Bruner II, G. C., & Al-Shuridah, O. (2009). The role of social influence on adoption of high tech innovations: The moderating effect of public/private consumption. *Journal of Business research, 62*(7), 706-712.
17. Lagna, A., & Ravishankar, M. N. (2022). Making the world a better place with fintech research. *Information Systems Journal, 32*(1), 61-102.
18. Lee, D. K. C., & Teo, E. G. (2015). Emergence of FinTech and the LASIC Principles. *Journal of Financial Perspectives, 3*(3).
19. Lee, J. M., & Kim, H. J. (2020). Determinants of adoption and continuance intentions toward Internet-only banks. *International Journal of Bank Marketing.*
20. Müller, J., & Kerényi, Á. (2019). The Need for Trust and Ethics in the Digital Age–Sunshine and Shadows in the FinTech World. *Financial and Economic Review, 18*(4), 5-34.
21. Nangin, M. A., Barus, I. R. G., & Wahyoedi, S. (2020). The effects of perceived ease of use, security, and promotion on trust and its implications on fintech adoption. *Journal of Consumer Sciences, 5*(2), 124-138.

22. Nasfi, N., Yunimar, Y., & Prawira, A. (2022). The Role Of Fintech In Sharia Rural Bank West Sumatra. *International Journal of Social and Management Studies, 3*(2), 13-19.

23. Oladapo, I. A., Hamoudah, M. M., Alam, M. M., Olaopa, O. R., & Muda, R. (2021). Customers' perceptions of FinTech adaptability in the Islamic banking sector: comparative study on Malaysia and Saudi Arabia. *Journal of Modelling in Management.*

24. Ozili, P. K. (2018). Impact of digital finance on financial inclusion and stability. *Borsa Istanbul Review, 18*(4), 329-340.

25. Pratama, J. (2021). Analysis of Factors Affecting Trust on the Use of FinTech (P2P Lending) in Indonesia. *Jurnal Sisfokom (Sistem Informasi dan Komputer), 10*(1), 79-85.

26. Roh, T., Yang, Y. S., Xiao, S., & Park, B. I. (2022). What makes consumers trust and adopt fintech? An empirical investigation in China. *Electronic Commerce Research,* 1-33.

27. Schneider, F. (2018). *China's digital nationalism.* Oxford University Press.

28. Shaikh, A. A. (2016). Examining consumers' intention, behavior, and beliefs in mobile banking adoption and continuous usage. *Jyväskylä studies in business and economics,* (172).

29. Stewart, H., & Jürjens, J. (2018). Data security and consumer trust in FinTech innovation in Germany. *Information & Computer Security.*

30. Woolley, S. C., & Howard, P. N. (Eds.). (2018). *Computational propaganda: Political parties, politicians, and political manipulation on social media.* Oxford University Press.

31. Zetsche, D. A., Buckley, R. P., Arner, D. W., & Barberis, J. N. (2017). From FinTech to TechFin: the regulatory challenges of data-driven finance. *NYUJL & Bus., 14,* 393.

9

Is Digital Currency a Payment Disruption Mechanism?

Vanishree Mysore Ramkrishna[1]* and Vyshnavi Loganathan[2]

[1]Surana Research & Consultancy Cell, Surana College (Autonomous), Bangalore, India
[2]Advance Tax Analyst, Ernest & Young – Global Delivery Services, India

Abstract

Digital economies are omnipresent, evident, and inhabit every sphere of human existence. Blockchain technology has changed how private currencies such as bitcoin and Ethereum are traded in open markets. To strengthen and protect the economic & financial system against such private currencies, the central banks around the world have leaped to introduce their own Central Bank Digital Currency (CBDC) for phasing out with high technology transformations. The present paper will be a first of its kind attempt to capture the perceptions and real-time issues of common people in the implementation of CBDC in a large country like India. As CBDC is still in its pilot phase of implementation, researchers have used the bottom-up approach to capture the requisite information from the common man view and the thematic analysis method was used to finalize the variables viz., financial literacy & inclusion, infrastructure, technical know-how, trust & belief in the system, and acceptance level for further discussion. The result analysis highlights, that government and implementing agencies of CBDC should ensure to reach the unreached population, especially in Tier-2 & 3 cities with proper technology infrastructure, and frequently hold awareness/orientation campaigns to realize the benefits of financial inclusion and easy adaptation of digital currency.

Keywords: Digital currency, CBDC, fiat currency, blockchain, financial inclusion

9.1 Introduction

Civilization existed even before money, but probably radical economic progress was witnessed through invention and mediations with various

*Corresponding author: vanishree.drc@suranacollege.edu.in; vanimysoreram@gmail.com

Mohd Naved, V. Ajantha Devi, and Aditya Kumar Gupta (eds.) Fintech and Cryptocurrency, (173–192)
© 2023 Scrivener Publishing LLC

forms of money. We have evinced the shift of medium of exchange from barter – coins – paper – cards – now to digital for easing the economic activities. The need for a standardized form of fiat currency with inherent value, dividable, homogeneous, liquid, rare, and stable value (Rose, 2015) had become inevitable to easily connect to the world, by enabling the smooth trade activities and investors to mass wealth creation. Eventhough fiat currency was very promising in all its existence, has a detriment position in illegal forms such as money laundering, tax evasion, financial fraud, bribery, white-collar crime, misappropriation, insurance and identity fraud, and so on. With the rise of fintech, net banking and online transfer of money have drastically changed the entire payment system with a high assurance of accountability and transparency.

India being a promising emerging market has grown remarkably in terms of trade and business activities. The country also has ventured into a huge space of fintech with a robust financial system in place. Though we have a traditional mode of payment systems such as cheques, withdrawals, drafts, money orders, letters of credit, gift cards, etc., this still did not seem to solve the problem of money transfer within the stipulated time and safety. As such, various modes of payments such as NEFT, internet banking, and electronic fund transfers became prominent, especially in pandemics. The extension of the mobile banking system gave tremendous acceptance of Unified Payment Systems (UPI), e-wallets such as Google Pay, Phone Pe, Paytm, etc. In addition, demonetization was one such event that disrupted regular payments and gave an acceleration for usage and extension of e-wallets. Around 93 percent of urban Indians have extensively used digital wallets both in-store and online, which is way ahead of 55 percent of the global average. Such a promising system has its own impediments in terms of infrastructure, financial literacy, trust and safety, and technology know-how, especially for the marginalized section of society.

Blockchain technology in private currencies such as bitcoin, Ethereum, stable coins, etc., have interrupted the strong existing financial system, and as a mandate, the central bank is exploring Central Banking Digital Currency (CBDC) as their form of electronic currency to stabilize the economic progression and reduce the usage of private currencies. Electronic currency sponsored and issued by the RBI is Central Bank Digital Currency (CBDC). As per Atlantic Council CBDC Tracker report, around eighty-seven countries (with a representation of over 90 percent of worldwide GDP) are in the pursuit of researching on CBDC as a full-fledge currency in the pilot program. In May 2020, around 35 countries are in the research phase, and 9 countries have already launched a digital currency of their own. Bahamas has launched its CBDC 'Sand Dollar' in 2020, Nigeria with 'e-Naira' in 2021, and countries such as China is in pipeline to launch their own CBDC in the winter Olympics.

In India, the Reserve Bank of India (RBI) seeks to begin a payment ecosystem that gives the go-ahead for a safe, swift, and low-cost, economical and cost-effective digital payments to every individual across the length and breadth of the country. The pilot launch of India's CBDC is awaited in the first quarter of 2022. In this paper, we have attempted to capture the transformational phase of fiat currency to digital currency in India. The core objective of our paper was to assess the level of awareness and acceptance of CBDC among the various community. Also, identify the issues and challenges to be addressed by the Government and policymakers while implementing such a technology-oriented system in a democratic country like India. This paper will be the first of its kind, as we investigated the entire transformation process through the lens of a bottom-up approach to geographical locations.

9.2 Review of Literature

Money is defined as an arrangement within a society, to use some material as a means of exchange, which plays an effective and efficient role that meets its requirements that can be accepted through the valid currency law (Yuneline, 2019). Digital payment has been defined in various literature as a platform that is used for making monetary transactions and its importance grows as this has become a great facilitator of e-commerce (Malusare Lalita Babulal, 2019), (Sahi *et al.*, 2021). India is still a developing country; in maximum rural areas, the literacy of technology is still only 6.5%. There seems to be tremendous growth, however, proper financial literacy is still required (Borkar, Avinash Galande, 2020). Financial literacy is the key to the growth and transformation of India into a cashless economy (Baghla, 2018). (Babulal, 2019) states the advantages of digital payments were found to be a time-saver, better accessibility, easy purchasing, etc. Few of the most frequent electronic payment systems in India includes Debit Cards, Credit Cards, but the use of Electronic Fund Transfers, Net Banking, Unified Payment Systems (UPI), e-commerce payment systems, internet banking where Paytm, Phone Pe, Jio Money, BHIM, Google pay which has been concluded in various pieces of literature as a part of the adoption of digital payments by (Bagola, 2018), (Byakod *et al.*, n.d.), (Ghosh, 2021), (Shailza & Sarkar, 2019). The better part is that even the lower income group of people are also moving towards digital (Bijapurkar *et al.*, 2020) in rural Karnataka as well (Byakod *et al.*, n.d.). The awareness, purpose of usage, and factors influencing the preference for digital payment systems in Coimbatore City are explained by (Krishnakumari & Pavithra, 2018). Similar variables perception of cash vs digital payments, online fraud experience, and trust are explained by (Shree *et al.*, 2021) to verify the acceptance of such digital currency.

Blockchain is a decentralized, digitized, public ledger of all cryptocurrencies (Kaur, 2020). Bitcoin, one of the most popular examples of cryptocurrency is defined as a peer-to-peer network by (Chris Rose, 2015). CBDCs would also potentially enable more real-time and cost-effective globalization of payment systems (Central Bank Digital Currency – Is This the Future of Money). As per the Fintech in India report on Powering Mobile Payments (2019) in the year 2016-17, there were around 1.5 million acceptable locations, and local merchants accepting digital payment has increased to 10 million within 2-3 years (Borkar, Avinash Galande, 2020).

In July, the Monetary Authority of Singapore in collaboration with JP Morgan Chase and Temasek said that they "successfully" settled payments in various currencies on the blockchain based network The bank's managing director has mentioned that he would be welcome the collaboration with China. The Bahamas started its "project sand dollar" pilot in its Exuma district on Dec. 27, 2019. The trial consisted of more than 1,000 respondents a month, and the nation plans to extend their program across all 700 of its islands before year's end. In 2018, Venezuela launched the petro, a cryptocurrency (allegedly backed by oil reserves) designated to provide help to citizens to cope with international sanctions and the dysfunctional nation's hyperinflation. The petro has been a flop, and the U.S. is offering a $5 million bounty for information leading to the capture of the initiative's leader, who has been indicted for drug trafficking and sanctions violations (HACKETT, 2020). For achieving the potential benefits of CBDC for public welfare while preserving financial stability along with public-private sector cooperation, there is a need for further exploration of CBDC design choices (Auer, *et al.*, 2021) and its micro to macro financial implications on a different segment of the population need to consider. The present paper explores the real-time perception and observation of the common man for the digital transformation of the new form of the currency system. The researcher has adopted the bottom-up approach to providing the dimension of various segments of the population with different age brackets, geographical regions, occupations, and levels of literacy.

9.3 Methodology and Sampling

The qualitative method opted for such study to understand the pulse of initiation of Indian CBDC version in near future, various stakeholder was involved from across the nation to collate the perspectives and their know how on digital currency era. Focus Group Discussion (FGD) survey method was used to collect requisite information as the topic of research was still niche.

Through this focus group, we have attempted to understand the perceptions, awareness, opinions, and ideology about Central Banking Digital Currency and their views on implementation. Attempted to identify the issues and challenges to be addressed by the Government and policymakers while implementing such a high technology-oriented system in a democratic country like India.

We clustered the entire population based on Tier-1, Tier-2, and Tier-3 cities covering both urban and rural populations. We covered 6 states with two districts (high privilege and under privilege districts) and further two villages/towns under each district. Table 9.1 shows the sample selection based on the geographical location of the participants. Further, moderators have adhered to gender balance in every survey, so totally we had 153 females, 276 males, and 8 transgenders participating in this survey. Because of the Covid situation, data were collected both in-person and online (through Google meet) for professional and educated classes.

A semi-structured questionnaire was designed to capture the required dataset and enough illustrations were done to demonstrate the process of implementation of CBDC in other countries and its learning for India. In addition, data were also captured to check their awareness of blockchain technology and the technical know-how of various operations.

Table 9.1 shows the sample selection based on the geographical location of respondents.

Apart from the above sample respondents we also have inputs polled from places such as Bareli, Vizag, Madurai, Kota, and Kolkata. Each group size for FGD varied between 5-6 members based on their consent for the interview and availability of time. Each FGD lasted for 15-20 minutes with a focus on capturing the level of awareness and acceptance new form of digital currency and the momentum of the Indian CBDC version. As the concept of CBDC is still novel, enough training and orientation were done to moderators and timely assistance was given by the researchers. Data were collected between November 2021 to February 2022. We have ensured to take the ethical consent (verbal) in their regional language from

Table 9.1 Sample framework and sample covered.

State	District	Village/Town		Sample covered
Karnataka	Bengalum	Dasanapura		
		Kadigeuahalli		
	Hubli-Dharwad	Agadi		
		Umachigi		Street Vendors
Andhra Pradesh	Hyderabad	Saidabad		Petty Shops
		Golconda		House Maids
	Kurnool	Ulchala		Students
		Konideia		Housewife
Maharashtra	Saugali	Haroli		Unemployed
		Kadamwadi		Corporate Workers
	Mumbai	Tirandaj		Civil Servants
		Aare		Retired Officers
Gujarat	Ahmedabad	Detroj		Teachers Professors
		Dholka		Drivers
	Janmagar	Fala		MSMEs
		Nani Matli		Entrepreneurs
Himachal Pradesh	Kullu	Manikam		NRIs
		Kais		
	Bilaspur	Bagi		
		Jamthal		

(Source: Authors')

each participant in every scheduled interview, explain the procedure of information gathered, confidentiality and privacy of data collected. Also, prior permission was taken to audio record all the survey responses from each group. As the respondents belong to various communities and states, questions were administrated in their regional language, and responses were entered in English.

We have used the thematic analysis method for analyzing the data collected. An inductive approach was followed for arriving at the theoretical framework to assess the level of awareness and acceptance of CBDC from selected respondents. Data both transcript and audio were intensely observed for familiarization of data collected and initial codes were developed on contents captured. Later, we moved into identifying the themes which access the objectives of the present study, and a rigorous review process was undertaken for the finalization of the themes. Five board themes viz., financial literacy & inclusion, infrastructure, technical knowhow, trust & belief in the system, and acceptance level were confirmed.

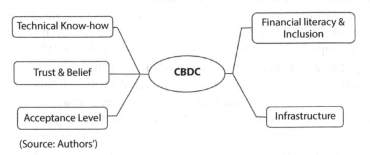

(Source: Authors')

After a defined discussion process, analysis was done based on the above-finalized themes. The themes address the awareness, acceptance, and foreseen real time-tested challenges for the implementation of such a massive technology-based system where the majority population is living in rural or semi-urban; uneducated and illiterate; with poor economic backgrounds.

However, the present study has not investigated the technical implementation process whether it's a blockchain technology or UPI-based. Distribution mechanism systems i.e., retail or wholesale or token-based CBDC, and tax-related infrastructure were not a part of the present study. We also observe that around 52 percent of the working-class population in metropolitan or cosmopolitan cities are people who have moved from smaller villages to tier 1 cities, where most of them have closely adopted or learned to adapt to the existing technology.

9.4   Results and Discussion

Based on the data captured through FGD and confirmed themes further results and discussion were derived.

9.4.1   Financial Literacy & Inclusion

India's economic growth rate was 8% in the year 2014–2015 and although is one of the fastest growing economies in the world, still financial literacy is low compared to other countries. Financial Literacy is defined as the capability to analyze, manage, and learn to earn or invest money (Lokesh Vijayvargy and Priti Bakhshi, 2018). It is considered one of the most important factors today for promoting financial inclusion, consumer protection, and lastly financial stability. Financial Inclusion on the other hand ensures necessary access to financial products and services in all sections of the society fairly and transparently are delivered. Financial literacy and inclusion need to go hand in hand to enable the common man to understand the needs and benefits of the products and services offered by formal financial institutions.

Financial literacy and inclusion are a global concern mainly in under-developed and developing economies, such as India. When it comes to making financial decisions, the common man understands the needs and benefits of the products and services offered by formal financial institutions. So, from the financial literacy perspective, it essentially involves two elements, one of access, and the other of literacy through which financial literacy and inclusion play a major factor (Lokesh Vijayvargy and Priti Bakhshi, 2018). It could be even more impactful if, its concepts have been taught in the curriculum in schools at an early stage and make personal finance part of basic education (Sharon Taylor & Suzanne Wagland, 2013).

In the present study, there were quite a lot of comments we received from our Focus Group Discussions (FGD). We had a few graduate students mention, "The place (Bareli and Golconda) 70-80% people will not be able to handle the shift to CBDC. The reason is they are not well educated. Literacy is not up to the mark, most of the elderly population still unable recognize the fiat currency notes, they try to identify through color combination or size of the paper currency!"

The lack of financial inclusion has also been mentioned by our respondents stating, "Even though it is made mandatory that the labour side have bank accounts, but even now if they have any problems they don't even know how to go to banks and sort it out. So, asking them to use the digital they would not prefer it. It won't penetrate to the lower level in most cases. Every implementation that happens it has reached the tier 1 cities and partial in tier 2."

"Basically, from the business point of view – I don't think this will work (Tirupur and Fala) because most businesses don't pay taxes and come under the bracket of unorganized. And, they think it is a real-time challenge to provide financial literacy because the population is so large."

There were a few who did not prefer the shift for the very reason of financial literacy and inclusion, "We are not sure what impact the e-currency would have. What will the people in rural side do where people cannot learn even if we give literacy?" shows the non-acceptance of the new currency system.

From the above analysis of literature and focus group discussions with our respondents, we understand that financial literacy and inclusion go hand in hand. As much as literacy is important, we see that inclusion is also lacking in a lot of tier 2 and tier 3 cities and other districts in India. From our study, we believe, both the factors are the two sides of the same coin which becomes a key factor in our research.

9.4.2   Infrastructure

Financial infrastructure and intermediaries play a 'central role' in the financial market by Director, China Central Depository & Clearing Co., Ltd (CCDC), China. (Yi, 2020). Every complex system requires an appropriate infrastructure with clarity as clear as crystal along with the resources, framework, power grid, required energy consumption, hardware, and software implementation, and much more to support an e-currency for an entire nation with a huge population as India.

Financial infrastructure and inclusion are defined as "the process of ensuring access to financial services and timely and adequate credit where needed by vulnerable groups such as weaker sections and low-income groups at an affordable cost" (Taufeeque A. Siddiqui, Kashif I. Siddiqui, 2020) which closely relates to understanding the importance of financial structure in the economic system in India.

An analysis of the recent trends in the expansion of financial infrastructure states that it is now well recognized that the banking system of a country is in its financial infrastructure and balanced development and availability of banking facilities in a country is crucial to its rapid, balanced, and inclusive economic development (Dr. Sukanya, 2016). Literature "stresses the role of financial institutions in the efficient allocation of financial resources required for the full use of resources for capital formation.

It has been highlighted that the role of financial development in promoting the efficient investment of financial resources in a country, crucial for its rapid economic growth. It also highlights the role of financial institutions in financing entrepreneurs engaged in technological innovations, a theme developed originally in 1949. From the above, we tend to understand that efficiently to help improvise the financial infrastructure of any country we need to further focus on a centralized banking system in the country.

As a step toward digital currency in India, the government of India has launched an electronic voucher-based digital platform system called "e-RUPI" which is a person-specific and purpose specific payment system. The launch and implementation of e-RUPI will be one of the most convenient methods for a cashless economy. This will be a prepaid gift voucher that can be redeemed at specific centres without any credit or debit card, a mobile app, or internet banking. The issuing entities will be onboarded by banks on its UPI platform. There seems to be a lot more positive impact and acceptance when the digital currency is launched via the UPI system rather than the mining of cryptocurrency. It would be most advisable to accept the approach via the UPI system. Alternatively, earlier studies state that a cashless and contactless digital payments system that could be delivered to mobile phones of beneficiaries in form of an SMS string or a QR Code could be more efficient and an easier way to adapt to the shift in terms of acceptance and implementation. Now, as it is still in the initial stages, it is quite unsure which technology is going to be implemented.

During a further discussion with respondents, a few pointers were raised related to the existing financial infrastructure available in the country, the infrastructure required for the implementation of CBDC, and the reach in the country to every individual making it accessible and efficient. A group from Andhra Pradesh states "As the government is still not able to provide electricity to reach all houses. They still feel it should be 70-30 with 30% cash. If the infrastructure is in place, we could go 100%. For example, if I'm hungry and I don't have a battery on my phone I won't be able to eat. Maybe a card system where we can directly access it". One of our respondents from Thrissur, Kerala district stated that "Even though it is made mandatory that the labor side have bank accounts, but even now if they have any problems they don't even know how to go to banks and sort it out. So, asking them to use the digital they would not prefer it. It won't penetrate to the lower level in most cases. Every implementation that happens has reached the tier 1 cities and partial in tier 2. We would like to shift but we don't see it practically possible". People still prefer hard cash as stated, "I would prefer mostly hard cash as well. It is because it is technology-based and we will have to depend on technology".

There were a few questions that we came across, "In Kulu, some of the mountain regions – some people don't even have a smartphone or a connection. They don't have resources, what will they know about e-currency?"

People have also faced personal experiences of infrastructural technicalities stating, "I don't want to take anything new. The reason being – from my experience (like Paytm) I try to use it, but some issues – no network as such. Unless I have cash in hand, I don't want to do any purchase."

People also believe that if digital currencies are implemented the cost for a common person would rise as they mention, "We will require resources such as internet, smartphones all the time which is now an expense to continue paying for connectivity. Digital technology is not completely reliable – we are not sure when it could collapse in terms of servers, etc. We should not panic in such cases."

From our FGD, we understand that people are still very skeptical about the existing resources available for the usage of e-currencies and digital payments. There are a huge labor class people in India who till the present day survive on hard cash. As this group of people still rely on cash, it is evident that they do not have any knowledge about the technology required for financial stability or usage presently. It seems clear that financial inclusion and providing them with infrastructure would be a challenging task. Providing infrastructure with the required resources in a cost-effective manner is also an important factor to consider. We also understand the law protecting the financial infrastructure needs to be in place. As one of our respondents who are students stated that "We don't yet have a Data protection law in our country and with the recent, IT act they passed, they said they will stop Facebook and implement a hierarchy – they were canceling the encryption – that was so much of data breach."

The educated class who participated in our FGD also stated that the current UPI system serves the purpose of digitization. The reach of infrastructure is very important such that the government needs to ensure that every individual from tier-3, tier-2, tier-1 cities, including districts and other rural places also has access to the required infrastructure.

One of the major concerns that stick in the minds of the educated class of the country is if India is going to be able to afford the cost of a digital currency whilst promoting and working rigorously towards making an impact.

9.4.3   Technical Know-How

CBDC will be backed by distributed ledger technology (DLT) but works on permissioned blockchain which will make it different from other permissionless cryptocurrencies (RBI Speech June 2021). CBDC ecosystem may have a homogenous risk for cyber-attacks as existing payment systems are exposed. As the country faces humongous problems relating to minor financial literacy levels, the increase in digital payments has high threats of fraud and data/transaction hacking issues. Before the implementation, the government should ensure that the people are well prepared and equipped with sufficient technical awareness/orientation interventions at various levels for large acceptance of such massive technology transformation and implementation.

Well-educated respondents have the awareness and acceptance of the digital currency. However, what resists them is the fact that if it will reach the tier 2 and tier 3 cities and people in rural districts such as, "If everyone has to go into the digital method, do the government has the infrastructure to handle the load of transactions? What if the server crashes suddenly? What if someone in the village wants to pay their loan at the last moment (because that's how loans are paid in villages) they try to get their daily wages and try to pay their loans, what if he misses it and interest is charged to him because the servers are down?"

This is further possible upon the evolution of super-fast internet, and telecommunication networks and ensuring the broader reach of sophisticated technology to the general public every conner for smooth transact on CBDC.

9.4.4   Trust and Belief

Central Bank Digital Currency (CBDC) is foreseen as the game changer to provide a big leap to the digital economy and offer benefits to its users in terms of liquidity, scalability, acceptance, ease of transactions with anonymity, and faster settlement. To ensure such transformation, trust and belief play a very significant role in its acceptance and usage. It should be noted that there are a few elements that revolve around sticking to the system of acceptance to work comprehensive and collaborative for change management. The majority 64 percent of the respondents felt that digital currency mechanisms can pose hurdles such as data privacy, security, and safety of transactions. There is always a high chance of hacking and data leaking recently evidenced in many cases. Even though RBI will issue and monitor the entire process of digital currency and conversion of digital to the physical form of currencies, there is a huge risk involving the trustworthiness of financial intermediaries and channels which supports such a system at large. Respondents from the rural side felt that with the existing system for withdrawing money from post-office/banks or even to open an account normally local broker at the village level charge heft amount and to withdraw their own money they collect money on every transaction! With this ground reality and no monitory system in place at ground level, how do you think digital currency systems are more trusted than existing systems? If something happens to our money whom to approach? When we don't have electricity or a smartphone or even reading ability itself, how do you think we can have trust or access to such a system?

These few questions were raised by respondents while interviews.

CBDC can have worries even about central banks losing control over the payment systems. Individuals with a higher level of education or income and status quo especially from Tier-1 cities are most likely to trust and change to any type of payment transaction. They are also open to private agencies managing and controlling the digital currency as most of these segments of the population are already one-way or other exposed to private currency or transactions. When we looked up to Tier 2 and Tier 3 or even semi-urban to the rural population of Tier -1 places, we barely have awareness or access to such payment systems. The working-class respondent from cosmopolitan or metro cities even though they extensively make use of digital payment mechanisms like Paytm, or phone pay find it very difficult to convince their people to transform fiat to digital mode. They feel very insecure if they don't have hard cash in form of paper or coins. It's a great challenge to convenience the rural and semi-urban population to shift from fiat to digital form of currency until and unless a strong Government system is placed properly for monitory entire flows of digital currency.

9.5   Acceptance of CBDC

There is various literature that has attempted to write a key definition of acceptance in terms of digital payment systems. However, it seems like acceptance is rather a variable that is mostly defined by numerous other factors that influence them than having keywords.

An empirical study done by (Shailza, Madhulika P. Sarkar, 2019) proves various factors impact the intention to adopt/accept such as compatibility, security, perceived risk, trust, usability, and mobility as studied. Literature by (Surabhi Koul, Sahil Singh Jasrotia, and Hari Govind Mishra, 2021) attempts to define acceptance of digital payments using the technology acceptance model (TAM) as a theoretical base to hypothesize and test an integrated model. It has been identified that along with the digital payment drive, a campaign in rural areas, and providing appropriate platforms RBI also needs to provide the right knowledge and skillset required on how to access the various digital payments.

The pandemic due to Covid-19 was an event that shook the entire globe in an unpredicted manner. It had disrupted almost all sectors of the economy leaving an unforgettable impact. One of the impacts it left was the push to marginalize cash transactions, but not so much to eradicate it (Sandeep Kaur, Nidhi Walia, 2021). However, there is a need for widespread behavioural change, financial literacy, and awareness and acceptance to grow. Due to the expansion of digital payments, the adoption received a lot of attention from academics and practitioners stating that various aspects influence their usage and acceptance. Perceived risk is one factor that seemed to be an obstacle to adoption (Alaa Mahdi Sahi, Haliyana Khalid, Alhamzah Fadhil Abbas, 2021).

Although there seems to be the adoption of digital payments, literature evidences the fact that the supply and usage of cash don't seem to reduce (Carlos A. Arango-Arango, Nicolás SuárezAriza, 2020). The question of why cash does not fade away through the adoption seems to be rising has been studied which proves that the convenience and ease of usage, made cash more reliable. There is evidence that it is a simultaneous growth in both the demand for cash and the digital payment network around the world, which helps show a positive impact of growth if the focus is turned towards one. Following the bottom-up approach of our paper, we also find evidence that only 18% of the population is connected, the remaining population is still at a slower pace in terms of adoption due to multiple factors such as infrastructure, low levels of trust, and risk. From the TAM model used in their paper to understand the acceptance of digital payments, it was found that various factors influence or have an impact on the acceptance or adoption of digital payments. constructs like social influence, perceived risk, and perceived ease are the prime factors driving the acceptance of digital wallets (Surabhi Koul, Sahil Singh Jasrotia, Hari Govind Mishra, 2021).

Taking into consideration the fact that the implementation of Central Banking Digital Currency in India is at its initiation stage and is completely inclusive of digitization, the question of acceptance is also an important factor to consider. We have attempted to analyze the acceptance in this paper through the qualitative method. The idea of CBDC has been a growing idea on its own in India and the scope of the study has started to grow. We also understand the concept is still sprouting, as such, the implementation is not disclosed by the RBI.

In terms of public opinion, there were quite a lot of comments we received from our Focus Group Discussions (FGD).

Though a lot of people in the country believe this shift is necessary, they still resist the shift at the moment. One of our respondents mentioned, "As the ruling govt has an upper hand as they will be regulating it, they will have an upper hand and it will be biased. In terms of regulation, holding rights. The point was who appoints the Governor of RBI- Central govt does. Even in a hypothetical situation they still believe there should be both." Another student from Madurai stated his reason why he wouldn't be ready to accept the shift at the moment, "My decision will be based on tax slabs. Personal commercial benefits. It is not about mentality or mindset; it is about the system where we are taxed for everything (not saying the system is wrong) there are some legal loopholes in the system. We need to reduce tax slabs. Jewelry, functions, etc everything happens only in cash." "We would like to shift but we don't see it practically possible. We are all for digitization, but we would prefer considering it works out."

One of the reasons they still feel the existence of cash is necessary is because they believe nothing is as impactful as a real-time experience stated by one of our students we interacted with, "Nothing would work as an experience. We still don't know what would happen. Anyway, not full. If we have the option, we will get to know the positives and negatives of both and if the negatives are too high; we will not be comfortable."

As previous literature states, financial literacy is also a key factor for acceptance "I would still mostly prefer hard cash. I don't want to record my transactions. We should have a clear understanding about it."

Looking a little deeper into the conventional mindset of Indians, the traditional old-fashioned mentality also makes a huge impact on the acceptance of digital payment systems. A few pointers as mentioned by our respondents: "I don't want to take anything new which I don't know. It can add value. But I am a little old-fashioned. In a case where everything is fine and people still go without cash, I will go with it. But right now, I do not have any idea about it so I will carry cash." "I am okay with the shift; I consider myself as a pretty tech guy with the available resources. If you go back to my place in my native – and tell them no cash allowed and only phone to make payments – you would see stars and they would not agree, it could be because of literacy and understanding. However, even in a situation given everything in hand, they will have questions due to their mindset; they will not be convinced why they need to shift. But their son will be okay with it. It will be the generation gap." "As an individual, I believe this shift is good, but from the place (Bareli) I come from 70-80% of people will not be able to handle the shift. The reason is they are not well educated. Literacy is not up to mark. They hold old school mentality, they resist change, just like how the farmer's thing happened." "As a student having access to technology, I would prefer to shift. However, to speak about my background (Thrissur, Kerala) – my parents would accept it, but my grandparents would not. However, in the districts and outskirts, it would be difficult." "They won't prefer in my place (Nagpur). For my parents as well, it is more convenient to carry cash and they are so accustomed to it that they wouldn't prefer to shift. But then it is a gradual shift. Even if the financial literacy is given and they don't understand the debit and credit side of what is going in or coming out from their account, even with gadgets – they don't know how to read it."

Besides, the disadvantages people still feel it is beneficial. "I would accept this change if it is better for the economy, for the development of the country. But most of the students prefer digital payment and the place as a whole would shift. Not for personal benefit, but for the benefit of the country in terms of money laundering, etc" "It would be very convenient for us if it is digitized." "The Benefit is basically that all transactions would be recorded and there would be no corruption. It can have an impact on the economy. The government should bridge the gap first and only then they will implement it." "Though Himachal is in India, they still live like a separate part. If there is a shift it is easier for me, If I have bundles of cash, for safety reasons digital currency would be easier. There will be fewer thefts. We will need to shift in the long run."

"The thought process behind is good. But the cons are higher than the pros by infinite times."

From the above analysis of literature and focus group discussions, we understand that there is a huge population that is aware of digital payment systems, one group of people have the resources, few others know the technical aspect of it, and few others are ready to accept it. However, all this is subjected to various factors. Though they believe it will have its benefits, it still comes with its disadvantages which need to be the focus of the government. From our study we believe, we can provide the right analysis required, focusing on the bottom-up approach.

9.6   Conclusion

CBDC is intended to complement the existing central bank medium of exchange. With the implementation of Central Banking Digital Currency, we believe this could make way for future developments. We intend to further study the implementation of CBDC – phase-wise strategic implementation with the help of global exhibits from other countries where the CBDC has been successfully implemented, possibly with minimal drawbacks.

Financial development and digitization are crucial for the rapid economic growth of an economy in promoting efficient individual or economic investment decisions of financial resources available in a country. A centralized banking system in the country helps improvise the financial development of any country. This paper helps understand and capture the transformation and emergence of Central Banking Digital Currency in India following a Bottom-Up Approach with a global perspective. It focuses on comprehending the current scenario of the digital payments system in India and various other factors that impact the same, such as Technical Know-how, Trust and Belief, Acceptance and Awareness Level, Financial Literacy and Inclusion, Infrastructure starting from tier 3 and tier 2 cities, move up the ladder in tier 1 cities and its influence on the emergence of CBDC.

The qualitative method through focus group discussion (FGDs) covering various geographic locations across the country focuses on respondents from tier 3 and tier 2 cities widely and is opted to understand the opinions of the common public regarding the implementation of CBDC. From our study we notice that there is one lane where digitization is growing as stated in previous pieces of literature; the other where digitization has its limitations. We believe that these limitations have given way too many illegal corrupt activities where a part of the country has been taking these as loopholes to escape the financial system. As such, from our study, we would like to highlight that the implementation of CBDC is required for the current scenario which would be a probable solution as this would mean that every penny will now be tracked by the RBI – highly regulated and that every rupee that goes in and comes out of every account is tracked and there is absolute transparency that it does not give way for any corruption or financial crimes. However, the further argument in this paper is that there is a gap that exists in the system which needs to be bridged.

Existing literature evidence facts to help understand the level of acceptance and awareness of digital payment systems and the growth of digitization in India. Whilst the growth of the digital world is rapidly expanding day by day, as stated previously we also note that there are a few drawbacks to each of the factors identified. Focus on identifiable factors such as technical know-how, trust, and belief, acceptance and awareness level, financial literacy and inclusion, and infrastructure are the need of the hour. Technical development and testing at the large to small scale level are required at every regional concentration. To ensure national security and financial security, the government implementing agencies taking such assignments of CBDC need to initially adopt basic models and test comprehensively to reduce the adverse impacts on monetary policy and the existing banking system.

With the implementation of Central Banking Digital Currency, we believe this could make way for future developments. We intend to further study the implementation of CBDC – phase-wise strategic implementation with the help of global exhibits from other countries where the CBDC has been successfully implemented, possibly with minimal drawbacks.

References

Arango-Arango, C. A., & Suárez-Ariza, N. (2020). Digital payments adoption and the demand for cash: New international evidence. Journal of Payments Strategy and Systems, 14(4), 392–410.

Baghla, A. (2018). A Study on the future of Digital Payments in India. In International Journal of Research and Analytical Reviews (Vol. 5, Issue 4). IJRAR- International Journal of Research and Analytical Reviews.

Bank, C. (n.d.). Digital Currency -- Is This the Future of Money. (n.d.). Speech: Central Bank Digital Currencies: Is this the Future of Money?

Bijapurkar, R., Shukla, R., Rai, P., & Sachdeva, V. (2020). Digital Payments Adoption in India, 2020. 2020, 1–7. https://www.linkedin.com/pulse/digital-payments-adoption-india-2020-anpci-report-ram-rastogi

Byakod, P. R., Chaya, U., Kulgude, P., Sharma, A., Sharma, P., & Mazumdar, C. Sen. (n.d.). (n.d.). A Study on Penetration of Digital Payment System in Selected Areas of Rural Karnataka. UAS - JMC.

Galande, M. A., & Borkar, D. S. (2021). Digital Payment: the Canvas of Indian Banking Financial System. In the European Journal of Molecular & Clinical .... European Journal of Molecular & Clinical Medicine. https://ejmcm.com/article_11443.html%0Ahttps://ejmcm.com/article_11443_8d2decd9d558c0da134cf233fc175e9c.pdf

Ghosh, G. (2021). Adoption of Digital Payment System by Consumer: A review of Literature. In Researchgate.Net (Vol. 9, Issue 2). International Journal of Creative Research Thoughts (IJCRT. https://www.research-gate.net/profile/Gourab-Ghosh-4/publication/349212193_Adoption_of_Digital_Payment_System_by_Consumer_A_review_of_Literature/links/602509b5299bf1cc26b9edb7/Adoption-of-Digital-Payment-System-byConsumer-A-review-of-Literature.pdf

Hackett, R. (2020). C H IN A ' S D R I V E F O R C U R R E N C Y D O M IN A N C E. F O R T U N E A U G U S T / S E P T E M B E R.

Kaur, M. (2019). Digital Currency and its Implications for India. In The Management Accountant Journal (Vol. 54, Issue 11). The Management Accountant Journal. https://doi.org/10.33516/maj.v54i11.64-67p

Kaur, S., & Walia, N. (2021). COVID-19 and adoption of digital payments in India. World Economics, 22(1), 149–160.

Koul, S., Jasrotia, S. S., & Mishra, H. G. (2021). Acceptance of digital payments among rural retailers in India. Journal of Payments Strategy and Systems, 15(2), 201–213.

Krishnakumari, R., & Pavithra, G. (2018). Digital Payment System: Awareness and Usage in Coimbatore City. In International Journal of Management and Social Science Research Review (Vol. 1, Issue 45). International Journal of Management and Social Science Research Review.

Malusare, L. (2019). Digital Payments Methods in India: A Study of Problems and Prospects. In International Journal of Scientific Research in Engineering and

Management (IJSREM) (Vol. 03, Issue 08). International Journal of Scientific Research in Engineering and Management (IJSREM.

Rahman, D., & Jasim, M. K. M. (n.d.). Dr. Ayub Khan Dawood. (2018). A critical review. International Journal of Engineering & Technology.

Rose, C. (2015). The Evolution Of Digital Currencies: Bitcoin, A Cryptocurrency Causing A Monetary Revolution. In International Business & Economics Research Journal (IBER) (Vol. 14, Issue 4). International Business & Economics Research Journal. https://doi.org/10.19030/iber.v14i4.9353

Sahi, A. M., Khalid, H., & Abbas, A. F. (2021). Digital payment adoption: a review (20152020). In Journal of Management Information and Decision Sciences (Vol. 24, Issue 7). Journal of Management Information and Decision Sciences.

Shailza, & Sarkar, M. P. (2019). Literature Review on Adoption of Digital Payment System. In Global Journal of Enterprise Information System (Vol. 11, Issue 3). Global Journal of Enterprise Information System. http://10.0.71.135/gjeis/2019 %0Ahttps://login.loginbiblio.poligran.edu.co/login?url=http://search.ebsco host.com/login.aspx?direct=true&db=iih&AN=140226705&site=ehost-live

Shree, S., Pratap, B., Saroy, R., & Dhal, S. (2021). Digital payments and consumer experience in India: a survey-based empirical study. In Journal of Banking and Financial Technology. Journal of Banking and Financial Technology. https://doi.org/10.1007/s42786-020-00024-z

Siddiqui, T. A., & Siddiqui, K. I. (2020). FinTech in India: An analysis on the impact of telecommunication on financial inclusion. In Strategic Change (Vol. 29, Issue 3). John Wiley & Sons. https://doi.org/10.1002/jsc.2331

Sivathanu, B. (2019). Adoption of digital payment systems in the era of demonetization in India: An empirical study. In Journal of Science and Technology Policy Management (Vol. 10, Issue 1). Journal of Science and Technology - Emerald Insight. https://doi.org/10.1108/JSTPM-07-2017-0033

Sukanya, N. (2016). Expansion of Financial Infrastructure in India-An Analysis of the Recent

Trends. Journal of Commerce and Management Thought, 7(3), 422. https://doi. org/10.5958/0976-478x.2016.00025.2

Vally, K. S., & Divya, K. H. (2018). A Study on Digital Payments in India with Perspective of Consumer"s Adoption. In International Journal of Pure and Applied Mathematics (Vol. 119, Issue 15). International Journal of Pure and Applied Mathematics.

Yi, D. (2020). Why financial infrastructures and intermediaries are actively promoting blockchain applications although it means disruption to them. In Journal of Securities Operations & Custody (Vol. 12, Issue 4). Journal of Securities Operations & Custody. http://libezproxy.iyte.edu.tr:81/login?url=http://search. ebscohost.com/login.aspx?direct=true&db=bsu&AN=146494147&site=eds-live

Yuneline, M. H. (2019). Analysis of cryptocurrency's characteristics from four perspectives. In Journal of Asian Business and Economic Studies (Vol. 26, Issue 2). Journal of Asian Business and Economic Studies. https://doi.org/10.1108/jabes-12-2018-0107

Investor Sentiment Driving Crypto-Trade in India

Sushant Waghmare[1]* and Dipesh Uike[2]

[1]Maharashtra National Law University, Nagpur, India
[2]Dr. Ambedkar Institute of Management Studies & Research, Deekshabhoomi, Nagpur, India

Abstract

The Indian market has become one of the largest cyprtocurrency markets in the world. The demand for the trade of cryptocurrencies is evident from the number of Indian exchanges that have taken root and grown in the past few years. The drivers instigating investor movement towards crypto-assets from the traditional option available among Indians is being evaluated in this study. The study aims to analyse and identify the key factors driving the investor sentiments towards trading in the highly volatile cryptocurrencies. It attempts to gain insight into the reasoning behind the investor decision to trade in them. Extensive review of literature sheds light on the factors driving investment in cryptocurrencies. It is evident that the awareness levels for crypto, the future of crypto investments and the potential returns that they are offering have created a huge interest among the general public. The reasoning behind trading and investing in cryptocurrencies are also unique in their nature. The adoption of taxation policies by the government although may seem like a deterrent however, the 'Fear-of-Missing-Out' or 'FOMO' seems to have caught hold of the investors in pushing such investment decisions. The sample consists of the retail investor and the investment advisors in India using the structured questionnaire. Stratified Sampling Technique was utilized for the purposes of this study. The Independent Samples t-test was used to analyse the data and final results were interpreted from them. The results showcase certain parameters such as awareness, promotion, global acceptance, future of investment, 'Fear-of-Missing-Out' or 'FOMO' etc. as some of the factors driving trade and investment in cryptocurrencies. There are significant differences in sentiments of Retail Investors and Investment Advisors. Gender also plays a role

---

**Corresponding author*: sushantwaghmare@gmail.com

Mohd Naved, V. Ajantha Devi, and Aditya Kumar Gupta (eds.) Fintech and Cryptocurrency, (193–220)
© 2023 Scrivener Publishing LLC

in sentiments driving these investment decisions and finally education levels of individuals are also critical as well.

Keywords: Cryptocurrency, retail investor, investment decision, investment advisor, fear-of-missing-out (FOMO), behavioural finance

10.1 Introduction

The word 'cryptocurrency' has taken up traction in almost all walks of life. Today, very few people remain who have not heard of the term. However, there are still many aspects and individuals who do not have an understanding of what 'cryptocurrency' means. The following chapter attempts to shed light on the terms such as Cryptocurrency, Digital Assets, Digital, Crypto-Trading and various other aspects related to cryptocurrency trading in India. At the outset, let us define the terminology for the purposes of comprehensive understanding of this chapter.

The Merriam-Webster Dictinary [1] defines Currency as circulation as a medium of exchange. It is also known as something of general use, acceptance, or prevalence for the purposes of exchange of goods and services. Similarly, Frankenfield [2] explains that cryptocurrency is a digital asset created on a network distributed among a large quantity of computers. The decentralized nature of the structure allows them to exist out of the ambit of the government and central control. This currency is created on the Blockchain. The Blockchain is further elaborated as 'Blockchain allows the recording and monitoring of transactions through the creation of an incontrovertible ledger on a business network [3]. Within the purview of the blockchain, assets of both physical and effervescent natures such as houses, cars, gold or copyrights, patents, etc. can be stored in it. Anything of actual or virtual value can be transacted upon in a blockchain network. Furthermore, the blockchain allows reduction in risk and savings for all involved. This enables speedy, secure and validated transactions across the blockchain network with minimal interference from the government or central control systems and authorities. Thus, it has become quite a favored means of investing and transactions among retail investors. In India, a retail investor is defined as someone who buys and sells shares of listed companies, mutual funds investments or other financial products and services through traditional or online brokerage firms or other types of investment accounts [4]. Generally, retail investors make use of investment advisors to conduct their transactions. Investment advisors are individuals or companies who provide financial investment advice relating to securities, shares, debentures and other investment opportunities to their clients. Although the terms may sound similar, investment advisers are different from financial advisors and should not be confused [5].

The increasing development and access to internet and fintech has enable cryptocurrency to make roadways into multiple countries and today, cryptocurrency adoption is growing at breakneck speeds. In 2021, it was reported that globally crypto ownership has increased to over 300 mn. users and about eighteen thousand businesses have also adopted it [6]. According to Chand [7], cryptocurrencies are showing widespread adoption and acceptance wherein India, USA, Russia, Nigeria and Brazil are the top five countries with maximum number of holders with over a 100 million holders in India alone.

The widespread adoption, acceptance and use of cryptocurrencies bear a few pertinent questions in mind. The researcher is motivated to pursue the questions such as who is investing in cryptocurrencies, the motivations behind such investments and the possible reasons and challenges spurring this change in investment and adoption behaviour. The changing market scenario, the possible growth that crypto assets offer and perhaps also a desire to dip one's toes into something new may be the reasoning behind this change in behaviour according to the author.

Therefore, the aime of the study is to analyse and identify the key factors driving the investor sentiments towards trading in the highly volatile cryptocurrencies. It attempts to gain insight into the reasoning behind the investor decision to trade in them and perhaps also to gain an insight into whether there are certain issues and challenges in such type of investments.

10.2   Review of Literature

10.2.1   Finance & Sentiments

Traditional investments used to be Public Provident Funds (PPFs), Bank Fixed Deposits, Recurring Deposits etc. Cleartax [8] with real-estate, gold, shares and debentures, mutual funds and ETFs becoming more popular in recent times. This change in investment behaviour displayed by people is a gradual acceptance of newer methodology for parking funds. Also, there are many other drivers such as the desire to maximize one's returns on money invested. These driving forces have helped in the development of a wholly new domain called as Behavioural Finance. Behavioural finance is a new field of science honing in on the minutiae of individual behaviour while investing in the stock market and the psychology involved therein [9].

Studies on Behavioural finance shows how cognitive & emotional factors affect the rational behaviour in investment decision.

Obenberger [10] and Tomola [11] have identified certain factors such as personal and financial needs, and certain types of information such as accounting information, brand image and other advisors in playing a key role in changing financial habits of investors. Maditinos *et al.* [12] realized through their work that many individuals rely upon news sources and media outlets to gauge their investment decisions from whereas, professional investors would focus more on the scientific analysis for their investment decisions. Odean [13], discovered that factors such as Anchoring, Representativeness and Availability bias had more influence on investment decision while others found that behavioural factors affect investment decisions as well.

The studies of Chandra [14] and Jayaraj [15] concluded that dogmatism, lack of confidence, frugality, precautionary attitude and information lop-sidedness play a critical role in investor decision as well which may lead one to interpret those psychological factors may also play a critical role in influencing investment decisions. Studies by Warren [16] and many others arrived at the realization the demographic factors have significant impact on investment decision.

From the above existing literature, it was found that behavioural factors had an influence on the investment decisions of individual investors in the financial markets, especially stock markets. The present study has considered the broad behavioural factors that had influence on individual investor decision making.

10.2.2   Cryptocurrency

The Independent Reserve [17], observed that cryptocurrency trading has been seeing a huge uptick in the markets around the world; their survey suggested that millions of people are flocking to sign up for trying their luck in crypto-assets every day.

Gainsbury [18] and Scholten *et al.* [19] wrote that cryptocurrencies are digital coins based on blockchain technology. The blockchain technology allows for validating transactions across peer-to-peer networks and allows for transactions on various different types of evolving systems. Crypto-trading is much more common place than one thinks and it shares many common traits Cryptocurrency trading has much in common with modern trading on the share-market and is an attractive playground for retail and institutional investors [19, 20]. It is a highly volatile, automated and continuous market. It runs twenty-four hours a day, seven days a week throughout the year. There are certain issues with valuations of the crypto-assets as well. Thus, it is more sentiment driven than any other type of market trade. The coin's value depends heavily on how the 'perceived value' of its future potential may seem to be. Such a project lacks the traditional valuation framework and return-on-investment models to evaluate the potential of profitability. Kraaijeveld (2020) discovered that many factors such as speculation, endorsements and social-media activity played a critical role in the acceptance and growth of cryptocurrencies. However, there was no strong predictability in how it may impact the value of the currencies. The prices of cryptocurrencies tend to fluctuate randomly; sometimes a coin may show a hundred percent surge within a few hours and return to its original price randomly [21]. The most powerful cryptocurrency such as the Bitcoin also experiences similar volatility [22]. This continuous and often unpredictable surge and slide within the markets tend to make it a highly risky investment. Cryptocurrencies have a tendency to be manipulated since many artificial push-up or pull-down of valuations can be done through misinformation, social-media speculation etc. [23]. These tendencies of the crypto-market tend to make it the poster-boy for government regulations and bans.

The traditional share market at least has certain hedges against Bull and Bear Markets. However, building a stable portfolio in crypto assets is quite difficult since there are no 'blue-chip' coins which can be considered as such. The valuation of altcoins is heavily dependent on the Bitcoin and yet at times surges and slides do not seem to be in tandem with it either [24]. This brings a new question to mind; it is possible maybe that cryptocurrencies are perhaps a newer form of gambling?

10.2.3 Addiction or Analysis?

Crypto investments have many common characteristics that may be compared to gambling, especially close to online gambling as observed by [15, 25, 26]. There is a significant portion of trading that ends up being pure luck in the case of crypto-trading. There is a huge level of inconsistent outcomes and returns and many a times based purely on luck and many authors [27–30] point out that even though the traditional share day-trading may conform to conventional analyses, crypto does not always tend to do so and hence, does not conform to pre-existing financial analyses. Melker [31] opined that majority of the crypto-traders booked losses and don't make high returns.

Arthur J. N. [27] found that gamblers and day-traders tend to have similar tendencies. This argument was supported by the findings

Mills & Nower [32] who found that gamblers and crypto traders show-case all behaviours associated with sports betting. Multiple authors such as Dixon [33], Conlin [34], Kraaijeveld [35], and Kumar [36] were in agreement that people who enjoy gambling and have a tendency to seek out novelty may be more attracted towards crypto-trading.

Crypto trading seems to be on the uptick continuously as the days go by. There is an illusory sentiment of control whenever certain crypto-traders invest in the coins of their choice. They believe that their faith in the coin will propel them towards higher and higher valuations. This has been competently defined by the works of Langer [37] and Wohl [38] who provided insight into the person's conviction that he/she could control the outcome of an event. This common characteristic of gambling. Crypto investors show signs of gambling such as strategizing, rituals even games of chance to support their trades and this is eerily similar to addictive behaviours as per [39–41]. Certain behaviours such as bias confirmation, self-belief etc. end up becoming promoters of actions and their repercussions. It is quite possible that these play a key role in confirmation of their perspective whenever they may make a positive trade. This might reinforce their biases [4, 43]. It may also be evident from the crypto-traders' behaviour that they are always pre-occupied with the trading itself. Continuous checking on the market status and inability to dis-engage from the activities of trading or monitoring investments may be considered as an addictive behaviour as well [44, 45].

Crypto-trading has similarities in share trading and so involves various shared day-to-day routines such as monitoring prices, buy and sell decisions, developments with respect to the coins under consideration and identifying new coins for future investment. However, since the crypto markets are operational continuously, the ability to disengage oneself from the trading activities becomes more and more difficult [33]. Thus, this is a highly time-consuming and risky commitment.

The above findings shed light in an otherwise dark area of financial investments. It seems that crypto-trading may be a subverted form of gambling. Now, it may end up creating a similar to a set of gambling addictive behaviours to many. It may also lead to psychological disturbances comparable to high level addicts and may require to be monitored since it may harm people. One needs to beware of the possible potentially harmful side-effects that may be almost alike to gambling addictions.

10.2.4   Fear of Missing Out (FOMO)

A new terminology called as the 'Fear of Missing Out (FOMO)' has been coined and become quite popular these days. The idea first came to light in the paper by Dr. Dan Herman. The abbreviation 'FOMO' was coined by Patrick McGinnis in 2004 through his article published in the American magazine 'The Harbus.' The idea points towards an intrinsic feeling of anxiety wherein people are sharing and enjoying a feeling of being part of something and you yourself are missing out on it. Often this is most observed in social media trends which primarily focus on the positive sides of one's life and therefore, others tend to feel that they are somehow less or incapable of being happy in their own lives. In the crypto context, FOMO means the feeling of missing out on a profitable investment opportunity. Both traders and investors feel this way since some assets rise in a matter of moments and suddenly become unattainable. Thus, this psychological factor is seen to be prevalent in crypto-trading because it is a twenty-four by seven open market for trade [45].

Przybylski *et al.* [46] cite FOMO as a primary driver instigating adoption of cryptocurrency investment among traders and generally it perverts the analysis towards a strong bias when making the trade. The thousands of coins with fluctuating spurts of acceleration do motivate a person to keep track of all the potential opportunities out there. However, if the trader had not taken a specific coin into consideration and it 'goes to the moon' then the FOMO resides strongly in his future decision making when investing. The near compulsion of trying one's luck and pre-occupation with trying to invest and make money pushes one to irrational boundaries while trading. This has largely been due to the impact that crypto has on the social media. The online presence of all these projects and the continuous push they make towards their coins ends up making someone feel as if he/she is missing out on a potentially great opportunity.

People are reluctant to sell their holdings at times because they believe that if they did not commit the trade or let it go consciously then they would be wracked with anxiety and regret This feeling of having to put in the effort and taking a chance is quite comparable to gamblers or lottery players [47–49].

The problem herein is that one may end up betting too much into a specific coin and if a loss occurs then they may lose their entire savings. A multitude of factors facilitate and deviate from crypto-trading. It is important for one to analyse the various aspects of such kind of trades. It is therefore, imperative that one makes use of discipline and rationale whenever making such trades. However, this evidently can be facilitated through the use of Investment Advisors as well. It bears mention that perhaps it is important to note that maybe expert advice can help minimize losses and maximize gains. This bears a deeper study which has been attempted through this research.

10.3 Research Methodology

10.3.1 Aim of the Study

The study aims to analyse and identify the key factors driving the investor sentiments towards trading in the highly volatile cryptocurrencies. It attempts to gain insight into the reasoning behind the investor decision to trade in them.

10.3.2 Objectives of the Study

1. To understand the impact of demographic factors on the sentiments driving crypto-trade.
2. To compare the perceptions of Retail Investors and Investment Advisors for crypto-trading.
3. To identify the critical factors where Retail Investors and Investment Advisors diverge with respect to their sentiments for trading in cryptocurrencies.

10.3.3 Sampling Methodology & Data Analysis

A sample of 150 total respondents was collected by the researcher. It consisted of 130 Retail Investors and 20 Investment Advisors. The sampling methodology was cluster sampling method and a structured questionnaire was used for collection of the data. SPSS Software was used for analysing the data and the Independent Samples t-test was made use of to test the significant differences between the demographic variables and also the Retail Investors and Investment Advisors.

The following hypotheses can be derived for the purposes of this study through the prescient literature review:

$H_0{}^1$: There is no significant difference between the sentiments driving Retail Investors and Investment Advisors during trading in cryptocurrencies.

Ha^1: There is a significant difference between the sentiments driving Retail Investors and Investment Advisors during trading in cryptocurrencies.

$H_0{}^2$: There is no significant difference between the sentiments driving male and female investors when trading in cryptocurrencies.

H_a^2: There is a significant difference between the sentiments driving Male and Female investors when trading in cryptocurrencies.

H_0^3: There is no significant difference between the sentiments driving Under-Graduate and Post-Graduate investors when trading in cryptocurrencies.

Ha^3: There is a significant difference between the sentiments driving Under-Graduate and Post-Graduate investors when trading in cryptocurrencies.

10.3.4 Limitations of the Study

The study is limited to the Retail Investors and Investment Advisors within the reachable ambit of the researcher. Another limitation was that these investors and advisors were interested and involved in crypto trading.

10.4 Data Analysis & Interpretation

The data was analysed on three fronts viz. (1) Retail Investors & Investment Advisors, (2) Gender and (3) Education levels. The Independent Samples t-test was utilized for analysing since each distinct category in the study. Sentiments driving investment decisions were taken into consideration while creating the questionnaire and they were the factors which were used for the purposes of analysis. The analysis is tabulated and interpreted in Table 10.1.

Table 10.1 displays the outcomes of the Independent Samples t-Test results comparing Retail Investors and Investment Advisors with each other. Since these are two distinct types of categories or groups of people who invest money it was the appropriate variable to study and evaluate for the purposes of their study. The investment behaviours with respect to their sentiments whenever evaluating whether to invest in cryptocurrencies or not is observed. We observe that there is a significant difference with respect to various factors as listed below:

There is a significant difference among Retail Investors and Investment Advisors with respect to the promotion levels of the crypto products. It is indicated by the p value. The p-value for this factors is $p=0.04$ which is less than $p=0.05$ therefore, we can infer that there is a significant difference.

There is a significant difference among Retail Investors and Investment Advisors with respect to the future of trading and the belief that crypto trading is the future of investment. The p-value for the factor is $p=0.002$

Table 10.1 Independent samples t-test for retail investors vs. investment advisors.

S.N.	Factors	Role	N	$\bar{x}$	σ	σ_M	p-value for unequal variances
1	I am aware of crypto markets	Retail investor	130	3.47	0.925	0.081	0.054
		Investment advisor	20	3.95	0.999	0.223	
2	I am aware of crypto investment opportunities	Retail investor	130	3.35	0.963	0.084	0.066
		Investment advisor	20	3.85	1.089	0.244	
3	I am aware of crypto is a profitable investment measure	Retail investor	130	3.35	0.870	0.076	0.089
		Investment advisor	20	3.65	0.671	0.150	
4	I am aware of crypto is a well promoted product	Retail investor	130	3.40	0.903	0.079	0.040
		Investment advisor	20	3.75	0.639	0.143	
5	I am aware of the various applications and websites for crypto investments	Retail investor	130	3.54	0.882	0.077	0.493
		Investment advisor	20	3.70	0.979	0.219	
6	Crypto is a trustworthy investment option	Retail investor	130	3.01	0.936	0.082	0.481
		Investment advisor	20	3.15	0.813	0.182	
7	My money is safe in crypto investments	Retail investor	130	2.92	0.845	0.074	0.110
		Investment advisor	20	3.20	0.696	0.156	

(Continued)

Table 10.1 Independent samples t-test for retail investors vs. investment advisors. (*Continued*)

S.N.	Factors	Role	N	$\bar{x}$	σ	σ_M	p-value for unequal variances
8	I believe that crypto investments are the future of investing	Retail investor	130	3.41	0.994	0.087	0.002
		Investment advisor	20	3.90	0.553	0.124	
9	I believe that crypto projects will take over the current market scenario	Retail investor	130	3.23	0.985	0.086	0.411
		Investment advisor	20	3.40	0.821	0.184	
10	I think that crypto might be able to evolve into complete global acceptance	Retail investor	130	3.44	0.988	0.087	0.030
		Investment advisor	20	3.10	0.553	0.124	
11	Crypto investment is good for quick and great returns	Retail investor	130	3.27	0.896	0.079	0.014
		Investment advisor	20	3.80	0.834	0.186	
12	Crypto investment is very popular these days so I believe it is necessary part of our portfolio	Retail investor	130	3.20	1.116	0.098	0.292
		Investment advisor	20	2.95	0.945	0.211	
13	Everyone says crypto is a viable option for investment so I also want to invest in it	Retail investor	130	3.18	0.861	0.075	0.897
		Investment advisor	20	3.15	1.137	0.254	

(*Continued*)

Table 10.1 Independent samples t-test for retail investors vs. investment advisors. (*Continued*)

S.N.	Factors	Role	N	$\bar{x}$	σ	$σ_M$	p-value for unequal variances
14	I am investing because I keep hearing people making huge profits in crypto	Retail investor	130	3.17	1.020	0.089	0.032
		Investment advisor	20	2.60	1.046	0.234	
15	If I don't invest in crypto I might lose out on possible future opportunities and profits	Retail investor	130	3.02	1.034	0.091	0.043
		Investment advisor	20	3.45	0.826	0.185	
16	Crypto tax is the first step of legalizing crypto investments	Retail investor	130	3.39	0.911	0.080	0.239
		Investment advisor	20	3.70	1.081	0.242	
17	Crypto tax is too high in India	Retail investor	130	3.74	0.822	0.072	0.153
		Investment advisor	20	4.05	0.887	0.198	
18	High Crypto tax will not stop me from investing in crypto	Retail investor	130	3.04	0.901	0.079	0.362
		Investment advisor	20	3.20	0.696	0.156	
19	Crypto tax rules and regulations are known to me	Retail investor	130	2.97	0.871	0.076	0.040
		Investment advisor	20	3.40	0.821	0.184	
20	Crypto tax rules and regulations are easy to understand and implement	Retail investor	130	2.91	0.792	0.069	0.730
		Investment advisor	20	2.85	0.671	0.150	

which is significantly less than p=0.05. Therefore, we can interpret that there is a significant difference.

There is a significant difference among Retail Investors and Investment Advisors with respect to global acceptance towards cryptocurrencies. The p-value for this factor is p=0.03 which is less than the p=0.05. It is therefore; appropriate to conclude that there is a significant difference.

There is a significant difference among Retail Investors and Investment Advisors with respect to returns from the investment in crypto products. The p-value for this factor is calculated as p=0.014. This is significantly less than p=0.05 thus, we may say that there is a significant difference.

There is a significant difference among Retail Investors and Investment Advisors with respect to how they are influenced by information from others. The p-value for this factor is calculated as p=0.032 which is less than p=0.05. Thus, it can be inferred that we there is a significant difference among the categories.

There is a significant difference among Retail Investors and Investment Advisors with respect to their knowledge of the Indian Crypto-Tax Laws. The p-value is calculated at p=0.040. Since, calculated p-value is less than p=0.05 which is the level of significance then we can interpret that there is a significant difference with respect to knowledge of tax laws among the two categories.

Our Hypothesis for this portion of the chapter was:

H_0^1: There is no significant difference between the sentiments driving Retail Investors and investment advisors during trading in cryptocurrencies.

Ha^1: There is a significant difference between the sentiments driving Retail Investors and investment advisors during trading in cryptocurrencies.

Since, we observe that there are various areas wherein there lies a significant difference regarding the sentiments of Retail Investors and Investment Advisors then we reject the Null Hypothesis and conclude that there is a significant difference between the sentiments driving trade in cryptocurrencies.

Our second motive was to observe if there is a significant difference between the male and female individuals whenever they wish to make an investment decision with respect to cryptocurrencies. The Independent Samples t-Test was used to infer whether there is a significant difference among the male and female individuals. The table for the evaluation is given in Table 10.2.

Table 10.2 Independent samples t-test for gender.

S.N.	Factors	Gender	N	x̄	σ	σ_M	p-value for unequal variances
1	I am aware of crypto markets	M	102	3.53	0.930	0.092	0.943
		F	48	3.54	0.988	0.143	
2	I am aware of crypto investment opportunities	M	102	3.32	0.881	0.087	0.119
		F	48	3.63	1.178	0.170	
3	I am aware of crypto is a profitable investment measure	M	102	3.29	0.929	0.092	0.016
		F	48	3.60	0.610	0.088	
4	I am aware of crypto is a well promoted product	M	102	3.31	0.965	0.096	0.001
		F	48	3.73	0.574	0.083	
5	I am aware of the various applications and websites for crypto investments	M	102	3.64	0.865	0.086	0.136
		F	48	3.40	0.939	0.136	
6	Crypto is a trustworthy investment option	M	102	2.84	0.972	0.096	0.000
		F	48	3.42	0.647	0.093	
7	My money is safe in crypto investments	M	102	2.90	0.896	0.089	0.222
		F	48	3.06	0.665	0.096	

(Continued)

Table 10.2 Independent samples t-test for gender. (*Continued*)

S.N.	Factors	Gender	N	$\bar{x}$	σ	σ_M	p-value for unequal variances
8	I believe that crypto investments are the future of investing	M	102	3.35	1.068	0.106	0.007
		F	48	3.73	0.610	0.088	
9	I believe that crypto projects will take over the current market scenario	M	102	3.16	1.051	0.104	0.041
		F	48	3.46	0.713	0.103	
10	I think that crypto might be able to evolve into complete global acceptance	M	102	3.29	1.086	0.108	0.018
		F	48	3.60	0.494	0.071	
11	Crypto investment is good for quick and great returns	M	102	3.32	0.956	0.095	0.729
		F	48	3.38	0.789	0.114	
12	Crypto investment is very popular these days so I believe it is necessary part of our portfolio	M	102	3.02	1.160	0.115	0.008
		F	48	3.48	0.875	0.126	
13	Everyone says crypto is a viable option for investment so I also want to invest in it	M	102	3.07	0.988	0.098	0.009
		F	48	3.42	0.613	0.088	
14	I am investing because I keep hearing people making huge profits in crypto	M	102	3.02	1.134	0.112	0.151
		F	48	3.25	0.786	0.113	

(*Continued*)

Table 10.2 Independent samples t-test for gender. (*Continued*)

S.N.	Factors	Gender	N	x̄	σ	σ_M	p-value for unequal variances
15	If I don't invest in crypto I might lose out on possible future opportunities and profits	M	102	2.92	1.087	0.108	0.003
		F	48	3.40	0.765	0.110	
16	Crypto tax is the first step of legalizing crypto investments	M	102	3.52	0.920	0.091	0.107
		F	48	3.25	0.957	0.138	
17	Crypto tax is too high in India	M	102	3.82	0.825	0.082	0.360
		F	48	3.69	0.854	0.123	
18	High Crypto tax will not stop me from investing in crypto	M	102	3.09	0.924	0.091	0.542
		F	48	3.00	0.772	0.111	
19	Crypto tax rules and regulations are known to me	M	102	3.03	0.895	0.089	0.954
		F	48	3.02	0.838	0.121	
20	Crypto tax rules and regulations are easy to understand and implement	M	102	2.93	0.761	0.075	0.482
		F	48	2.83	0.808	0.117	

We note the following observations:

Investment decision with respect to gender does differ significantly. The investment decision sentiment varies with respect to the profitability of crypto investments. The calculated p-value shows that p=0.016 which is significantly less than the p=0.05, our level of significance. Thus, we may interpret that there is significant difference among them.

Another significant difference among male and female investors with reference to how well the cryptocurrencies are promoted. The calculated p-value shows that p=0.001 and since this is well below the significance level of p=0.05 we may infer that there is a significant difference regarding the sentiments for promotion.

Trustworthiness of the crypto investments show a calculated p-value of p=0.000 which is significantly less than the p=0.05. Therefore, we can interpret that there is a significant difference regarding the trustworthiness of the investment in cryptocurrencies.

There is also a significant difference regarding the future of investments. The sentiments show that the male and female investors differ significantly with respect to this factor. The calculate p-value is p=0.007. This is a significantly less than p=0.005. Therefore, we may conclude that there is a significant difference among them.

There is a significant difference with respect to the males and females in the sentiment for how crypto-projects will be taking over the market scenario for investment opportunities. The calculated p-value is p=0.041 and this is much less than the p=0.05 which is the level of significance. Therefore, we may determine that there is a significant difference among them.

The global acceptability of cryptocurrencies is also a major sentiment driving investment in crypto products. We observe that there is a significant difference among male and female investors in this as well. The calculate p-value is p=0.018 which is significantly less than p=0.05. Therefore, we may say that there is a significant difference with respect to global acceptability of these products.

The popularity of crypto investments is also a driver for crypto investments and also its importance as a portion of the investment portfolio is also critical. There is a significant difference among sentiments for both males and females in these as well. The calculate p-value is p=0.008. This is significantly less than p=0.005 thus, there is a significant difference with respect this factor among males and females.

The sentiments of others pushing for the viability of crypto investments are also a driver for crypto investments. The male and females investors differ on this factor as well. The calculated p-value is p=0.009. Thus, we may interpret that there is a significant difference with respect to this specific factor.

There is a significant difference among male and female investors which are interested in crypto investments. The driver for 'Fear-of-Missing-Out' or 'FOMO' is also a significant one. Since many don't wish to lose out on the opportunities and potential profits that are offered by crypto investments. The calculated p-value is p=0.003 which is significantly less than the threshold of p=0.05. Thus, we may conclude that there is a significant difference among male and female investors with this sentiment.

Our Hypothesis for this portion of the chapter was:

H_0^2: There is no significant difference between the sentiments driving Male and Female investors when trading in cryptocurrencies. **[REJECTED]**

H_a^2: There is a significant difference between the sentiments driving Male and Female investors when trading in cryptocurrencies.

Here, we observe that since there are multiple factors or sentiments with respect to which male and female investors are driven to invest in cryptocurrencies we may easily conclude that the Null Hypothesis is rejected. We may interpret that there is a significant difference with respect to the male and female investors' sentiments while investing in cryptocurrencies.

The final portion of the data analysis focuses on the Education Levels of the crypto-investors. The level of education one has also plays a key role in how they invest their money. Thus, the outcome of this analysis was conducted using the Independent Samples t-test again since the grouping of the sample respondents was according to the education levels. The Under-Graduate or Bachelors' Degree holders are denoted by 'UG' and the Post-Graduates or Masters' Degree holders are denoted by 'PG'. The output is given in Table 10.3.

The sentiment for safety of investments is observed to be a bone of contention among the Under-Graduate and Post-Graduate investors. They differ with respect to this factor. The calculated p-value is p=0.009. This is much below or less than the p-value for significance which is p=0.05. Thus, we may say that there is a significant difference with respect to this factor or sentiment.

The push from social-media or peers is another driver for investment decision and it seems once again that there is a difference among Under-Graduate and Post-Graduate investors. The calculated p-value is p=0.02 which is less than the p-value for significance which is p=0.05. Thus, we may say that there is a significant difference among them.

Table 10.3 Independent samples t-test for education levels.

S.N.	Factors	Education	N	$\bar{x}$	σ	$σ_M$	p-value for unequal variances
1	I am aware of crypto markets	Under-Graduate	19	3.26	0.933	0.214	0.190
		Post-Graduate	131	3.57	0.945	0.083	
2	I am aware of crypto investment opportunities	Under-Graduate	19	3.26	0.933	0.214	0.445
		Post-Graduate	131	3.44	1.001	0.087	
3	I am aware of crypto is a profitable investment measure	Under-Graduate	19	3.32	0.671	0.154	0.610
		Post-Graduate	131	3.40	0.875	0.076	
4	I am aware of crypto is a well promoted product	Under-Graduate	19	3.32	0.671	0.154	0.394
		Post-Graduate	131	3.47	0.906	0.079	
5	I am aware of the various applications and websites for crypto investments	Under-Graduate	19	3.42	0.902	0.207	0.497
		Post-Graduate	131	3.58	0.894	0.078	
6	Crypto is a trustworthy investment option	Under-Graduate	19	3.32	0.946	0.217	0.165
		Post-Graduate	131	2.98	0.911	0.080	
7	My money is safe in crypto investments	Under-Graduate	19	3.26	0.452	0.104	0.009
		Post-Graduate	131	2.91	0.863	0.075	

(*Continued*)

Table 10.3 Independent samples t-test for education levels. (*Continued*)

S.N.	Factors	Education	N	x̄	σ	σ_M	p-value for unequal variances
8	I believe that crypto investments are the future of investing	Under-Graduate	19	3.16	1.015	0.233	0.157
		Post-Graduate	131	3.52	0.947	0.083	
9	I believe that crypto projects will take over the current market scenario	Under-Graduate	19	3.11	0.994	0.228	0.492
		Post-Graduate	131	3.27	0.961	0.084	
10	I think that crypto might be able to evolve into complete global acceptance	Under-Graduate	19	3.58	1.170	0.268	0.456
		Post-Graduate	131	3.37	0.913	0.080	
11	Crypto investment is good for quick and great returns	Under-Graduate	19	3.37	1.012	0.232	0.895
		Post-Graduate	131	3.34	0.891	0.078	
12	Crypto investment is very popular these days so I believe it is necessary part of our portfolio	Under-Graduate	19	3.37	0.895	0.205	0.319
		Post-Graduate	131	3.14	1.122	0.098	
13	Everyone says crypto is a viable option for investment so I also want to invest in it	Under-Graduate	19	3.53	0.612	0.140	0.020
		Post-Graduate	131	3.13	0.923	0.081	

(*Continued*)

Table 10.3 Independent samples t-test for education levels. (*Continued*)

S.N.	Factors	Education	N	$\bar{x}$	σ	$σ_M$	p-value for unequal variances
14	I am investing because I keep hearing people making huge profits in crypto	Under-Graduate	19	3.37	1.012	0.232	0.219
		Post-Graduate	131	3.05	1.040	0.091	
15	If I don't invest in crypto I might lose out on possible future opportunities and profits	Under-Graduate	19	2.84	1.167	0.268	0.357
		Post-Graduate	131	3.11	0.994	0.087	
16	Crypto tax is the first step of legalizing crypto investments	Under-Graduate	19	3.58	0.607	0.139	0.314
		Post-Graduate	131	3.41	0.976	0.085	
17	Crypto tax is too high in India	Under-Graduate	19	4.11	0.658	0.151	0.035
		Post-Graduate	131	3.73	0.849	0.074	
18	High Crypto tax will not stop me from investing in crypto	Under-Graduate	19	3.32	0.885	0.203	0.190
		Post-Graduate	131	3.02	0.872	0.076	
19	Crypto tax rules and regulations are known to me	Under-Graduate	19	3.00	0.943	0.216	0.895
		Post-Graduate	131	3.03	0.868	0.076	
20	Crypto tax rules and regulations are easy to understand and implement	Under-Graduate	19	2.63	0.761	0.175	0.114
		Post-Graduate	131	2.94	0.772	0.067	

Finally, the analysis shows that there is a significant difference among the Under-Graduate and Post-Graduate investors with respect to the level of taxation that has been implemented upon crypto investments. The calculated p-value for this sentiment or factor is p=0.035 which is less than the p-value for significance which is p=0.05. Thus, we may say that taxation levels as a sentiment for driving investments in cryptocurrencies is another area where a significant difference is observed.

The final hypothesis of the study was:

$H_0{}^3$: There is no significant difference between the sentiments driving graduate and post-graduate investors when trading in cryptocurrencies. [REJECTED]

Ha^3: There is a significant difference between the sentiments driving Under-Graduate and Post-Graduate investors when trading in cryptocurrencies.

The factors for safety of investments in cryptocurrencies, the sentiments of peers or other driving investments in crypto and finally the taxation levels of the government seem to be the major concerns wherein the Under-Graduate and Post-Graduate investors seem to differ. These are equally important areas wherein there is a significant difference among them. Thus, we may infer that the Null Hypothesis is rejected and conclude that there is a significant difference between the sentiments of Under-Graduate and Post-Graduate investors.

10.5   Conclusions, Suggestions & Recommendations

Cryptocurrencies have taken up the interest of millions of people across the globe and has broken into the mindsets of the general populace. It may happen over the course of a few years that even more people would jump on the wagon for Crypto investments spurred on by the gains or potential gains that they may wish to achieve. However, it is not completely without risk. It is quite possible that these trades may have certain features of gambling as well. The exceptional risk and outstanding rewards promoted by the crypto investments have an impact on the psychology of the investors. The huge popularity it has gained on social media platforms enables crypto investment and crypto projects to promote themselves without any inhibitions. Its unique 24/7/365 i.e. twenty-four hours a day, seven days a week and 365 days a year open nature makes it a prime candidate for preoccupying the minds and money of millions or people. A certain disclaimer should be given however that the crypto trading is extremely vicious and fluctuates at times without rhyme or reason. These factors tug at the heart-strings of investors and keep them motivated to keep looking at their investments on a daily almost addictive basis. Amateurs may have promoted the game but even the professionals have been burnt by this monster and the influence of media attention, social media, peers and FOMO sentiments cannot be overlooked. There is a need to regulate the cryptocurrency market however, the regulations at this juncture do not seem to be the most acceptable among the demographics. There's a huge discrepancy that has not yet been addressed when considering crypto investments.

The data shows that there are various factors along which the Retail Investors and Investment Advisors are at loggerheads. The areas where they differ are on how the promotions of the cryptocurrencies are done. The future of the cryptocurrencies as a medium of trade is also an area where there is a difference in sentiments. Also we observe that the belief that crypto-trading is the future is definitely the trend that has taken an uptick as well. As slowly but steadily the global acceptance of cryptocurrencies and crypto-trade catches on, we will see even more adoption and trade being conducted in this area. The p-value for this promotion is $p=0.04$ which is less than $p=0.05$ therefore, while that for crypto as the future of trading is seen to be $p=0.002$. Along with this we see that global acceptance towards cryptocurrencies is $p=0.03$ that for potential returns is $p=0.014$. The manner in which both are influenced by information from others has a $p=0.032$; while knowledge levels among Retail Investors and Investment Advisors of the Indian Crypto-Tax Laws shows $p=0.040$. Since, calculated p-value is less than $p=0.05$ which is the level of significance for these above mentioned factors we can interpret that there is a significant difference among Retail Investors and Investment Advisors.

Gender has a key role in today's world. The quick adoption of any product, service or trend by either of the genders does play a crucial role in making or breaking that product or service or trend. Therefore, it is imperative that one takes into consideration the way both males and females are reacting to it. It is noted from the analysis that we see that there is a difference of sentiments with respect to profitability of crypto investments, the way in which crypto is promoted also appeals differently to males and females and these sentiments can be key drivers influencing investment decisions. There is a factor of trustworthiness of crypto investments and also on how it is promoted. These sentiments are going to play a critical role in determining whether one puts in his/her hard-earned money into such a volatile entity. There is also a difference of opinion on the matter of whether crypto-trading will be the future of investments as well and definitely a significant difference on whether the market will accept new crypto-projects. As slowly and steadily the cryptocurrencies gain a global acceptance among the general populace then this adoption and utilization will grow tremendously. It will be impossible to ignore the place of crypto-assets in one's portfolio of investments at that time. Currently, the viability of crypto investments is a thorn in the side of pro-crypto sentiment. . The driver for 'Fear-of-Missing-Out' or 'FOMO' is also a significant one. Since many don't wish to lose out on the opportunities and potential profits that are offered by crypto investments. The calculations show that $p=0.016$ for profitability while the promotion of crypto showcases a $p=0.001$. Another couple of areas like trustworthiness of crypto investments, the future of these investments and the uptake of crypto-projects in the market all have $p=0.000$, $p=0.007$ and $p=0.041$ respectively. The global acceptability of cryptocurrencies as the driver for investments along with its importance to be included in one's portfolio of investments is at $p=0.018$ and $p=0.008$; also in the case of viability of crypto investments we observe $p=0.009$. Finally the interest levels among male and female investors with respect to the crypto investments also differs greatly with $p=0.03$. These are all below the significance threshold of $p=0.05$. Therefore, we may conclude that these factors do impact investment decisions.

The Education Levels of individuals have a vital influence on how one chooses to invest. The sentiments for safety of investments and the overall push that social media has in the crypto space are certain sentiments where we see a certain amount of conflict among Under-Graduate and Post-Graduate investors. There is also a difference with reference to the taxation levels of the crypto investments and this also plays a decisive role in investment decision. The calculate p-values for these factors have turned out to be $p=0.009$ for safety of investments, $p=0.02$ for influence of social media and $p=0.035$ for taxation levels among these type of investors respectively.

The landscape of investments and investment products is changing rapidly. The cryptocurrencies have captured the imagination of millions of people who in turn have invested billions of their hard-earned money. This is where the factors like trust, Fear-of-Missing-Out, greed for returns etc. provides a motivating force for pushing these products. It must also be noted that these factors are endorsed by the future potential, viability and global market acceptance of crypto investments. It is necessary to note however, that there are various areas where there is a difference of opinion and perhaps it is those very same areas where crypto-project makers, crypto-investors, investment advisors and others can focus upon to streamline their investment decision process. Crypto is an emotional, as well as, a fiduciary investment option as the crypto taxation is being taken up by various countries with a vengeance. This however, has not deterred the crypto investor. Thus, perhaps the 'Fear-of-Missing-Out' or FOMO which is heavily driven through social media and one's peers is a driving sentiment spurring investment decisions as well.

References

1. Merriam-Webster. (2022, April 16). https://www.merriam-webster.com/dictionary/currency. Retrieved April 16, 2022, from https://www.merriam-webster.com/dictionary/currency: https://www.merriam-webster.com/dictionary/currency

2. Frankenfield, J. (2022, January 11). https://www.investopedia.com/terms/c/cryptocurrency.asp. Retrieved January 11, 2022, from https://www.investopedia.com/terms/c/cryptocurrency.asp: https://www.investopedia.com/terms/c/cryptocurrency.asp

3. IBM. (2022, April 16). https://www.ibm.com/topics/what-is-blockchain. Retrieved April 16, 2022, from https://www.ibm.com/topics/what-is-blockchain: https://www.ibm.com/topics/what-is-blockchain

4. ETMakets. (2019, December 26). https://economictimes.indiatimes.com/markets/stocks/news/how-is-a-retail-investor-defined-in-india/articleshow/72979017.cms. Retrieved December 26, 2019, from https://economictimes.indiatimes.com/markets/stocks/news/how-is-a-retail-investor-defined-in-india/articleshow/72979017.cms: https://economictimes.indiatimes.com/markets/stocks/news/how-is-a-retail-investor-defined-in-india/articleshow/72979017.cms

5. FINRA. (2022, April 16). https://www.finra.org/investors/learn-to-invest/choosing-investment-professional/investment-advisers#:~:text=What%20they%20are%3A%20An%20investment,and%20should%20not%20be%20confused. Retrieved April 16, 2022, from https://www.finra.org/investors/learn-to-invest/choosing-investment-professional/investment-advisers#:~:text=What%20they%20are%3A%20An%20investment,and%20should%20not%20be%20confused.: https://www.finra.org/investors/learn-to-invest/choosing-investment-professional/investment-advisers#:~:text=What%20they%20are%3A%20An%20investment,and%20should%20not%20be%20confused.

6. triple-A. (2022, April 16). https://triple-a.io/crypto-ownership/. Retrieved April 16, 2022, from https://triple-a.io/crypto-ownership/: https://triple-a.io/crypto-ownership/

7. Chand, M. (2021, October 21). https://www.c-sharpcorner.com/article/top-10-countries-with-the-most-cryptocurrency-holders/. Retrieved April 16, 2022, from https://www.c-sharpcorner.com/article/top-10-countries-with-the-most-cryptocurrency-holders/: https://www.c-sharpcorner.com/article/top-10-countries-with-the-most-cryptocurrency-holders/

8. Cleartax. (2022, January 11). https://cleartax.in/s/top-6-safe-investments-india. Retrieved April 16, 2022, from https://cleartax.in/s/top-6-safe-invest ments-india: https://cleartax.in/s/top-6-safe-investments-india

9. Fromlet, H. (2001). Behavioural Finance- Theory and Practical Application. Business Economics, 34-42.

10. Obenberger, N. &. (1994). Factors influencing individual investor behaviour. Financial Analysts Journal, 63-68.

11. Tomola, M. (2013). Factors influencing investment decisions in capital market: A study of individual Investors in Nigeria. Organizations & Markets in Emerging Economies, 15-28.

12. Maditinos, D. C. (2011). The impact of intellectual capital on firms' market value and financial performance. Journal of Intellectual Capital, 132-151.

13. Odean, T. (1998). Are investors reluctant to realize their losses? Journal of Finance, 1775-1798.

14. Chandra, A. &. (2011). Determinants of Individual Investor Behaviour: An Orthogonal Linear Transformation Approach. MPRA.

15. Jayaraj, S. (2013). The factor model for determining the individual investment behaviour in India. IOSR Journal of Economics and Finance, 21-32.

16. Warren. (1990). Using demographic and life style analysis to segment individual investors: A segmentation Approach. Journal of Behavioural Finance, 170-179.

17. Independent Reserve. (2020). Cryptocurrency index. Cryptocurrency Index: IRCI.

18. Gainsbury, S. &. (2017). How blockchain and cryptocurrency technology could revolutionize online gambling. Gaming Law Review, 482–492.

19. Scholten, O. J. (2020). Inside the decentralised casino: A longitudinal study of actual cryptocurrency gambling transactions. Plos One.

20. Granero, R. T.-A.-P.-M. (2012). Gambling on the stock market: An unexplored issue. . Comprehensive Psychiatry, 666–673.

21. Kim, H. J. (2020). Comparison of psychological status and investment style between bitcoin investors and share investors. Frontiers in Psychology.

22. Meng, J. &. (2020). Understanding gambling behavior and risk attitudes using cryptocurrency based casino blockchain data: Gambling behaviour and risk attitudes. . Royal Society Open Science.a

23. Dahham, A. Z. (2020). Effects of volatility and trend indicator for improving price prediction of cryptocurrency. IOP Conference Series: Materials Science and Engineering.

24. Kamps, J. &. (2018). To the moon: Defining and detecting cryptocurrency pump-and-dumps. Crime Science, 1–18.

25. Balakrishnan, A. (2021, March 10). Retrieved March 10, 2021, from https://freebitco.in/site/blogs/bitcoin/how-altcoins-aretied-to-bitcoin/: https://freebitco.in/site/blogs/bitcoin/how-altcoins-aretied-to-bitcoin/

26. Millar, S. I. (2018). Cryptocurrency expands online gambling. Gaming Law Review, 174–174.

27. Mills, D. J. (2019). Preliminary findings on cryptocurrency trading among regular gamblers: A new risk for problem gambling. Addictive Behaviors, 136–140.

28. Arthur, J. N. (2016). Day traders in South Australia: Similarities and differences with traditional gamblers. Journal of Gambling Studies, 855–866.

29. Arthur, J. N. (2015). Is there a relationship between participation in gambling activities and participation in high-risk stock trading? Journal of Gambling Business and Economics, 34–53.

30. Barber, B. M. (2009). Just how much do individual investors lose by trading? Review of Financial Studies, 609–632.

31. Melker, S. (2019). Day trading bitcoin: Why 95% of traders lose money and fail. https://cointelegraph.com/news/day-trading-bitcoin-why-95-of-traders-lose-money-and-fail. Accessed 10th March 2021.

32. Melker, S. (2021, March 10). https://cointelegraph.com/news/day-trading bitcoin-why-95-of-traders-lose-money-and-fail. Retrieved April 16, 2022, from https://cointelegraph.com/news/day-tradingbitcoin-why-95-of-traders-lose-money-and-fail: https://cointelegraph.com/news/day-tradingbitcoin-why-95-of-traders-lose-money-and-fail

33. Mills, D. J. (2019). Preliminary findings on cryptocurrency trading among regular gamblers: A new risk for problem gambling. Addictive Behaviors, 136–140.

34. Dixon, M. R. (2018). What characterizes excessive online stock trading? A qualitative study. Journal of Gambling Issues, 8–26.

35. Conlin, A. K. (2015). Personality traits and stock market participation. Journal of Empirical Finance, 34–50.

36. Kraaijeveld, O. &. (2020). The predictive power of public Twitter sentiment for forecasting cryptocurrency prices. Journal of International Financial Markets, Institutions and Money

37. Kumar, A. (2009). Who gambles in the stock market? The Journal of Finance, 1889–1933.

38. Langer, E. J. (1975). The illusion of control. Journal of Personality and Social Psychology, 311–328.

39. Jefferson, S. &. (2003). A new instrument to measure cognitive distortions in video lottery terminal users. The Informational Biases Scale (IBS). Journal of Gambling Studies, 387–403.

40. Lambos, C. &. (2007). Numerical reasoning ability and irrational beliefs in problem gambling. International Gambling Studies.

41. Joukhador, J. B. (2004). Superstitious beliefs in gambling among problem and non-problem gamblers: Preliminary data. Journal of Gambling Studies, 171–180.

42. Blanco, F. M. (2011). Making the uncontrollable seem controllable: The role of action in the illusion of control. The Quarterly Journal of Experimental Psychology, 1290–1304.

43. Matute, H. (1996). Illusion of control: Detecting response-outcome independence in analytic but not in naturalistic conditions. Psychological Science, 289–293.
44. Browne, M. &. (2020). Measuring behavioural dependence in gambling: A case for removing harmful consequences from the assessment of problem gambling pathology. Journal of Gambling Studies, 1027–1044
45. Griffiths, M. D. (2005). A 'components' model of addiction within a biopsychosocial framework. Journal of Substance Use, 191–197.
46. Ma, J. (2022, April 16). https://academy.binance.com/en/glossary/fear-of-missing-out. Retrieved April 16, 2022, from https://academy.binance.com/en/glossary/fear-of-missing-out: https://academy.binance.com/en/glossary/fear-of-missing-out
47. Przybylski, A. M. (2013). Motivational, emotional, and behavioral correlates of fear of missing out. Computers in Human Behavior, 1841–1848.
48. Schwartz, B. W. (2002). Maximizing vertus satisficing: Happiness is a matter of choice. Journal of Personality and Social Psychology, 1178–1197.
49. Bar-Hillel, M. &. (1996). Why are people reluctant to exchange lottery tickets?. Journal of Personality and Social Psychology, 17–27.

11

Applications of Digital Technologies and Artificial Intelligence in Cryptocurrency - A Multi-Dimensional Perspective

W. Jaisingh[1]*, Preethi N.[2] and R. K. Kavitha[3]

[1]*School of Information Science, Presidency University, Bangalore, Karnataka, India*
[2]*Department of Data Science, Christ University, Bangalore, Karnataka, India*
[3]*Department of Computer Applications, Kumaraguru College of Technology, Coimbatore, Tamil Nadu, India*

Abstract

The paradigm shift requires spreading the light of decentralized ledger technology, extraordinarily implementing cryptocurrencies, and being visible as a game-changer. Blockchain technology, along with cryptocurrencies like Bitcoin, Ethereum, and Litecoin, is a tool for global economic transformation that is rapidly gaining traction in the finance industry. However, these technologies have had low popularity in the consumer market. Many platforms have been misunderstood and ignored when there is an obvious hole in among them.

The basic idea behind cryptocurrency is that it is a network-based, totally virtual exchange medium that utilizes cryptographic algorithms such as Secure Hash Algorithm 2 (SHA-2) and Message Digest 5 (MD5) to secure the data. Transactions within the blockchain era are secure, transparent, traceable, and irreversible. Cryptocurrencies have gained a reputation in practically all sectors, including the monetary sector, due to these properties. The uncertainty and dynamism of their expenses, however, hazard investments substantially despite cryptocurrencies' growing popularity amongst approval bodies. Studying cryptocurrency charge prediction is fast becoming a trending subject matter in the global research community. Several device mastering and deep mastering algorithms, like Gated Recurrence Units (GRUs), Neural nets (NNs), and nearly short-term memory, were employed by the scientists to analyze and forecast cryptocurrency prices.

As a part of this chapter, we discuss numerous aspects of cryptographic protection and their related issues. Specifically, the research addresses the state-of-the-art

*Corresponding author: jaisinghw@gmail.com

Mohd Naved, V. Ajantha Devi, and Aditya Kumar Gupta (eds.) Fintech and Cryptocurrency, (221–250)
© 2023 Scrivener Publishing LLC

by examining the underlying consensus mechanism, cryptocurrency, attack style, and applications of cryptocurrencies from a unique perspective. Secondly, we investigate the usability of blockchain generation by examining the behavioral factors that influence customers' decision to use blockchain-based technology. To identify the best crypto mining strategy, the research employs an Analytic Hierarchy Process (AHP) and Fuzzy-TOPSIS hybrid analytics framework. Furthermore, it identifies the top-quality mining methods by evaluating providers' overall performance during cryptocurrency mining.

Keywords: Cryptocurrency, FinTech technologies, blockchain, security attacks, hybrid analytics approach, sensitivity analysis, machine learning, deep learning

11.1 Introduction

The application of cryptocurrencies is transforming finance in a manner that can be viewed as a game-changer in light of decentralized ledger technology. The underlying paradigm of cryptocurrencies ensures their widespread acceptance within global economic markets with characteristics such as transparency, immutability, auditability, and anonymity. In response, global stakeholders, legislators, and regulators are seeking to diversify their investment portfolios by investing in cryptocurrencies. A slew of sophisticated cryptocurrencies has emerged following the fine-tuned success of Bitcoin [1]. These cryptocurrencies rely on regulatory loopholes to fuel a wide array of financial bubbles. The rate of financial return of these economic bubbles is at a record high, despite the potential for contagious financial instability caused by them.

Volatility is the result of the fact that the market capitalization and returns on these cryptocurrencies are based on speculative projections and are extremely volatile [2]. Inspire primarily by the technological breakthrough behind a significant number of cryptocurrencies, Blockchain allows peer-to-peer fund transfers in a trustless decentralized computing environment. By creating cryptographic communication among end-users, it supports sensitive interactions without implementing a centralized governance infrastructure. A wide variety of solutions can be enabled by blockchain technology, from public digital ledgers to private ledgers with permission. Utilizing asymmetric key encryption and zero-knowledge proof, this method also reduces retroactive data changes. Generally, blockchains can be divided into two types based on their access to governance services: public and private [3, 4].

It is possible to modify cryptocurrencies to give them sophisticated capabilities in the financial ecosystem. Cryptocurrencies are representations of certain Blockchain categories. Security concerns, financial instability, and a lack of de facto norms are among the factors that have raised serious concerns about cryptocurrency. According to the market capitalization of cryptocurrencies, they offer a new paradigm of safe financial transactions, though cryptocurrencies tend to be vulnerable to heterogeneity due to their particular challenges [5]. An important source of security risks stems from cybercriminals motivated by money. The exploitation of vulnerabilities in intermediaries or underlying services is another important factor contributing to this problem. The Ethereum platform has been exposed to some smart contract vulnerabilities, including the 2016 attack on the Decentralized Autonomous Organization (DAO), which cost approximately USD 60 million, the 2017 attack on the Parity wallet, which cost approximately USD 31 million, and the 2018 attack on the DNS, which cost approximately USD 17 million. Cryptocurrency security is influenced by many factors, and it can be difficult to pinpoint the exact type of problem, but trust breaches, private keys, and data management are the most critical factors [6].

11.2 State-of-the-Art Review

In the past, there were also auxiliary or alternative digital currencies. In contrast, an open-source currency with no central point of trust that relies on a third party is a novel and revolutionary concept.

The use of consensus mechanisms in cryptocurrency systems is critical to achieving higher performance and greater security. Following this, we will examine several consensus mechanisms concerning cryptocurrencies, including their strengths, weaknesses, and issues that affect cryptocurrency security.

Proof-of-Work and Naor [7] offer a distributed consensus-based mechanism called Work [7]. Any networking service that uses PoW (such as e-mail) requires a considerable level of computation before it can be utilized. In the past, it was used to combat DoS assaults and to prevent service exploitation (e.g., spam) on networks. It became popular in cryptocurrencies in the late 2000s, particularly in Bitcoin [8]. To attach blocks created by full nodes to the Blockchain in Bitcoins, a significant amount of computational time is devoted to calculating the random nonce. Based on the previous block's hash, this nonce computes the current block's hash [9].

- Requestors (clients) and service providers (servers) work directly with each other via the challenge-response method.

Providers may issue challenges to the requesting party in the form of items in a set that have certain properties [10]. Requestors must then respond to the challenge by providing an appropriate response, which must be transmitted to the provider. Due to its creation on the spot, the complexity of the challenge can be changed to fit the provider's current load. In the case of challenge-response-based strategies, there is usually an upper bound if there is a solution known to the requester.

- Verification based on a solution: In this methodology, the requester and the provider do not have to be related immediately. It is important that the supplier self-imposes the problem before approaching the requester for a solution. The supplier then conducts an in-depth analysis of the issue, double-checks the selection of the problem, and recommends a solution. Iterative probabilistic processes underlie most of the techniques, including HashCash [11]. Based on known solution-based approaches, there is a small difference in variance between them and unbounded probabilistic approaches.

11.3 Application Areas of Cryptocurrencies

The use of crypto-currencies can be applied in a variety of contexts. In the following subsections [12] we discover some of the domain researchers' recommended applications (as shown in Figure 11.1).

11.3.1 Fundraising and Investments

The use of cryptocurrency as a tool to raise funding for products and services is being considered by start-ups and established companies, which could revolutionize the entire fund-raising process. When Blockchain Capital launched the first tokenized hedge-chain security token, BCAP, in October 2013 [13], it set a precedent for the industry. By avoiding financial intermediaries, users can send money quickly and cheaply with cryptocurrency. In addition to helping encourage ethical business practices, cryptocurrency transactions are transparent. From 2013 to 2020, the market capitalization of Bitcoin is shown in Figure 11.2 [14]. Cryptocurrencies can be used to collect funds in several ways, including initial coin offerings (ICOs), which have gained much attention in recent years. Several

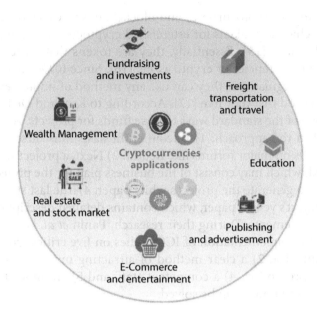

Figure 11.1 Cryptocurrencies in practice [9].

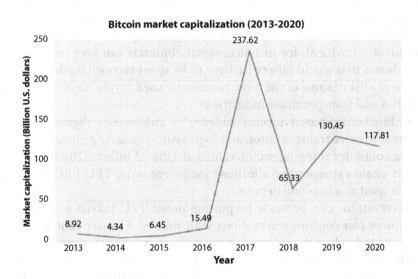

Figure 11.2 The Bitcoin market capitalization over the next five years (2013–2020) [9].

companies in the cryptocurrency and Blockchain space use tokens to raise funds by exchanging tokens for established cryptocurrency units or some other legal tender [15]. Essentially, they are tokens that represent newly created cryptocurrencies or crypto assets [16]. Since ICOs are not subject to any formal regulations, they can use any method of implementation or working method that they like [17]. According to Kaal and Dell'Ebra [18], ICOs are one of the standard ways to raise funds for projects. A set of steps is included in the approach: 1) Bitcoin enthusiasts must first create concepts for ICOs on major forums like Reddit. 2) Next, a project white paper is generated, which may consist of the business plan for the project. 3) The next step is to generate the project's white paper. 4) The last step is to prepare the project's yellow paper, which contains detailed descriptions of the project's requirements. During their research, Panin *et al.* [19] found that the successful implementation of ICOs relies on five critical components: 1) a brilliant idea, 2) a clear method of attracting investors, 3) effective methods of promotion, 4) a competent staff, and 5) an understanding of the problem and how it can be solved.

11.3.2   Freight Transportation and Travel

Since cryptocurrency is becoming more popular among retailers, consumers can use it to pay for tickets, where consumers can conduct transactions. Transportation and logistics are poised to benefit greatly from blockchain-based technologies in a variety of ways. By automating tasks like invoice payment, for instance, smart contracts can save hundreds of man-hours that would otherwise have to be spent reconciling documents. Below is a list of some of the most commonly used cryptocurrencies in the logistics and transportation industries:

A Blockchain-based project called 300 cubits uses digital booking deposits to solve transportation and logic issues, including ghost bookings in the container shipping sector valued at US$ 23 billion [20]. To reduce supply chain expenses and eliminate inefficient ones, TEU ERC20 Utility coin is used as a booking deposit.

Reservations can be made by putting down TEU tokens as a deposit, and liners can confirm reservations with tokens. A smart contract completes its task when the contract's expectations and circumstances are met.

Mobile wallet platforms such as Dovu offer rewards that consumers can redeem for mobility-related products or services in their ecosystems [21]. Blockchain-based networks enable users to connect their cars and share data while maintaining privacy and security.

11.3.3   Education

As cryptocurrencies become more widely accepted as a form of payment in the education industry, they are becoming more widely used. Online platforms make learning easier for students, and cryptocurrencies can be used for certifications. A growing number of cryptocurrencies have seized market niches for education-related products, including educational websites, holistic institutions, audiobooks, and webinars. The following are some of the most widely used cryptocurrency technologies in education:

- Academic Token is a recognized educational institution that teaches Blockchain development to its students [22]. By providing Blockchain development courses, the institution is addressing the shortage of Blockchain developers. To make use of this, users can use cryptocurrency in order to purchase training programs, educational opportunities, and online study materials.
- Tokens of Success Life [23] are used for the payment of personal, educational, and professional development. Reduced fees for personal, professional, and educational courses will help reduce the cost of living, thereby alleviating the problem of the slow job market and income growth. By developing and meeting the demands of the adult education market, the project also improves policies and training programs.

11.3.4   Publication and Advertising as Means of Communication

Organizations that use cryptocurrencies for advertising reap significant benefits. Direct exchange can be used by advertisers to construct consumer profiles and promote to them based on their wants and preferences. By identifying the source and handling parties of the products, customers can verify the legitimacy of the products they purchase. The use of cryptocurrencies by publishing houses and social media platforms is also increasing, as participants can be validated with cryptocurrencies. Publishers and advertising agencies are among the most popular users of Affiliate Coin. Affiliate Markets have been revolutionized thanks to the use of smart contracts [24]. The Affiliate Coin solves the problem of uncertainty surrounding the proper usage of funds for brands. Furthermore, smart contracts can resolve issues associated with disputed payments, as well as reduce the chances of advertisement fraud.

11.3.5   E-Commerce and Entertainment

By using cryptocurrency, non-financial data specific to a particular transaction can be kept in an immutable record and re-used to make payments and fulfill orders through e-commerce. In addition to providing cost savings, security, and transparency, cryptocurrencies also ensure corporate growth and consumer privacy [25]. In addition, cryptocurrencies are uniquely suited to handle supply chain communication, which e-commerce relies on to increase efficiency because cryptocurrencies offer traceability of transactions or payments. Additionally, the entertainment and media industries could also benefit from cryptocurrency applications. Payments are made with cryptocurrency because it is safer and faster than other payment options. The use of mobile devices to earn money has made Augmented Reality (AR) applications increasingly popular. Blockchain technology has simplified and accelerated loyalty payments, eliminating the need for expensive intermediaries. Using smart contracts, parties can agree on terms and conditions and have those terms and conditions implemented automatically. The music industry now receives royalties much faster, since musicians do not have to wait months for them. Further, smart contracts allow content producers to specify the terms and conditions of their collaborations instead of accepting what streaming services offer. The cryptocurrency-based entertainment technologies Zimrii and OPUS are popular [26].

11.3.6   Real Estate and Stock Market

There are several industries that have begun to embrace cryptocurrencies, including real estate and equities. A nation's economy can be revolutionized by legislative procedures if they provide substantial benefits in this area. Tokenizing real estate and trading it online without intermediaries using cryptocurrencies can be done quickly and efficiently. By reducing transaction costs (such as registration fees, inspection fees, and professional fees) [27], this decentralized transaction method will help reduce transaction costs. The method will also provide all participants with liquidity and fractional ownership. As prices are derived from multiple sources, cryptocurrency can reduce trading costs and speed up executions in stock markets.

11.3.7   Trained Financial Planners

A cryptocurrency can be considered the next step in wealth management. Retail investors throughout the world are seeking ways to manage their money in an unrestricted manner using cryptocurrency. As an example, SwissBorg provides investors with the option to invest in local currencies and manage cryptocurrency assets. To help stakeholders become a part of the ecosystem, a variety of tools are being developed for crypto-asset management. These tools could assist those without a deep understanding of the details of the process. Businesses will benefit from smooth asset management, resulting in the steady growth of cryptocurrency market capitalization [28, 29].

11.4 Financial Transaction Using Blockchain Technology

11.4.1 Introduction

Blockchain technology is regarded as an extremely safe and secure platform for recording transactions. DLT, smart contracts, and other blockchain technologies, which include IBM Hyperledger and Ethereum, are built into blockchain mechanisms and provide services to a variety of other technologies.

Its complex characteristics and unique structure have drawn the attention of blockchain technology experts, leading to the development of new material. Legislation and legitimacy are the first axioms in the user's perspective, followed by factors such as social impact, technological design, and user experience [30]. Moreover, it is important to take into account trust and danger. Customers perceive blockchain technology as the most dangerous. To prevent this from happening, technology must have enough confidence to advance in a highly competitive market [30, 31].

In contrast, implementing new technology is a lengthy and costly process. Millions of dollars have been lost as a result of information technology implementation errors [32], highlighting the importance of accurate market forecasts. Even so, gaining real or intangible benefits from IT adoption or implementation has become a key concern for many companies [33]. As a result of customer feedback, new technologies are viewed as important by clients. The inventors are given a few technical feasibility comments before moving forward with developing the firm's concept. The likelihood of acceptance can also be enhanced with more data and forecasts [34]. Attitudes can predict a customer's actual usage of a technology by measuring their behavioral intentions.

When it comes to improving customer performance, the central objective of IT is to leverage technology: the greatest need lies in applying appropriate technology to various duties [35, 36]. In the future, blockchain technology can be an important technology that will be required by the market. Blockchain technology can be used to expand many industries in the future. Adoption of blockchain technology may improve service quality as well [37].

Many new platforms are using blockchain technology, especially in the financial industry. On the other hand, customer utilization was lower than expected [30]. There is a question as to why customers are reluctant to use cryptocurrency based on blockchain technology while many people still use traditional banking services, which are slow, costly, and don't provide privacy or control [38].

11.4.2 Technology Acceptance Model

The study focuses on customer behavior in connection with blockchain-based bitcoin transactions. As such, we should look into using the TAM model. However, TAM should not be used as a sole instrument for proper assessment. The present study will use an integrated model.

TA Based on the Theory of Reasoned Action paradigm [39], information technology is used in a variety of settings in different workplaces. Following these theories (TRA and TAM), behavior is defined by the purpose for which an individual acts. A strong relationship was observed between the behavior and the intention [40]. Individuals' intentions are described as their attitude toward new technology as reflected in their actions.

In order to ascertain or influence information technology attitudes and behaviors, Davis examines the external environment that influences perceived ease of use (PEoU) and perceived value (PU). PEoU has a direct influence on PU according to the TAM, which defines them as separate variables. The TAM model is based on the concept that behaviour intention provides the user with an optional perspective to choose from. This user-friendly model aids them in analyzing stages and procedures to make the best decisions regarding their acceptance [40–42].

11.4.3 External Constructs

11.4.3.1 Trust (T)

A consumer's trust, or their level of comfort, confidence, and security as they use technology, can be defined as comfort, confidence, and security.

Several factors influence people's willingness to adopt technology, including trust, security, and privacy [43]. Trusted systems that are adaptable to the inevitable fluctuations in trust can handle the evolution of social interactions over time [44]. During the development stage of new systems for internet purchases and online activities, customer trust plays a major role, according to Keen [45]. By improving customer trust, electronic banking systems reduced the risks of online shopping by lessening customer distrust. While increasing institutional dependence, banks must reduce the likelihood of usage risk in their transaction systems [46]. In electronic commerce, trust is paramount. To combat consumers' perceptions of risk and insecurity, a truss bridge needs to be constructed that allows them to feel comfortable interacting over a new channel with a distant, often unknown provider [47].

Conversely, trust is the foundation for customer-vendor relationships. Keeping the communication channel active and sustainable requires maintaining the trust of the commercial partner. Trustworthy partnerships are characterized by this feature that might reduce the risks of danger [48]. An important part of customer preparation is trust; similarly, protection against negative acts is also the building of trust, which is accomplished by monitoring customer activities in advance to ensure additional protection and security [49].

A Technology is more likely to gain trust and reassurance about its safety if people have a positive attitude about it. Despite controlling for trust [50], this study shows a high partial correlation between risk and acceptability. According to McCloskey and Weaver, trust is one of the strongest factors that make things easier to use. You demonstrate that you believe that online shopping is simple when a customer trusts you with their financial and personal information [41].

When a customer's trust is eroded, he or she becomes less likely to take chances, and the risk of dishonesty increases. Taking risks and being unable to control the outcome are situations that call for trust. The blockchain should have a low risk likelihood, and the level of trust should be high. Trust is the study's central theme, and this characteristic has a substantial indirect impact on customer behavior. Accessible technologies have a direct effect on attitudes and the PEoU when it comes to trust. A customer's trust can influence their decision to select a particular technology or service [51]. There was not enough faith in blockchain technology among the technical and financial markets until today. Those benefits are considered outweighed by the risks [30]. Moreover, many people assume that blockchain technology is hard to understand and administer. In addition, proof of stake (PoS) might strengthen the trust chain if trust is established through a blockchain-based consensus system. Hyperledger is also a blockchain platform with a collaborative management system to ensure user trust and data confidentiality [52, 53].

11.4.3.2   Support (RS) for Regulatory Standards

Legislative frameworks are implement by governments so that they can monitor and ensure that both consumers and service providers are adhering to their contractual agreements and avoiding violations [54].

A country's rule of law is essential for e-business, monitoring quality of service, and authorizing and implementing new technologies. This law ensures that the process runs smoothly and fairly. Similar to client behavior in regards to blockchain technology and cryptocurrencies, so can be said about their technology applications. Regulating is not possible without reducing or eliminating uncertainty. Government restrictions and directions may influence customers' willingness to trust technology. In addition, there are issues with the internationalization of cryptocurrency, such as the absence of government regulation [55–57].

The impact of government regulation on technology improvement is double: the first is through taxation and other decisions, and the other is through changes in the environment within which technology innovation takes place [56]. For ensuring the authenticity and authorisation of the entities associated with blockchains, policies, laws, and regulations are essential.

11.4.3.3   Experience (E)

Knowledge and experience are the characteristics that support customers' use of new technologies [58]. Customer behavior is more likely to be trustworthy when their experience level is high [59]. There is substantial evidence to suggest that experience impacts trust. It is possible that this variable may have a large impact and increase or decrease depending on the experience level of the individual [60].

For any new technology to be used effectively, customers must have an appropriate level of experience and understanding [61]. It is possible for a user's aptitudes and previous experiences to influence their ability to use new technology, particularly after a short training period that facilitates and enhances their control and usage of the various systems. Researchers have found that users' enthusiasm for new technology increases interaction and makes it easier to use [62]. The correlation analysis conducted by Fazio and Zanna in 1978 examined and assessed experience as a continuous variable. As a result of their behavioural experiences, people's attitudes are determined by their experiences: the more an attitude predicts subsequent behavior, the more influence it has on individuals, and the more certain they are in their views [63]. Computer applications may benefit from the experience of the industry in terms of productivity gains and high-performance.

11.4.3.4   Social Influence (SI)

An individual's perception of what they should be doing is shaped by a set of standards, roles, memberships, and values [60].

Online services that include social influence allow customers to connect with the platform in a timely manner to get a sufficient experience, while maintaining their loyalty to the company or technology [60]. Additionally, social influence is unique in that it reflects how much trust people have in technology and can significantly influence it.

This interaction and communication created an environment in which the customer was encouraged to investigate, evaluate risk levels, and decide whether to utilize the service or not. Assessing the influence of social influences on blockchain technology will allow us to gain a better understanding of customer behavior towards blockchain technology and the benefits it is expected to provide.

User behavior is significantly affected by new technology and social elements. Numerous studies and approaches have examined the role of social impact in predicting consumer behavior [60, 64]. Due to its social component, studies have shown that social media has a crucial role in the utility of technology. Collaboration was also enhanced by social factors, which led to a feeling of support [65]. According to the TRA model, both subjective norms and attitudes can influence user behavioral intentions. A social environment that combines IT features with customer decisions impacts users' decisions and behavior directly [66, 67].

11.4.3.5   Design (D)

Navigation, appearance, and layout are technical attributes that affect how users use a system [68].

The design of mobile applications has the potential to influence behavior and alter expectations because they are used on a daily basis [68]. The research of DeLone and McLean focused extensively on the factors affecting the success of technical systems. In order to alter the quality of the system and information, the authors hypothesized that quality measurements, which have a substantial impact on implementation and design quality standards, can be utilized [69].

As a result of slow response times, slow hardware, and inefficient software, people are still wary of adopting new technology. The design of a difficult website can also result in an inaccessible system and high traffic on the website. Designers should therefore pay special attention to how their websites are built. Having a user-friendly interface will facilitate adoption and ease of use due to positive attitudes and experience [59].

11.4.4 Summary

A wide range of secure transaction and service alternatives are available using blockchain technology, which has recently exploded on the global stage. Blockchain technology hasn't been well embraced, and real utilization remains low thanks to aversion from clients. A study analyzes how well Blockchain technology can be used by customers and identifies characteristics that influence their acceptance of bitcoin transactions using blockchain-based applications. There is a low adoption rate for blockchain technology. This new model opens up a new perspective on blockchain technology and contributes to its adoption given the emergence of new technologies and the limited resources for research and development.

11.5 An Analysis of Cryptocurrency Mining Using a Hybrid Approach

11.5.1 Introduction

In the mining industry today, Bitcoin (BTC) is a revolutionary digital asset and is referred to as a cryptocurrency. It was first published in 2008 by Nakamoto Satoshi as a peer-to-peer (P2P) electronic cash system. Since then, BTC has become the world's most popular cryptocurrency. Mining bitcoins might be thought of as a reward for participating. Blockchains are distributed ledgers in which transactions are verified by cryptographic network nodes and recorded in a distributed ledger known as a cryptocurrency [70]. Cryptocurrencies can be exchanged over-the-counter as well as for goods, services, and other cryptocurrencies.

Bitcoin mining was once the cheapest method of obtaining Bitcoins on the blockchain for programmers. The value of 17.8 million BTCs increased to USD 332 billion for a market value of USD 19,783 in December 2017. A variety of mining techniques have been developed as alternatives to purchasing BTC directly from a cryptocurrency exchange as a result of its growing popularity. Since the price of acquiring a BTC is so much higher than the average mining cost, individual investors from all backgrounds choose alternative cryptocurrency mining tactics, including cloud-based mining and hosted mining.

After losing faith in cloud mining services, many individuals began mining cryptocurrency themselves by purchasing the necessary hardware and utilities. The practice is known as home mining. On the other hand, individual investors had to improve their equipment or install more energy-intensive mining machines to reduce the difficulty of hashing. Several private investors converted their home mining operations into large-scale bitcoin mining farms after investing in technology infrastructure and utilities, thereby increasing the mining capacity.

The third option is called hosted mining, and it is used by many professional investors in addition to cloud mining and home mining. The advantage of this strategy over cloud mining is that investors have greater control over miners at the mining facilities of the service provider. Instead of paying for the tenant's running costs, the hosting provider covers all costs and offers maintenance management technical support. Host mining also offers advantages such as reduced pool membership fees and access to the latest mining technology provided by cryptocurrency miner manufacturers.

11.5.2   Cryptocurrency Mining Strategies

There is little evidence linking bitcoin mining and cryptocurrency investing or portfolio diversification. BTC, cryptocurrency price prediction, hedging, and portfolio diversification with BTCs have been examined previously.

First, let's review Bitcoin basics. Satoshi [70] describes Bitcoin as an electronic cash system that works without any centralized authority via a cryptographic protocol. The entire network is responsible for BTC mining in open-source systems. The use of a decentralized network of computers is sufficient to record digitally signed transactions.

Having bitcoins produced by mining requires a proof-of-work protocol to prevent denial-of-service attacks. The system monitors the speed of computers to prevent denial-of-service attacks. With the help of this peer-to-peer network, a distributed timestamp server can be established [6, 20]. A collection of cryptographic hash functions called SHA-256 is used for hashing blocks created by miners. As soon as the hashing produces a valid block, it is chained together. A high number of blocks too quickly increases the difficulty, generating more BTC and requiring more hashes to create blocks [71].

Many studies have been conducted on cryptocurrency mining, including studies focused on technical aspects of blockchain technologies as well as their operating mechanisms, such as cryptovirology, cybersecurity, energy efficiency, optimizing mining algorithms, creating cryptocurrency mining malware systems, discovering covert cryptocurrency mining, mobile mining, crypto-jacking, mining ASIC pricing, and other blockchain-related topics. Kim examined the effects of Bitcoin rewards, mining difficulty, transaction costs, discount costs, and pooling costs on mining efficiency using a Multi-Leader Multi-Follower Stackelberg Game Model [72]. A system-level simulation conducted by him revealed that the game technique is more fair and efficient than other BTC schemes. Haghighat and Shajari [73] tested the hypothesis that the majority of the network's computational power (51) could be provided by BTC mining pools with lower hashing power. According to Easley et al. [74], a game-theoretic model was developed in order to analyze BTC transactions from mining to market. Additionally, they highlighted that the balance of BTC's blockchain is a complex balancing act between user and miner activity and imbalances in input and outflow from pools of participants that could do significant damage.

11.5.3 Summary and Discussion

Bitcoin investments are successful only if the best cryptocurrency mining plan is developed and implemented. The performance of cryptocurrency mining service providers is assessed using a hybrid analytics approach. Business analytics is an area that has received little attention until now.

Compared with cloud mining and home mining, a hosted mining plan offers some specific advantages as well as some risks to investors. With the second, you get a greater level of technological capabilities and a more flexible contract at a smaller price than with the first. Compared to home mining, cloud mining and hosted mining solutions have shorter contracts, thus reducing investment risks. Professional cloud mining services, on the other hand, use new technology to replace old miners in order to manage the increasing difficulty of hashing.

Developing an effective cryptocurrency mining strategy requires monitoring price changes, global economic conditions, advances in mining technology, and transparency and trustworthiness within mining services and cybersecurity. An understanding of the cryptocurrency market and the ecosystem is necessary in order to develop and implement a smart mining strategy.

11.6   Forecasting Cryptocurrency Price Using Convolutional Neural Networks

11.6.1   Introduction

Remarkable growth has been experienced by the bitcoin market over the past few months. Since the beginning of the year, cryptocurrency market capitalizations have risen steadily. Because of this incident [75], bitcoin has become a major financial asset and electronic payment system. Since Bitcoin [76], perhaps the most well-known cryptocurrency, was created, P2P payment systems have attracted a lot of attention from investors and researchers. The advantages of cryptocurrencies over traditional cash systems, including decentralization, high security, and reduced transaction costs, cannot be overstated [77]. At the end of September 2019, cryptocurrencies had reached $300 billion in market capitalization, with Bitcoin accounting for almost $200 billion. In addition, there are approximately 2,000 types of cryptocurrencies that are available to the public for trading.

In order to maximize gains and minimize losses, cryptocurrencies are in need of reliable forecasting models. A prediction of price movement can assist in preventing speculators from spreading false information. Despite this, it is notoriously difficult to predict traditional financial data time series due to markets' random properties. Cryptocurrencies, as a type of digital asset, present a challenge to research due to their lack of correlation with traditional investments [78, 79].

A high prediction accuracy has been achieved by the ARIMA model when forecasting bitcoin prices over short time spans (e.g., two days). For longer-term predictions, the prediction errors were significant when the model was trained for a longer period of time (e.g., 9 days). GARCH models are compared with stochastic volatility models (SV) in [80]. Results suggest SV models are more resilient to price swings than GARCH models. Our analyses determined that SV-t was the optimal Bitcoin model, while GARCH-t was the optimal Litecoin model (i.e., SV-t was the most effective Bitcoin model, while GARCH-t was the most effective Litecoin model). They tested 12 different GARCH-based models, using log-returns of exchange rates of seven popular cryptocurrencies. Chu, Chan, Nadarajah, and Osterrieder found that the IGARCH and GJRGARCH models were the most volatile.

11.6.2   Assistive Technologies in Machine Learning and Deep Learning

Models using machine learning (ML) and deep learning (DL) are much more effective at analyzing non-linear multivariate data than standard time-series models and remain more robust to noise. The regression problem is inextricably linked to time-series data prediction in ML and DL algorithms [81]. Traditional econometric and statistical models in many cases do not perform as well as classical ML models. Multilayer perceptrons, Bayesian networks, and SVMs have shown promising results when it comes to cryptocurrency and stock market prediction, for example [82]. Furthermore, some studies have used machine learning techniques and sentiment analysis to analyze bitcoin volatility [83]. These methods are not without limitations, including a small sample size and misinformation's influence.

As well as contributing to ML as a whole, DL has made major contributions to speech recognition, computer vision, and natural language processing. Through DL, time-series predictions can be made. Nevertheless, there are very few studies that use DL approaches to estimate bitcoin prices. Research has demonstrated that DL is capable of detecting the chaotic dynamics of cryptocurrency markets. A long-short term memory (LSTM) network has greater predictability than generalized regression neural networks, according to [84] (GRNN). Research [85] also showed recurrent neural networks (RNN) with gated recurring units (GRU) and LSTM outperformed typical machine learning (ML) models. GRU's recurrent dropout model outperformed the baseline by a significant margin in predicting bitcoin prices. According to the study [86], CNN's were also used to predict long-term crude oil prices with reasonable accuracy, demonstrating CNN's ability to predict cryptocurrency prices. In reality, most of these techniques rely on simple RNNs or CNN variations. However, few studies have been conducted on the potential use of composite DL models to predict bitcoin prices. Several of these studies concentrate primarily on Bitcoin's price and ignore other cryptocurrencies or its relationships with other cryptocurrencies.

11.6.3   Convolutional Neural Networks with Weighted and Attentive Memory Channels

WAMC is built primarily from three modules: Attentive Memory, Channel-wise Weighting, and Convolution & Pooling. Below is a description of each module.

11.6.3.1   Attentive Memory Module

A component of Attentive Memory is a GRU, and another component is a self-attentive component. Time-series data dependencies are handled by the GRU component using a reset gate Rt and an update gate Ut, respectively. Gate 1 also gets input from the current time step input Xt as well as the previous time step's hidden state St– 1.

An update gate that is close to 1 will suppress more information from previous time steps, so it is important to note this. Whenever elements in Ut are close to zero, the new hidden state approaches the candidate hidden state. GRU, on the other hand, overcomes the gradient vanishing problem in RNNs, as well as improves the capturing of dependencies in lengthy sequences of data.

It also emphasizes the importance of self-attention in the module attentive memory. Using the hidden state within the GRU component, we can encode long-term and short-term dependencies. However, the GRU component sometimes struggles to recognize instances that have occurred at distinct delayed positions. Attention processes explicitly enhance the ability to select essential information from various delayed positions, as demonstrated in [87].

11.6.3.2   Convolution & Pooling Module

Recurrent Neural Networks (RNN) and Artificial Neural Networks (ANN) are capable of capturing non-linear mappings and time dependences, but the extent of their connectivity limits their abilities [88, 89]. In comparison to traditional ANNs and RNNs, CNNs connect neurons by sharing weights locally, allowing them to find local information faster. An alternative definition of a local receptive field is a group of neighbouring neurons. By combining convolutional layers and pooling layers, CNN reduces the parameters and reduces the impact of overfitting. A convolutional 2-D layer with a maximum-pooling layer is used in this module.

11.6.4   Summary and Discussion

Weighted and Attentive Memory Channels (WAMCS) is a machine-learning approach to predicting cryptocurrency price fluctuations and daily closes. Channel-wise Weighting is composed of an Attentive Memory module, a Pooling & Convolution module, and a Channel-wise Memory Channel. As part of enhancing the ability to model complicated dynamics, such as those seen on the bitcoin market, independently, adaptive memory establishment, channel-wise recalibrating, convolution and pooling processes are being utilized. The historical price data of four major cryptocurrencies have been used extensively in testing. As for price regression, the experiments found the model to be more accurate and less error-prone than other commonly used methods when compared to others.

11.7 Blockchain Technology and Cryptocurrencies for the Collaborative Economy

11.7.1 Introduction

This part examines how machine learning algorithms and the Weighted and Attentive Memory Channels model can be used to forecast daily close prices and fluctuations of cryptocurrencies. Weighted & Attentive Memory models include channel-wise weighting, convolution, and pooling. In the example of bitcoin markets, all of these processes are involved in increasing the ability to capture the complexity of market movements like those observed in these markets, including attentive memory establishment and channel-wise recalibrating. Four major cryptocurrencies have been used to conduct a large number of experiments. In the experiments, the price regression model was more accurate and less prone to error than the other methods for predicting price movements.

In Despite its near-vernacular status, CE is an economic model whose size and scope have increased dramatically with time. Exchanges between peers, between organizations, and between organizations and peers have all increased as a result [90]. Blockchain technology has also been developed due to tremendous advances in computer science and mathematics [91]. As a result of this technology, true peer-to-peer trading has increased with minimal middlemen involved.

Studies about the interdependence between blockchain technology and the CE are few and far between in terms of technological advances and the facilitation of peer-to-peer exchanges. Since the literature on this subject is relatively scarce, the purpose of this article is to review the research on the topic to better understand how blockchain technology is contributing to the development of collaborative practices.

It is the purpose of this research to gain an initial understanding of the occurrences that may not be well known, using an exploratory descriptive approach. In addition to serving as a basis for new ideas and hypotheses, the design enables the development of new perspectives. Since CE technology and blockchain technology are still in their nascent stages of research, this article intends to compile some of the most recent evidence on the use of blockchain technology in collaborative activities to better understand its effect. Technology such as this could stimulate CE growth by decentralizing transactions and exchanging value. Thus, blockchain technology could facilitate the diffusion of this new socioeconomic model, reshaping actors, systems, and roles.

11.7.2   Collaborative Economy and Digital Platforms

Various terms for the sharing economy include collaborative consumption, on-demand economy, on-demand services, group economy, independent economy, peer economy, gig economy, and platform economy [92]. A new socio-economic model is best described using the term "collaborative economy" in this study [93]. The fact that it can accommodate both redistribution and mutualization makes it popular also [94]. Redistribution refers to trades that require ownership transfer, whereas mutualization is access to resources without ownership transfer [95]. CE enables mutualization via new traffic systems that involve peers and Internet connections, as stated by Ertz *et al.* (2019b) [94]. Consumers who participate in CEs become suppliers and service providers, changing the structure of the market exchange, and they also change their role as consumers. The CE involves not only monetary transactions, but also the sale, exchange, and donation of goods [96]. "Means of exchanging resources between consumers that can allow them to exchange resources or services directly or via a mediator, temporarily or permanently," Ertz *et al.* (2016) [97] simplify these two aspects by defining collaborative consumption within the CE as: "The exchange of temporary or permanent resources or services between two consumers or a mediator (both direct and indirect)," This mediator could have a variety of levels of mediation experience, ranging from facilitating interactions to coordinating all aspects of these encounters. Organizations, offline channels, and multi-channel systems are the most common platforms for the implementation of these activities.

Therefore, CE [98] is essentially a peer-to-peer economic model. As a result of the CE's arrival, the retail and consumer service industries have been affected severely. There is evidence of this in many sectors, including food, lodging, transportation, and access to goods and services [99]. CE does indeed involve networks of connected individuals and communities instead of relying on centralized institutions to change how people produce, consume, finance, and learn. Collaboration in production, collaboration in education, collaboration in finance, and collaboration in consumption are the four major divisions of CE [100]. Researchers define CE as a practice other than traditional trade, such as trading, renting, pooling, or sharing.

11.7.3 Emergence of Collaborative Consumption

Massive interaction has become possible thanks to collaboration platforms. Three parties are identified by Hawlitschek, Notheisen, and Teubner [101] as being involved in these transactions:

A User seeking to acquire, use, or acquire the product or service through a variety of means (for instance, a tenant or a passenger). Supplier (for instance, a host on Airbnb, or a Turo or Uber driver) who offers a private service or resource that is often underutilized and underused, and offers it for sale, donation, swapping, or rental.

11.7.3.1 Promoting the Diffusion of Collaborative Practices

Due to technology advancements that enable peer-to-peer communication, collaborative activities are becoming more widespread. Collaboration practices and peer-to-peer sharing activities existed before digital platforms, but technical advances have played an important role in the development of CE. Some examples of technological advancements that contributed to the development of CE include online payment methods, social networking sites, and georeferenced sites. The blockchain can pave the way for huge, largely unexplored developments in CE, much like the potential of information and communication technologies earlier. As a result, Baller, Dutta, and Lanvin note that blockchain enables individuals to monetize their resources securely while creating distributed and sharing economy applications [102].

11.7.4 Summary

Blockchain technology has enhanced new forms of consumption and market processes, which have expanded its scope beyond digital currency. It seems premature to conclude that blockchain technology will lead to accelerated CE development based on the information provided. It appears that technology is having a significant impact on collaborative practices and the ecosystem that supports them in numerous ways. Digital platform users are able to create value directly with each other without a middleman using blockchain technology. Additionally, the blockchain can prevent the development of quasi-monopolistic and predatory organizations as well as guarantee the safety of transactions and ensure the solvency of all parties involved.

11.8 Conclusions

Recently, computer science, cryptocurrency, and the technologies that support them have been considered important achievements. The fields began as a hobby for scholars, but have grown into a full-fledged area with fresh and exciting potential in adjacent fields. Traditional methods of processing electronic financial transactions are problematic, but these systems offer an innovative solution. On the other hand, they also pose security risks and complications.

References

1. Nakamoto, S., 2008. Re: Bitcoin P2P e-cash paper. The Cryptography Mailing List.
2. Vidal, T.A.d.C., 2020. How exchange platform attacks impact the cryptocurrency and traditional markets Ph.D. thesis.
3. Lohachab, A., 2021. A perspective on using blockchain for ensuring security in smart card systems. In: Research Anthology on Blockchain Technology in Business, Healthcare, Education, and Government. IGI Global, pp. 529–558.
4. Gupta, B.B., Quamara, M., 2019. Smart Card Security: Applications, Attacks, and Countermeasures. CRC Press.
5. Zhang, R., Preneel, B., 2019. Lay down the common metrics: evaluating proof-of–work consensus protocols' security. In: 2019 IEEE Symposium on Security and Privacy (SP). IEEE, pp. 175–192.
6. Chen, H., Pendleton, M., Njilla, L., Xu, S., 2020. A survey on ethereum systems security: vulnerabilities, attacks, and defenses. ACM Comput. Surv. (CSUR) 53 (3), 1–43.
7. Dwork, C., Naor, M., 1992. Pricing via processing or combatting junk mail. In: Annual International Cryptology Conference. Springer, pp. 139–147.
8. Nakamoto, S., 2008. Re: Bitcoin P2P e-cash Paper. The Cryptography Mailing List.
9. Sidharth Quamara*, Awadhesh Kumar Singh, "A systematic survey on security concerns in cryptocurrencies: State-of-the-art and perspectives", Computers & Security 113 (2022) 102548.
10. Feng, W.C., Kaiser, E., 2011. System and Methods of Determining Computational Puzzle Difficulty for Challenge-Response Authentication. US Patent App. 13/050,123.
11. Back A.. Hashcash-amortizable publicly auditable cost-functions. Available http:// www.hashcash.org/papers/amortizable.pdf 2002.

12. Lohachab, A., 2021. A perspective on using blockchain for ensuring security in smart card systems. In: Research Anthology on Blockchain Technology in Business, Healthcare, Education, and Government. IGI Global, pp. 529–558.

13. Arsov, D., *et al.*, 2017. Periodic Table of Cryptocurrencies: Blockchain Categorization. Available at SSRN 3095169.

14. Statista, 2020. https://www.statista.com/capitalization/. Accessed: September 2020.

15. Fisch, C., 2019. Initial coin offerings (ICOs) to finance new ventures. J. Bus. Venturing 34 (1), 1–22.

16. Fenu, G., Marchesi, L., Marchesi, M., Tonelli, R., 2018. The ICO phenomenon and its relationships with Ethereum smart contract environment. In: 2018 International Workshop on Blockchain Oriented Software Engineering (IWBOSE). IEEE, pp. 26–32.

17. Panin, A., Kemell, K.K., Hara, V., 2019. Initial coin offering (ICO) as a fundraising strategy: a multiple case study on success factors. In: International Conference on Software Business. Springer, pp. 237–251.

18. Kaal, W.A., Dell'Erba, M., 2017. Initial Coin Offerings: Emer ging Practices, Risk Factors, and Red Flags. Verlag CH Beck (2018), 17-18.

19. Panin, A., Kemell, K.K., Hara, V., 2019. Initial coin offering (ICO) as a fundraising strategy: a multiple case study on success factors. In: International Conference on Software Business. Springer, pp. 237–251.

20. Peronja, I., Lenac, K., Glavinović, R., 2020. Blockchain technology in maritime industry. Pomorstvo 34 (1), 178–184.

21. Gohwong, S.G., 2018a. The state of the art of cryptocurrencies. Asian Adm. Manage. Rev. 1 (2).

22. Ante L., Meyer A.. Cross-listings of blockchain-based tokens issued through initial coin offerings: do liquidity and specific cryptocurrency exchanges matter? 2020.

23. Somin, S., Gordon, G., Altshuler, Y., 2018. Network analysis of ERC20 tokens trading on Ethereum blockchain. In: International Conference on Complex Systems. Springer, pp. 439–450.

24. Abraham, L., Guegan, D., 2019. The Other Side of the Coin: Risks of the Libra Blockchain. University Ca'Foscari of Venice, Dept of Economics Research Paper Series No 30.

25. Gupta, B.B., Quamara, M., 2018. A dynamic security policies generation model for access control in smart card based applications. In: International Symposium on Cyberspace Safety and Security. Springer, pp. 132–143.

26. Chen, Y.P., Ko, J.C., 2019. CryptoAR wallet: a blockchain cryptocurrency wallet application that uses augmented reality for on-chain user data display. In: Proceedings of the 21st International Conference on Human-Computer Interaction with Mobile Devices and Services, pp. 1–5.

27. Karamitsos, I., Papadaki, M., Al Barghuthi, N.B., 2018. Design of the blockchain smart contract: a use case for real estate. J. Inf. Secur. 9 (3), 177–190.

28. Swissborg. https://www.swissborg.com/ Accessed: June 2020; 2020.
29. R. Houben, A. Snyers, Cryptocurrencies and Blockchain: Legal Context and Implications for Financial Crime, Money Laundering and Tax Evasion, Policy Department for Economic, Scientific and Quality of Life Policies - European Parliamnt, 2018.
30. A. Wunsche, Technological Disruption of Capital Markets and Reporting? an Introduction to Blockchain, Chartered Professional Accountants Canada, Canada, 2016.
31. M.S. Cunningham, The Major Dimensions of Perceived Risk. Risk Taking Information Handling in Consumer Behavior, i.h.i.c. behavior, 1967.
32. V. Venkatesh, H. Bala, Technology acceptance model 3 and a research agenda on interventions, Decis. Sci. J. 39 (2) (2008) 273–315.
33. J.S. Jasperson, P.E. Carter, R.W. Zmud, A comprehensive conceptualization of postadoptive behaviors associated with information technology enabled work systems, MIS Q. 29 (3) (2005) 525–557.
34. L.G. Tornatzky, M. Fleischer, A. Chakrabarti, The processes of technological innovation 10, Lexington Books, 1990, p. 2013. Issues in organization and management series.
35. S.A. Salloum, et al., Exploring students' acceptance of E-learning through the development of a comprehensive technology acceptance model, IEEE Access 7 (2019) 128445–128462.
36. D.L. Goodhue, R.L. Thompson, Task-technology fit and individual performance, MIS Q. (1995) 213–236.
37. T. Aste, P. Tasca, T. Di Matteo, Blockchain technologies: the foreseeable impact on society and industry, Computer 50 (9) (2017) 18–28.
38. C. Martins, T. Oliveira, A. Popovic, Understanding the Internet banking adoption: a unified theory of acceptance and use of technology and perceived risk application, Int. J. Inf. Manag. 34 (1) (2014) 1–13.
39. F.D. Davis, R.P. Bagozzi, P.R. Warshaw, User acceptance of computer technology: a comparison of two theoretical models, Manag. Sci. 35 (8) (1989 - Aug) 982–1003.
40. F.D. Davis, A Technology Acceptance Model for Empirically Testing New End-User Information Systems: Theory and Results, Massachusetts Institute of Technology, 1985.
41. D.W. McCloskey, The importance of ease of use, usefulness, and trust to online consumers: an examination of the technology acceptance model with older customers, J. Organ. End User Comput. 18 (3) (2006) 47–65.
42. S.L. Jarvenpaa, et al., Consumer trust in an Internet store, Inf. Technol. Manag. Sci. 1 (1–2) (2000) 45–71.
43. E.D. Matemba, G. Li, Consumers' willingness to adopt and use WeChat wallet: an empirical study in South Africa, Technol. Soc. 53 (2018) 55–68.
44. G. Fortino, et al., Using blockchain for reputation-based cooperation in federated IoT domains, in: International Symposium on Intelligent and Distributed Computing, Springer, 2019.

45. P.G. Keen, Are you ready for thetrust'economy? Computerworld 31 (16) (1997), 80-80.
46. A. Kesharwani, S. Singh Bisht, The impact of trust and perceived risk on internet banking adoption in India: an extension of technology acceptance model, Int. J. Bank Market. 30 (4) (2012) 303–322.
47. D.H. McKnight, V. Choudhury, C. Kacmar, Developing and validating trust measures for e-commerce: an integrative typology, Inf. Syst. Res. 13 (3) (2002) 334–359.
48. P. Ratnasingham, The importance of trust in electronic commerce, Internet Res. 8 (4) (1998) 313–321.
49. R.C. Mayer, J.H. Davis, F.D. Schoorman, An integrative model of organizational trust, Acad. Manag. Rev. 20 (3) (1995) 709–734.
50. J.R. Eiser, S. Miles, L.J. Frewer, Trust, perceived risk, and attitudes toward food technologies 1, J. Appl. Soc. Psychol. 32 (11) (2002) 2423–2433.
51. A. Kesharwani, S. Singh Bisht, The impact of trust and perceived risk on internet banking adoption in India: an extension of technology acceptance model, Int. J. Bank Market. 30 (4) (2012) 303–322.
52. G. Fortino, et al., A reputation capital and blockchain-based model to support group formation processes in the internet of things, in: 2019 6th International Conference on Control, Decision and Information Technologies (CoDIT), IEEE, 2019.
53. S. Demirkan, I. Demirkan, A. McKee, Blockchain technology in the future of business cyber security and accounting, J. Manag. Analy. (2020) 1–20.
54. New York Codes, R.A.R., Regulations of the Superintendent of Financial Services Part 200. Virtual Currencies, New York State Department Of Financial Services, 2015. 55. 55.
55. G . Peters, E. Panayi, A. Chapelle, Trends in cryptocurrencies and blockchain technologies: a monetary theory and regulation perspective, J. Finan. Perspect. (2015).
56. O.E. Williamson, Organizational Innovation: the Transaction Cost Approach, University of Pennsylvania, Center for the Study of Organizational Innovation, 1980.
57. W. Viriyasitavat, D. Hoonsopon, Blockchain characteristics and consensus in modern business processes, J. Ind. Inf. Integr. 13 (2019) 32–39.
58. G. Hackbarth, et al., Computer playfulness and anxiety: positive and negative mediators of the system experience effect on perceived ease of use, Inf. Manag. Sci. 40 (3) (2003) 221–232.
59. C.-L. Hsu, H.-P. Lu, management, Why do people play on-line games? An extended TAM with social influences and flow experience, Inf. Manag. 41 (7) (2004) 853–868.
60. W. Chaouali, I.B. Yahia, N. Souiden, The interplay of counter-conformity motivation, social influence, and trust in customers' intention to adopt Internet banking services: the case of an emerging country, J. Retailing Consum. Serv. 28 (2016) 209–218.

61. A.A. Alalwan, *et al.*, Examining adoption of mobile internet in Saudi Arabia: extending TAM with perceived enjoyment, innovativeness and trust, Technol. Soc. 55 (2018) 100–110.

62. F. Kanwal, M. Rehman, Factors affecting e-learning adoption in developing countries–empirical evidence from Pakistan's higher education sector, IEEE Access 5 (2017) 10968–10978.

63. R.H. Fazio, M.P. Zanna, Attitudinal qualities relating to the strength of the attitudebehavior relationship, J. Exp. Soc. Psychol. 14 (4) (1978) 398–408.

64. G.S. Howard, A.L. Mendelow, Discretionary use of computers: an empirically derived explanatory model, Decis. Sci. J. 22 (2) (1991) 241–265.

65. W.M. Alenazy, W.M. Al-Rahmi, M.S. Khan, Validation of TAM Model on Social Media Use for Collaborative Learning to Enhance Collaborative Authoring, IEEE Access, 2019.

66. J. Fulk, Y. Connie Yuan, Social construction of communication technology, Int. Encycl. Org. Commun. (2017) 1–19.

67. J. Fulk, J. Schmitz, D. Ryu, Cognitive elements in the social construction of communication technology, Manag. Commun. Q. 8 (3) (1995) 259–288.

68. T. Zhou, Y. Lu, B. Wang, The relative importance of website design quality and service quality in determining consumers' online repurchase behavior, Inf. Syst. Manag. 26 (4) (2009) 327–337.

69. W.H. DeLone, E.R. McLean, Information systems success: the quest for the dependent variable, Inf. Syst. Res. 3 (1) (1992) 60–95.

70. N. Satoshi, A peer-to-peer electronic cash system, Bitcoin (2008).

71. S. Barber, X. Boyen, E. Shi, E. Uzun, Bitter to better - how to make bitcoin a better currency, in: A.D. Keromytis (Ed.), Financial Cryptography and Data Security. F.C. 2012. Lecture Notes in Computer Science, Vol. 7397, Springer, Berlin, Heidelberg, 2012.

72. S. Kim, A novel bitcoin mining scheme based on the multi-leader multi-follower Stackelberg game model, IEEE Access 6 (2018) 48902–48912.

73. A.T. Haghighat, M. Shajari, Block withholding game among bitcoin mining pools, Futur. Gener. Comput. Syst. 97 (2019) 482–491.

74. D. Easley, M. O'Hara, S. Basu, From mining to markets: the evolution of bitcoin transaction fees, J. Financ. Econ. 134 (1) (2019) 91–109.

75. Balcilar, M., Bouri, E., Gupta, R., & Roubaud, D. (2017). Can volume predict bitcoin returns and volatility? a quantiles-based approach. Economic Modelling, 64, 74–81.

76. Nakamoto, S. (2019). Bitcoin: A peer-to-peer electronic cash system. Technical Report Manubot.

77. Mukhopadhyay, U., Skjellum, A., Hambolu, O., Oakley, J., Yu, L., & Brooks, R. (2016). A brief survey of cryptocurrency systems. In 2016 14th annual conference on privacy, security and trust (PST) (pp. 745–752). IEEE.

78. Kristjanpoller, W., & Minutolo, M. C. (2018). A hybrid volatility forecasting framework integrating garch, artificial neural network, technical analysis and principal components analysis. Expert Systems with Applications, 109, 1–11.

79. Chuen, D. L. K., Guo, L., & Wang, Y. (2017). Cryptocurrency: A new investment opportunity? The Journal of Alternative Investments, 20, 16–40.
80. Tiwari, A. K., Kumar, S., & Pathak, R. (2019). Modelling the dynamics of bitcoin and litecoin: Garch versus stochastic volatility models. Applied Economics, 51, 4073–4082.
81. Chu, J., Chan, S., Nadarajah, S., & Osterrieder, J. (2017). Garch modelling of cryptocurrencies. Journal of Risk and Financial Management, 10, 17.
82. Peng, Y., Albuquerque, P. H. M., Camboim de Sa, ′ J. M., Padula, A. J. A., & Montenegro, M. R. (2018). The best of two worlds: Forecasting high frequency volatility for cryptocurrencies and traditional currencies with support vector regression. Expert Systems with Applications, 97, 177–192.
83. Matta, M., Lunesu, I., & Marchesi, M. (2015). Bitcoin spread prediction using social and web search media. In: UMAP workshops (pp. 1–10).
84. Lahmiri, S., & Bekiros, S. (2019). Cryptocurrency forecasting with deep learning chaotic neural networks. Chaos, Solitons & Fractals, 118, 35–40.
85. Dutta, A., Kumar, S., & Basu, M. (2020). A gated recurrent unit approach to bitcoin price prediction. Journal of Risk and Financial Management, 13, 23.
86. Luo, Z., Cai, X., Tanaka, K., Takiguchi, T., Kinkyo, T., & Hamori, S. (2019). Can we forecast daily oil futures prices? Experimental evidence from convolutional neural networks. Journal of Tisk and Financial Management, 12, 9.
87. Liang, Y., Ke, S., Zhang, J., Yi, X., & Zheng, Y. (2018). Geoman: Multi-level attention networks for geo-sensory time series prediction. In IJCAI (pp. 3428–3434).
88. Ertz, M., Hallegatte, D., & Bousquet, J. (2019a). La reconfiguration de l'échange marchand. Tour d'horizon, enjeux et perspectives (pp. 113e131). Quebec, Canada: Les Presses de l'Universite du Qu ebec.
89. Roos, D., & Hahn, R. (2019). Understanding collaborative consumption: An extension of the theory of planned behavior with value-based personal norms. Journal of Business Ethics, 158.
90. Ertz, M., Durif, F., & Arcand, M. (2016). Collaborative consumption: Conceptual snapshot at a buzzword. Journal of Entrepreneurship Education, 19(2), 1-23.
91. Ghilal, A., & Nach, H. (2019). La technologie de la chaîne de blocs: Fondements et applications. In M. Ertz, D. Hallegatte, & J. Bousquet (Eds.), La reconfiguration de l'echange marchand. Tour d'horizon, enjeux et perspectives (pp. 113-131).
92. Botsman, R. (2015). Defining the sharing economy: What is collaborative consumption-and what isn't. Fast company. Retrieved from https://www.fastcompany.com/3046119/defining-the-sharing-economy-what-is-collaborative-consumption-and-what-isnt.
93. Tussyadiah, I. P., & Pesonen, J. (2018). Drivers and barriers of peer-to-peer accommodation stayean exploratory study with American and Finnish travellers. Current Issues in Tourism, 21(6), 703-720.

94. Ertz, M., Durif, F., & Arcand, M. (2019b). A conceptual perspective on collaborative consumption. Academy of Marketing Science Review, 9, 27e41. https://doi. org/10.1007/s13162-018-0121-3.
95. Acquier, A., Daudigeos, T., & Pinkse, J. (2017). Promises and paradoxes of the sharing economy: An organizing framework. Technological Forecasting and Social Change, 125, 1-10.
96. Botsman, R., & Rogers, R. (2010). What's mine is yours. New York, USA: Penguin Press.
97. Ertz, M., Durif, F., & Arcand, M. (2016). Collaborative consumption: Conceptual snapshot at a buzzword. Journal of Entrepreneurship Education, 19(2), 1-23.
98. Belk, R. (2014). You are what you can access: Sharing and collaborative consumption online. Journal of Business Research, 67(8), 1595-1600.
99. Correa, J. C., Garzon, W., Brooker, P., Sakarkar, G., Carranza, S. A., Yunado, L., et al. (2019). Evaluation of collaborative consumption of food delivery services through web mining techniques. Journal of Retailing and Consumer Services, 46, 45-50.
100. Botsman, R. (2013). The sharing economy lacks A shared definition. Fast Company. Retrieved from http://www.fastcoexist.com/3022028/the-sharingeconomy-lacksa-shared-definition.
101. Hawlitschek, F., Notheisen, B., & Teubner, T. (2018). The limits of trust-free systems: A literature review on blockchain technology and trust in the sharing economy. Electronic Commerce Research and Applications, 29, 50-63.
102. Baller, S., Dutta, S., & Lanvin, B. (2016). Global information technology report 2016. Geneva, Suisse: Ouranos.

12

A Study on the Influence of Personality on Savings and Investment in Cryptos

K. Manimekalai[1]*, T. Satheeshkumar[2] and G. Manokaran[3]

[1]Department of Computer Applications, Sri GVG Visalakshi College for Women, Udumalpet, Tamil Nadu, India
[2]Department of Management Studies, Dr. N.G.P. Institute of Technology, Kalapatti, Coimbatore, Tamil Nadu, India
[3]School of Management, Sree Saraswathi Thyagaraja College, Pollachi, Tamil Nadu, India

Abstract

Crypto currency is a digital currency that can be usedin the same waylike traditional currencyas a second hand. It uses encryption to secure its transactions, control the growth of a single form of coin, and track every transaction across the whole network. A survey of 434 Indian investors was conducted. In addition to socio-demographic characteristics study related to the human populations gender, income, age, and education, financial behavior (savings, investment) were collected and analyzed. The purpose to invest in crypto currencies is impervious by socio-demographic characteristics or financial literacy. This study looks into the impact of behavioral and socio-demographic characteristics on investors' intentions to invest in crypto currencies. This article creates an attempt to scan the impact of investors' personalities on their investment behaviour. Financial advisors would benefit from studying the elements that control the behaviour of investors belonging to an assortment of personality groups in order to edify individual investors found on their personality type and create investor programs for them.

Keywords: Cryptocurrency, investment, multi dimesnional scaling, personality, saving

Corresponding author: gvgmanimekalai@gmail.com

Mohd Naved, V. Ajantha Devi, and Aditya Kumar Gupta (eds.) Fintech and Cryptocurrency, (251–276)
© 2023 Scrivener Publishing LLC

12.1 Introduction

Investment decision is the accountability of individuals and how much capital is invest in the search of making profit. With the passage of time Investment decision making changes in terms of variegations and trading frequencies (He, Liao, Bi & Guo, 2019). For investment decisions, an efficient decision-making method is crucial. Matured and veteran investors prefer high assortment, hold low risk portfolios, trade less repetitively and this investment skill becomes inadequate at an age of 70 (Sadi & et al., 2011). The steadiness of investment choice is based on efficient investment return strategy development (Rutkauskas & Stasytyte, 2008). Investors need to know the shared distributions that show possible grades of their investment decisions, since they don't know the final outcome of their investment decisions (Zhou & Xu, 2020).

Money is something that every living human being on this planet values highly, and its history stretches back to ancient times when gold, silver, and other metal coins were used to purchase products and other necessities. Before the commencement of the monetary system, the Barter System was the prime mode of commerce, with people exchanging items for other commodities that met their specific needs or requirements. Gradually, the barter system gave way to the monetary system, and many currencies emerged, which were adopted by a choice of governments around the world. Paper Money replaced metal coins as the primary medium of exchange because it was cushy to transport from one location to another and the availability of great denominations in printed paper form aided major firms in carrying out large transactions.

Cash transactions had vanished by the mid-twentieth century. At that time, the invention of plastic money, that solved security issues for instance larceny or theft of large amount of money. Rather than keeping significant quantities of cash on hand, people found it easier to carry a plastic card readily available to use for multiple purchases.

Later on, through the advancement of technology and the origination of the Internet, Internet banking was born, and with the improvement of mobile phone technology, can now effortlessly access services such as mobile banking or mobile payment gateways, where all transactions can be all the way through with just one click on our phone. We no longer need to carry anything other than a smart phone; the rest will be taken care of by superior technology. Till now, there is a need for explicit amount of cash printed or imprint by the government, which would be held in reserve in a bank through which we would conduct all of our transactions, which is a centralized system. However, we have upgraded one step further, and a decentralizedtype of currency known as Crypto currency has emerged, which is like wised used in transactions for various purposes.

Crypto currencybeing a digital currencyis designed for a regular use as a normal currency in transactions. It makes use of cryptography and block-chain technology to defend its exchanges, edgeup the development of a specific type of coin, and to track all transactions across the entire network.

Today's financial services industry is exceedingly diversified, endowed with the investors diverse choice of investment options. Investors can develop their own capital by means of appropriate investment methods and financial planning that determine to increase the economic growth. Economic growth is one of the most fundamental variables determining people's value of life in a country. Income, Savings, and Investment are three variables that facilitate and measure an economy's growth.

Personality refers to a person's dynamic and organized set of characteristics that determine his cognitions, motives, and acts in a variety of situations. Their activities are heavily influenced by their personality. The investor's decision was impacted by the individual's personality.

Since domestic saving rates are inversely correlated with investment rates and the banking system's ability to lend money, they are a key indicator of economic development in any nation. Despite having more money, people lack the knowledge on where, when, and how to invest it.

Investors have cognitive and emotional flaws that cause them to make poor financial decisions. Behavioral finance academics have demonstrated scientifically over the last few years that investors do not always act logically. They have behavioral biases that cause them to make systematic errors while processing information for financial decisions. Age, income, education, and marital status, according to empirical research, all influence an individual's investment decision.

12.2   Literature Review

Personality is a feelings, thoughts, behaviours and motives to every individuals and determined how individuals recognize and react to the environment (Gillen & Kim, 2014). Ahmed (2020) defines about the personality qualitiesof an individual as a combination of cognitive, perceptual, distinguishing emotional and motivational characteristics. The above mentioned personality traits will have an effect on the decision making of every investors agreeing to the circumstances. With the actualization about behavioural finance, that has end up honestly axiomatic to that amount an investor's strengthen adapt is abundantly bend with the aid of his personality (Bapat, 2020). Durand, Newby and Sanghani (2008), Durand, Newby, Peggs and Siekierka (2010), acknowledged that there is a close relationship between the personality, investment choices, and outcomes (investment performance). Jalal, Zeb, and Fayyaz, (2019) recommend that the personality traits are unruffledwith five principles, namely, replicability, comprehensiveness, external correlates, source traits and multiple levels. The five principles afterwardswere coined as Big-Five factors or Five-Factor Model (FFM). The FFM orchestrate personality traits into Extraversion (E), Conscientiousness (C), Agreeableness (A), Neuroticism (N) and Openness to experience (O) (Ahmad, 2020). It has been experiential that thinking and behavioural pattern of individuals determined the individuals personality (Allport, 1961). According to researchers the financial literacy influence the potential investor's decision. Most often, financial literacy is seen as a specialised sort of consumer expertise on how to successfully manage one's financial affairs or as a type of human capital specifically related to personal finances. To disclose why people act the way they do, the Big Five personality theory offers a clear foundation for understanding others and fostering connections.

Outspokenness to new experiences, conscientiousness, extroversion, agreeableness, and neuroticism are considered as every bit of characteristics of the OCEAN.

12.2.1 Openness to Experience

The inclination to explore new things is referred to as openness to experience. Openness speaks about general curiosity, an interest and appreciation to new experiences, emotions, art, adventures and new ideas (McCrae, Costa & Martin, 2005). Folkswho score high on openness have a sturdy imagination and are stretchy in their behaviour. In investors, openness also relates to perilousactions or gambling. Investment-Specific Result: Openness was found to be connected to the gathering of information as it is related to natural curiosity and the interest in creating new experiences (Costa & McCrae, 1992).

Openness, as well as emotional stability are also linked to high risk acceptance in successful professional traders (Fenton-O'Creevy, Nicholson, Soane, & Willman, 2011) and to long-term investing (Mayfield, Perdue, & Wooten, 2008). Kleine, Peschke and Wagner (2019) foundout that individuals who invest in collectibles, another non-traditional investment, scored higher on openness than a control group. A person with a high level of openness has a stunning imagination, enjoys variety, and is eager to learn novel things. A person with a low level of openness has a preference routine and stays in their comfort zone.

This characteristic possesses qualities like insight and originality. Those who excel at this quality also have a extensive range of interests. They are willing to learn new things and fix in novel activities because they are inquisitive about the world and other people. A high level of this personality valuebuilds a person more creative and risk-taking. Low scorers on this trait are more conventional and may have trouble thinking abstractly.

Those of this nature are adaptable and have aninclination for novel ideas and ideals. They are amenable to new ethnic, political, and social ideas. Simplicity is preferred above ambiguity by them. They are inquisitive, imaginative, and unique. They are more liable to have the same opinion with statements such as "I am quick to understand things," "I have a vivid imagination," and "I have wonderful ideas," among others (Pan and Statman, 2013). For the reason that of their high levels of confidence, these investors have a propensity to buy and sell stocks. In the Lahore market, (Zaidi and Tauni et al., 2012) discovered no association between overconfidence bias and openness.

Bashir et al. (2013) discovered that openness had a considerable positive connection with herding, implication that investors with this quality will seek fresh investing information and be more overconfident. Sadi et al. (2011) discovered a noteworthy positive association sandwiched between openness and hindsight bias, the same as openness and overconfidence. There was furthermore link between openness and the availability bias in the opposite direction. Jamshidinavid et al., (2012) revealed that openness had a considerable positive connection with overconfidence and herding. According to (Kowert and Hermann et al., 1997), the investor's openness attribute has a high association with risk taking.

Openness was found to be significantly connected to both accuracy and confidence by (Schaefer et al. 2004). The link amid openness and accuracy suggested that this variety of person is interested in learning from a variety of sources. Folks with this personality trait were more likely to employ in long-term investing, according to (Mayfield et al., 2008), although openness did not appear to predict short-term investing in the study. Investors with the openness attribute, on the other hand, are more possible to have short-term investing goals, according to (Akhtar and Batool, 2012). Large openness, (Nicholson et al. 2005), accordingly states thatitis associated with a stronger proclivity to take high risks.

12.2.2 Conscientiousness

Conscientiousness conveys a person's approach to completing a task. Conscientiousness illustrates the tendency to be orderly, responsible and dependable (John & Srivastava, 1999). Investment-Specific Result: Conscientiousness was found to be the most imperative personality trait for money management and self-control regarding financial behaviour. Donnelly *et al.* (2012) give you an idea about that conscientious individual have a more positive financial attitude and future orientation. A person with a high level of conscientiousness use up time planning ahead, complete jobs hurriedly, pays seal consideration to details, and have a preference to plan ahead to absolute work well. A person with a low level of thoroughness favours spontaneity superior than timetables and dislikes them. They have a first choice to be disorganized and impediment on crucial duties.

The major behaviour of this persona category is self-discipline, competence, order and dutifulness. Conscientious persons are responsible, trusted, stable, structured and reliable. Those with this character tend to agree with statements like, "I keep a schedule, I am always prepared, and I pay attention to details," and they are much organised (Pan and Statman, 2013). Investors with this personality variety are more likely to think their own investments are greater to those of their colleagues. Zaidi and Tauni (2012) establish that there was a positive affiliation stuck between superciliousness prejudice and conscientiousness, involve that the investors who were well thought-out, responsible, highly well-organized and dutiful succumb to overconfidence bias. Lin (2011) found that the trait conscientiousness had a positive relative with overconfidence and disposition effect implying that the investors with this trait cautiously sold the winning stocks in advance. Overconfidence and conscientiousness have a strong positive correlation, according to correlation studies. Sadi *et al.* (2011) found that there was a reverse correlation between conscientiousness and randomness favouritism in the stock market. Jamshidinavid *et al.* (2012) found that conscientiousness have a considerable positive relationship with disposition effect and overconfidence in the stock market, implying that these kinds of investors were cautious and According to Jamshidinavid *et al.* (2012), conscientiousness have a substantial positive link with self-importance in the stock market and disposition effect, indicating that these investors tended to be vigilant and certain and to base their verdict on their own financial knowledge.

Pan and Statman (2013) found that high risk tolerance interrelated to low levels of conscientiousness. Conscientiousness had a direct correlation with the tendency to regret. High inclination for maximization was positively interconnected with conscientiousness. Trust position low on conscientiousness. The tendency to quality success towards luck over skill was prominent amongst those with low conscientiousness. Conscientiousness did not appreciably forecast accuracy, confidence, or overconfidence, according to Schaefer *et al.* (2004). According to research by Durand, Newby, Tant, and Trepongkaruna (2013), these investors have a propensity to lower risk. According to Akhtar and Batool (2012), conscientious investors are more probable to have short-term investment goals.

This dimension is characterised by high levels of thoughts, well-built impulse control, and goal-directed behaviours. Highly thorough individuals are frequently well thought-out and detail-oriented. They plan to the lead, take into account how their behaviour affects other people, and keep track of deadlines.

12.2.3   Extroversion

The method a person pulls their energy and interacts with people is referred to as extroversion. Extraversion illustrates the tendency to be extrovert and sociable (John & Srivastava, 1999). High extraversion personality types might actively try to find out other people's attention. Investment-Specific Result: Extraversion was bringing into being to influence financial preferences as well as investment performance and choices (Durand *et al.*, 2013; Oehler & Wedlich, 2017). Mayfield, Perdue and Wooten (2008) found that extraversion is linked to short-term investing, while Durand *et al.* (2013) linked it to overconfidence. A person who is highly unreservedobtain motivated from socializing, have the benefit of initiating discussions, has a large numeral of friends, and discover it easy to get together new people. Those who are low on the companionability scale, on the other hand, have preferenceloneliness and are exhausted by extreme socializing. They also look down onundersized talk and find it sturdy to strike up a discussion with them.

Excitability, friendliness, loquaciousness, hostility, and high levels of excitingself-expression are all characteristics of extraversion (or extroversion). People with high extraversion tend to be extrovert and do well in societal situations. When they are around other people, they feel energised and happy. Low extraverts (or introverts) are less extroverted and are less extroverted in social circumstances. In order to "recharge" after participating in social events, introverts frequently need some time alone and in silence.

Extraversion also had a substantial optimisticassociation with superciliousness and herding, meaning that investors with this personality trait would be more to be expected to follow others' advice and stay on top of declining equities in the look forward to of a re-emerge. In Pakistan, (Bashir *et al.*, 2013) investigated the relationship between Big Five personality traits and behavioural biases such as disposition effect, overconfidence, and herding. Extraversion showed a strong positive influence on overconfidence, according to the SEM findings. The link between overconfidence and extraversion was also shown to be considerably favourable, according to the consequence of the correlation. Sadi *et al.*, (2011) examine the impact of personality factors on top of behavioural errors such as accessibility bias, randomness bias, escalation of commitment, hindsight bias, and overconfidence in Tehran investors. Extraversion and hindsight bias were found to have a substantial positive relationship, according to the findings.

12.2.4   Aggreeableness

Agreeableness refers to how a person interrelates with others and whether or not they have a proclivity intended for cooperation and compassion. Being agreeable exist viewed as having understanding and having faith in other people. A near to the ground score on agreeableness might show competitive behaviour or an untrustworthy individual. Agreeableness has been linked to risk distaste and has been linked to a lower probability of advance in higher risk investments, such as shares (Investment-Specific Result, Dohmen *et al.*, 2011). (Brown & Taylor, 2014). A person who is highly agreeable has empathy for others and enjoys assisting them. A person with a low level of this feature is unconcerned with other people's feelings and frequently disagrees.

Faith, munificence, responsiveness, affection, and other prosaically actions are included in this persona characteristic. High obligingness individuals are further cooperative, whereas near to the ground agreeableness individuals are more competitive and even calculating.

Individuals with this personality type are more likely to respect their peers and be honest in their interactions with others. According to (Sadi *et al.*, 2011), their major traits are modesty, directness, and trust. They are usually very adaptable to the desires of others. According to (Jamshidinavid *et al.*, 2012), investors with this mentality tend to follow peer recommendations, which can lead to herding tendencies. According to Zaidi and Tauni, (2012), there is a positive association sandwiched between overconfidence bias and agreeableness, meaning so as to those investors who are giving, ready to lend a hand, cooperative, nice, type, and conciliation are prone to overconfidence prejudice. Pan and Statman *et al.*, (2013) discovered with the intention of overconfidence and a high tendency for maximization were associated to agreeable nature indirectly. On the agreeableness scale, trust ranked high. Those with high agreeableness had a tendency to attribute success to chance rather than skill. According to (Schaefer *et al.*, 2004), agreeableness did not significantly forecast self-confidence, accurateness, or superciliousness. According to (Nicholson *et al.*, 2005), low agreeableness reduces apprehension about unfavourable decision outcomes.

12.2.5 Neuroticism

The capability to staysteady and balanced is referred in the direction of as neuroticism. Neuroticism is the affinity to experience negative sentiment and being hassled out easily. Those who have a high level of neuroticism are prone to apprehension and worry easily. Someone with a low altitude of neuroticism is emotionally safe and does not worry frequently. Low scores on neuroticism relay to a high control over the individual's emotions. Investment-Specific Result: Andreas Oehler, Wendt, Wedlich and Horn (2018) found that neuroticism in business student investors show the way to a less risky investment portfolio. Similarly, high neuroticism is correlated to being less able to deal with money compared to highly conscientious individuals (Donnelly, Iyer, & Howell, 2012). In addition, Gambetti and Giusberti (2012) found that anxiety which is related to neuroticism is negatively associated with stock trend predictability. Durand *et al.* (2013) can show in their study that neuroticism is linked to frequent trading, as investors are fewer anxious about their trading results.

Neuroticism manifests as sadness, irritability, and emotional instability. Mood swings, worry, irritability, and melancholy are frequent traits among those who rate this characteristic highly. More emotionally stable and resilient people are those that score poorly on this trait.

Impulsivity, depression, nervousness, and wrath are some of its key characteristics. Neuroticisms are self-centered as well as seek out greater objectives (Sadi *et al.*, 2011). This personality range is characterised by nervousness, anxiety, and emotional instability (Jamshidinavid *et al.*, 2012). (Zaidi and Tauni *et al.*, 2012) discovered a negative association between overconfidence bias and neuroticism, meaning that tense, worried, emotionally distressed, and sad Lahore investors were less self-confident than others. Lin (2011) discovered that neuroticism had a substantial optimistic relationship by means of herding and disposition effect.

Neuroticism had a physically powerful beneficial impact on herding in the stock market, according to SEM data (Bashir *et al.*, 2013), sensing that investors with this feature would advance based on peer recommendations.

The association analyses as well demonstrated that neuroticism and herding have a substantial positive association. Sadi *et al.* (2011) discovered a substantial positive link stuck between neuroticism and escalation of commitment, as well as between neuroticism and randomness bias. Jamshidinavid *et al.*, (2012) discovered with the purpose of neuroticism had a substantial positive association with disposition effect and herding. Individuals with this personality feature were found to keep away from short term investing (Mayfield *et al.*, 2008). Low neuroticism, according to (Nicholson *et al.*, 2005) prevented worry over poor choice outcomes.

12.3   Objectives of the Research

- Determine the extent to which people are aware of crypto currencies and how they think about it.
- To determine whether people are willing to invest in crypto currencies.
- To give the impression of being into the future of crypto currencies in India from the perspective of the common civilization.
- On the way to study the investment decision-making process and distinct personality qualities that influences an investor's attitude toward their investment portfolio.
- To determine the effect of investing goals on personality attributes.
- To determine how investing intentions affect behavioural characteristics.

12.4   Methodolgy

Data was collected from beginning to end a structured questionnaire to answer the various objectives framed for the study. The big five inventory questionnaire was used to analyse the individual characteristics of the investors. The data was collected through Google forms from about 434 respondents over a period of one month. The data collected were analysed using various tools in the SPSS software and their results are tabulated for Discussion.

Multi Dimensional Scaling (MDS) is a way of envisage the level of likeness of individual cases of a dataset. The pair wise "distances" between a set of n items or people are converted hooked on a configuration of n point that are mapped onto an abstract Cartesian space using MDS. More technically, MDS refers to a set of connected ordination techniques used in information visualization, in particular to put on view the information contained in a distance matrix.

The main function of Multi Dimensional Scaling (MDS) is to re-project the objects (sites) in reduced dimension ordination space. As previously mentioned, the lack of independence prevents the use of the axis scores in subsequent analyses. The main advantage of MDS over other ordination methods is that, in comparison to eigen-based ordinations, it typically represents the ordering connections between items within a given set of dimensions better. MDS creates a configuration of objects specifically for a specified number of additional axes, as opposed to eigen-based analyses, which rotate all of the original axes so that each axis optimises the variance retained by that axes. As a result, the configuration from an MDS is optimised for just two dimensions when a two-dimensional ordination is required, as opposed to the eigen-based object configurations, which are independent of the number of dimensions you plan to plot.

The data cloud is more intensely focussed and orientated and hence more "successful" in terms of being able to represent many variables by only a few new variables the stronger the links between the variables (species) are.

The "reduced data" can be employed in further statistical studies because the resulting principle components (axes) and scores (new variable values) are independent of one another. For instance, in a typical linear modelling technique, principle component 1 (as one measure of the community) could be regressed against an environmental variable (such as height or rainfall). Similar to this, several correlated predictor variables that would otherwise violate multi-collinearity could be boiled down to one or two orthogonal predictors for use in linear modelling. In order to use principle components analysis as either responses or predictors in linear modelling, this intermediary step is frequently used.

Analysis and Findings

Table 12.1 shows the awareness level on the various factors studied related to crypto currencies.

Table 12.1 reveals the awareness of the respondents is not significant, whereas drawing conclusion is very difficult. On the whole the respondents Awareness on hash graphs, block chains, and other technology that supports crypto currency and Awareness on the differentiation between the terms "proof of work" and "proof of stake" are slightly lower. Whereas the Awareness on its stand such as ethereum, NXT, Omni, and waves.

Table 12.1 Awareness level on the various factors studied related to crypto currencies.

Particulars	Very high	High	Neutral	Low	Very low
Awareness on hash graphs, block chains, and other technology that supports crypto currency	23	79	212	61	59
	5.3%	18.2%	48.8%	14.1%	13.6%
Awareness on the difference between the terms "proof of work" and "proof of stake"	21	86	173	113	41
	4.8%	19.8%	39.9%	26.1%	9.4%
Can recognize the difference between crypto coins and crypto tokens	37	103	157	92	45
	8.5%	23.2%	36.7%	21.2%	10.4%
Awareness on platforms such as ethereum, NXT, Omni, and waves	24	100	189	59	62
	5.5%	23.0%	42.5%	13.6%	14.3%
Awareness on crypto currencies operate in an open and independent network	53	115	155	76	35
	12.2%	26.5%	35.7%	17.5%	8.1%

Awareness on crypto currencies function in an open and independent set of connectionsis slightly higher.

Willingness to Invest In Crypto Currencies
Table 12.2 shows the attitude, transactions security and control, decentralization and perceived easiness of use of crypto currencies.

Table 12.2 clearly shows the respondents attitude towards transaction, security & control and perceived easiness of make use ofthe positive side. The respondents agree that they were able to transfer money worldwide money through crypto currency, Respondents agree crypto currency consent to to easily transact money, Respondents agree crypto currency permit to transfer money steadily, Respondents agree crypto currency allows to control his money, Respondents agree crypto currency decentralization enables, Respondents agree crypto currency allows to do transactions quicker, Respondents agree crypto currency do not have anagreement with any authority, Respondents agree crypto currency there is no central authority that has custody of their deposit, Respondents agree crypto currency is simple to use, Respondents agree inlearning how to use Crypto currency is simple for them, Respondents agree crypto currency effortlessly convert flat currency into Crypto currencies and vice versa, Further Respondents agree crypto currency is effortless for respondents to obtain and discover new tools.

Future of Crypto Currencies In India
Table 12.3 shows the future of crypto currencies in India through the attitude to use of crypto currencies.

Table 12.3 clearly shows that with the passing of time the future of crypto currencies will grow in India.

Objectives of Savings
To understand the objective of savings a Multidimensional scale tool was used in SPSS to plot the map in a two dimensional space. It is revealed in Figure 12.1.

The locations of the stimuli in the combined n-dimensional space are referred to as the "coordinates". **Here we can rename the Dimension 1 as hierarchy of needs and Dimension 2 as tenure of investment.** The above analysis clearly shows the mid set of the respondents is very traditional, where their objective of saving is for children's education and building a house. Whereas, the two dimensional spatial shows that saving for retirement and health is on the same horizon. Further, the figure reveals saving for long term is the least.

Table 12.2 Attitude, transactions security and control, decentralization and perceived ease of use of crypto currencies.

S. no	Particulars	Strongly agree	Agree	Neither agree nor disagree	Disagree	Strongly disagree
1.	I can instantly transfer money through crypto currency	42	122	176	39	55
		9.7%	28.1%	40.6%	9.0%	12.7%
2.	I can transfer money worldwide money through crypto currency	82	153	101	65	33
		18.9%	35.3%	23.3%	15.0%	7.6%
3.	Crypto currency allows me to easily transact money	71	117	155	55	36
		16.4%	27.0%	35.7%	12.7%	8.3%
4.	Crypto currency allows me to transfer money securely	31	128	181	41	53
		7.1%	29.5%	41.7%	9.4%	12.2%
5.	Crypto currency enables me to control my money	49	91	168	96	30
		11.3%	21.0%	38.7%	22.1%	6.9%
6.	Crypto currency decentralization enables me to do transactions faster	20	113	189	43	69
		4.6%	26.0%	43.5%	9.9%	15.9%

(Continued)

Table 12.2 Attitude, transactions security and control, decentralization and perceived ease of use of crypto currencies. (*Continued*)

S. no	Particulars	Strongly agree	Agree	Neither agree nor disagree	Disagree	Strongly disagree
7.	Crypto currency, I do not have to deal with any authority	30	146	137	99	22
		6.9%	33.6%	31.6%	22.8%	5.1%
8.	Crypto currency, there is no central authority that has custody of my deposit	47	129	163	67	28
		10.8%	29.7%	37.6%	15.4%	6.5%
9.	Crypto currency is easy to use	51	80	174	67	62
		11.8%	18.4%	40.1%	15.4%	14.3%
10.	Learning how to use Crypto currency is easy for me	34	127	138	103	32
		7.8%	29.3%	31.8%	23.7%	7.4%
11.	I can easily convert flat money into Crypto currencies and vice versa	33	96	181	92	32
		7.6%	22.1%	41.2%	21.2%	7.4%
12.	It is easy for me to get and learn new tools for Crypto currency	54	153	126	72	29
		12.4%	35.3%	29.0%	16.6%	6.7%

Table 12.3 Future of crypto currencies in India through the attitude to use of crypto currencies.

Usage behaviour	Often	All times	Sometimes	Rarely	Never
Frequency of use	55	13	119	125	122
	12.7%	3.0%	27.4%	28.8%	28.1%
Buy goods	57	17	80	158	122
	13.1%	3.9%	18.4%	36.4%	28.1%
International transfers	45	17	141	114	117
	10.4%	3.9%	32.5%	26.3%	27.0%

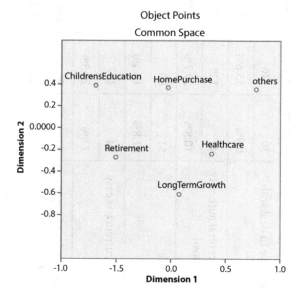

Figure 12.1 Objectives of savings.

Options of Savings

To understand the options for savings a Multidimensional scale tool was used in SPSS to plot the map in a two dimensional space. It is depicted in Figure 12.2.

The "coordinates" are the points in the combined n-dimensional space where the stimuli have been placed. **Here we can rename the Dimension 1 as Risk & Knowledge and Dimension 2 as traditional way of investing.**

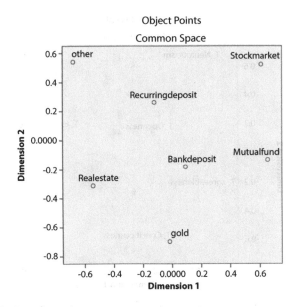

Figure 12.2 Options for savings.

The result of the plot derived as a result of the Multi-dimensional scaling reflects the mind-set of the respondent. This study reveals that the respondents are very traditional when it comes to the option of savings. The figure clearly shows that investment in gold is at the bottom of the figure in the y-axis where we have named it as traditional way of investing. Further the study reveals that respondent feel that investing in gold required less knowledge and the risk involved is also less.

Personality and Preference to invest
Figure 12.3 shows the Personality and Preference to invest.
The "coordinates" are the points in the combined n-dimensional space where the stimuli have been placed. **Here we can rename the Dimension 1 as Risk Taking Propensity and Dimension 2 as preference to invest.** The study reveals that respondents with high Neuroticism are willing to invest in crypto currencies, as the previous study reveals, individuals with neuroticism personality feature were found to avoid short term investing and prevented worry over poor choice outcomes. Whereas, respondents score on conscientiousness wasbring into being to be the most important personality trait for money management and self-control relating to financial behaviour.

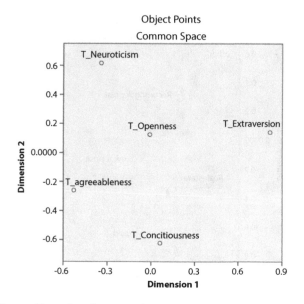

Figure 12.3 Personality and preference to invest.

12.5 Discussion

The study on the influence of personality on savings and investment in crypto currencies, revealed that the respondentsawareness is not significant, whereas drawing conclusion is very difficult. On the whole the respondents Awareness on hash graphs, block chains, and other technology that supports crypto currency and Awareness on the dissimilarity between the terms "proof of work" and "proof of stake" are slightly lower. Further, the Awareness on platforms for instance ethereum, NXT, Omni, and waves and awareness on crypto currencies function in an open and independent network are slightly higher.

On analysing the willingness to invest in crypto currencies the study revealed that respondents attitude towards transaction, security & control and perceived ease of use are on the positive side. The respondents agree that they were able to transfer money worldwide money through crypto currency, Respondents agree crypto currency allows to easily transact money, Respondents agree crypto currency agree to transfer money securely, Respondents agree crypto currency allows to control his money, Respondents agree crypto currency decentralization enables, Respondents agree crypto currency agree to do transactions faster Respondents agree crypto currency do not have to deal with any authority, Respondents agree crypto currency readily available is no central authority that has custody of their deposit, Respondents agree crypto currency is easy to use, Respondents agree Learning how to use Crypto currency is trouble-free for them, Respondents agree crypto currency effortlessly convert flat money into Crypto currencies and vice versa, Further Respondents agree crypto currency is easy for respondents to get hold of and learn new tools.

On analysing the future of crypto currencies in India through the attitude to use of crypto currencies with the maturity of the market and the awareness coping up and with the various regulations and willingness of the government to formalise crypto currencies usage will grow in India.

References

Ahmad, F. (2020). Personality traits as predictor of cognitive biases: moderating role of riskattitude. Qualitative Research in Financial Markets.

Akhtar, M. N., and Batool, I. (2012). Psychological factors, information asymmetry and investment decision making. Actual problems of economics, (130), 200–205.

AleksandrasVytautas RUTKAUSKAS and Viktorija STASYTYTĖ, (2008) stratification of stock profitabilities – the framework for investors' possibilities research in the market, INTELLECTUAL ECONOMICS, No. 1(3), p. 65–72

Allais, P. M. (1953). Le Comportment de l'HommeRationneldevant Le Risque: Critique des PostulatsetAxiomes. deL'EcoleAmericaine. Econometrica, 21, 503–546.

Allport, G.W. (1961). Pattern and growth in personality. New York: Holt, Rinehart & Wilson.

Altman, M. (2018). Implications of behavioural economics for financial literacy and public policy. The Journal of Socio-Economics, 41(5), 677-690.

Andreas Oehler & Stefan Wendt & Florian Wedlich & Matthias Horn. (2018). "Investors' Personality Influences Investment Decisions: Experimental Evidence on Extraversion and Neuroticism," Journal of Behavioral Finance, Taylor & Francis Journals, vol. 19(1), pages 30-48.

Asada, A., Basheerb, M. F., Irfanc, M., Jiangd, J., & Tahir, R. (2020). Open-Innovation and Knowledge Management in Small and Medium-Sized Enterprises (SMEs): The role of External Knowledge and Internal Innovation. Revista Argentina de ClínicaPsicológica, 29(4), 80-90.

Awais, M., Laber, M. F., Rasheed, N., & Khursheed, A. (2016). Impact of Financial Literacy and Investment Experience on Risk Tolerance and Investment Decisions: Empirical Evidence from Pakistan. International Journal of Economics and Financial Issues, 6(1), 73-79.

Ballantine, J., & Stray, S. (1998). Financial appraisal and the IS/IT investment decision making process. Journal of Information Technology, 13(1), 3-14.

Bapat, D. (2020). Antecedents to responsible financial management behavior among young adults: moderating role of financial risk tolerance. International Journal of Bank Marketing.

Barnewall, M. M. (1987). Psychological characteristics of the individual investor. ICFA Continuing Education Series, 1987(2), 62-71.

Barrick, M. R., and Mount, M. K. (1991). The big five personality dimensions and job performance: a meta-analysis. Personnel psychology, 44(1), 1-26.

Bashir, T., Azam, N., Butt, A. A., Javed, A., and Tanvir, A. (2013). Are Behavioral Biases Influenced by Demographic Characteristics and Personality Traits? Evidence from Pakistan. European Scientific Journal, 9(29), 277-293.

Blanchet-Scalliet, C., El Karoui, N., Jeanblanc, M., &Martellini, L. (2008). Optimal investment decisions when time-horizon is uncertain. Journal of Mathematical Economics, 44(11), 1100-1113.

Block, J. (1995). A contrarian view of the five-factor approach to personality description. Psychological bulletin, 117(2), 187.

Bongomin, G. O. C., Munene, J. C., Ntayi, J. M., & Malinga, C. A. (2018). Nexus between financial literacy and financial inclusion. International Journal of Bank Marketing.

Brown, S. J., Walker, K., Gannon, T. A., Keown, K. (2013). Developing a theory of empathy and cognitions in sex offenders. Journal of Sexual Aggression, 19(3), 275–294.

Camgoz, S. M., Karan, M. B., & Ergeneli, A. (2012). Relationship between the Big-Five personality and the financial performance of fund managers. Diversity, Conflict, and Leadership, 1(13), 137-152.

Charles, A., and Kasilingam, R. (2014a). Do Investors' Emotions Determine their Investment Personality?.Parikalpana: KIIT Journal of Management, 10(2).

Charles, A., and Kasilingam, R. (2014b). Do Framing Effects of Investors Determine their Investment Personality?.Anvesha, 7(2), 38-45

Conrad J. Kasperson, Franklin and Marshall College (1978), Scientific Creativity: A Relationship with Information Channels, Psychology of the Scientist, 42 (3) 691-694

Costa Jr, P. T., and McCrae, R. R. (1992). Neo personality inventory–revised (neo-pi-r) and neo five-factor inventory (neo-ffi) professional manual. Odessa, FL: Psychological Assessment Resources.

DeYoung, C. G. (2006). Higher-order factors of the Big Five in a multi-informant sample. Journal of personality and social psychology, 91(6), 1138.

DeYoung, C. G., Quilty, L. C., and Peterson, J. B. (2007). Between facets and domains: aspects of the Big Five. Journal of personality and social psychology, 93(5), 880

Digman, J. M. (1990). Personality structure: Emergence of the five-factor model. Annual review of psychology, 41(1), 417-440.

Disney, R., & Gathergood, J. (2013). Financial literacy and consumer credit portfolios. Journal of Banking & Finance, 37(7), 2246-2254.

Donnelly, C., Elliott, B., Ackland, T., Doyle, T., Beiser, T., Finch, C., Cochrane, J. L., Dempsey, A., & Lloyd, D. (2012). An anterior cruciate ligament injury prevention framework: Incorporating the recent evidence. Research in Sports Medicine, 20(3-4), 239-262.

Durand, R. B., Newby, R., and Sanghani, J. (2008). An intimate portrait of the individual investor. The Journal of Behavioral Finance, 9(4), 193-208.

Durand, R. B., Newby, R., Peggs, L., & Siekierka, M. (2010). Personality (Working Paper). Crawley: University of Western Australia.

Durand, R., Newby, R., Tant, K., and Trepongkaruna, S. (2013). Overconfidence, overreaction and personality. Review of Behavioral Finance, 5(2), 104-133.

Durand, R.B., Newby, R., & Sanghani, J. (2018). An intimate portrait of the individual investor. The Journal of Behavioral Finance, 9(4), 193–208.

Durand, R.B., Newby, R., Peggs, L. and Siekierka, M. (2013), Personality, Journal of Behavioral Finance, 14(2), 116-133.

Eysenck, H. J. (1991). Dimensions of personality: 16, 5 or 3?—Criteria for a taxonomic paradigm. Personality and individual differences, 12(8), 773-790.

Fenton-O'Creevy, M., Nicholson, N., Soane, E., and Willman, P. (2004). Traders: Risks, decisions and management in financial markets. Oxford University Press.

Gambetti, E., & Giusberti, F. (2012). The effect of anger and anxiety traits on investment decisions. Journal of Economic Psychology, 33(6), 1059–1069

Gillen, M., & Kim, H. (2014). Older adults' receipt of financial help: Does personality matter?. Journal of Family and Economic Issues, 35(2), 178-189.

Goldberg, L. R. (1990). An alternative description of personality: the big-five factor structure. Journal of personality and social psychology, 59(6), 1216.

Grable, J., & Lytton, R. H. (1999). Financial risk tolerance revisited: the development of a risk assessment instrument☆. Financial services review, 8(3), 163-181.

Hafeez, M. H., Basheer, M. F., Rafique, M., & Siddiqui, S. H. (2018). Exploring the Links between TQM Practices, Business Innovativeness and Firm Performance: An Emerging Market Perspective. Pakistan Journal of Social Sciences (PJSS), 38(2).

Hameed, W. U., Basheer, M. F., Iqbal, J., Anwar, A., & Ahmad, H. K. (2018). Determinants of Firm's open innovation performance and the role of R & D department: an empirical evidence from Malaysian SME's. Journal of Global Entrepreneurship Research, 8(1), 1-20.

Hameed, W., Nawaz, M., Basheer, M. F., & Waseem, M. (1819). The Effect of AmanahIkhtiar Malaysia (AIM) on Microenterprise Success in Sabah State Malaysia. Dialogue, 6462(14), 2.

He, Y., Liao, N., Bi, J., & Guo, L. (2019). Investment decision-making optimization of energy efficiency retrofit measures in multiple buildings under financing budgetary restraint. Journal of Cleaner Production, 215, 1078-1094.

Jalal, R. N. U. D., Zeb, N., & Fayyaz, U. E. (2019). The effect of personality traits on employee job satisfaction with moderating role of Islamic work ethics. The Journal of Asian Finance, Economics, and Business, 6(2), 161-171.

Jamshidinavid, B., Chavoshani, M., and Amiri, S. (2012). The Impact of Demographic and Psychological Characteristics on the Investment Prejudices in Tehran Stock. European Journal of Business and Social Sciences, 1(5), 41-53.

John, O. P., & Srivastava, S. (1999). The Big Five Trait taxonomy: History, measurement, and theoretical perspectives. In L. A. Pervin& O. P. John (Eds.), Handbook of personality: Theory and research (pp. 102–138). Guilford Press.

Keller, C., & Siegrist, M. (2006). Investing in stocks: The influence of financial risk attitude and valuesrelated money and stock market attitudes. Journal of Economic Psychology, 27(2), 285-303.

Khan, D. (2020). Cognitive Driven Biases, Investment Decision Making: The Moderating Role of Financial Literacy. Investment Decision Making: The Moderating Role of Financial Literacy (January 5, 2020).

Komarraju, M., Karau, S. J., Schmeck, R. R., &Avdic, A. (2011). The Big Five personality traits, learning styles, and academic achievement. Personality and Individual Differences, 51(4), 472-477.

Kowert, P. A., and Hermann, M. G. (1997). Who takes risks? Daring and caution in foreign policy making. Journal of Conflict Resolution, 41(5), 611 - 637.

Krishnan, R., & Beena, F. (2009). Measurement of conformity to behavior finance concepts and association with individual personality. IUP Journal of Behavioral Finance, 6(3/4), 25.

Kumari, S., Chandra, B., & Pattanayak, J. K. (2019). Personality traits and motivation of individual investors towards herding behaviour in Indian stock market. Kybernetes.

Lauriola, M., Gioggi, A., & Saggino, A. (2001). The Big Five and the intention to choose a university faculty: An exploratory study of high school students. Rassegna di psicologia, 18, 133-141.

Lin, H. W. (2011). Elucidating the influence of demographics and psychological traits on investment biases. World Academy of Science, Engineering and Technology, 77, 145-150.

Lo, A. W., Repin, D. V., and Steenbarger, B. N. (2005). Fear and greed in financial markets: A clinical study of day-traders (No. w11243). National Bureau of Economic Research.

Lusardi, A. (2015). Financial literacy: Do people know the ABCs of finance?. Public understanding of science, 24(3), 260-271.

Marcolin, S., & Abraham, A. (2006). Financial literacy research: Current literature and future opportunities.

Markowitz, H. (1952). Portfolio selection. The Journal of Finance, VII, 77–91.

Mayfield, C., Perdue, G., and Wooten, K. (2008). Investment management and personality type. Financial Services Review, 17(3), 219-236.

McAdams, D. P. (1992). The Five-Factor model in personality: A critical appraisal. Journal of personality, 60(2), 329-361.

McCrae, R. R., & Costa, Jr, P. T. (2007). Brief versions of the NEO-PI-3. Journal of individual differences, 28(3), 116-128.

McCrae, R. R., and Costa Jr, P. T. (1997). Personality trait structure as a human universal. American psychologist, 52(5), 509.

McCrae, R. R., and Costa, P. T. (2004). A contemplated revision of the NEO Five-Factor Inventory. Personality and Individual Differences, 36(3), 587-596.

McCrae, R. R., and John, O. P. (1992). An introduction to the five-factor model and its applications. Journal of personality, 60(2), 175-215.

McDougall, W. (1932). Of the words character and personality. Journal of Personality, 1(1), 3-16.

Muneer, S., Basheer, M. F., Shabbir, R., & Zeb, A. (1819). Does Information Technology (IT) Expeditethe Internal Audit System? Determinants of Internal Audit Effectives: Evidence from Pakistani Banking Industry. Dialogue, 14(2), 145.

Myers, I. B., McCaulley, M. H., and Most, R. (1985). Manual, a guide to the development and use of the Myers-Briggs type indicator. Consulting Psychologists Press.

Neumann, J. V., & Morgenstern, O. (2004). Theory of games and economic behavior. Princeton Univ. Press.

Nga,J. K.H., & Leong, K.Y. (2013). The influence of personality trait and demographic on financial decision making among generation Y. Young Consumers, 14(3), 230-243.

Nicholson, N., Soane, E., Fenton O'Creevy, M., and Willman, P. (2005). Personality and domain specific risk taking. Journal of Risk Research, 8(2), 157-176.

Nisar, Q. A., Basheer, M. F., Hussain, M. S., & Waqas, A. (2021). The Role of Leaders' Emotional Sincerity towards Followers' Trust: Leaders' Integrity & Quality Relationship. Journal of Contemporary Issues in Business and Government, 27(1), 472-479.

Nuseir, M. T., Basheer, M. F., & Aljumah, A. (2020). Antecedents of entrepreneurial intentions in smart city of Neom Saudi Arabia: Does the entrepreneurial education on artificial intelligence matter?. Cogent Business & Management, 7(1), 1825041.

Pak, O., & Mahmood, M. (2015). Impact of personality on risk tolerance and investment decisions. International Journal of Commerce and Management, 25(4), 370-384.

Pan, C. H., and Statman, M. (2013). Investor Personality in Investor Questionnaires. Journal of Investment Consulting, 14(1), 48-56.

Pompian, M. M., and Longo, J. M. (2004). A new paradigm for practical application of behavioral finance: creating investment programs based on personality type and gender to produce better investment outcomes. The Journal of Wealth Management, 7(2), 9-15.

Previn, L. A. (1994). A critical analysis of current trail theory. Psychological Inquiry, 5, 103–113

Riley Jr, W. B., & Chow, K. V. (1992). Asset allocation and individual risk aversion. Financial Analysts Journal, 48(6), 32-37.

Rotter, J. B. (1966). Generalized expectancies for internal versus external control of reinforcement. Psychological monographs: General and applied, 80(1), 1.

Ryckman, R. (2008). Theories of personality. Ninth edition, Thomson Wadsworth Press.

Sadi, R., Asl, H. G., Rostami, M. R., Gholipour, A., and Gholipour, F. (2011). Behavioral Finance: The Explanation of Investors' Personality and Perceptual Biases Effects on Financial Decisions. International journal of economics and finance, 3(5), 234-241.

Sadiq, M. N., & Khan, R. A. A. (2019). Impact of Personality Traits on Investment Intention: The Mediating Role of Risk Behaviour and the Moderating Role of Financial Literacy. Journal of Finance and Economics Research, 4(1), 1-18.

Salgado, J. F. (1997). The five factor model of personality and job performance in the European Community. Journal of Applied Psychology, 82(1), 30-43.

Schaefer, P. S., Williams, C. C., Goodie, A. S., and Campbell, W. K. (2004). Overconfidence and the big five. Journal of Research in Personality, 38(5), 473-480.

Sneed, C. D., McCrae, R. R., and Funder, D. C. (1998). Lay conceptions of the five-factor model and its indicators. Personality and Social Psychology Bulletin,24(2), 115-126.

Sreedevi, V. R., and Chitra, K. (2011). Does personality traits influence the choice of investment?. The IUP Journal of Behavioral Finance, 8(2), 47-57.

Thomas Bailard, David Biehl and Ronald Kaiser. (1986) Personal Money Management, 5th edition. Science Research Associates: Chicago.

Thomas, T., and Rajendran, G. (2012) BB and K Five-way Model and Investment Behavior of Individual Investors: Evidence from India, International Journal of Economics and Management, 6(1), 115–127.

Thomas Dohmen, Armin Falk, David Huffman, UweSunde, Jürgen Schupp, Gert G. Wagner (2011), Individual Risk Attitudes: Measurement, Determinants, and Behavioral Consequences, Journal of the European Economic Association, Volume 9, Issue 3, 1 June, Pages 522–550.

Wang, H., Zhang, J., Wang, L., & Liu, S. (2014). Emotion and investment returns: Situation and Personality as moderators in a stock market. Social Behaviour and Personality: An International journal, 42(4), 561-570. 2737| NaveedaZeb Impact of Personality Traits on Investment Decision with Moderating Role of Financial Literacy

Yan, R., Basheer, M. F., Irfan, M., & Rana, T. N. (2020). Role of Psychological factors in Employee Well-being and Employee Performance: An Empirical Evidence from Pakistan. Revista Argentina de ClínicaPsicológica, 29(5), 638.

Zahra, M., Hameed, W. U., Fiaz, M., & Basheer, M. F. (2019). Information technology capability a tool to expedite higher organizational performance. UCP Management Review (UCPMR), 3(1), 94-112.

Zaidi, F. B., and Tauni, M. Z. (2012). Influence of Investor's Personality Traits and Demographics on Overconfidence Bias. Institute of Interdisciplinary Business Research, 4(6), 730-746.

Zhou, W., & Xu, Z. (2020). Investment Decision Making Based on the Asymmetric Hesitant Fuzzy Sigmoid Preference Relations. In Qualitative Investment Decision-Making Methods under Hesitant Fuzzy Environments (pp. 21-48). Springer, Cham.

Zvaríková, K., & Majerová, J. (2014). Financial literacy in the Slovak Republic. Procedia-Social and Behavioral Sciences, 10, 1106-1115.

13

Deep Neural Network in Security: A Novel Robust CAPTCHA Model

Manasi Chhibber, Rashmi Gandhi*, Aakanshi Gupta and Ashok Kumar Yadav

Department of Computer Science and Engineering, Amity School of Engineering & Technology, Amity University Noida, Uttar Pradesh, India

Abstract

The CAPTCHA verifies that the user is a human by using a password to strengthen personal identification security on the web services. Web services can be made vulnerable by automated attacks on websites. CAPTCHA is a well-known security method for protecting websites from being attacked by automated attack tools. When a CAPTCHA is given a high level of distortion to make it resistant to automated attacks, it becomes difficult for humans to recognise it. The problem can be addressed in a variety of ways using a neural network. Deep learning models Dense net, Mobile Net, and VGG were used to test the security in the presented research work. To assess the model's fitness, the models performed batch normalisation using the required additional layer. With loss and accuracy, the best model is visualised. The experimental findings confirmed the neural network's superiority over the current state-of-the-art technique for captcha recognition.

Keywords: Security, deep learning models, captcha, dense net, mobile net, VGG, neural network

13.1 Introduction

CAPTCHA involves generating random alpha-numeric images that are used to block out non-human access to a website [12]. CAPTCHA helps in protecting you from password decryption and spam by requesting you to complete a fairly simple test that verifies that you are in fact a person rather than a computer system attempting to access an account that is password-protected. Challenge-response authentication is the name for this

---

*Corresponding author: rashmibehal@gmail.com

Mohd Naved, V. Ajantha Devi, and Aditya Kumar Gupta (eds.) *Fintech and Cryptocurrency*, (277–302)
© 2023 Scrivener Publishing LLC

sort of security technique. Every activity that we get involved in over the internet has some kind of digital footprint associated with it. In order to avoid unauthorized access and prevent spammers, CAPTCHAs do come handy. They may defend your website against less sophisticated evil bots, but they are not the ideal solution to the bot problem. They don't differentiate between real people and bots, and they force every visitor to solve them. They can be time-consuming and difficult at times [1]. Because of this discomfort, users may choose to visit websites that do not use CAPTCHAs. Also, with the advent of smart tools & technologies, it's getting tougher to block out the unwanted.

New age artificially intelligent systems [27] have the ability to pass through these security measures. Although machine learning techniques are extensively used and have demonstrated to be highly effective, they are heavily reliant on manually created features, which necessitates a significant amount of effort on the part of domain experts. Since a result, deep learning approaches [22, 23] have lately attracted interest, as they have the potential to decrease feature defining work while achieving relatively more accurate performance. Image identification, object detection, and segmentation are some of the most common image analysis tasks that can be performed using CNNs [2, 16]. Text from images can be read using these neural networks by first segmenting the image and then identifying and classifying each character one by one. When employing CNNs, [14] we apply filters. Filters enable us to the take advantage of a given image's spatial localization by establishing a local connection pattern across neurons. The process of multiplying two functions pointwise to create a third function is called convolution. Our picture pixels matrix is one of the functions, and our filter is the other one. The dot product of these two matrices is obtained by sliding our filter across the complete picture. A "Feature Map" is the resultant matrix. Multiple convolutional layers collect information from the picture, followed by an output layer that tells us the categorization.

By the means of this chapter, we also present a comparative study with numerous transfer learning models [3, 24]. Transfer learning [26] is an amazing technique for representing features from a previously learned model without having to build a new model from start. A previously trained model is generally developed on a very huge dataset like ImageNet, and the weights acquired from the trained model may be utilized with your own neural network [7] for any other similar application [35]. These freshly constructed models can be utilized to make predictions on relatively new jobs or to train models for related applications. This method not only cuts down on training time, but it also minimizes generalization error.

Here we have used DenseNet, MobileNet and VGG16 models for comparison. A DenseNet [4] is analogous to a convolutional neural network that uses Dense Blocks to link multiple layers straight up to one another, which results in dense connections between the layers. MobileNets are structured on a streamlined design. VGG16 is a simple and popularly used CNN architecture which is also used in ImageNet for visual object detection. Among these all, CNN architecture provided the highest accuracy.

13.2 Literature Review

A CAPTCHA Decoder should essentially take in an image consisting of alpha-numeric characters and once the neural network-based algorithms [7] are applied, it should be able to decrypt the image and output all the characters present in it, sequentially. Not only it can help people with disabilities to perform day-to-day internet surfing but also, we can bring into light that CAPTCHAs are not the most secure way of blocking out undesired website visitors [13].

In the past, there has been some extensive work done in this domain. A unique decoding method as per the multi-population genetic algorithm was suggested by Chen Ru, Yang Jing, Hu Rong-gui and Huang Shu-guang (2013). The experimental findings have shown that the unique LSTM-RNN [18] decoding method may increase the recognition accuracy of combined CAPTCHA. Yujin Shu and Yongjin Xu (2019) proposed an entire deep CNN-RNN [18] network model, which was built by researching the captcha recognition technology, which can aid in the recognition of 4-character long text-based CAPTCHA. Their CNN-RNN algorithm initially creates a deep residual convolutional neural network in order to completely extract the input captcha picture properties [7]. The generated variant RNN network is then used to obtain the deep internal properties of the captcha [18]. The studies are showing 99% accurate results. Asadullah Kehar, Rafaqat Hussain Arain and Riaz Ahmed Shaikh (2020) applied several digital image processing techniques while preprocessing and steps involving segmentation. A CNN was used for the decoding process. They were successful in obtaining an accuracy of 77.5% on 3-letter long CAPTCHAs. Jun Chen, Xiangyang Luo, Liyan Zhu, Qikun Zhang and Yong Gan (2021) presented a text CAPTCHA cracking approach based on a style transfer network [3, 25]. It proposed to separate the structure and style of fonts of characters in a new way. Although these results are promising, but we've managed to work extensively on transfer learning models [24].

13.2.1 Convolutional Neural Networks

Artificial intelligence has made significant progress. To reach astonishing outcomes, researchers study on a range of components in the field. Computer vision is among numerous fields in this category. The objective of this discipline is to enable machines to see the environment in the same manner that humans do, and for utilizing that knowledge for tasks like picture and video recognition, image analysis and categorization, media reconstruction, recommendation systems, NLP, etc.

A CNN/ConvNet [14, 15, 19] is a form of Deep Learning system [20] which can prioritize and distinguish between the numerous things present in an image. ConvNet requires far less pre-processing than other classification algorithms. Contrary to basic approaches, which need hand-engineering of filters [17], ConvNets may acquire these features with sufficient training. The design of a ConvNet, which is analogous to the connecting structure of neurons in the human brain, was inspired by the organisation of the visual cortex. In the receptive field, individual neurons are capable of responding to stimuli. To cover the whole visual field, a set of comparable fields might be employed. By using the proper filters, a ConvNet can detect the spatial and temporal relationships in a picture. Because there are fewer factors to worry about and the weights may be reused, the architecture offers a better fit on the dataset. Alternatively, the network might be trained to specifically recognize the image's complexity. The ConvNet's [17, 19] task is to keep essential properties for accurate prediction while compressing the pictures into a format that is simpler to examine. For an architecture to learn features and still be scalable to massive datasets, this is essential. The distinguishing feature of convolutional neural networks is their capacity to simultaneously learn several filters tailored to a training dataset while adhering to a predetermined predictive modelling objective, such as image categorization. As a result, very specific qualities show on input photos that may be recognized anywhere.

A convolutional neural network has four different types of layers: the convolutional layer, the pooling layer, the ReLU correction layer, and the fully connected layer. The fundamental building elements are convolutional layers. A filter is applied to a feature. The result of applying a filter to an input and receiving an activation is convolution. A feature map is formed when the same filter is applied to an input repeatedly, presenting the locations and intensities of a recognized feature in an input, such as an image. The pooling layer is frequently sandwiched between two convolution layers, receiving many feature maps and applying the pooling operation to each one. The pooling procedure reduces the size of the photos while maintaining their essential properties. This increases network efficiency and prevents over-learning. A real non-linear function is referred to as a Rectified Linear Units (ReLU). All negative values obtained as the inputs are replaced by zeros with the help of the ReLU correction layer. It serves as an activating mechanism. A neural network's fully connected layer is often the last layer. An input vector is transformed into a new output vector by this layer. In order to do this, the incoming input values are subjected to a linear combination and maybe an activation function. The chance that the provided image corresponds to a certain class is represented by each component of the vector. Weight values are learned in the same manner as convolutional neural networks by back-propagation of the gradient during the training phase.

The prime pros of Convolutional Neural Network include:

1. They boost deep learning research significantly [20].
2. They may be picturized as basic function probabilistic models that could be used as image features extractors in downstream applications [17].
3. CNN's main advantage over models preceding it is that it detects vital characteristics without the need for human interaction.

The major cons include:

1. Visual transformers are already sweeping CNNs out. They have much faster training speeds.
2. CNNs [15] are still vulnerable to adversarial assaults, rotations, and reflections, among other things.
3. They lack a sense of memory state and are restricted in their sequential modelling.

13.2.2 Transfer Learning

Given the significant computational and time resources required to develop neural network models for these problems, including the significant improvements in skill which they provide on associated incidents [30], it is a common deep learning technique to use pre-trained models as the beginning point [24, 26, 32] for computer vision and NLP tasks [21, 29]. As explained in transfer learning [26], we train a baseline network on a base dataset and task, then repurpose or transfer the obtained features to a second targeted system that will be trained on a target dataset and task. This tactic is more likely to be successful if the attributes are general, that is, applicable to both the basis and the target occupations, as opposed to being exclusive to the base job.

Transfer learning [25, 30, 33] may be applied to your own predictive modelling challenges. The following are two popular approaches to using it:

a) Creating a Model Approach

Choose a source task. In order to demonstrate your understanding of the ideas learnt when mapping input to output data, you must choose a relevant predictive modelling issue with a significant amount of data in which the input data, output data, and/or concepts are all related in some manner.

Create a source model. After that, you must make a trained model for the initial mission. The model must perform better than a naïve model in order to demonstrate that any feature learning has taken place.

Adjust the model. Optionally, you may need to adapt or improve your model to the I/O pair data available for your task.

b) Pre-Trained Model Methodology

Select a source model. A pre-trained source model is selected from the available models. Many laboratories publish models for large and rewarding datasets that can be included in a pool of selectable candidate models.

Reuse the model. You can then use the pre-trained model as a starting point for the model for the second task of interest. This may include using the entire model or part of the model, depending on the modeling technique used. *Adjust the model.* Optionally, you may need to adapt or improve your model to the I/O pair data available for your task.

Transfer learning is a performance-enhancing improvement [30, 32]. In general, the benefits of utilizing transfer learning in the domain are not clear until the model has been constructed and validated [31]. In their chapter on transfer learning, Lisa Torrey and Jude Shavlik discuss three potential benefits of employing transfer learning:

A better start. The initial competence on the original model is higher than it would be otherwise (before improving the model).

A steeper incline. The rate of skill increment during source model learning is steeper than it would be otherwise.

Asymptote goes higher. The trained model's converged learning goes on higher than it would be otherwise.

The prime pros of transfer learning models [3, 28, 34] include:

1. Getting rid of the necessity for a huge collection of labelled training data for each new model.
2. Improving Machine Learning design and implementation performance for many models.

3. A broader approach to automated problem solving that makes use of several methods to address new difficulties.
4. Instead of real-world situations, models can be taught in simulated environments.

The major cons include:

1. The composition of the training data utilized by your pre-trained model should be similar to the data you will confront during testing, or it should not differ significantly.
2. The quantity of training data for transfer learning should be chosen in such a way that the model is not overfit.
3. One cannot confidently remove layers to lower the number of parameters.

13.3   Proposed Approach

13.3.1   Data Pre-Processing and Exploratory Analysis

The complete workflow is described in detail in Figure 13.1.

The images from the dataset were first read in grayscale. Adaptive thresholding [8] and image dilation [9] was done to show a more contrasting image of the characters. The image was segmented in 5 parts, thus separating out all the characters. Then, all the images were scaled/normalized. The frequency of all the characters in the overall dataset was calculated. The labels were one-hot encoded so that training process could be done. By creating fresh and varied examples for training datasets, picture data creation was carried out in order to improve the performance and outcomes of machine learning models. Some key procedures are explained in detail below.

13.3.2   Data Acquisition

The data was acquired form Kaggle. Wilhelmy, Rodrigo, and Horacio Rosas contributed the dataset in 2013 as the dataset of CAPTCHAs. As shown in Figure 13.2, the images consisted of five alpha-numeric characters. All of them were in grayscale. 1070 pictures were present in the dataset.

a) Adaptive Thresholding
The threshold value is calculated using the adaptive thresholding [8] approach, which produces different threshold values for different locations.

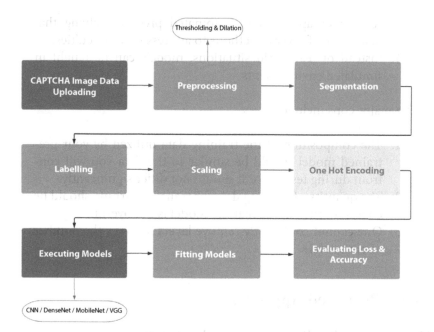

Figure 13.1 Proposed workflow.

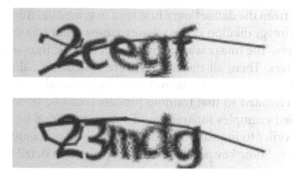

Figure 13.2 Images in the dataset.

It is used to distinguish desired foreground visual items from the backdrop based on the pixel intensities of every area. To calculate T in the arithmetic mean, each pixel nearby makes the same contribution. Additionally, the Gaussian mean reduces the contribution of pixels beyond the region's coordinate centre to the computation of T overall. The general formula to compute is presented in equation 13.1.

$$T = mean(I_L) - C \tag{13.1}$$

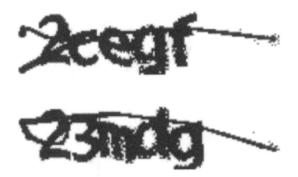

Figure 13.3 Images after applying adaptive thresholding.

The local sub-region of the picture, is what we may utilize to fine-tune the threshold value T. The mean is either the arithmetic or Gaussian mean. The images obtained after applying adaptive thresholding look like the ones presented in Figure 13.3.

b) Image Dilation
Dilation is the process of adding pixels to the edges of components in a picture. It is one of the operations in mathematical morphology [9]. The output value for a certain pixel is determined by taking the average value of all the pixels nearby. In a binary image, a pixel is set to 1 if any of its neighbors also have a value of 1. Morphological dilatation fills up tiny spaces in objects and makes things more visible. Solid designs become larger and lines get thicker. This operation can be represented mathematically as presented in equation 13.2.

$$A \oplus B \qquad (13.2)$$

Here, is the input image that is converted to binary and is the structuring element or the kernel. We use 2D convolution of the input picture with the kernel in this case. In reality, the kernel is a square matrix. The dilated image is the outcome of the given formula as shown in Figure 13.4.

c) Segmentation
The segmentation of images was performed in order to separate out characters. This was done using slicing operations in python. Once the individual characters were separated out, the image label was also split into five parts and those segmented images were labelled individually. Now, these

Figure 13.4 Images after dilation.

labelled images consisting of only a single character were used for the model training. This step made it feasible for the model to learn the characteristics of all the alphabets or numbers present in the original images. Figure 13.5 shows how the preprocessed images were taken, sliced, and labelled again to create a dataset of individual character images for model training.

The frequency of occurrence of different characters in the dataset is visualized in Figure 13.6 and the exact count can be checked in Table 13.1.

d) One Hot Encoding
We occasionally find columns in datasets that have categorical features, such as parameter color, which may have categorical parameters such as black and white. These labels have no preferred order, and because the input is string labeled, the machine learning model cannot operate with it. We can assign a specific number to these labels, for example, black and white are mapped to 0 and 1, respectively. This is called label encoding. However, when 1>0, our model will begin to favor the white parameter, despite the fact that both categories are equally relevant in the dataset. To tackle this problem, we should use the One Hot Encoding approach [10]. Separate columns for black and white labels will be constructed using this method. As a result, anytime the color black is used, a 1 will be placed in the black column and a 0 in the white column, and vice versa. In our case, all the characters' labels were one hot encoded.

e) Image Data Generation
The model was fit on the training data produced after image data generation. The image augmentation approach is an excellent method for increasing

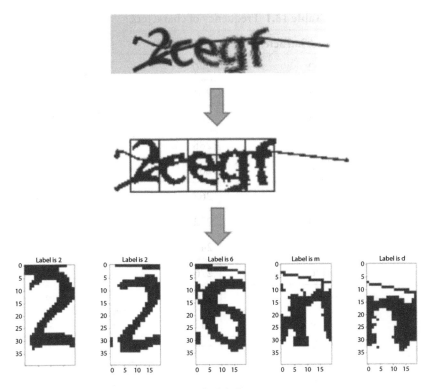

Figure 13.5 Performing segmentation and relabeling.

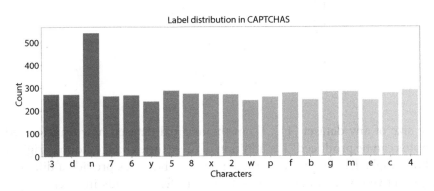

Figure 13.6 Distribution of characters in CAPTCHA images.

Table 13.1 Frequency of characters.

Characters	Count
2	270
3	271
4	289
5	288
6	267
7	262
8	272
b	247
c	276
d	269
e	245
f	277
g	281
m	282
n	540
p	259
w	244
x	271
y	240

the size of any dataset [11]. From the original dataset, new transformed photos can be produced. The addition of these little changes to the original photographs has no effect on the target class but does provide a different perspective on catching the object in real life. This aids in integrating a level of variety in the dataset, allowing the ML model to generalize more effectively on previously unknown data. In addition, when trained on new, slightly changed photos, the model becomes more resilient. Some altered

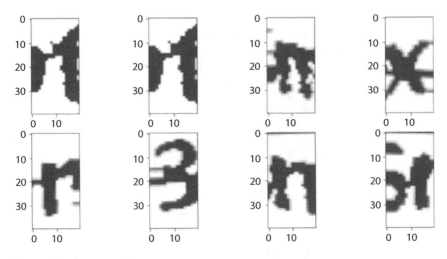

Figure 13.7 Augmented images.

images generated using this technique are shown in Figure 13.7. The pre-processing is shown from Figure 13.2 to Figure 13.7.

13.4   Results and Discussions

There are different CAPTCHA images (3/4/5 letters) are available. In this work, experiments are performed on 5 letters. Synthetically data was generated and then trained with 1070 CAPTCHA images. Letters created 5*1070 = 5350 random images for training. The experimental work is performed on 80-20 ratio for testing and validation. The generated CAPTCHA images were then segmented into 5 characters. All images were successfully segmented. The hyperparameter specifications are depicted in Table 13.2.

13.4.1   CNN

CNN based diagnosis unit filter bank is used for verification. For each class, CNN classified filtered misclassification samples independently. The resultant captcha category was detected or not based on performance compared to previous work, but it worked with limited data. The complexity of CNN architecture is being overcome with the enhanced Crossover Optimization (ICRMBO) algorithm [26]. CNN [6, 15] eliminates manual work via encoding methods. The Figure 13.2 shows the complete framework of the

Table 13.2 Hyperparameters specifications.

Model name	Epochs	Optimizer	Loss function	Metrics	Activation function	Splitting ratio	Batch size	Image size
CNN	150	Adam	Categorical Cross Entropy	Accuracy	ReLU & Softmax	80:20	32	40 X 20
DenseNet	20	Adam	Categorical Cross Entropy	Accuracy	ReLU & Softmax	80:20	32	256 X 256
MobileNet	20	Adam	Categorical Cross Entropy	Accuracy	ReLU & Softmax	80:20	32	256 X 256
VGG16	20	Adam	Categorical Cross Entropy	Accuracy	ReLU & Softmax	80:20	32	256 X 256

proposed model being used. Another, most used activation function that is quite easy to compute and does not have the problem of saturation and does not cause the Vanishing Gradient Problem in CNN is the "ReLu". The CNN training processing results are depicted in Table 13.3 and classification report is in Table 13.4. Figure 13.8 shows the CNN accuracy and CNN loss function [16].

Table 13.3 CNN training process.

Epoch	Loss	Accuracy	Validation loss	Validation accuracy
1	2.9725	0.1405	3.3706	0.0533
2	1.9756	0.4052	4.4760	0.0654
3	1.5806	0.5502	3.3472	0.1206
4	1.2329	0.6607	1.5664	0.5897
5	1.0905	0.7030	0.7039	0.8355
6	0.9483	0.7445	0.6000	0.8393
7	0.8461	0.7727	0.5477	0.8607
8	0.8106	0.7778	0.5389	0.8514
9	0.7401	0.8047	0.4913	0.8766
10	0.7537	0.7947	0.4907	0.8757
11	0.6591	0.8318	0.4939	0.8729
12	0.6793	0.8306	0.4577	0.8897
13	0.6299	0.8348	0.4678	0.8897
14	0.6006	0.8329	0.4431	0.8888
15	0.5923	0.8379	0.4311	0.8907
16	0.5689	0.8408	0.4345	0.8972
17	0.5757	0.8390	0.4485	0.8888
18	0.5617	0.8464	0.4250	0.8935
19	0.5247	0.8627	0.4324	0.8916
20	0.5664	0.8503	0.4379	0.8953

Table 13.4 CNN classification report.

Character	Precision	Recall	F1-Score	Support
2	0.92	0.94	0.93	49
3	0.95	1.00	0.97	53
4	1.00	0.97	0.99	68
5	0.96	0.95	0.96	57
6	1.00	0.98	0.99	52
7	0.93	0.93	0.93	58
8	0.94	0.98	0.96	50
b	0.96	0.96	0.96	53
c	0.90	0.92	0.91	50
d	0.85	0.87	0.86	61
e	1.00	0.89	0.94	36
f	0.96	0.93	0.95	57
g	0.92	0.95	0.94	63
m	0.93	0.50	0.65	54
n	0.76	0.92	0.83	104
p	0.94	0.94	0.94	65
w	0.95	0.93	0.94	44
x	0.92	0.92	0.92	53
y	0.87	0.93	0.90	43

13.4.2 DenseNet

Huang *et al.* discussed an efficient architecture, where input and output layers are connected with short connections. The main pros of this type of networks are good flow of gradients and information in all around networks [21, 42]. Further, performance is increased consistently, without any overfitting and degradation. So, these can be performed well with fewer parameters and less computation. The proposed model has been trained for 15 epochs with batch size = 32 and the Figure 13.9 shows the trained

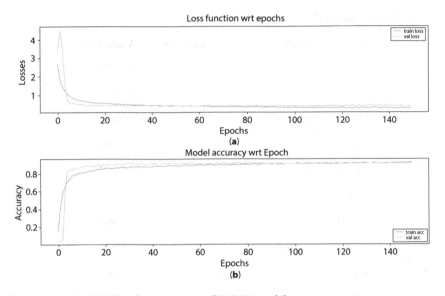

Figure 13.8 (a) CNN loss function curve. (b) CNN model accuracy curve.

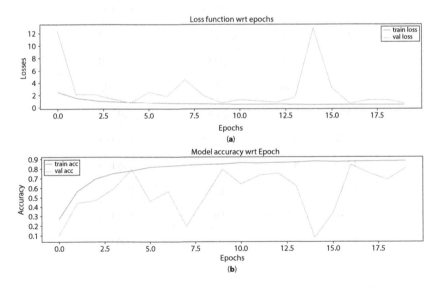

Figure 13.9 (a) DenseNet loss function curve. (b) DenseNet model accuracy curve.

model accuracy and trained loss for test dataset. The training accuracy comes out to be 80.71% and the loss of 68.89% The model gives good and comparable results as the MobileNet model. The DenseNet training processing results with accuracy and validation loss and validation accuracy are depicted epoch-wise in Table 13.5.

Table 13.5 DenseNet training process.

Epoch	Loss	Accuracy	Validation loss	Validation accuracy
1	2.4300	0.2691	12.3071	0.0938
2	1.4761	0.5612	2.1059	0.4356
3	1.0830	0.6914	2.0788	0.4650
4	0.8921	0.7497	1.4102	0.5890
5	0.8029	0.7777	0.7290	0.7907
6	0.6934	0.8127	2.4152	0.4545
7	0.6454	0.8247	1.7855	0.5606
8	0.6108	0.8367	4.4762	0.1894
9	0.5597	0.8402	1.9655	0.4915
10	0.5532	0.8465	0.7144	0.7926
11	0.4907	0.8625	1.2253	0.6392
12	0.5139	0.8569	0.9835	0.7292
13	0.4861	0.8597	0.8249	0.7500
14	0.4715	0.8667	1.6232	0.6193
15	0.4253	0.8783	12.7892	0.0729
16	0.4461	0.8726	3.1716	0.3314
17	0.4466	0.8724	0.5881	0.8400
18	0.4139	0.8766	1.1775	0.7528
19	0.4258	0.8752	1.1985	0.6856
20	0.4026	0.8797	0.7066	0.8030

It is used as an activation function in between the hidden layer and the choice of the activation function for the output layer depends upon the type of the prediction problem. Thus, to underrate the loss function and to make it correct and optimized predictions as possible changes need to be made in the weights and other parameters like the learning rate of the model.

13.4.3   MobileNet

Figure 13.10 presented next shows the validation and training loss and accuracy vs 15 epochs for the various pre-trained models from where the proposed model gives the highest training accuracy and the highest validation accuracy for the MobileNet [5] as pre-trained model for feature extraction. Performance indicators like precision, accuracy, recall, and F1 score can be used to assess the model's strength. The ratio of number of accurately predicted photos to the total number of predictions can be used to calculate the accuracy. The hyperparameter tuning of the proposed model with MobileNet as convolutional base is also done for various optimizers Adam, SGD, Adagrad, Adadelta and RMSprop and the results have been analysed. Fine-tuning of the pre-trained model MobileNet is accomplished in the second suggested model by unfreezing the top layers of the convolutional base and retraining the network with a low learning rate and SGD optimizer. The suggested model's comprehensive framework is shown in Figure 13.7. The model's accuracy can be increased by fine-tuning. Unfreezing the few top layers of the convolutional base and retraining the network with a modest learning rate are the main components of fine-tuning.

Following the formation of the model, the number of layers to be trained on our dataset is determined. Despite our objective of preserving most of what the original MobileNet learned from ImageNet by freezing the weights in many layers, particularly the early ones, we still need to train

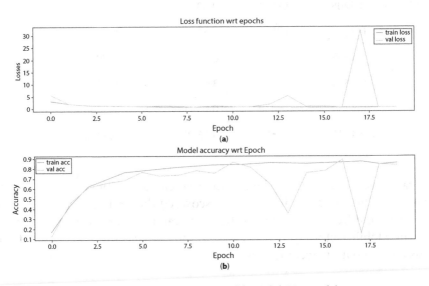

Figure 13.10 (a) MobileNet loss function curve. (b). MobileNet model accuracy curve.

Table 13.6 MobileNet training process.

Epoch	Loss	Accuracy	Validation loss	Validation accuracy
1	2.9329	0.1671	5.4715	0.1259
2	1.8845	0.4320	1.8362	0.4555
3	1.2812	0.6202	1.3102	0.6108
4	1.0847	0.6928	1.1356	0.6553
5	0.8744	0.7603	1.1031	0.6828
6	0.8074	0.7798	0.7936	0.7652
7	0.7562	0.7934	1.1186	0.7273
8	0.6805	0.8132	1.0164	0.7358
9	0.6374	0.8226	0.7115	0.7784
10	0.6004	0.8378	0.9950	0.7509
11	0.5821	0.8374	0.5228	0.8617
12	0.5721	0.8444	0.6898	0.8087
13	0.5173	0.8578	1.7734	0.6496
14	0.5277	0.8501	5.1469	0.3485
15	0.5208	0.8501	0.8341	0.7576
16	0.4865	0.8562	0.8532	0.7822
17	0.4993	0.8583	0.4044	0.8892
18	0.4614	0.8700	31.8383	0.1553
19	0.5354	0.8444	0.6044	0.8400
20	0.4931	0.8571	0.5528	0.8352

certain layers since the model has to learn characteristics about this new data set. After some testing, it was discovered that training only the final 23 layers and freezing the rest of the layers can produce acceptable results.

The Mobile Net training processing results with accuracy and validation loss and validation accuracy are depicted epoch-wise in Table 13.6.

13.4.4   VGG16

VGG16 is a 16-layer CNN model [14] developed by researchers from the University of Oxford. The model has been trained for 15 epochs with batch size = 32 and the Figure 13.11 shows the training accuracy vs the validation accuracy and training loss vs the validation loss respectively for the captcha dataset. The model gives a good training accuracy of 74.22%, however, the validation accuracy is quite less as compared to the training loss is around 99.46% but the model seems too overfit. The VGG16 training processing results with accuracy and validation loss and validation accuracy are depicted epoch-wise in Table 13.7.

Figure 13.12 and 13.13 presents decoded captchas with validation accuracy and loss. Table 13.8 presents the best accuracy and loss of each model.

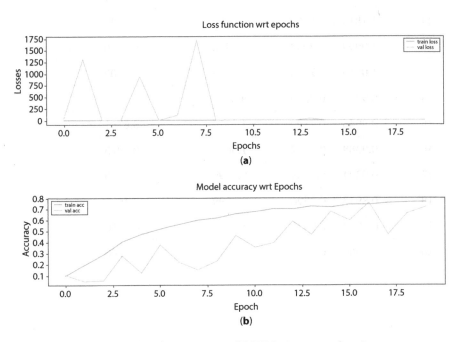

Figure 13.11 (a) VGG16 loss function curve. (b) VGG16 accuracy function curve.

Table 13.7 VGG16 training process.

Epoch	Loss	Accuracy	Validation loss	Validation accuracy
1	2.9045	0.0957	40.2459	0.1013
2	2.5863	0.1922	1307.7281	0.0464
3	2.3476	0.2872	12.4215	0.0521
4	1.9877	0.4080	2.7994	0.2803
5	1.7697	0.4740	938.6497	0.1231
6	1.6186	0.5210	2.0259	0.3759
7	1.5068	0.5638	110.7636	0.2178
8	1.3909	0.6005	1705.3021	0.1515
9	1.3157	0.6212	4.1092	0.2273
10	1.2379	0.6559	2.0136	0.4621
11	1.1816	0.6750	2.2760	0.3523
12	1.0999	0.7032	2.5250	0.3930
13	1.0515	0.7043	1.6795	0.5900
14	0.9955	0.7300	46.7504	0.4688
15	0.9946	0.7199	1.9572	0.6761
16	0.9388	0.7427	1.3696	0.5975
17	0.9204	0.7469	0.8395	0.7585
18	0.8937	0.7596	2.1399	0.4697
19	0.8770	0.7622	1.0941	0.6610
20	0.8564	0.7685	1.0141	0.7206

2g783

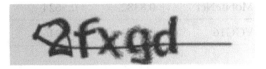

2fxgd

88bgx

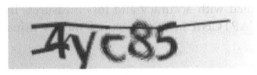

4yc85

Figure 13.12 Decoded CAPTCHAs.

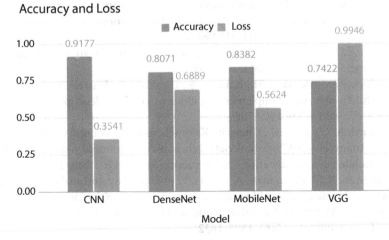

Figure 13.13 Accuracy and loss comparison.

Table 13.8 Accuracy and loss comparison.

Model name	Accuracy	Loss
CNN	0.9177	0.3541
DenseNet	0.8071	0.6889
MobileNet	0.8382	0.5624
VGG16	0.7422	0.9946

13.5 Conclusion

In this study, CAPTCHA which is used in the cryptocurrency and other vital issues of security have been implemented using three different deep learning and transfer learning models. The outcome of the experimental results validate the best approach for recognition is CNN. The comparison between CNN and other models (DenseNet, MobileNet, and VGG16) has been performed with accuracy and loss measures. In the future, we can utilize the CAPTCHA in more secured way by using the upcoming technologies.

References

1. Bursztein, E., Martin, M., & Mitchell, J. (2011, October). Text-based CAPTCHA strengths and weaknesses. In Proceedings of the 18th ACM conference on Computer and communications security (pp. 125-138).
2. O'Shea, K., & Nash, R. (2015). An introduction to convolutional neural networks. arXiv preprint arXiv:1511.08458.
3. Weiss, K., Khoshgoftaar, T. M., & Wang, D. (2016). A survey of transfer learning. Journal of Big data, 3(1), 1-40.
4. Iandola, F., Moskewicz, M., Karayev, S., Girshick, R., Darrell, T., & Keutzer, K. (2014). Densenet: Implementing efficient convnet descriptor pyramids. arXiv preprint arXiv:1404.1869.
5. Howard, A. G., Zhu, M., Chen, B., Kalenichenko, D., Wang, W., Weyand, T., ... & Adam, H. (2017). Mobilenets: Efficient convolutional neural networks for mobile vision applications. arXiv preprint arXiv:1704.04861.
6. Simonyan, K., & Zisserman, A. (2014). Very deep convolutional networks for large-scale image recognition. arXiv preprint arXiv:1409.1556.
7. Bishop, C. M. (1994). Neural networks and their applications. Review of scientific instruments, 65(6), 1803-1832.

8. Roy, P., Dutta, S., Dey, N., Dey, G., Chakraborty, S., & Ray, R. (2014, July). Adaptive thresholding: A comparative study. In 2014 International conference on control, Instrumentation, communication and Computational Technologies (ICCICCT) (pp. 1182-1186). IEEE.

9. Tambe, S. B., Kulhare, D., Nirmal, M. D., & Prajapati, G. (2013). Image processing (IP) through erosion and dilation methods.

10. Seger, C. (2018). An investigation of categorical variable encoding techniques in machine learning: binary versus one-hot and feature hashing.

11. Schraml, D. (2019, September). Physically based synthetic image generation for machine learning: a review of pertinent literature. In Photonics and Education in Measurement Science 2019 (Vol. 11144, p. 111440J). International Society for Optics and Photonics.

12. Ahn, L. V., Blum, M., Hopper, N. J., & Langford, J. (2003, May). CAPTCHA: Using hard AI problems for security. In International conference on the theory and applications of cryptographic techniques (pp. 294-311). Springer, Berlin, Heidelberg.

13. Wang, P., Gao, H., Shi, Z., Yuan, Z., & Hu, J. (2020). Simple and easy: Transfer learning-based attacks to text CAPTCHA. IEEE Access, 8, 59044-59058.

14. Albawi, S., Mohammed, T. A., & Al-Zawi, S. (2017, August). Understanding of a convolutional neural network. In 2017 international conference on engineering and technology (ICET) (pp. 1-6). Ieee.

15. Kattenborn, T., Leitloff, J., Schiefer, F., & Hinz, S. (2021). Review on Convolutional Neural Networks (CNN) in vegetation remote sensing. ISPRS Journal of Photogrammetry and Remote Sensing, 173, 24-49.

16. Wu, J. (2017). Introduction to convolutional neural networks. National Key Lab for Novel Software Technology. Nanjing University. China, 5(23), 495.

17. Chauhan, R., Ghanshala, K. K., & Joshi, R. C. (2018, December). Convolutional neural network (CNN) for image detection and recognition. In 2018 First International Conference on Secure Cyber Computing and Communication (ICSCCC) (pp. 278-282). IEEE.

18. Banerjee, I., Ling, Y., Chen, M. C., Hasan, S. A., Langlotz, C. P., Moradzadeh, N., ... & Lungren, M. P. (2019). Comparative effectiveness of convolutional neural network (CNN) and recurrent neural network (RNN) architectures for radiology text report classification. Artificial intelligence in medicine, 97, 79-88.

19. Zou, L., Yu, S., Meng, T., Zhang, Z., Liang, X., & Xie, Y. (2019). A technical review of convolutional neural network-based mammographic breast cancer diagnosis. Computational and mathematical methods in medicine, 2019.

20. Bernal, J., Kushibar, K., Asfaw, D. S., Valverde, S., Oliver, A., Martí, R., & Lladó, X. (2019). Deep convolutional neural networks for brain image analysis on magnetic resonance imaging: a review. Artificial intelligence in medicine, 95, 64-81.

21. Kalchbrenner, N., Grefenstette, E., & Blunsom, P. (2014). A convolutional neural network for modelling sentences. arXiv preprint arXiv:1404.2188.

22. Mohakud, R., & Dash, R. (2021). Survey on hyperparameter optimization using nature-inspired algorithm of deep convolution neural network. In Intelligent and Cloud Computing (pp. 737-744). Springer, Singapore.

23. Kim, P. (2017). Convolutional neural network. In MATLAB deep learning (pp. 121-147). Apress, Berkeley, CA.

24. Torrey, L., & Shavlik, J. (2010). Transfer learning. In Handbook of research on machine learning applications and trends: algorithms, methods, and techniques (pp. 242-264). IGI global.

25. Pan, S. J., & Yang, Q. (2009). A survey on transfer learning. IEEE Transactions on knowledge and data engineering, 22(10), 1345-1359.

26. Ying, W., Zhang, Y., Huang, J., & Yang, Q. (2018, July). Transfer learning via learning to transfer. In International Conference on Machine Learning (pp. 5085-5094). PMLR.

27. Tan, C., Sun, F., Kong, T., Zhang, W., Yang, C., & Liu, C. (2018, October). A survey on deep transfer learning. In International conference on artificial neural networks (pp. 270-279). Springer, Cham.

28. Bengio, Y. (2012, June). Deep learning of representations for unsupervised and transfer learning. In Proceedings of ICML workshop on unsupervised and transfer learning (pp. 17-36). JMLR Workshop and Conference Proceedings.

29. Ruder, S., Peters, M. E., Swayamdipta, S., & Wolf, T. (2019, June). Transfer learning in natural language processing. In Proceedings of the 2019 conference of the North American chapter of the association for computational linguistics: Tutorials (pp. 15-18).

30. Pan, S. J., Kwok, J. T., & Yang, Q. (2008, July). Transfer learning via dimensionality reduction. In AAAI (Vol. 8, pp. 677-682).

31. Cao, B., Pan, S. J., Zhang, Y., Yeung, D. Y., & Yang, Q. (2010, July). Adaptive transfer learning. In proceedings of the AAAI Conference on Artificial Intelligence (Vol. 24, No. 1, pp. 407-412).

32. Shao, L., Zhu, F., & Li, X. (2014). Transfer learning for visual categorization: A survey. IEEE transactions on neural networks and learning systems, 26(5), 1019-1034.

33. Raina, R., Battle, A., Lee, H., Packer, B., & Ng, A. Y. (2007, June). Self-taught learning: transfer learning from unlabeled data. In Proceedings of the 24th international conference on Machine learning (pp. 759-766).

34. Niu, S., Liu, Y., Wang, J., & Song, H. (2020). A decade survey of transfer learning (2010–2020). IEEE Transactions on Artificial Intelligence, 1(2), 151-166.

35. Long, M., Zhu, H., Wang, J., & Jordan, M. I. (2017, July). Deep transfer learning with joint adaptation networks. In International conference on machine learning (pp. 2208-2217). PMLR.

14

Customer's Perception of Voice Bot Assistance in the Banking Industry in Malaysia

**Manimekalai Jambulingam[1]*, Indhumathi Sinnasamy[2]
and Magiswary Dorasamy[3]**

*[1]Taylors Business School, Subang Jaya, Selangor, Malaysia
[2]Asia Pacific University, Bukit Jalil, Kuala Lumpur, Malaysia
[3]Multimedia University, Cyberjaya, Kuala Lumpur, Malaysia*

Abstract

The purpose of the study is to investigate customers' perceptions of implementing voice bot technology in the banking industry. The pandemic environment has led to limited face-to-face interaction with customers and reduced instances of visiting the banks. Some of the challenges that customers face is the unavailability of officers to service them and the long waiting time. Banks should ensure to provide personalized 24/7 services to retain their customers. To meet these demands, many banks in Malaysia are now on the verge of introducing voice bots to engage their customers 24/7. The study has adopted a qualitative method. The study revealed that convenience, time-saving, and perceived enjoyment are factors that drive the adoption of voice bots in the banking industry. The study adds value to academic literature for future researchers and it provides practical recommendations to implement voice bots smoothly and efficiently in the banking industry.

Keywords: Artificial intelligence, voice bot, banking industry, trust, natural language processing, customer satisfaction, and perceived risk

14.1 Introduction

The present generation's preferences and expectations of services offered are driven by advanced Artificial Technologies that can provide convenience, time-saving and unique customer experiences. As such consumers

---

*Corresponding author: Manimekalai.Jambulingam@taylors.edu.my

Mohd Naved, V. Ajantha Devi, and Aditya Kumar Gupta (eds.) Fintech and Cryptocurrency, (303–324)

leave the stressful decision to an external source of computation [1]. From groceries to stock market trades, search for the best price and element contents are left to assistant bots such as Google Assistant, Amazon's Alexa, and Siri from apple [2]. According to eMarketer, 35.6 million Americans depend on a voice digital assistant like Google Home or Amazon Echo at least once a month. According to market chatbot statistics, usage of AI voice bit will increase 3 times in the next 5 years [3]. In today's technology-driven world, people are so busy with their daily routines, that they have very little time as well as knowledge to manage their finances. The lack of time as well as knowledge motivates them to look out for assistance to manage their finances quickly and efficiently on a daily basis. In 2017, American Express introduced Amazon's Echo to assist customers to check their bank balances and allow them to make transactions using a voice bot. In United States, Bank of America (BofA), the largest banking institutions introduced Erica, an AI-driven virtual financial assistant in late 2018. Erica's capabilities include assisting clients to make better financial decisions by analyzing their spending habits and financial behavioral pattern to provide them with personalized guidance and proactive insights. Thus, for banking industries to remain relevant and competitive, it is imperative to move to the next level of service by introducing artificial intelligence and interactive voice bot to assist with customer service.

14.2   Problem Statement

Artificial intelligence changed the business world rapidly, with the banking industry not being left behind. Artificial intelligence conversational interfaces such as voice bots have been a trending topic in recent years. Siri and Google assistants are the most recognized voice bots and chatbots' conversational interfaces. The recent prediction from EMarketer shows that conversational AI adoption is increasing tremendously. The statistics show that 64.2 percent of those aged between 25 to 34 utilized voice bots in 2021 and by 2022, 49.2 percent will use a voice assistant. It also predicted that by 2025, 48.2 percent of the US population will use conversation AI. The present generations are demanding 24/7, instant, and unique customer experiences in the banking industry. Being a digitally native generation, they seek seamless financial experiences catered to their lifestyle preferences and favor services that are quick to adopt new technologies that make their lives easier and simpler. To cater to these growing expectations of customers, in recent years banking industries have taken a big step toward developing and improving their customer service through artificial intelligence technologies. At the moment, the banking industry has been using chatbots and personal banking apps driven by artificial intelligence to assist customers. The apps allow customers to perform banking tasks on their smart mobile devices without any face-to-face interactions with banking staff. As voice bot usage is gaining traction in all service sectors, the banking industry is also at the forefront to leverage the use of voice bots to cater to customers' daily banking activities. To move forward, most players in the industry start by introducing voice bots for common repetitive tasks and general queries, like direct debits, standing orders, account statements request, reminders on upcoming payments, PIN and password reset, transaction limits, and various payment issues. In Asian countries, there are many studies focused on AI presence in marketing research on customer environment and consumer decision-making process with very few studies focused on voice bots and their services in the service industry. This research aims to gain knowledge and findings on consumers' perception to adopt voice bots in the banking service industry.

14.3 What is a Voice Bot?

Voice bots are chatbots that are voice-enabled i.e. AI-based software that allows voice interactions with devices and services, alleviating users' inconvenience from the endless frustrating web and phone navigations while offering a more seamless and faster two-way communication. Voice bots are a form of Conversational Banking. Conversation Banking is an intelligent way of interacting with non-human interfaces through voice, text, live chats, or visual engagement tools at various platforms to cater to banking needs. The main goal is to understand customer needs and offer the best possible solution in a personalized manner even before they ask for it. Most well-known voice assistants in the world are Samsung Bixby, Siri (Apple), Alexa (Amazon), and Google Assistant. In the banking space, we have Bank of America (Erica), Ally Bank (Ally Assist), and Kotak Mahindra Bank (KEYA), to name just a few.

The underlying technology for conversational bots initially started with a simple predefined conversation whereby customers or users are given a selection of questions with the bot responding to these queries and information requests based on predefined answers. With the advancement of technology and the use of artificial intelligence (AI) and natural language processing (NLP), bots are able to act much more flexibly and at times to even formulate answers on their own and offer responses in an almost human-like manner. It converts human voice to text using the Speech to

Text (STT) engine. The AI technology then helps to identify key markers or otherwise called intents in the speech and provides a suitable response. The Text to Speech (TTS) engine then converts the response (text) to audio or voice to conclude the interaction [4]. The continued use of the bots optimizes the NLP function, thereby enabling the bot to operate more and more effectively.

Figure 14.1 shows how NLP which enables bots to convert users' speech into structured data to be understood by a machine comprise of Natural Language Understanding (NLU) and Natural Language Generation (NLG). NLU focuses on intent recognition, basically on comprehending the intention and meaning of human speech. This is done by recognizing patterns in unstructured speech input to extract information. For example: "I would like to apply for a car loan in the Kuala Lumpur main branch". The bot must understand that the customer wants to apply for a car loan and not a housing loan. In addition, the preferred branch must be "Kuala Lumpur" and not any other branch. After the intent is detected, it will move on to the processing step which can be in various forms and would include completion of other information such as "car price", "loan amount", "tenure". Thereafter, the system will communicate with other systems to search for eligibility of the loan. Based on these, there may be a necessity to generate responses, request for further information or communicate outcomes. Figure 14.2 shows the components of the voice bot.

NLG is the domain that generates responses whereby it converts the machine-produced structured data into a human readable text that a user will understand. This involves the structuring of responses in a narrative manner, applying grammar rules and spell checks, and inputting the responses in a language template to ensure a natural conversational response.

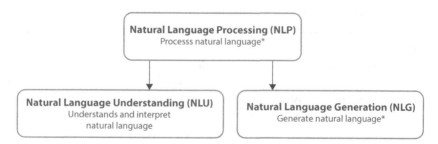

Figure 14.1 Voice bot Architecture. *Natural language refers to the way humans communicate with each other, which is complex, with an infinite number of phrasing possibilities. As voice bots evolve from defined to free communication, natural language processing makes all the difference.

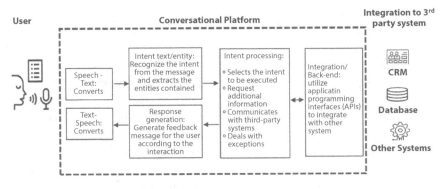

Figure 14.2 Components of a voice bot.

The connection of voice bots to the third-party systems can be designed very flexibly via application programming interfaces (APIs). By connecting third-party systems, voice bots can fetch data from other applications, both inside and outside the organization in a fully automated manner, thus generating real added value.

14.3.1   Characteristics of a Voice Bot

What is a well-designed voice bot? Voice bots are aimed at bridging the gaps in customer services at various contact points. The changing customer behavior which focuses on an instant, seamless and unique customer experience makes traditional banking less attractive, inefficient, cumbersome, and time-exhausting. Voice bots can handle these evolving customers' expectations to become the first choice of support for many. In that context, let us explore the characteristic that makes a voice bot well designed.

- 24 hours: Available around the clock for conversation with customers, even outside office hours and public holidays
- Instant: Instantly responds to customer's query without any delay or requiring them to wait in a queue
- Improved sales performance: Able to remember customer preferences, and history, learns from customer responses, propose services and products and effectively cross-sell and up-sell
- Omni channel: Available across different channels and provides consistent experience irrespective of the channel of communication or touchpoint

- Enhanced customer experience: Provides inputs, follow up on queries, and improvises thus enhancing customer experience
- Improved efficiency: Improves efficiency, reduces Turn Around Time, able to perform routine tasks quickly, allows employees to focus on more complex tasks by completing user interactions successfully with minimal human intervention.
- Multi-language capability: Able to interpret commonly conversed languages
- Simple interface: Eases communication with simple and easy-to-understand interfaces

14.3.2   Why are Voice Bots Becoming Popular?

Changing consumer behavior, essentially all boils down to customer experience With the spread of conversational trends across most industries, voice bots are key to the banking sector's digital journey to stay ahead of the curve and gain a competitive edge in delivering the next generation of customer service & engagement.

The key factors influencing this increase in trend are:

- The shift of customer behavior and preferences towards digital channels
  Customers are no longer interested to walk into a bank to do their banking. Availability of branches is no longer a key choice for customers. With accessibility for mobile devices, customers are switching to the internet and mobile apps for any sort of transaction. They want to complete all their task and needs in a click at their own comfort space without needing to allocate time, beat traffic, and walk into a branch.
- Increase in expectations in service level, speed, and unique customer experience
  The standard of service and customer experience offered by technology, e-commerce, and fintech companies have lifted customers' expectations and customers now seek the same hyper-personalized, unique and convenient service they get from Amazon, Netflix, Ali Pay, etc.
- The younger generation gets accustomed to voice interfaces
  For Millennials and Gen-Z, the first fully digital generation, banking is an experience. They seek seamless financial

experiences catered to their lifestyle preferences. Being a digitally native generation, they expect more from technology and are quick to adopt new technologies that make their lives easier. To entice and retain them as customers, banks have to constantly innovate with new digital technologies to provide tip top and unique customer experience. Putting their feet in early will allow banks to secure this market share and retain a competitive edge.

- The accelerated digitalization of retail banks contributed to the Covid-19 pandemic.

  According to BCG experts in the study "Global Retail Banking 2021: The Front-to-Back Digital Retail Bank", the pandemic has accelerated the digitalization of retail banks by 3-4 years, stimulating an active transition of customers from traditional banking channels to digital ones. Online banking grew by 23% and mobile banking by 30% respectively. BCG experts predicted that the usage of mobile banking trend will continue to grow by 19 percent and the number of calls from the customer to the banks will decrease by 26 percent by the end of the pandemic.

14.3.3 Benefits of a Voice Bot from the Bank's Perspective

- Reduce Cost: A properly implemented voice bot can significantly lower costs, and increase productivity and efficiency. Bots enable consistent quality of services being offered regardless of the circumstances. They help to reduce costs by servicing more customers without the need to increase their overheads. Virtual customer assistants can help curtail inbound queries by anything up to 40%, and often deliver first call resolution (FCR) rates far in excess of live agents [5]. A single bot can communicate with many different customers at the same time while providing a personalized response to them thus significantly reducing cost while delivering satisfactory customer experiences powered by greater analytical capabilities.

- Increase Revenue: As the voice bot can communicate with many customers concurrently, this increases the chances of the services being translated into sales thus driving revenue. The real-time, omnichannel, smart interaction voice bot which offers a seamless and personalized customer experience, will enhance customer satisfaction and increase the chances of customers coming back for more services which leads to higher customer retention and ultimately a higher bottom line.

- Improved employee productivity: Voice bot allows the automation of a large fraction of calls, emails, SMS, social media messages, and other communication channels which would require human intervention otherwise. This enables employees to focus on more complex and higher skilled tasks and roles while the voice bot provides support by handling and speeding up tedious, repetitive, and mundane tasks/requests which can be time-consuming. By working hand in hand, voice bots and humans can provide a better and higher quality customer user experience.

- Expand to new channels: Voice bot can generate leads, qualify leads, schedule meetings, promote new products, provide personalized advice and support and increase engagement and digital sales. Essentially, the voice bot becomes another channel (in addition to traditional channels) for sales conversions and engagement of customers without the need to deploy new resources which would require additional cost, training, and management, making sales and marketing activities a lot easier and efficient.

- Reduce Error: It is inevitable for humans to make mistakes. There are instances where customers or employees accidentally provide inaccurate information or allow their emotions to cloud their logic and decision-making. Voice bots whilst not perfect, assist to lower the possibilities of mistakes and errors via human interactions. They offer consistent service and are far more dependable for retrieving policies, data, answers to FAQs, and more. Additionally, there are audit logs in place for regulatory purposes or to investigate customer complaints.

- The need for Data & Personalization: Banks already have lots of customer data. However, these data are not capitalized or organized in a way it can be used for customer attraction, acquisition, and retention, and sometimes these data are just data without any insights. So basically, they have data, but just maybe not the 'right data' which will help them tap into to offer better and innovative products and solutions to customers. Voice bots collect data that can be stored and accessed by many parties and systems. Data that is collected from human interactions may not be complete or may only be accessed and found useful by the parties who acquired the data. Banks that understand the importance of personalization in this current dynamic technological era where their main customers are millennials and Gen-Z will understand the need for data. An effective personalization would need (i) gathering data and gaining insights into customer behavior via these collected data to provide the personalization and (ii) making available a platform to have the personalized conversation. Voice bots play a crucial role in banks' data collection and their personalization strategy.

14.3.4   Benefits of a Voice Bot from the Customer's Perspective

- Available 24/7: Voice bots never sleep. They are available 24/7, 365 days even on holidays, a feature the current digital savvy's 'always connected' customers expect. It is at their convenience over different channels, and it is available immediately without long wait times. Banks with voice bots have a competitive edge as an effective and efficient voice bot can provide high-quality 24/7 support and will likely attract and retain their customers.
- Enhanced Customer Experience: Customers these days look for speed, ease, and convenience rather than price. Voice bots simplify the process of users finding the information that they require. Customers just need to ask for the information and the voice bot can help them refine their searches through their responses and the ongoing conversations. After experiencing favorable exposure to various virtual assistants on their digital devices, users are seeking the same convenience and comfort in their banking services. As customers are happier, the banks get highly satisfied customers who keep coming back.
- Increase Loyalty: When an organization delivers a quick, seamless, and frictionless experience that customers demand, it strengthens the connections to the organization and customers will repay with loyalty. They are also more likely to make recommendations to families and friends. Loyal customers

help an organization grow and increase its profit. The profit of the business increased from 25% to 95% by increasing 5% of customer retention and the same effect on profit as decreasing operating costs by 10% [6]. The payoff of implementing an efficient voice bot that is responsive and conversational can be greatly significant.

- Consistent answers: How often have one ended up talking to many different customer service agents to solve one issue or to get information on one single product? This is a normal scenario in any contact center or even branch. This results in the customers having to repeat themselves multiple times and receiving discrepancies and inconsistencies in answers and sometimes even needing to deal with impatient and annoyed agents. This may be due to the different levels of experience of the employees, the employees being new in their job, or the employee simply having a tough day at work. Voice bots meanwhile function on the pre-determined framework and retrieve their responses from a single source of library. This mostly eliminates the inconsistencies in the responses provided. Moreover, they are not influenced by emotions and can consistently always provide the same level of services.

14.3.5   Opportunities for Voice Bots in Banking

A fully integrated, scalable, and trainable chatbot solution will allow banks to automate key customer interactions across various functions, channels, and request types:

- Customer Service: Simple FAQs to reduce call centers' traffic. Voice bot can assist customers with a variety of simple requests conversationally and securely ranging from reviewing an account, reporting lost cards or making payments, resetting PIN, locating a branch/ATM, etc. This enables a 24-hour service to customers with immediate response whilst enabling greater efficiency at Customer Contact Centres by allowing employees to focus on more complex tasks.
- Customer Acquisition: Voice bots can be used to boost cross-selling/upselling among existing customers, offer personalized products and services based on historical

transactions and user profiles as well as help potential customers in right-sizing products and services based on their needs during the onboarding process. This can increase lead generation, accelerate customer acquisition and assist to reduce application drop-offs.

- Provide Financial management: An effective voice bot will have access to all customers' information and profile. It can learn from customers' interactions and transactional behavior, provide credit scores, set and manage budgets, and give them a deeper awareness of their banking activities. With all this information, voice bots can guide and advise customers on their cash management, enabling them to make smarter decisions and boost their financial health. They can play the role of a financial advisor by offering personalized financial advice which is usually reserved for the wealthier customers. This can be very useful for people who don't have easy access to financial advice services due to their budget or location. As customers cultivate better financial habits, there will be opportunities to offer new innovative products to them even before they know they would need it.

- Wealth Management: As stated earlier, voice bots incessantly analyze large amount of data. This generates valuable insights that enables effective personalized advisory and guidance for customers. It can assist customers to identify unique investment options and portfolio strategies based on the insights gathered thus providing and proposing investment opportunities that are personalized and highly attractive based on each customer's unique behavior and requirements. This personalization increases the chances of success rate. Furthermore, customers also won't have any restrictions on the number of conversations they can have with the bot.

14.3.6   Use Cases: Bank Voice Bots Currently Available Around the World

- Erica, by Bank of America
  Bank of America (BofA), one of the largest banking and financial institutions in the United States, introduced Erica, an AI-driven virtual financial assistant in late 2018. Erica had 6.3 million users and 15.5 million interactions by early 2019.

When the pandemic hit the U.S., BofA updated Erica to process more than 60,000 inquiries related to COVID-19, according to the voice bot. A year later, Erica reported that the number of users increased to 19.5 million, and 100 million interactions were recorded with 90% efficacy [7]. Erica has answered more than 250 million questions since it launched [8]. Erica's capabilities include assisting clients make better financial decisions, by analyzing their habits and financial behavioral patterns to provide them with personalized guidance and proactive insights.

- Ally Assist, Ally Bank
  In 2015 Ally bank launched a chat box with Ally Assist within the bank's Mobile App. Ally Assist interacts with customers by speech or text and it performs a wide range of tasks such as P2P transactions, Transfers, and initiating payments and deposits. It also helps the customers analyze their spending/saving patterns and generate detailed account information of customers. Ally Assist provides information on customer service queries using natural language [9].

- Santandar UK
  In 2015, Santander was the first UK bank to launch voice banking for its iOS users of the Smart Bank app. The introductory phase is aimed at helping customers get to grips with the basic features, by providing the ability to ask about their card spending. In 2017, it enhanced functionality in the Smart Bank app to enable customers to fully service their accounts. This includes advanced features such as the ability to make payments, report lost cards, set up account alerts, and answer a broad range of questions about their spending [22].

- KEYA, Kotak Mahindra Bank
  Keya is an intelligent voice bot that changes the customers' preferred voice text and it can understand a customer's request quickly and guide the conversations toward a prompt response. The technology enabled us to answer a range of bank-related queries such as credit, debit card and car loans, house loans, and fixed deposits and perform tasks like paying bills and ordering cheque book. The usage of voice bots increased up to 1.2 million out of 1.7 million average calls in a month. Since Keya's chat box launched it has handled 3.5 million inquiries from one million users with 93percent accuracy [10].

- Oleg, Tinkoff Bank
  Tinkoff is a branchless online financial ecosystem, centered around lifestyle banking. It helps customers review and organize personal spending, invest savings, obtain loyalty card bonuses and make reservations – for example, book a restaurant or a cinema trip. Tinkoff provides its services through its app and its website. Launched in June 2019, Oleg is a personal voice assistant designed to help Tinkoff customers with their daily routines. It attempts to do this through certain learned actions. These operations include paying phone bills, paying credit card bills, presenting the customer's income and expenses, advising on financial issues, updating personal information in Tinkoff, and talking about several subjects. It also recognizes and protects against calls from fraudsters and spammers. Tinkoff claims that for Tinkoff Mobile subscribers, Oleg is able to answer calls and talk and joke with the caller, translating audio messages into written text [23].
- Ugi, Garanti BBVA
  Ugi, launched in 2015 is Turkey's first smart banking assistant. With Ugi on the Garanti BBVA Mobile home page, support can be obtained for more than 200 banking transactions, from money transfers to account and card queries. Users can ask Ugi via voice or text. Since implemented in 2015, when Garanti BBVA's smart assistant said "hello" for the first time, 5.6 million customers have interacted with Ugi more than 64 million times. As of July 2020, with the addition of its written communication capability, the usage rates of Ugi increased by 70% on a monthly basis. The rate of Ugi's correct understanding and accurate guidance reached 83%. Today, more than 650,000 customers a month actively communicate with Ugi [11].

14.4 Call to Action

Voice technology continues to gain popularity and momentum in this new digital era, driven by expectations from digitally savvy consumers. For banks to remain relevant and gain a competitive edge, it's imperative that they keep abreast of the trends in voice technology and how they are attracting and retaining customers to drive business. As customers become more familiar and comfortable with voice-driven technology, it will become a necessary expectation for them. Banks must continuously enhance and improve their voice technology to keep up with these new and dynamic expectations.

14.5   Literature Review

Voice bot is a new AI technology and is still in the infancy stage of implementation in the banking industry compared to e-marketing. The Capgemini Digital survey discovered that 24 percent of 5000 respondents said they preferred to use voice bots rather than websites [12]. The study found that 51 percent of respondents use the voice assistant's app on their smartphone and 35 percent said they used voice bots to buy groceries, clothing, and home care products. Google, Microsoft, Apple, and Amazon have linked voice assistants to their delivery systems for their consumers' convenience. The world's biggest leader in online shopping, amazon earned the trust of its customers for its effective services. Now it started offering services through home voice bot assistance which is linked to warehouses and vastly distributed systems to cater to millions of customers. Voice bot increases happiness for their consumers by timesaving on searching and providing value convenience [13]. Shevat (2017) stated that consumers recognized the benefits of using voice bots and they are confident that the voice bots can determine the best possible attributes of the available alternatives [14].

Weerabahu et al., (2019) found that chatbot technology increased customer satisfaction and provides solutions to day-to-day issues compared to call centers which are time-consuming and inefficient in Sri Lanka [15]. Wirtz et al., (2018) stated that the "intention of using new technology depends on the cognitive evaluation of ease of use and perceived usefulness" [3]. Recent studies show that consumer adoption of new technology depends on their enjoyment of using the speaker and ease of use to process the information. Firms are focusing on the hedonism of voice bots while reducing the perceptions of security risks [15, 16]. Makridakis (2017) identified that once the customer purchase things through the voice bot, it creates trust that voice assistance chooses a better option for them and they may be afraid of their own choice not being the best [17]. In 2018, professor, Tim Wu wrote in New York Times, "Tyranny of Convenience". It was stated that: "Today, convenience is the most undervalued and least understood force of the world". "Convenience in decision making is not a new thing". This has been practiced for a long time and it is evidenced in the literature [18]. Convenience is the key influencer of the adoption of AI bot technologies among customers [19].

Additionally, consumer perception is a crucial component of consumers' willingness to adopt new technology. Consumer perception is an important marketing tool that articulates consumers' awareness, consciousness, and belief about a new product or service (Dictionary, 2018). The consumers' positive and negative perceptions will affect the adoption of new technologies. Therefore, the study aims to investigate customers' perceptions of the adoption of voice bot technology in the banking industry.

14.6 Research Methodology

The study adopted a mixed-method approach. 80 respondents participated in the survey and 20 respondents participated in the interview section. The qualitative method has been chosen to explore the depth of the topic. 20 respondents aged from 21 to 32 participated in the study. Among them 11 are male and 9 of them female. The semi-structured interview was conducted on the perception of adopting voice bots in the banking industry. The interview was conducted in a group of 20. The research instruments are based on ease of use, perceived usefulness, security, convenience, and trust which are derived from the literature. The researcher explained what is a chatbot and voice bot and how it is used in the banking industry. The respondents answered that they are all aware of chatbots but were not familiar with voice bots. The following questions are asked to explore the perception of voice bots in the banking industry.

1. Have you used any voice bot such as Siri and google assistant?
   They said they used the voice assistant to control home electronic devices, listen to music, and talk to someone while they are driving.
2. Have you used mobile banking apps for your banking transactions?
   Among the respondents, 12 of them said that they have been using a mobile app for transactions. They felt it is easy to transfer and it is secure. Others said they are not willing to take the risk and they don't trust the mobile app. They are more comfortable using online banking services.
3. What do you think if the voice bot can replace a customer service executive in the near future?

Most of them were excited and said it is interesting. They said they are able to make transfers any time and it is a very convenient and very useful voice assistance bot. Without the need to type or enter numbers in the system. it is going to be easy for them. However, eight of the respondents said they won't use it because they are afraid of security, and they don't want to take risks related to financial matters. Most of them said it saves a lot of time, and they perform any transfers anytime through the app. Two respondents further asked whether the voice is going to be a female voice or a male voice. Many of them doubted whether the voice bot can recognize their language and the ascent of the speech. A few of them said they may not use it because they are afraid the voice bot cannot understand their language. Most of them preferred to use voice assistance instead of using a chatbot and find chatbots to be boring. They believe it is cumbersome and time-consuming.

4. Do you think it is going to be more comfortable using voice bots for some basic tasks such as balance checking and making payments?

Most of them said they believe it is going to be easy and convenient. Some said it is going to be fun to use the app for transactions by voice assistant and save a lot of time. Some respondents said that there is human touch when they talk to voice bots and also they do things fast compared to chatbot conversation. Four of them said that they are not confident in using the voice bot for transactions. They may use it for getting information. They cannot trust the app and they do not want to use it for financial transactions. The findings concluded that pleasure, convenience, time-saving, and perceived ease of use are the driving force for consumers to use voice bots in the banking industry in the future. Perceived risk, language recognition, data security, and lack of trust and confidence are the avoiding factors preventing them from using voice bots.

14.7 Descriptive Analysis

Survey questions were sent out to 100 respondents. Only 80 respondents returned the survey questions. Table 14.1 shows respondents' demographic and descriptive analysis. Among the respondent 38.75 percent of them are female and 61.25 percent were male. 76 percent of them belong to the age group between 21 to 26 and 24 percent of them are from the 27 to 31 age group. Among the respondents, 65 percent of them have used a chat bot and 35 percent of them have never used a chat bot. 63.75 percent of them have used a voice bot and 32.25 percent never used it before. 67.25 percent of them used banking transactions through the mobile app and 32.75 percent of them never used the mobile app. 68.75 percent of them said they are willing to use voice bot assistance, 23.75 percent of them said they are

Table 14.1 Respondents' profile.

Gender	Percentage
Female	38.75
Male	61.25
Age	
21- 26	76
27 to 32	24
Have you used Chat bot?	
No	35
Yes	65
Have you used Voice assistant?	
Yes	63.75
No	36.25
Have you used a mobile app for transactions	
Yes	67.5
No	32.5
Will you use in future voice assistant bot in banking transactions	
Yes	68.75
No	23.75
Not sure	7.5

not going to use voice bot assistance and 7.5 percent of them are not sure about it.

Figure 14.3 shows that 21.25 percent of them used a voice assistant to choose a song, 15.25 percent of them used to get information, 25 percent of them used to control devices in their home,13.75 percent of them used for entertainment,17.25 percent used to call someone while driving and 6.25 percent of them used to read the message for them.

Figure 14.4 shows the respondents' opinions on using voice bots. 27.27 percent of them using for convenience, 34,55 percent of them for saving time, 15.36 percent of them want to multitask, 14.55 percent feel it is easy to use and 7.27 percent said it gives pleasure to them.

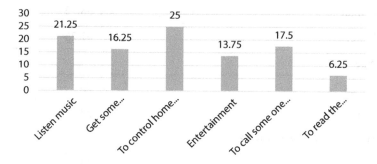

Figure 14.3 Voice bot usage of the respondents.

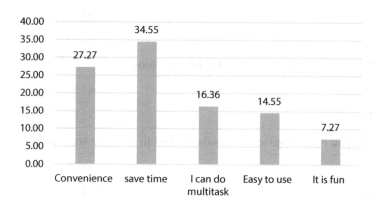

Figure 14.4 Reasons for using voice bots in banking transactions.

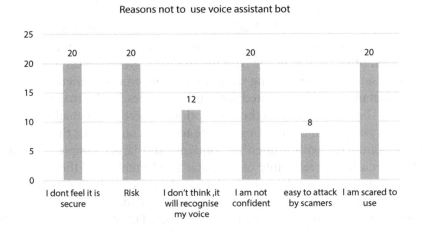

Figure 14.5 Reasons not to use voice bot in banking transactions.

Figure 14.5 shows the reasons for not using the voice bot. 20 percent of them feel that it is not secure, 20 percent of them do not want to face any risk, 12 percent of them doubt it will recognize their voice/accent, 8 percent of them feel easy for scammers to attack, and 20 percent of them are not confident in using the voice bot for banking transactions.

14.8   Discussion and Conclusion

The study revealed that perceived risk, trust, security, language recognition, and scams are the main concern of customers making the decision not to adopt voice bot assistance in banking transactions. Nevertheless, we find that the majority of the respondents are willing to adopt voice bot assistance in the banking industry. The finding is in line with previous studies that the voice bot can save a lot of time, allows multitasking, and have trust it makes the right decision [17]; provide convenience [18], and enjoyment [15].

The study also contributed to the theory of social presence in the context of voice bots in virtual environments. Previous studies show that social presence has a significant impact on customer satisfaction by 60 percent within a computer-mediated form of communication [20]. Hassaein and Head (2007) found that implementing voice assistant and pictures increase the user's satisfaction and experience [21]. A voice bot recognizes speech and interprets language commands while providing a human touch and the feeling of interacting with a real person. The study shows there is a significant impact on customer satisfaction and pleasure in using voice bots in the banking industry. Perceived risk, trust, and fear of language recognition are the concern of customers regarding the adoption of voice bots in the banking industry. Nevertheless, the present generation's decision-making depends on convenience. Therefore, voice bot assistance may be adopted without any issues by the majority of the people. The study discussed the description of voice bot, it challenges consumers' perception of adopting it. Due to time constraints, the study has to be conducted with limited respondents and larger sample size could have given higher reliability of the data. The limitation of the research is that not many respondents had taken part in the study due to time and many of them were not aware of voice bot assistance. Larger sample size could have given higher reliability of the data. Future research should be conducted with a larger number of samples and various age groups of people.

References

1. U. Gretzel, "The transformation of consumer behavior," in The Routledge Handbook of Tourism Marketing-n Tourism Business Frontiers, D. R. Fesenmaier, Ed. London : Taylors & Francis, pp. 31–40.
2. K. N. Lemon and P. C. Verhoef, "Understanding customer experience throughout the customer journey," *Journal of Marketing*, vol. 80, no. 6, pp. 69–96, 2015.
3. R. Chotia, A. Tyagi, N. Ayyagari, and A. C. Fernandes, "100 best chatbot statistics for 2022 [latest BOT statistics]," *Verloop.io*, 04-Jul-2022. [Online]. Available: https://verloop.io/blog/100-best-chatbot-statistics/#h-market-chatbot-statistics. [Accessed: 15-July-2022].
4. S. B. Banerjee, "Voice bot in enhancing the future of Banking System," *C-Zentrix*. [Online]. Available: https://www.c-zentrix.com/us/blog/voice-bot-in-enhancing-the-future-of-banking-system.
5. "Chatbots: The definitive guide," *Conversational AI Platform for Enterprise - Teneo | Artificial Solutions*, 21-Jun-2022. [Online]. Available: https://www.artificial-solutions.com/chatbots.
6. S. Chambers, "The importance of customer loyalty," *Nicereply*, 11-May-2020. [Online]. Available: https://www.nicereply.com/blog/the-importance-of-customer-loyalty/.

7. M. Shahab, "A deeper look into what makes a successful chatbot with Bank of America's Erica," *Tearsheet*, 26-Aug-2021. [Online]. Available: https://tearsheet.co/artificial-intelligence/a-deeper-look-into-what-makes-a-successful-chatbot-with-bank-of-americas-erica/.

8. E. H. Schwartz, "Bank of America's Virtual assistant Erica explodes in popularity," *Voicebot.ai*, 21-Apr-2021. [Online]. Available: https://voicebot.ai/2021/04/21/bank-of-americas-virtual-assistant-erica-explodes-in-popularity/.

9. J. Marous, "Meet 11 of the most interesting chatbots in banking," *The Financial Brand*, 14-Mar-2018. [Online]. Available: https://thefinancialbrand.com/71251/chatbots-banking-trends-ai-cx/.

10. Dr. Shalini Sayiwal and Asst.Prof., Alankar P.G.Girls College, Jaipur. (2021). Chatbots in Banking Industry: A Case Study. *Journal of Emerging Technologies and Innovative Research (JETIR)*, vol.7 no.6, June 2020. [Online]. Availabe : JETIR2006221.pdf

11. A. R. Rodríguez, "Garanti BBVA interacts with more than 650,000 customers a month with its smart assistant Ugi," *NEWS BBVA*, 30-Dec-2021. [Online]. Available: https://www.bbva.com/en/tr/garanti-bbva-interacts-with-more-than-650000-customers-a-month-with-its-smart-assistant-ugi/.

12. Sengupta, A. Empathetic intelligence: how smart voice assistants are driving consumer convenience, Capgemini Research Institute, 2018, available at: www.capgemini.com/2018/09/voice-assistants-driving-consumer-convenience/ (accessed 17 January 2022).

13. A. V. Whillans, E. W. Dunn, P. Smeets, R. Bekkers, and M. I. Norton, "Buying time promotes happiness," *Proceedings of the National Academy of Sciences*, vol. 114, no. 32, pp. 8523–8527, 2017.

14. Shevat, A., Designing Bots: Creating Conversational Experiences, "O'Reilly Media, 2017.

15. D. Weerabahu, A. Gamage, C. Dulakshi, G. U. Ganegoda, and T. Sandanayake, "Digital assistant for Supporting Bank Customer Service," *Communications in Computer and Information Science*, pp. 177–186, 2019.

16. P. Klaus and J. Zaichkowsky, "Ai Voice Bots: A services marketing research agenda," *Journal of Services Marketing*, vol. 34, no. 3, pp. 389–398, 2020.

17. S. Makridakis, "The forthcoming Artificial Intelligence (AI) revolution: Its impact on society and firms," *Futures*, vol. 90, pp. 46–60, 2017.

18. J. E. Collier and S. E. Kimes, "Only if it is convenient," *Journal of Service Research*, vol. 15, no. 1, pp. 39–51, 2012.

19. D. Grewal, A. L. Roggeveen, and J. Nordfält, "The future of retailing," *Journal of Retailing*, vol. 93, no. 1, pp. 1–6, 2017.

20. C. N. Gunawardena and F. J. Zittle, "Social presence as a predictor of satisfaction within a computer-mediated conferencing environment," *American Journal of Distance Education*, vol. 11, no. 3, pp. 8–26, 1997.

21. K. Hassanein and M. Head, "Manipulating perceived social presence through the web interface and its impact on attitude towards online shopping," *International Journal of Human-Computer Studies*, vol. 65, no. 8, pp. 689–708, 2007.

22. "About Santander UK," *Santander UK*, 22-Mar-2015. [Online]. Available: https://www.santander.co.uk/about-santander/media-centre/press-releases/santander-becomes-first-uk-bank-to-launch-voice-banking. [Accessed: 12-April-2022].

23. "Тинькофф - финансовые услуги для физических и юридических лиц," *Тинькофф Банк*. [Online]. Available: https://www.tinkoff.ru/about/news/06102015-tinkoff-named-the-largest-digital-bank-eng/. [Accessed: 15-April -2022].

15

Application of Technology Acceptance Model (TAM) in Fintech Mobile Applications for Banking

Tabitha Durai and F. Lallawmawmi*

Department of Commerce, Madras Christian College, University of Madras, Chennai, India

Abstract

The rising prominence of Fintech payment services has a great impact on banking. It is increasingly becoming a global trend. Mobile payment applications and gateways are a well-liked use of Fintech services for banking. Of course, contactless payments are much more appreciated in today's world. This research paper aims to study the factors that influence customers' usage of Fintech services for banking. A descriptive and analytical study was conducted through a structured Questionnaire. The Technology Acceptance Model is used to examine the extent to the perceived usefulness, brand image, and perceived risk influence the usage of Fintech. The data have been analyzed and hypotheses have been tested by using statistical measures and quantitative methods. This study identified three factors Perceived usefulness, Brand image, and Perceived risk which influence the usage of Fintech services for banking. Perceived usefulness is the most enabling influencing factor on the usage of Fintech services. The results show that perceived usefulness and brand image have a significant positive influence on the usage of Fintech services, while perceived risks do not significantly affect the usage of Fintech services. It is expected that the findings of this empirical study would have enabled adding to the present contributions on the subject.

Keywords: Fintech, banking, fintech services, mobile banking, mobile payment, perceived usefulness, brand image, perceived risks

*Corresponding author: awmi251098@gmail.com

Mohd Naved, V. Ajantha Devi, and Aditya Kumar Gupta (eds.) Fintech and Cryptocurrency, (325–350)

15.1 Introduction

Financial Technologies (Fintech) have transformed banking and financial services operations worldwide during the past years. The emerging importance of fintech (Financial Technology) applications greatly impacts the banking and finance sectors in many ways. The advancements in Fintech have a dramatic effect on traditional banking and financial services sectors in terms of operations. It was originally applied for back-end systems and is now used in many additional applications such as mobile payments, online banking, fund management as well as stock trading. In a nutshell, the basic process of payment methods has been transformed through the use of digital technology and the financial ecosystem has been changed by Fintech [1]. The rising technologies and the fintech companies use digital tools to transform the way we bank and evolve the banking industry from physical to digital and then to hybrid banking models. With the help of fintech banking services, self-service capabilities provide bank customers with operational processes such as checking account balances, transferring money, opening new accounts, opting for loans, and buy insurance, etc. digitally [2]. FinTech is increasingly becoming a global trend and is now attracting the attention of FinTech regulators in the past, present, and future in the financial and banking industries. Nowadays, FinTech is an industry that uses Information Technology concentrated on smartphones/mobile phones to improve financial system efficiency [3].

The term 'Fintech' is derived by joining two words which are 'financial' and 'technology'. FinTech indicates the use of digital technology to come up with innovative financial products and services such as mobile payment, online banking, big data, alternative finance and overall financial management [4]. Fintech refers to new technology that seeks to improve and automate the delivery and use of financial services and products. When it emerged in the 21st Century, the term 'Fintech' was introduced as a technology employed in the back-end systems of established financial institutions and banks [5]. Now, it encompasses several applications that are consumer-based which leads to more consumer-oriented services. By 2019, through this technology, you can manage funds, trade stocks and even pay for insurance, etc [4]. Fintech services are software, algorithms and applications that are used on both computers and smartphones. It also includes hardware in the same cases. Fintech platforms enable a variety of financial activities like money transfers, depositing checks, paying bills or applying for financial aid. They also include developing and using crypto exchanges and encompass technically intricate concepts like peer-to-peer (P2P) lending [6].

There are many different types of fintech, some of the most popular examples are: (a) Mobile payment and wallet apps like Google pay, PayPal, Apple Pay, Square, and Venmo allow users to send one another money from their mobile devices through a linked bank account or card [7]; (b) Crowdfunding platforms such as Kickstarter and GoFundMe, have replaced traditional funding options by allowing platform users to invest their money in businesses, products and individuals, and allow them to cross geographical boundaries by in contact with global markets and investors [8, 9]; (c) Cryptocurrency and blockchain technologies are some of the most well-known examples of fintech. Cryptocurrency exchanges such as Coinbase and Gemini, allow users to buy or sell cryptocurrencies (bitcoins), these currencies are stored in a decentralized manner under which money transactions are verified using blockchain technologies [8, 9]; (d) Robo-advisors such as Betterment and Ellevest, are online investment-management services, consist of algorithm-based portfolio recommendations and management to lower costs and increase efficiency [8, 9]; (e) Stock trading apps such as Robinhood and Acorns allow investors to trade stocks from anywhere with their mobile devices instead of visiting stockbrokers [8]; (f) Insurtech companies are engaging with traditional insurance companies to automate the procedures at it entirely and allowing them to expand claim-coverages [9].

The latest Fintech business model research hotspots are mobile payments, P2P lending, crowdfunding and microfinance [10]. The most popular Fintech service to have been used was in the banking and payments category in 2019 [11]. In 2021, digital banking and bill payments were the most dominant uses of fintech services [12]. Mobile banking was already gaining popularity even before the outbreak of coronavirus in 2019, but the disruptions and restrictions caused by Covid-19 have moved banking through mobile from novelty to necessity [13]. Mobile payment applications and gateways are a well-liked use of fintech services that enable banking through mobile devices/smartphones without the need for physical contact between the bank and its customers [1]. They come under the most prevalent uses of fintech services to conduct banking activities without appearing physically in the bank [9]. Fintech services like mobile payments consist in making payments and transactions between individuals easily, fast, and convenient, anytime and anywhere, using a mobile phone/smartphone. It also provides greater security for users in the interactions derived from money transactions [14]. The development and exploitation of new technologies make opportunities, exclusively for numerous local economies, to promote their products globally at low cost, anticipating a bigger share not only from local markets but also from the global travel market and following the same path when it comes to financial transactions [10].

Fintech services like mobile/digital banking apps (Fintech payment services) can warn customers when they spend more than they have in their account and allow them to set controls on their cards to restrict spending. Banking apps can also make it easy to transfer money and reach customer service representatives with the tap of a button [13]. Some of the benefits of mobile banking apps are: (a) Mobile banking apps enable banking from anywhere at any time and make it convenient for the customers; (b) Mobile banking apps guarantee paramount safety and security for all money transactions. Cybersecurity and multi-layer encryption are important for mobile banking apps; (c) Mobile banking apps make it easier to monitor the flow of money to and from an account by giving all the information in a single app; (d) Customers who use mobile banking have better access and control of their financial transactions which make them more likely to catch any suspicious activities and to prevent any kind of frauds; (e) Mobile banking is sustainable in terms of energy and saving time, they are also environment-friendly since they save unnecessary paperwork unlike traditional banking [15]; (f) Mobile banking enables to set up of automatic payments for regular utility bills; (g) It reduces the risk of counterfeit currency with digital fund transfers and restricts the circulation of black money; (h) Mobile banking apps strengthen privacy and security for the users [16].

The advantages of mobile banking/payment service for both bank institutions and customers include easy access anywhere, availability on 24 hours basis, control over your money, and reduction in the cost of handling banking transactions [17]. The main advantage of Fintech services/ applications like mobile banking to both customers and banks is the opportunity of being on the same page. When a bank meets its customers' expectations and satisfies their needs, it attracts more customers to the bank and speeds up its growth. A large number of mobile banking users proves that Fintech services/applications have a lot of advantages for banking. Among the advantages of mobile/online banking is that users need less time to perform simple money transactions. All the customers need is the internet since no branch visit is needed. They can check their accounts, access information and get notifications about the bank news at any time. There are also benefits of fintech services like mobile banking apps for banks themselves. Banks can serve customers at any time since customers can access and check their accounts, and make money transactions independently everywhere at any time. Fintech services also help banks in time-saving and give more time to assist those customers who need personal attention which improves the workflow. Other benefits of Fintech services for banks are saving on operational costs, reducing costs by going paperless and saving money on printing [18].

Using mobile payment services requires the user to open an account at his or her bank and receive payment instruments such as card, etc. that are linked to the account from the issuing bank to pay merchants online or offline. Mobile payment services can be separated into Fintech payment service that links with financial institutions through IT companies and existing payment service that directly links to financial institutions. In both services, payments are made directly to the service provider or through an integrated payment agency, that supports both existing payment services and Fintech payment services. However, traditional payment services have some limitations and problems when compared to the Fintech payment services even though they use IT technology like Fintech payment services. Fintech payment service allows user to use an independent customized payment service that is not dependent on the payment service of the financial institution but that is personalized to the convenience of the user of specific financial institution. Unlike traditional payment services, Fintech payment service providers can customize payment services according to the needs of the user as well as the merchants, and it has more diverse purposes and methods of use [19].

Fintech competitors are intruding on the traditional business of banks, even though banks are conforming to the digital world. New competitors are allowed to use hard (codifiable) information to erode the traditional relationship between bank and client, based on soft information (the knowledge gained from bank and client relationships). Still, in order to avoid compliance costs, utmost new competitors stay clear of asking for a banking license and try to skim profitable business from banks. Implicit advantage of the new entrants lies in exploiting the distrust towards banks that millennials have developed at the same moment that they offer digital services with which the youngish generation is at ease [20]. Payments and particularly retail-related payments areas seem most open to Fintech. This core area of banking is being wanted by technology firms and payment specialists such as Google, Apple and PayPal. Banks have maintained their central role in payments until now. The payments innovators have developed in joint ventures or other types of alliances with traditional banks, as they are not typically independent of banks [21].

Technology Acceptance Model (TAM) is often used for the technology users' acceptance testing. It was introduced in 1989 by Davis in his PhD thesis. There are two objectives described by Davis, the first is to improve the understanding of the user acceptance process and the second is that TAM provides a theoretical basis for practical user acceptance testing [22]. TAM has become one of the most widely used models in the field of information technology adoption research because it explains the difference in consumer willingness to adopt information technology and can be specified and improved according to the analysis problem [23].

TAM has been used to study Technology Acceptance Model of Financial Technology in Micro, Small, and Medium Enterprises (MSME) in 2020 [22]. In this research, the researchers included external variables such as level of education, business age and business size to predict Perceived Usefulness (PU) and Perceived Ease of Use (PEOU). Zhongqing Hu, Shuai Ding, Shizheng Li, Luting Chen and Shanlin Lang [23] used TAM to analysed the key factors influencing the adaptation of Fintech services through empirical research as well as the behavioural intentions of users. Data was collected from 387 randomly selected active customers of the Hefei Science and Technology Rural Commercial Bank who had used Fintech services of the bank and analysed through structural equation model (SEM) to test the hypothesis including the relationships of all latent variables. They found that brand image, government support, user innovation and user's trust in fintech services have positive impact on the adaptation fintech services while perceived ease of use has no significant influence on user's attitudes for adaptation of fintech services. Li Min Chuang, Chun Chu Liu and Hsiao Kuang Kao [26] also applied TAM in order to understand the consumer behavioural intentions in using Fintech service and found brand and service trust, perceived usefulness, perceived ease of use and attitudes towards using have a significant positive effect on behavioural intention to use.

In the Unified Theory of Acceptance and Use of Technology (UTAUT) by Tun-Pin Chong *et al.* [24] TAM has been used to examine the extent to that perceived usefulness, perceived ease of use, social influence, personal innovativeness, security concerns, perceived enjoyment and demographic profile affect the intention to adopt Fintech in 2019. They found out that all the constructs that are mentioned above had a significant and positive relationship with the intention to adopt Fintech in Malaysia. Kavitha Lal, M. Suvarchala Rani and P. Rajini [39] studied to identify the influencing factors on the Bank customer adoption of Fintech in Hyderabad. A sample size of 101 was collected and analysed using ANOVA, Exploratory Factor Analysis (EFA) and Multi Variant Regression Model. The study found that the most enabling influencing factor was Conducive among three factors such as Conducive, Adaptability and Security, which was identified. Ivanka Vasenska, Preslav Dimitrov, Blagovesta Koyundzhiyska-Davidkova,

Vladislav Krastev,Pavol Durana and Ioulia Poulaki [10] studied to present a survey analysis of Fintech utilization of individual customers before and after COVID-19 pandemic in Bulgaria using statistical measures and quantitative methods including ANOVA and two-sample paired t-tests and Levene's test. The research targeted 242 Bulgarian adult and found that majority of the respondents are less familiar with Fintech services before the COVID-19 crisis, however some of them were planning to change their attitudes towards the adaptation of fintech services and use it more after COVID-19 pandemic.

15.1.1   Significance of the Study

Fintech services like mobile payment/banking apps are incredibly convenient and powerful tools which give an important advantage to customers. Mobile banking has made money transactions user-friendly and virtual access much faster for the customers. Fintech services like mobile banking/payment apps became more common as users became comfortable with the technology and find it useful in their day-to-day life. Contactless payments are much more appreciated in today's world which makes mobile banking apps popular among banks' customers. Therefore, the current research attempted to identify the factors that influence customers' usage of Fintech services for banking. The findings could provide the Fintech sphere with information to target, diversify, and popularize their products better on the market. It could also provide users assessment and empirical framework for banks to adopt new and user-oriented services.

15.1.2   Research Objectives

Fintech has become an important and interesting topic given the fast-growing change in information technology. The development of Fintech such as mobile banking has contributed to the increasing advancement in technology productivity. The services offered by the financial institutions continue to challenge and cater to the attitudes of consumers who are accepting of new technology products to gain market opportunities [24]. It is used to determine the adoption of Fintech services. Studies on the usage of Fintech and the factors that influence the usage of Fintech among bank customers are very limited. Hence, the current study aims to explore the various factors that influence customers' usage of Fintech applications for banking. The present study identifies the most enabling influencing factor on the usage of Fintech services for banking. The study also identifies whether the various factors have a significant positive influence on the usage of Fintech services for banking.

15.1.3 Hypotheses of the Study

In this study, TAM is used as the foundation and referenced relevant literature. The Technology Acceptance Model (TAM) developed by Davis, is an adaptation of the Theory of Reasoned Action (TRA). It defines perceived usefulness and perceived ease of use as two determinants of individuals' attitude toward the behavioural intention and usage of technology [25]. Technology Acceptance Model (TAM) was proposed from the perspective of behavioural science, self-efficacy theory and integrating expectation theory, it is mainly used to study the individuals' behavioural intentions to use technology [23]. The TAM assumes that the key determinant of behavioural intentions of an individual depends on their beliefs about their subjective evaluation of the usefulness of the technology and their own ability to use a piece of technology [26].

15.1.3.1 *Perceived Usefulness Toward the Usage of Fintech*

According to the Technology Acceptance Model (TAM), perceived usefulness is a factor widely used in the process of information system adoption and is defined as the degree to which a consumer using this new technology would improve their work efficiency [27]. A large number of empirical studies on the adoption of information technology during the last decade have shown that perceived usefulness and ease of use can have a positive impact on users' intentions [23]. In the TAM, perceived usefulness is the level of confidence a person has in using a specific system to augment his or her performance in a job or task. In other words, it leads to the consumer's attitude toward the performance concerning the outcome of the experience [24]. Perceived ease of use is the level of a person who believes that online transactions through mobile banking would be effortless [28]. People assess the consequences of their behaviour in terms of perceived usefulness and their behavioural choices are based on the attractiveness of the perceived usefulness [29]. Hence, the following hypothesis is proposed.

Hypothesis 1 ($H_{0\,1}$) = Perceived usefulness has a significant positive effect on the consumers' usage of fintech services.

15.1.3.2   Brand Image Toward the Usage of Fintech

The brand effect of service providers plays a positive role in promoting users' achievements of their intended purposes and thus has a significant influence on the provision of reliable services to users [30]. A large number of studies on Fintech proved that brand image has an important influence on users' perceptions of quality, value and satisfaction [31]. According to psychological research results, a decent brand image can create trust among users [32]. Therefore, brand image is the guarantee of products and services, which enables users to clearly define the service orientation of the enterprise, improves user recognition and satisfaction, helps enterprises and users build a solid relationship, and ultimately affects customer recognition and builds trust [33]. Hence, the following hypothesis is proposed.

Hypothesis 2 (H_0 2) = Brand Image has a significant positive effect on the consumers' usage of fintech services.

15.1.3.3   Perceived Risks Toward the Usage of Fintech

Perceived risk refers to the form of lack of trust, and most scholars believe that perceived risk is the main factor that negatively affects the adoption of technology [34]. In this paper, perceived risk refers to the financial risk as well as privacy risk that users perceive when they choose fintech services for banking. The users are more concerned about the misuse of their personal information when using fintech services for banking which may lead to more serious consequences. Based on these considerations, perceived risks arising from the use of fintech can significantly affect the willingness of users to use financial technology for banking [35]. Hence, the following hypothesis is proposed.

Hypothesis 3 (H_0 3) = Perceived Risk (PR) has a significant positive effect on the frequency of usage of fintech services.

TAM has become one of the most widely used models in the field of information technology adoption research because it clearly explains the difference in consumers' willingness to adopt information technology and can be improved, and also specified according to the analysis problem [23]. Many scholars have focused on factors that affect the use of new technologies, including ease of use, result demonstrability, relative advantage, visibility, compatibility, image, trialability and voluntariness. The perceived usefulness and perceived ease of use would affect the individuals' behavioural intention of the use of new technologies and would also be affected by the external variables including individual characteristics, organizational support and system characteristics [25].

15.2   Methods and Measures

The current study aims to establish individual customers' utilization of fintech services for banking. This is a descriptive and analytical study based on primary data and secondary data. A structured questionnaire was administered using Google forms to collect primary data. The questionnaire was adapted from multiple literature reviews. Journals, websites, newspapers and books were used as secondary data sources.

The population evaluation is based on the results of a survey questionnaire conducted on 100 respondents. This study implemented the convenience sampling method to get a bigger size of sample. Balter and Brunet [36] stated that the use of new technologies such as social networking sites can be effective for the study of "hard-to-reach" populations. Thus, this study was conducted using Google form, which was distributed through social networking sites. The pros and cons of online surveys have been studied and applied as compared to other data collection methods. Online surveys have the advantages of being faster, cheaper, more accurate, and independent in the cases of time and space when compared to other data collection methods such as face-to-face, telephone, and mail surveys [10]. The disadvantage of online surveys is that investigators can encounter problems as regards sampling when conducting online research [10]. The study recommends that it is necessary to outline the demographic factors of the respondents in terms of their gender, age, and occupation. The sample characteristics of the respondents such as gender, age, occupation and the frequency of the usage of fintech services have been analyzed by using descriptive statistics percentage analysis.

The data have been analyzed and hypotheses have been tested by using valid statistical tools using IBM SPSS Statistics 22. Data and results have been interpreted based on the resulting output. It also includes the option to carry out more advanced statical processing as well as to create scripts to automate analysis. Multi Variant Regression Model and ANOVA were used to test the hypotheses. Bryn Farnsworth [37] stated that SPSS (Statistical Package for the Social Sciences) is possibly the most widely used statistical software package. It offers the capability to easily compile descriptive statistics, parametric and non-parametric analyses. It also offers the ability to easily compile graphical depictions of results through the graphical user interface (GUI). It also includes the option to carry out more advanced statical processing as well as to create scripts to automate analysis.

It is inevitable to use the tools provided by statistical methodology in the collection, summary, and analysis of empirical data. The 5 points Likert-type Scale (i.e., strongly disagree (1), disagree (2), neutral (3), agree (4), and strongly agree (5)) is applied in the questionnaire that was distributed to gather data. The Likert scale provides five possible answers to a question or statement which is used to let the participants to indicate how much they agree or disagree regarding the particular question or statement [38].

15.2.1 Instrument Development

This paper made full reference to the problems of research scholars in relevant research and made adjustments and expansions according to the characteristics of Fintech services studied as shown in Table 15.1. Perceived usefulness and ease of use (PU), Brand Image (BI) and Perceived Risk (PR) were adopted from Zhongqing Hu *et al.* (2019), Li-Min Chuang *et al.* (2016) and Kavitha Lal *et al.* (2020) [23, 26, 39]. The scale consisted

Table 15.1 Measurement instruments relating to factors of Fintech.

Latent variables	Measurement instruments	Sources
Perceived Usefulness (PU)	Useful	Zhongqing Hu *et al.* (2019), Kavitha Lal *et al.* (2020), and Li-Min Chuang *et al.* (2016);
	Easy to use	
	Save time	
	Convenient	
	Availability	
	Meet service needs	
Brand Image (BI)	Good services system	Zhongqing Hu *et al.* (2019) and Kavitha Lal *et al.* (2020)
	Maintain data security	
	Good reputation	
Perceived Risk (PR)	Cyberattacks	Kavitha Lal *et al.* (2020).
	Money can be stolen	

of three latent variables as external influencing factors and each variable was composed of three to six measurement variables. Likert Scale was used in the questionnaire to express the item of each measurement variable. Participants were obliged to express their attitudes according to their true opinion. The five options were: strongly agree, agree, neutral, disagree and strongly disagree.

The Technology Acceptance Model (TAM) is used to examine the extent to that perceived usefulness, brand image and perceived risk influence the usage of fintech services for banking.

This paper studies the influence and relationship of the frequency of usage of fintech services for banking and conducts in-depth research and discussion on it through a technology acceptance model (TAM). The TAM explains the relationship between behavioural intention that predicts a user's acceptance of information technology [40]. TAM posits that if innovation or technology enhances an individual's performance, it is considered useful and the person will be more likely to adopt the service, technology or behaviour. The results of numerous studies have supported the reliability and validity of the perceived usefulness and perceived ease of use variables in the Technology Acceptance Model [41].

15.3   Results

The findings of statistical analysis are presented in this section i.e., to identify the various fintech services or applications used for banking and to study the factors that influence consumers' usage of Fintech Applications.

15.3.1   Demographic Profile of the Respondents

Based on the demographic factors, a general conclusion could be made that young and student female tend to respond to such online surveys, especially through social media. Another general conclusion regarding the survey, results could be that women tend to participate in such surveys due to the fact that women are perceived as more caring, concerned and sensitive, while men are perceived as more independent, reasonable and strong such differences have been created by society. As for the frequency of the fintech services usage, frequent users are described for a relatively high proportion, which indicates that the popularizing rate of fintech payment services is relatively high at present.

In Table 15.2, 60% are females and the majority of the respondents, that is 80% are in the age group of 20-30, while 1% of the total respondents are in the age group of 'above 50'. Most of the participants are students, that is 43% of the total respondents. An analysis related to the frequency of the usage of fintech services for banking shows that 49% of the respondents use fintech services monthly while there is none for 'never' option.

Table 15.2 Demographic profile of the respondents.

Demographic variable	Category	Percentage
Gender	Male	40%
	Female	60%
Age	Below 20	5%
	20 – 30	80%
	30 – 40	9%
	40 – 50	5%
	Above 50	1%
Occupation	Student	43%
	Government Employee	8%
	Private Employee	11%
	Self-Employed	20%
	Housewife	4%
	Other	14%
Fintech Services Usage (such as Google Pay, PayPal, Apple Pay,etc)	Daily	16%
	Weekly	29%
	Monthly	49%
	Yearly	6%
	Never	0%

Source: Computed data.

15.3.2   Factors Influencing Fintech under Technology Acceptance Model (TAM)

The five-point Likert Scale is considered an interval scale and the mean is very significant. This paper calculated descriptive statistics – Means and standard deviation for the influencing factors. The means were interpreted as follows:

Strongly disagree = 1.00 – 1.79 (Lower limit – Upper limit), Disagree = 1.80 – 2.59, Neutral = 2.6 – 3.39, Agree = 3.4 – 4.19, Strongly agree = 4.20 – 5.00.

In Table 15.3, the mean from the first statement under PU (Perceived usefulness) category is 4.56 which means that the majority of the respondents strongly agreed that fintech services are 'useful'. The mean from the second statement under PU category is 4.51 which indicates that the majority of the respondents strongly agreed that fintech services are 'easy to use'. As from the third statement under PU category, the mean is 4.60 which shows that the majority of the respondents strongly agreed that fintech services 'save time'. In the fourth statement under PU category is 4.32 which means that the majority of the respondents strongly agreed that fintech services are 'convenient'. The mean in the fifth statement under the PU category is 4.02 which shows that the majority of the respondents are agreed that fintech services are 'available at any time'. Meanwhile, the last statement under the PU category is 4.10 which shows that the majority of the respondents agreed that fintech services 'meet their service needs'.

In the first statement under BI (Brand Image), the mean is 4.00 that indicates the majority of the respondents are agreed that fintech services have 'good services system'. The mean from the second statement under BI is 3.88 that means the majority of the respondents agreed that fintech services 'maintain data security'. The mean is also 3.88 in the last statement under BI category that indicates that the majority of the respondents agreed fintech services have 'good reputation'.

The mean from the first one statement under PR (Perceived Risks) is 2.97 that means the majority of the respondents are neutral as to whether 'cyber attacks' can be happen or not in fintech services. The last one statement under PR is 2.78 which shows that the majority of the respondent are also neutral about 'money can be stolen' in fintech services.

Table 15.3 Descriptive statistics for factors influencing Fintech under Technology Acceptance Model (TAM).

Factors/latent variables		N	Minimum	Maximum	Mean		Std. deviation
		Statistic	Statistic	Statistic	Statistic	Std. error	Statistic
Percieved Usefulness (PU)	Useful	100	3	5	4.56	.054	.538
	Easy to use	100	3	5	4.51	.059	.595
	Save time	100	3	5	4.60	.053	.532
	Convenient	100	2	5	4.32	.066	.665
	Availability	100	2	5	4.02	.078	.778
	Meet service needs	100	3	5	4.10	.061	.611
Brand Image (BI)	Good service system	100	3	5	4.00	.067	.667
	Maintain data security	100	2	5	3.88	.076	.756
	Good reputation	100	2	5	3.88	.074	.742
Percieved Risks (PR)	Cyber attacks can happen	100	1	5	2.97	.081	.810
	Money can be stolen	100	1	5	2.78	.089	.894
	Valid N (listwise)	100					

Source: Computed data.

15.3.2.1 Prominent Factors under Technology Acceptance Model (TAM) that Influence the Usage of Fintech

This study used one sample statistic- t-test to identify the most enabling influencing factor among the three factors such as Perceived usefulness, Brand image and Security which influence the usage of Fintech.

In Table 15.4, the mean of the Perceived usefulness (PU) factor is the highest among the three factors which indicate that perceived usefulness (PU) is the most enabling influencing factor for the usage of fintech services. Therefore, Perceived usefulness is the most enabling influencing factor for the usage of Fintech Payment services for banking which is followed by Brand Image (BI) factor and Perceived risk (PR) is the least enabling influencing factor, among the three factors, for the usage of fintech services for banking.

Table 15.4 One sample statistics for prominent factors under Technology Acceptance Model (TAM) that influence the usage of Fintech.

	N	Mean	Std. deviation	Std. error mean
Perceived usefulness	100	4.3517	.46293	.04629
Brand image	100	3.9200	.66349	.06635
Perceived risk	100	2.8750	.77321	.07732

Source: Computed data.

15.3.3 Technology Acceptance Model and the Usage of Fintech

There are three factors: Perceived Usefulness, Brand Image and Perceived Risks. This part of the study tends to test the hypotheses of the three factors towards the usage of Fintech services/applications for banking.

15.3.3.1 Perceived Usefulness Toward the Usage of Fintech

Based on the previous analysis, perceived usefulness has influenced the users' intention towards the use of Fintech services as individuals are able to avoid making needless mistakes throughout the commencement of jobs with the assistance of FinTech services. Furthermore, perceived usefulness has a constructive outcome in influencing the usage of Fintech services since users will measure the satisfaction of conducting financial transactions through a technological platform [24]. The 'usefulness' of technology acceptance factors has a significant positive effect on the usage of fintech services for banking. Users believe that the benefits provided by Fintech services are useful, easy to use, save time, convenient, available and meet service needs, which is helpful for increasing customers' usage of fintech services for banking. When the users believe that Fintech services are more useful, easy to use, save time, convenient, available and meet their service needs for their work, their attitude toward using Fintech services and the frequency of their usage of Fintech services are also higher.

Hypothesis 1 (H_{01}): Perceived usefulness (PU) has a significant positive effect on the usage of fintech services.

The main goal is to determine the most effective factors that influence consumers' usage of Fintech services for banking. To identify the Perceived Usefulness of the usage of Fintech, the regression model used takes the Usage of Fintech as the dependent variable and the Perceived usefulness (PU) factors of Fintech as independent variables viz., Meet service needs, Save Time, Availability, Useful, Convenient, Easy to Use. The hypothesis for the study is:

In Table 15.5, the p-value (probability value) is 0.003 and the value of F is 3.622. From the ANOVA at a 5% level of significance, the p-value is less than 0.05. Thus, the null hypothesis in this situation is rejected and the alternative hypothesis is accepted. Here, when the p-value is less than 0.010, that indicates strong evidence against the null hypothesis. Therefore, it is proved that Perceived usefulness (PU) has a significant positive effect on the usage of fintech services. This result means that if the users' view regarding the usefulness of the Fintech payment services is more positive, then their general attitude toward the frequency of the usage of Fintech Payment services will be higher.

Table 15.5 ANOVA results for usage of fintech and perceived usefulness factor.

Model		Sum of squares	df	Mean square	F	Sig.
1	Regression	11.887	6	1.981	3.622	.003[b]
	Residual	50.863	93	.547		
	Total	62.750	99			

[a]Dependent Variable: Usage of Fintech services
[b]Predictors: (Constant), Meet service needs, Save Time, Availability, Useful, Convenient, Easy to Use
Source: Computed data.

15.3.3.2 Brand Image Toward the Usage of Fintech

The brand and service reputation of enterprises have positive effects on the trustworthiness of users. The cognition of trust and experiences when using Fintech will directly affect the customers' usage of Fintech services [26]. In the context of Fintech applications, the perception of the users of the brand has been conceptualized and seen as a precondition for organizational trust. In the process of using Fintech services, private personal information is needed to be provided by the users. A good brand image can improve users' trust since it reduces risk effectively [23]. When the brand and service trust of users/customers is higher, the attitude toward purchasing the services is more positive. Customers will have a positive attitude toward the service providers when they believe that the information provided by the service providers/enterprises is honest [25]. Hence, the definition of 'brand image/trust' in this study is the degree of influence that the service providers' reputation, data security and service system have on the customers' frequency of usage of Fintech services for banking.

Hypothesis 2 (H_{02}) = Brand Image (BI) has a significant positive effect on the frequency of usage of fintech services.

The regression model used takes the Usage of Fintech as the dependent variable and the Brand Image (BI) factors of Fintech as independent variables viz., Good Reputation, Good service system, and Maintaining data security to identify the Brand Image toward the usage of Fintech.

From the ANOVA at a 5% level of significance, the p-value in Table 15.6 is less than 0.05. In Table 15.6, the p-value is 0.016 and the value of F is 3.597. Thus, the null hypoothesis in this situation is rejected and the alternative hypothesis is accepted. Therefore, it is proved that Brand Image (BI)

Table 15.6 ANOVA results for usage of fintech and brand image factor.

Model		Sum of squares	df	Mean square	F	Sig.
1	Regression	6.341	3	2.114	3.597	.016[b]
	Residual	56.409	96	.588		
	Total	62.750	99			

[a]Dependent Variable: Usage of Fintech services
[b]Predictors: (Constant), Good reputation, Good service system, Maintain data security
Source: Computed data.

has a significant positive effect on the usage of fintech services. This result means that if users have a higher trust level in brand image toward using Fintech Payment services, then their attitude toward the frequency of the usage of fintech Payment services will be more positive.

15.3.3.3   Perceived Risks Toward the Usage of Fintech

Previous studies show that security concerns have become a barrier to the use of fintech services like mobile payments as this type of transaction needs the exposure of financial information which is highly personal and sensitive [24]. Mohammad K. Al Nawayseh [42] stated that perceived risks make customers more reluctant to use Fintech, thereby decreasing their intention to use Fintech services/applications. Moreover, due to the intangibility of Fintech applications, the perceived risks of cyber threats and monetary loss inhibit users from using Fintech services. Fintech services usually involve technologies such as the Internet of Things, big data and cloud computing, thus there are some potential risks for users in receiving Fintech services [23]. According to the previous research findings, perceived risk is negatively related to the use of Fintech services/applications and has an opposite influence on the customers' behavioural intention of the use of Fintech [42].

Hypothesis 3 (H_{03}) = Perceived Risk (PR) has a significant positive effect on the frequency of usage of fintech services.

The multivariate regression used takes the usage of Fintech as the dependent variable and the Perceived Risks (PR) factors such as money can be stolen and cyber-attacks as independent variables.

In Table 15.7, the p-value is 0.118 and the value of F is 2.185. From the ANOVA at the 5% level of significance, the p-value is more than 0.05. Thus, the null hypothesis in this situation is accepted and the alternative

Table 15.7 ANOVA results for usage of fintech and perceived risks factor.

Model		Sum of squares	df	Mean square	F	Sig.
1	Regression	2.705	2	1.352	2.185	.118[b]
	Residual	60.045	97	.619		
	Total	62.750	99			

[a]Dependent Variable: Usage of Fintech services
[b]Predictors: (Constant), Money can be stolen, Cyber Attacks
Source: Computed data.

hypothesis is rejected. Therefore, it is proved that Perceived Risks (PR) do not significant positive effect on the usage of fintech services. This result means that the users still use fintech services for banking even though they highly believe that there can be cyber-attacked and money stolen.

15.4 Discussion

This paper discusses the factors which influence consumers' usage of Fintech mobile services/applications for banking. The findings of this research show that Perceived Usefulness is the most enabling influencing factor that has a significant impact on the customers' usage of Fintech services. This result is consistent with the research results of Kavitha Lal, et al., (2020) [39]. This finding of the study demonstrated that the majority of the respondents are inclined towards Fintech mobile services/applications for banking because of their usefulness, ease to use, time-saving, convenience, availability and services provided.

The first hypothesis test of the study shows that Perceived Usefulness has a significant impact on the consumers' usage of Fintech mobile applications for banking which is consistent with the previous research results of Zhongqing Hu, et al., (2019), Li-Min Chuang, et al., (2016) and Kavitha Lal, et al., (2020) [23, 26, 39]. This result confirms that customers' positive attitude toward using Fintech Services will increase if the Fintech service enables customers to conveniently, efficiently, and quickly obtain relevant information on performing money transactions under real-time and local restrictions [26].

In the second hypothesis, the finding shows that Brand Image has a significant impact on the consumers' usage of Fintech services/applications, unlike the research results of [Kavitha Lal, M. Suvarchala Rani & P. Rajini (2020) [39]. This result is aligned with the research results of Zhongqing Hu, et al., (2019) and Li-Min Chuang, et al., (2016) [23, 26]. This result shows that consumers' attitudes toward using Fintech services will be more positive if customers have higher brand and service trust toward using Fintech services/applications [23].

Meanwhile, the third and last hypothesis test of the study shows that Perceived Risks do not significantly affect the usage of Fintech services, unlike the hypothesis and the research by Zhongqing Hu, et al., 2019 [20], but this result is in accordance with the previous hypothesis and the research by Kavitha Lal, et al., (2020) [39]. The age group of the respondents may be considered as the reason which Perceived risk is not as a more enabling factor as Perceived usefulness and Brand image factors.

It is observed that most of the respondents are between 20 to 30 which can be interpreted that the younger generation is not much concerned about the security issues related to Fintech while they perform financial transactions using Fintech services/applications. The findings could provide the FINTECH sphere with information to target, diversify, and popularize their products better on the market. It could also provide user assessment and empirical framework for banks to adopt new and user-oriented services.

Moreover, these findings also indicate that individuals' usage of Fintech payment services is more influenced by their perceived usefulness than their perceived risks. The high expected value from using Fintech payment services should inspire financial institutions to provide new models, strategies and financial services in the field of Fintech services. However, Fintech service providers should not fail to care about the risk associated with their services, focus on building risk-free Fintech services and should increase security awareness as customers will later have these concerns [42]. Based on the demographic factors, a general conclusion could be made that young women tend to respond to such online surveys, especially through social media. Another general conclusion regarding the survey, results could be that women tend to participate in such surveys due to the fact that women are perceived as more caring, concerned and sensitive, while men are perceived as more independent, reasonable and strong such differences have been created by the society [10].

The current study identified the usage frequency of Fintech services/applications for banking. According to Zhongqing Hu et al., Tun-Pin Chong et al. and Mohammad K. Al nawayseh [23, 24, 39], the study was based on the users' behavioural intentions. It would have been better if the influencing factors on the frequency of consumers' usage of Fintech services/applications would have been included, and the current study was an attempt to fill this gap. Fintech services became more common as users became comfortable with the technology. In today's world, of course, contactless payments are much more appreciated [43]. The covid-19 pandemic forces consumers to use Fintech services as a convenient and safe tool to conduct financial transactions [44]. It is anticipated that FINTECH will play an important role alongside traditional banks, even replacing their functions in the near future [10].

Suggestions for Future Research

The current study focuses on the factors influencing the consumers' usage of Fintech services/applications for banking. Further research could use multiple dimensions, such as Attitude, Intention, and Government Support to investigate the role of rules and regulations made by the Government in Fintech Adoption. These aspects could be investigated by subsequent studies and utilising larger samples from around the world to understand Fintech adoption and its relation to the actual usage of Fintech services for banking.

15.5   Conclusion

Financial transaction services are one of the largest rapidly growing fintech services. From the study, it was clear that fintech services almost become a necessity for the majority of the respondents due to the advantages it provides along with the operations. Contactless payments are much more appreciated in these days which makes fintech payment services popular among banks' customers. Thus, the study's main objective is to observe factors and their significance in contributing to the users of fintech services for banking. It is expected that the findings of this empirical study, based on a reliable sample and effective statistical analysis would have enabled adding to the present contributions on the subject.

This study identified three factors Perceived usefulness (PU), Brand image (BI), and Perceived risk (PR) which influence the usage of Fintech payment services for banking. Perceived usefulness is the most enabling influencing factor on the usage of Fintech services for banking followed by the Brand image (BI) factor while Perceived risk (PR) is the least enabling influencing factor among the three factors on the usage of Fintech payment services for banking. The findings of the study demonstrated that the majority of the respondents are inclined towards Fintech mobile services because of their usefulness, ease to use, time-saving, convenience, availability and services provided. The most important findings of the research are that Perceived usefulness and Brand image have a significantly positive impact on the usage of fintech services while Perceived risks do not significantly influence the usage of fintech services for banking. The findings showed that when the users' view regarding the usefulness of the Fintech payment services is more positive and have a higher trust level in brand image toward using Fintech payment services, then their general attitude toward the frequency of the usage of Fintech payment services will be higher.

The study focuses on the factors influencing the consumers' usage of Fintech payment services/applications for banking. However, the influencing factors in this study have certain limitations. This paper has not studied psychological factors, such as social influences. Risks from multiple dimensions such as financial risks and privacy risks should also analyse.

A comprehensive and effective assessment will help to better analyze the usage of Fintech payment services for banking.

References

1. Rashmi Dabbeeru & D.N. Rao, *Fintech Applications in Banking and Financial Services Industry in India*, SSRN. https://ssrn.com/abstract=3881967, 2021.
2. Bala Parthasarathy & Armaan Joshi, *5 Ways Fintech Is Transforming Banking in India*, Forbes Advisor, 2021
3. Mercurius Broto Legowo, Steph Subanidja & Fangky Antoneus Sorongan, *FinTech and Bank: Past, Present, and Future ,Jurnal Teknik Komputer AMIK BSI*, Volume 7, No.1, 2021.
4. Nikunj Gundaniya, *Article -What is Fintech and how it has impacted banking?*, Digipay. Guru, 2020.
5. Julia Kagan, Financial Technology-Fintech https://www.investopedia.com/terms/f/fintech.asp, 2020.
6. Stephanie Walden, *What is Fintech and how does it affect how I bank?*, Forbes Advisor, August 3 2020.
7. Amber Murakami-Fester, *What Are Peer-to-Peer Payments?*, Nerdwallet, https://www.nerdwallet.com/article/banking/p2p-payment-systems, 2021.
8. Sean Peek, *What Is Fintech? Definition, Evolution and Examples*, https://www.uschamber.com/co/run/business-financing/what-is-fintech, 2020.
9. Neelam Tyagi, *What is Fintech? Examples and Applications?*, https://www.analyticssteps.com/blogs/what-fintech-examples-and-applications, 2021.
10. Ivanka Vasenska, Preslav Dimitrov, Blagovesta Koyundzhiyska-Davidkova, Vladislav Krastev, Pavol Durana & Ioulia Poulaki, *Financial Transactions Using FINTECH during the COVID-19 Crisis in Bulgaria.* Risks Volume 9 Issue 48, 2021.
11. Gary Hwa, *Eight ways Fintech adoption remains on the rise*, https://www.ey.com/en_in/financial-services/eight-ways-fintech-adoption-remains-on-the-rise#:~:text=The%20most%20popular%20FinTech%20service,saying%20they%20have%20done%20so, 2019.
12. Rey Mashayekhi, *Nearly 90% of Americans now use fintech—with boomers the fastest-growing demo*, https://fortune.com/2021/10/12/plaid-fintech-use-adoption-us-consumers-baby-boomers/, 2021.
13. Mary Wisniewski, *7 key benefits of mobile banking in 2022*, Bankrate, https://www.bankrate.com/banking/checking/benefits-of-mobile-banking/, 2022.
14. Francisco Liebana-Cabanillas, Francisco Munoz-Leiva, Juan Sanchez-Fernandez, *Comparative Study among New Payment Systems and Future Trends in Mobile Payments.* https://www.researchgate.net/publication/290795449, 2014.
15. Digibank, *Mobile Banking: Benefits of downloading a bank account app*, https://www.dbs.com/digibank/in/articles/save/benefits-of-mobile-banking-app, 2021.

16. Nelito Solutions that perform, *What is Digital banking, its benefits and future?*, https://www.nelito.com/blog/what-is-digital-banking-its-benefits-and-future.html, 2021.

17. Matthew N. O. Sadiku, Mahamadou Tembely, and Sarhan M. Musa, 2017, *Mobile Banking*, International Journals of Advanced Research in Computer Science and Software Engineering ISSN: 2277-128X (Volume-7, Issue-6), 2017

18. Markiyan Prokhako, *How Do Mobile and Online Banking Services Benefit Your Bank?*, KindGreek, https://kindgeek.com/blog/post/how-do-mobile-and-online-banking-services-benefit-your-bank#text1, 2020.

19. (Jungho Kang, *Mobile payment in Fintech environment: trends, security challenges, and services. Hum. Cent. Comput. Inf. Sci.* **8,** 32 (2018). https://doi.org/10.1186/s13673-018-0155-4, 30 October 2018).

20. Xavier Vives, *The impact of Fintech on Banking*, IESE Business School, Sections 2.2.1 and 4.1.5 of Vives, 2016

21. Arnoud W.A Boot, *The Future of Banking: From Scale & Scope Economies to Fintech*, University of Amsterdam and CEPR, University of Amsterdam, Amsterdam Center for Law & Economics (ACLE), Plantage Muidergracht 12, 1018 TV Amsterdam, The Netherlands, e-mail: a.w.a.boot@uva.nl., 2016

22. Pupung PURNAMASARI, Irena Paramita PRAMONO, Ria HARYATININGSIH, Shahifol Arbi ISMAIL, & Rohami SHAFIE, *Technology Acceptance Model of Financial Technology in Micro, Small, and Medium Enterprises (MSME) in Indonesia*, Journal of Asian Finance, Economics and Business Vol 7 No 10 (2020) 981–988, 2020.

23. Zhongqing Hu, Shuai Ding, Shizheng Li, Luting Chen & Shanlin Yang, *Adoption Intention of Fintech Services for Bank Users: An Empirical Examination with an Extended Technology Acceptance Model.* Symmetry, Volume 11, Issue 3. 2019.

24. Tun-Pin Chong, Keng-Soon William Choo, Yen-San Yip, Pui-Yee Chan, Hong-Leong Julian Tech, Shwu-Shing Ng, *An Adoption Of Fintech Service In Malaysia*, South East Asia Journal of Contemporary Business, Economics and Law, Vol. 18, Issue 5(February) ISSN 2289-1560, 2019.

25. Arun Khatri, Nakul Gupta & Anupama Parashar, *Application of Technology Acceptance Model (Tam) In Fintech services*, International Journal of Management (IJM), Volume 11, Issue 12, December 2020, pp.3520-3548, Article ID: IJM_11_12_328, https://iaeme.com/Home/issue/IJM?Volume=11&Issue=12, 2020.

26. Li-Min Chuang, Chun-Chu Liu & Hsiao-Kuang Kao, *The Adoption of Fintech Service: TAM perspective*, International Journal of Management and Administrative Sciences (IJMAS) (ISSN: 2225-7225) Vol. 3, No. 07, (01-15), 2016.

27. Fred D.Davis, *A Technology Acceptance Model for Empirically Testing New End-User Information Systems*, Theory and Results. PhD. Thesis, Massachusetts Institute of Technology, Cambridge, 1985.

28. Davis, F. D., *Perceived usefulness, perceived ease of use, and user acceptance of information technology*. MIS Quarterly, 13(3), 1989.
29. Mahmood Jasim Alsamydai, Saad Galib Yassen, Husam Mustafa Alnaimi, Dima Mousa Dajani & Ihab Ali Al-Qirem (2014), *The Factors Influencing Customer Usage Of Mobile Banking Services in Jordan*, International Journal of Business Management & Research (IJBMR) ISSN(P): 2249-6920; ISSN(E): 2249-8036 Vol. 4, Issue 2, Apr 2014, 63-78, April 2014.
30. Eunil Park, Heetae Kim, and Jay Y.ohm, *Understanding driver adoption of car navigation systems using the extended technology acceptance model*, Behaviour & Information Technology, Volume 34, Issue 7, 2014.
31. Stephen L. Shapiro, Lamar Reams, Kevin Kam Fung So ,*Is it worth the price? The role of perceived financial risk, identification, and perceived value in purchasing pay-per-view broadcasts of combat sports*, Sport Management Review, Elsevier, vol. 22(2), pages 235-246, 2019.
32. Kun Chang Lee and Nambo Chung, *Understanding Factors Affecting Trust in and Satisfaction with Mobile Banking in Korea: A Modified Delone and Mclean's Model Perspective*. Interacting with Computers 21(5-6): 385-392, 2009.
33. Nikoletta-Theofania Siamagka, George Christodoulides, and Nina Michaelidou, Aikaterini ValvI, *Determinants of social media adoption by B2B organizations*, Industrial Marketing Management, Volume 51, November 2015, Pages 89-99, 2015.
34. Pallab Sikdar and Munish Makkad, *Online banking adoption: A factor validation and satisfaction causation study in the context of Indian banking customers*, International Journal of Bank Marketing 33(6):785, 2015.
35. Srividya K. Bansal, Ajay Bansal, & M. Brian Blake, *Trust-based Dynamic Web service Composition using Social Network Analysis*. IEEE International Workshop on Business Applications of Social Network Analysis, BASNA 2010 [5730308], 2010.
36. Baltar, Fabiola, and Ignasi Brunet, *Social research 2.0: Virtual snowball sampling method using Facebook* . Internet Research 22, 2012.
37. Bryn Farnsworth, *The Top 7 Statistical Tools You Need to Make Your Data Shine*, IMOTIONS, Blog/statistical tools, 2019.
38. Dr.Saul McLeod, *Likert Scale Definition, Examples and Analysis*, SimplyPsyschology.org, Research Method/Attitude Measurement/Likert Scale, 2008.
39. Kavitha Lal, M. Suvarchala Rani & P. Rajini, *Factors that Influence the Customer Adoption of Fintech in Hyderabad*, International Journal of Recent Technology and Engineering (IJRTE) ISSN: 2277-3878, Volume-8 Issue-5, 2020.
40. Chuang Li Min, Chun-Chu Liu, & Kao, Hsiao Kuang Kao, *The adoption of fintech service: Tam perspective*, International Journal of Management and Administrative Sciences, 3(7), 2016.

41. Wallace, L. G., & Sheetz, S. D., *The adoption of software measures: A technology acceptance model (tam) perspective.* Information and Management, 51(2), 249–259, 2014.

42. Mohammad K. Al nawayseh ,*FinTech in COVID-19 and Beyond: What Factors Are Affecting Customers' Choice of FinTech Applications?*, Journal of Open Innovation: Technology, Market, and Complexity, 6, 153; doi:10.3390/joitmc6040153 www.mdpi.com/journal/joitmc, 2020.

43. Kristen Jason and Alison Arthur ,*Mobile Payments: What are the benefits?*, Alacriti.com, 2020.

44. Minh le, *Examining factors that boost intention and loyalty to use Fintech post-COVID-19 lockdown as a new normal behaviour*, University of Economics Ho Chi Minh City, researchgate, 2021.

16

Upsurge of Robo Advisors: Integrating Customer Acceptance

C. Nagadeepa[1]*, Reenu Mohan[1], Antonio Peregrino Huaman Osorio[2] and Willian Josue Fernandez Celestino[2]

[1]Department of Commerce, Kristu Jayanti College Autonomus, Bangalore India
[2]Universidad Nacional Santiago Antunez de Mayolo, Huaraz, Peru

Abstract

The rise of fintech in the digital community opens the door for companies to introduce robo advisors. Robo Advisors have emerged as a result of technological advances, and it is important to use Robo Advisors to manage and direct projects in the financial industry. The portfolio management service is critical for the efficient distribution and use of the surplus of economic activity in large markets. These robots are programmed to eliminate the dangers of prejudice and human error. This research article is about exploring the strengths and weaknesses of robo advisers, and as opportunities and threats, especially when compared to traditional financial advisors and a research framework to understand the acceptance of robo-advisors by investors. The findings of this study provide relevant research on financial institutions, banks, policy makers, asset managers, FinTech developers and financial advisors to increase the acquisition of Robo Advisors through the adoption of sustainable services.

Keywords: Robo-advisor, technology acceptance, FinTech, financial advisor

16.1 Introduction

The financial sector is an important link in economic activity. The financial sector is an information-intensive sector, which can change rapidly if you respond to technological advances. As a result, rules may be ignored or

*Corresponding author: cnagadeepa@gmail.com

Mohd Naved, V. Ajantha Devi, and Aditya Kumar Gupta (eds.) Fintech and Cryptocurrency, (351–382)

expired immediately, leading to unintended consequences. The financial sector provides a variety of services such as Price exchange is a payment method; Mediation-the process of transferring funds from depositors to borrowers; Risk transfer is a method of pricing and sharing risks; Liquidity-the ability to convert goods into cash with minimal loss of value.

Banks and Economy

Banks perform various functions in the economy. First and foremost, banks address the information related problems between investors and borrowers with the latest monitoring and ensure the proper use of investors' funds. However, due to maturity differences between their assets and liabilities, banks are less likely to operate and system risks. Third, banks are contributing to economic growth. Further, they play a vital role in corporate governance. The importance of the various roles and activities of banks varies greatly from country to country but however, banks remain very important in the economic system.

Banks can fulfill a normal deposit as a source of income by borrowing directly from the financial markets. Not only that, they can issue short term securities such as commercial paper and/or bonds; or they can temporarily borrow the collateral they have at other institutions to get cash. The most important role of a bank is to become the bridge between lenders with borrowers.

They are important in the domestic and international payment system and they make money by lending money to the neediest. Banks recoup extra money from the financial system, and lend the money by way of various trade securities. Banks play a vital role in the formation of monetary policy, which is one of the most important tools for achieving economic growth of a country without inflation by the government. Not only that, banks are important in controlling supply of money at the national level, while the banks facilitate the ease of flow of money in the money markets in which they operate.

The Rise of the Machines

These phrases appear to be the title of a movie or series or video game rather than financial terms. There is hot talk about the rise of computers in asset management which are human free technology. However, the story was featured on the cover of TIME magazine over 30 years ago. For the first time, the possibility for human like robots and digital solutions to take over the economy was clearly demonstrated. At the same time, technological change was taking its toll on many industries, including music, publishing, photographic technology and retail. Also, since the 2008 financial crisis, the financial industry has been in serious danger of collapse.

It is noteworthy, however, that the financial sector is not unaware in the use of technology. Capital has been innovating in capturing individual profits through new technologies. One of the best examples for these technologies is distant market which is gradually used by the entire world. M2M (Machine to machine), IoT are the combination of smart technology connected devices and their interaction is operated by the human being without human intervention. The introduction of the smartphone was the same technological change that had a profound effect on customer behavior and expectations of the banking service. As a result, it should come as no surprise that FinTech have come up with the new technology and idea of automating/human-free asset management process. It is not the question of is it mandatory, but how effective we can use this effectively to make ease of our work [1].

Artificial Intelligence

Artificial intelligence is a branch of computer science that aims to build intelligent machines that mimic human behavior. Learning, decision-making, planning, and speech recognition are all human AI machines designed to perform. Artificial intelligence allows machines to improve their performance continuously without the need of humans to give specific instructions on how to do so. AI technology is superhuman in operation, which is operating faster and more precisely than humans.

Computers and algorithms are used to develop and mimic human intelligence in Artificial Intelligence (AI). It is a fully functional machine. In general, any analysis such as data analysis or market analysis are done on the basis of information presented in a computer program not based on the natural intelligence of a machine [2]. Automation's promise of better performance and lower cost efficiency has further enhanced digital performance as a major industry practice [3].

Creating alpha, improving efficiency, improving product and distribution of content, and risk management are all pillars of AI transformation. Beyond business, AI may be used to mimic complex risks and perform stress tests. Traditional risk factor analysis can be challenged using the AI risk model, which demonstrates the benefits and drawbacks of each type of decision support tool.

Big data and Artificial Intelligence competence in fintech market will vary depending on the investment style and process. High-frequency quant/systematic /automated trading relies exclusively on powerful computers to analyze data sources, detect patterns, and generate information at speeds that humans cannot match. Investor perceptions of companies can be enhanced by AI, which is an integral part of their management operations. AI is used by a growing number of third-party providers to analyze corporate risks in ESG problems including water pressure. AI can be used to collect data and to develop anonymous or unlimited data. Artificial intelligence (AI) has the power to fundamentally alter how businesses are organized. If not handled appropriately, it might cause significant environmental harm.

Advantages of Artificial Intelligence

A potent instrument that is widely used in financial services is artificial intelligence (AI). If businesses use it with enough diligence, creativity, and care, it has a great potential to have a beneficial impact. The use of AI in the financial services industry has various advantages.

- It can improve firms' efficiency through cost reduction
- It helps in productivity enhancement; therefore, firms can achieve higher profitability via enhanced automated decision-making process and execution.
- It minimizes errors caused by human's psychological cues and emotional cues
- It improves the quality as it has mass market potential which can arrayed across industry
- Helps senior management to review and evaluate high quality data generated by a company.
- It enables the multi-tasking activities and executes hitherto tasks in lower cost.
- It can work endlessly (24x7) without breaks and faster than human.

AI trading software can absorb a lot of data to learn about the world and predict financial markets. To understand trends around the world, they can use everything from books, tweets, news reports, financial data, salary numbers, and international monetary policy.

High-frequency trading (HFT), which allows traders to place millions of orders and scan multiple markets in just seconds, respond to opportunities in ways that people simply cannot. Investment management firms rely on computers to make transactions for years. About 9% of all the funds, with a total of $ 197 billion under management, rely on large mathematical models created by data scientists. These types, on the other hand, remain stable, require individual involvement, and do not work well as the market changes. As a result, money is flowing more and more into virtual reality models that study large amounts of data and evolve over time. Automation, efficiency, competitiveness, and ultimately savings are key features of bank chatbots.

Conversational Robo-advisor: This service uses dialogue to learn about the risk characteristics of investors and then gives the best portfolio advice. Investment management firms have depended on computers to execute transactions for years. Around 9% of all funds, with a total of $197 billion under management, rely on huge statistical models created by data scientists. These models, on the other hand, are frequently stagnant, require human involvement, and perform poorly when the market changes. As a result, money is increasingly flowing towards actual artificial intelligence models that study enormous amounts of data and develop over time.

16.2   Chatbots

AI and ML are becoming inevitable in many industries. One of the main applications of digital technologies are customer service and chat bots- the best example of such technology. Automation, efficiency, a competitive edge, and ultimately savings are the main drivers for chatbots in banking. Chatbots are AI powered interactive messaging device via chat interface [4].

16.2.1   Benefits of Using Chatbots in Banks

With the advent of chatbots, the focus of bank has shifted from existing products to existing customers. Chat bots used in banking industry enhances productivity and the notable benefits are:

- Being smart and enhances productivity of bank personnel as not all the customer's problems requires the help of humans.
- Benefited with personalized assistance and improves relationship with clients conveniently by advanced chat banks and mobile banks services.
- Improved clients experience through growing personalized collaborations.by providing services according to individual customer's needs. Further, it improves user's interaction and reduces friction from non-affiliated banking channels.
- It detects fraud, money laundering and systemic misconduct.
- Database customer information, as chat banking improves by contacting every individual client. The banks can able to answer client's complex questions with lower cost.

- Reduced costs associated with maintaining and improving customer service standards, as business grows, and customer numbers increase
- Improves work efficiency and increases job satisfaction of employees. The improved operating procedures allow customer service to get information sit on the phone with the help of chatbots and allows staffs to focus on high value/important jobs
- Make decisions that are more personal and more specific about who the relationship manager should be in contact with and what messages should be delivered.
- Real-time customer service which simplifies the process of scrutiny of data and reduces human error in deducting frauds.
- Improved storage and retrieval levels can be achieved through problem-solving process.

16.3 Robo-Advisor

A robo-advisor is an automated platform that uses computer algorithms to manage financial portfolios and deliver financial planning services. A robo advisor is a type of AI based digital financial advisor helps in asset management without personal involvement. This AI based Advisors are developed and built to provide digital advice based on client's investment goals and their risk tolerance level. Robo-advisors are digital forums that provide an automated, financial guide driven by an algorithm without human guidance. Robo-advisors are suitable for hand-free and novice investors. It is becoming popular because it is cost-effective, simple way of investing platform and avoids human professionals.

A regular robo adviser takes an online interview to ask questions about client's financial position and future aspirations/plan. Based on the collected information robo advisors provide recommendations and invest automatically. Robo-advisors are built to perform with minimal human involvement. Many robo advisers are used to perform basic financial services, relying on a simple basic question to determine investment behavior of the investors. There are many more common robo advisors in the market which includes automated investment and advisor, wealth management advisor and digitalized consulting forums etc. Regardless of the name, it all refers to fintech (investment technology) applications for investment management.

16.3.1   Robo-Adviser – A Brief History

People around the world are crazy about superheroes, like superheroes, "financial superheroes" like robo-advisors have backstories. The automated wealth management and investing solutions are provided robo advisors which are used to make financial services. While bankers were strutting around Wall Street carrying beautiful leather briefcases and perfectly fitted jackets, 29-year-old Jon Stein had an idea and made the decision to take on Wall Street's "wolves" with a cutting-edge new financial product. The story of Robo advisors can be traced back to 2005-2006, when the first financial technology company Mint, explored an automated financial management solution.

2008 was a difficult year for the financial sector. The collapse of the sub-prime mortgage market served as the primary trigger for the onset of the global financial crisis. Wall Street was swiftly destroyed by the domino effect. Even Lehman Brothers, a 169-year-old financial business that many believed was too big to fail, eventually declared bankrupt. While the investment firms were currently experiencing severe losses, a new financial trend was subtly developing.

The idea of carefully controlling his fortune wasn't something Jon usually agreed with. He opened seven different brokerage accounts, invested a lot of time and effort in tracking and timing the market, but ultimately unable to outperform his competitors who simply followed the market.

The world is undoubtedly becoming more convenient and affordable, he reasoned, so why was investment moving in the opposite way, becoming ever more challenging? Why wasn't there a financial agency that could have just advised him on where to put his money and then carried it out without any further action?

With his roommate and other pals, Jon Stein signed a straightforward Betterment founding agreement in August 2008. Betterment was designed from the standpoint of improved customer experience, enhancing the customer's operational convenience and overall user experience, with the goal of helping people live better lives utilizing a more convenient investing solution. A new "smart" investing option known as a robo-advisor entered the financial industry at this time.

Betterment and Wealthfront, both established the words first Robo-advisors in late 2008 [5]. Jon Stein and Andy Rachleff and Dan Carroll, are considered the first quarterly consultants in the retail sector [6]. The first robo-advisory services emerged in Europe a few years later. It encouraged the creation of more robo advising platforms in 2009. Around the same period, pioneers like Betterment, Wealthfront, and Future Advisor debuted. Future Advisor was the first robo advisor in the world to connect directly to retirement accounts, and Betterment, which began as a cash and investing company before becoming the largest robo advisor in the world five years after its introduction.

Robo advising platforms have been introduced all around the world over the years. With early adopters including Pintec Technology, China Merchants Bank, and CreditEase, China saw the launch of its first robo adviser in 2015. In the UK, Moneyfarm launched its wealth management platform in 2016. Niche robo advising platforms targeting specific investment demographics were later developed in North America; one such company is Ellevest, which is run by women.

16.3.2 Historic Account of Robo Advisors

- In 2011 UK launched Nutmeg [7],
- Quirion was launched in Germany in 2013 [8]. Surprisingly,

Even if banks were not among the first beneficiaries, the beginnings of robo-advice may have been traced back to the initial origins or asset managers. Asset managers in particular, and robo advising services, present significant possibilities (Becchi *et al.* 2018). They can readily divert a portion of their client's funds to digital advising services, lowering the entry hurdle for new clients. It shouldn't be surprising that Vanguard, in terms of assets managed, owns the largest robo-consultant. The quarterly counseling's principal objective was to undermine banks advising services by giving brokers and other clients access to reasonable financial guidance in order to help them make wise investment choices [9]. Today, we can see that, instead of underestimating financial institutions like banks, robo-advisory deals with them primarily. According to the institutional economy in the FinTech sector [10], investors are very cautious because of the difficulties of control and trust, such as behavioral risks. Despite the financial crisis, banks continue to be more profitable than startups. In addition, banks are trying to tackle the problem of new skepticism through mixed-use models that include people and robo advisors.

Although the original business models were very simple, they focused on understanding customer risk and ETF-based stock advice and bond portfolio. Over time, counseling became more complex as new categories of assets, operating funds, tax improvements, and other factors were added. However, according to a 2018 survey, the investment process for quarterly advisers was straightforward at the time [10]. Investors were asked a few questions that were commonly used to assess risk preferences of their interest towards investment, but this does not appear to be sufficient in classifying active risk to make the apt investment recommendations. In that view, we believe that the quarterly counseling industry is in its early stages, and that further growth is needed.

16.3.3   Robo-Advisor Versus FA (Financial Advisor)

Table 16.1 provides the highlights of the basic difference between a human advisor and a robot advisor.

Table 16.1 Robo advisors vs financial advisors.

Feature	Financial advisor	Robo-advisor
Cost	It is combination of both percent of assets managed, hourly fee. It varies depending upon various firms/concern.	Basically, based on the Percentage of assets managed will be charged. It may vary from 0.25% to 10%.
Scope of service	FA provides range of financial services	Investors investing plan and based on their goal planning
Ease of signing up and maintenance	FA initially involves consultation, and then meetings over time. Usually it will have human touch.	It is very easy and quick to access via online. Further, it very adjustable at any time.
Excel in	FA is good for the task which requires a specialized expertise or unique task.	Automation makes investing easier for tedious and mundane tasks.
Superpower	The best financial advisors motivates the investors toward their financial objection and goal	It is specialised for tax-loss harvesting option.

16.3.4   Robo Advisors in Market

Private robo-advisors have raised more than $1.32 billion worldwide since 2012 across 119 equity transactions. Robo-advisors are the largest subset of wealth technology businesses, receiving about 30% of all funding.

Betterment, Personal Capital, and Wealthfront are three of the biggest robo-advisor companies in terms of total funding and among the first. Despite dominating in the US, they have obstacles to growth abroad because of a complex legal environment, varying investing patterns, and other entry-level restrictions. New early-stage robo-advisors have been launching in numerous markets and at least 17 other nations outside of the US because they have seen the business opportunity there.

Automated investments cover a wide range of concepts, including high frequency trading, algorithm trading, autonomous asset management, and automated stock trading [11]. Robotic asset management and investment counselling are both on the rise as trends in the market.

In the 1990s, the FinCEN Artificial Intelligence System (FAIS) was already in operation to anticipate potential money laundering. One of the first financial institutions to deploy chatbots, Ally Bank introduced Ally Assist in 2015 to allow the customers personal account management assistance.

Ally Bank introduced Ally Assist in 2015 to give customers un-interrupted personal account management assistance. It allows the various customer services such as bill payments, money transfers, and queries regarding account information, which can comfortably access through the mobile app.

RPA was first added to the Insurance Industry Data Repository in 2013 by Xchanging, a long-standing service provider in the insurance market in London. It had 13 automated processes in its insurance industry within two years. According to the company, this eliminated human mistake and cut down on application processing time by more than 90%.

Erica is a new AI-powered financial assistant from Bank of America. By delivering notifications, providing balance details, saving advice, sharing credit report updates, paying off debts, and assisting consumers in making sensible financial decisions, this chatbot has successfully addressed the banking needs of its users. It also offers personalized and speedy transactions.

Robo Advisor Global Share – A bird eye view:
The trend toward becoming digital has virtually eliminated any room for the financial services business as well. The introduction of the Robo-Advisor Market was made possible by the market's rapid digitalization and the adoption of cutting-edge technology, but it has also helped the sector maintain its place by acting as a major factor in driving up demand for the technology. Due to the service's low cost and almost complete lack of human engagement, several major players have chosen to invest in it rather

than investing heavily in labour costs. The service has been able to meet customer demand digitally by providing a complete site of solutions and using algorithmic computations. Since 2012, 57 percent of the global deal share has gone to US-based robo-advisors. The UK scored second place with 9 percent, followed by China and Germany.

Wacai, a Chinese robo-advisor and personal wealth management technology startup, received the two largest robo-advisor transactions outside of the US. A 50 million dollar Series B was raised by the firm in 4th quarter of 2014, and a $80M Series B-II was raised in 3rd quarter of 2015. With a $37.5M Series C in Q4 2016 and a $32M Series B in Q2 2014 that includes Armada Investment Group, Pentech Ventures, Balderton Capital, and other investors, UK-based Nutmeg closed the third and fourth largest deals [12] The Use of Digital Technology and Automation in Wealth Management are creating the Growth Opportunities for the Robo Advisory Market Globally [7, 11, 12].

Even though the industry is anticipated to expand during the forecasted period, a shortage of human knowledge at nearly all levels may function as a market restraint. The market's expansion is anticipated to be constrained by security and compliance issues. Other constraints that can limit market growth include a lack of direct customer interaction or individualized support, rising risk profiles brought on by shifting variables like retirement and income, and an inability to adjust to shifting conditions in real time. However, the market has a chance thanks to the assistance of the government and unrealized potential in the developing market. The market is given a chance by the numerous technical developments, including the incorporation of AI into digital investing platforms.

The Global Robo-Advisor Market is divided into following categories

1. Based on Geography,
2. Based on Services, and
3. Based on Automation Mode.

Based on Geography it is divided into

- North America;
- Asia Pacific;
- Europe and
- Rest of the world

Due to the presence of key market participants like Betterment and Vanguard there, North America is the top region in the robo-advisor business. The increasing robot advisory usage among investors is contributing to the region's rising need for technology. Due to a rise in the acceptability of digital technology in the region, Asia-Pacific is expected to take the second position in the lead [12].

Based on the automation mode, the market is divided into

- Fully Automated Robo-advisor financial services and
- Semi-Automated

Wealth management firms and investors employ both of these methods to obtain financial services, but completely automated is anticipated to rise over the projected period due to the financial services market's rapid digitalization.

Based on Service the market is divided into

- Investment Advisor services
- Wealth Management services
- TAX-Loss Harvesting services
- Personal Finance Advisor services

All of the technologically enabled services are currently in use, but due to the market dominance of wealth management and investment advisors as well as the comprehensive and simple digital use of the service, tax loss harvesting, and personal financial advisors are expected to grow in the coming years.

The market for robo advisory services is anticipated to expand as a result of product developments, corporate expansion, and acquisitions by major industry participants, as well as rising robo advisory acceptance for the convenience of using financial services. As user preference for traditional advisers continues to climb, users typically believe that human advisors are the best choice under volatile market conditions.

At a robust CAGR of 39.9%, it is predicted that the global robo advice industry will generate $59,344.5 million between 2021 and 2028 [13], up from $4,600.0 million in 2020. The Asia-Pacific Robo advisory market is expected to show an increase of 41.7 % CAGR, bringing in $19,518.4 million, according to the geographical analysis of the market.

Robo Advisory Market – Impact of COVID19

Investors understand the value of online services for investments thanks to the COVID-19 epidemic. Customers who once chose to visit a bank branch, now prefer to speak with a humanoid advisor and are gradually changing their behaviour. This is because when governments decided to implement a lockdown, banks closed their relevant sections. Frequently, customers were spending more time on alternative services that may provide a satisfactory customer experience because they did not anticipate such a significant change. The COVID-19 had a favourable effect on the robo advisory business. Since the COVID-19 outbreak, there have been increasing global fears, which, when paired with the ongoing conflict over oil prices, have alarmed investors all around the world [12].

The majority of digital advisor-managed portfolios outperformed each other amid market fluctuations, according to backend benchmarking, which analyses performance by opening portfolios at top robo-advisors. The number of users on an online wealth management platform or robo advising in wealth management has doubled as the coronavirus forces more and more advisers into lockdown mode. According to wealth management businesses, advisers are spending time managing customers who have been negatively impacted by the coronavirus on a human and financial level. The way that robo-advisors communicate will differ slightly from how traditional advice firms do it. Through email, push notifications, and in-app notifications, they will need to rely on the digital collaboration tools at their disposal. Innovative solutions could help robo-advisors provide the human touch necessary to allay customers' fears during trying times. These tools might include chat functionality or video conferences to communicate with a team of advisors. As examples of premium services, Betterment and Personal Capital already offer financial advisor access.

Why Should You Go For a Robo-Advisor?
A personal wealth advisor can be a great option if you need confirmation or personal discussion before investing. If a person wants personal advice or affirmation before making an investment, a financial advisor/counsellor may be their best choice. However, a Robo-advisor is the best option if he/she desires for simple transactions and quick access. Even the paid robos have fairly affordable prices, with the typical charge ranging between 10 bps and 50 bps [14]. The extensive range of services, including investment tracking, make robos well worth the cost. They will undoubtedly shape wealth management in the future, one can reasonably anticipate. As they gain the confidence of financial investors, they will also notice an expanding user base.

Understanding Robo-Advisors Betterment, the first advisor for the quarter, was established with the aim of evaluating the assets as per the client's requirement. Its main aim is to serve an online interface to manage idle investments, purchases and hosting them. To expand its offers to customers, Betterment purchased Makara, a robo consultant platform that manufactures and manages bitcoin portfolios, in 2022.

Since the early 2000s, human resource managers have been using automated portfolio distribution tools. However, before Betterment was introduced, they were the only ones who could afford the technology, so customers who wanted to benefit from this success had to hire a financial advisor.

16.3.5   How Robo-Advisors Work?

A robo-responsibility advisor's responsibility is to build customers' investment portfolio and to manage them. Figure 16.1 shows the step by step working process of robo-advisor.

Step 1: Creation of Account & Questionnaire: The first step in opening an account with a robo-advisor is to create a login. After that, a new client of a robo-advisor fills out an online questionnaire to provide their basic information, covers their financial objectives such as time frame, risk tolerance, and the amount of money that they wants to save.

Figure 16.1 Working process of robo advisor.

Step 2: Analysing the Proposals: The next step is an algorithm is applied by robo-advisors on such survey questionnaire. The answers provided by the client will assist the robo-advisor decide how to distribute their funds. A lot of robo-advisors adopt a strategy known as modern portfolio theory, or MPT. The proposals are analyzed to select appropriate product.

Step 3: Appropriate Investment Option: After the analyzing stage, Robo-advisors will give an asset allocation strategy and assist the client/customer in creating diversified investment portfolio that will satisfies the clients investment objectives.

Step 4: Confirmation/Rejection of the option: Once the receipt of robo-advisors option, client can either confirm about the investment option or they can reject the advice. If they reject, robo-advisor can further give another option based on their modified requirement.

Step 5: Automated Rebalance of portfolio: Once the clients funds are invested, the robo-advisor will automatically update their portfolio to best fit with achieving your goals as market conditions change or as you invest additional money. The term "rebalancing" more accurately describes this periodic purchasing and selling. By doing this, it will be made sure to stay inside the desired allocation. The robo-advisor will thereafter maintain client's target allocation using those contributions.

16.3.6   Types of Robo-Advisor

Robo-advisors can be grouped in four different ways: according to their technological proficiency, revenue model, advisory segment and by its scope.

a. Technical aptitude: There are two primary sorts of robo-advisors based on technical aptitudes
- The simplistic Robo advisor and
- the comprehensive robo advisors

a.1. Simplistic Robo-advisor: Basic/simplistic robo advisors create a portfolio using traditional profiling. A quick questionnaire is required to filled by investors in order to evaluate their risk tolerance. This basic information is assessed in light of the investor's objective and goal while creating a portfolio.

a.2. Comprehensive advisors: This type of advisors provide an in-depth understanding of investor profiles using artificial intelligence (AI) and data to predict investors behavior beyond the general risk profile questions. In this category, the data provides the robot with information about investors actual net worth, existing debts, spending habits, and behaviour in a variety of contexts, while the AI is always learning about investor and the best investments for their profile [15]. INDwealth, CUBE Wealth and Arthayantra are comprehensive advisors which uses ML to provide real-time personalised advice to the investors.

b. Revenue source: Some robos receive fees or commission from the product owners and advisory fees from the investors for providing financial advice. Since its revenue may affect its suggestions, the former has a conflict of interest [11]. Because it does not rely on the manufacturer for its revenue, the latter is free from any such conflicts. As a result, it is exclusively loyal to customers. Thus, investors alone are the object of its loyalty. The advisory fee might be anything between 10 and 50 basis points [16], while a human advisor typically charges 100 basis points in commission.

c. Advisor Segment based: Robo-advisors can also be categorised based on the range of tasks they are capable of performing. Based on the robot advisory segments, it is grouped as automated fund base advisor, equity based advisor and scope based advisor.

    c.1.Fund-based robo advisor offer recommendations to clients based on their risk and financial goals. Investments can only be made in funds (not in other assets). The commission will be charged based on fund distribution and it is the principal source of income for these consultants, who hardly ever charge their clients. They are perfect for inexperienced and novice investors who want guidance on how to assemble their portfolios but don't want to trade equities themselves.
    A few examples of these type of advisors are Scripbox, Kuvera and Fisdom.

    c.2.Equity based advisors: Equity-based "Robo advisors" platforms primarily focus on stocks portfolios. Through a variety of brokers, they provide fund execution. They also provide a portfolio mix for investments based on a particular industry or investment approach. Smallcase, Marketmojo are famous equity based advisors. These platforms frequently levy a predetermined fee for each transaction or on an annual basis. Investors that have a rudimentary understanding of the equities market and are prepared to take on moderate to high levels of risk in order to maximise their portfolios should seek out these advisers. Tauro Wealth, Marketmojo, and Smallcase are well-known equity-based Robo advisors.

d. Scope Based advisors: Robo advisors can be grouped based on the many tasks that they perform. The majority of robot advisors in India today only provide guidance on investment trusts, while other robot advisors do so for a variety of financial instruments and assets. The majority of robo consultants build portable portfolios for their clients using contemporary portfolio theory (or another approach). Robo Advisors use a measuring band for this. There is a precise weight assigned to each category of commodities or each individual security, together with the accompanying tolerance. The obligation to hold 30% of developing market shares, 30% of strong domestic shares, 40% of government bonds, and a corridor of 5% of each asset, for instance, could be part of a distribution strategy. This kind of redesign was formerly controversial due to its time commitment and potential cost-effectiveness.

16.3.7   Top Robo-Advisors

Specialized top robot advisors are listed in the following Table 16.2.

Table 16.2 Specialized top robo advisors.

Good In	Robo-advisor
Access to financial advisor	Betterment
Saving plans	Wealthfront
Minimum investment of $2000	SigFig
Beginners in investment	Ally
Low fees	Charles Schwab
Goal driven investment	Ellevest
Banking features and automated investment	TD Ameritrade
CFP access and fee free investment	SoFi
Best retirement planning	Fidelity
Socially responsible investment	Wealthsimple

Minibites of leading Robo advisors:
Betterment: It is an online based investment company, launched in 2008 and Betterment Everyday was launched in 2019. This was apt for customers

cash management option and provided services like checking and providing savings account options. Betterment aimed to become the preferred personal finance manager by having no account minimum and a 0.25 percent annual fee [17].

Wealthfront: Betterment and Wealthfront are the equally competitive leading robo-advisors in this industry. In 2018, Wealthfront made history by becoming the first robo-advisor to provide free, individualised financial planning to its consumers. Wealthfront does not, however, provide access to human financial counsellors for aid with regards to investing, in contrast to Betterment. Although better than the Betterment's $0 minimum amount, Wealthfront has a comparatively low $500 account minimum and a similarly low 0.25 percent yearly advising charge. This is best for the people who require access to human financial counsellors but yet desire inexpensive costs and a savings plan [18].

SigFig: It's a robo investing service provider called SigFig which combines financial advisors with money management software. The product from SigFig has several tiers, making it ideal for novice investors. Customers' complete investment portfolio is gathered in one location through its free portfolio tracker, which has no minimum investment requirement. Compared to Betterment and Wealthfront, it requires a minimum investment amount of $2,000 and with a lesser yearly charges of 0.25 percent. Further it covers, tax loss harvesting, rebalancing of customer's portfolios, and live adviser chat etc. as its features. This is the best robo advisor those who seek human advisor with minimum account balance of 2000$.

Charles Schwab: Charles Schwab Intelligent Portfolios, a leading robo-advising rival, excels in providing clients with a personalised financial plans. Investors are asked to submit a form in which they identify their personal objectives and risk tolerance. Schwab Intelligent Portfolios provides no management or account fees with a $5,000 minimum balance; nevertheless, consumers must pay expense ratios based on investments, which are typically still less expensive than the other competing robo-advisor's fees. This is suitable for people who seek customized robo advice with low fees.

Ellevest: Ellevest is a robo adviser service provider targeted specially for female investors, however it accepts users of any gender. Ellevest began its operations in 2017, succeeded by attempting to reduce gender differences in wealth. Each client's gender-specific needs are taken into account while calculating financial objective and targets using a proprietary algorithm, and best for goal-based investment seekers with low fees which does not expect minimum balance. Its monthly fees ranges between 1 to 9$ for their services.

Ally: One of the cheapest robo-advising solutions is "Ally Invest Managed Portfolios". It has a $100 minimum investment requirement and an average portfolio expense ratio of 0.7%. The service does not impose advisory fees, rebalancing fees or rebalancing investment fee, but it does mandate that clients retain at least 30% of their portfolios in interest-earning cash. This is the best robo advisors for the beginners.

TD Ameritrade: On October 6, 2020, Charles Schwab acquired TD Ameritrade, although the brokerage intends to carry on as usual for the time being. With its extensive range of offerings, including its Web Platform for all investing levels and the think or swim platform for sophisticated traders, TD Ameritrade appeals to both experienced investors and beginners. The best option for people who desire a variety of apps for different trading skill levels and objectives. TD Ameritrade offers a $0 account minimum, whereas Essential Portfolios have a $500 minimum (the entry-level robo-advisor option). Additionally, it provides no-cost per-leg options, ETFs, and stock trading commissions in the US. There is a $0.65 per contract cost for option trading [18].

SoFi: SoFi was launched in 2011 as a platform for student loans, SoFi has since then grown to provide personal loans, home loans, wealth management services, and administration of personal finances designed to attract young investors. SoFi charges no fees and have a $1 minimum account balance because it targets youngsters, fee-conscious customers. This is the best robo advisors for the youngsters with low fees and certified financial planners who can access it for free of cost.

Fidelity: Fidelity provides clients with services ranging from sound investment tools to financial planning and guidance. Its client assets total $7.6 trillion and 30 million unique clients. With a $10 account minimum, $0 in commission transactions, and $0 in fees, Fidelity is a top robo advising rival. Fidelity Go, the company's robo-advisor, only allows customers to invest in Fidelity Flex mutual funds. This is best for the clients who don't mind on limited investment option with low access fees and provides best retirement plans for their clients.

Wealthsimple: Wealthsimple is a relatively young participant in the robo-advice business; it first debuted in Canada in 2014 before expanding to the US in 2017. With the support of a group of financial professionals, Wealthsimple provides a socially conscious investment choice. Wealthsimple is gaining popularity among investors who value putting their investments here due to its $0 account minimum and 0.5 percent cost structure for balances up to $99,999. Wealthsimple is the greatest choice for investors interested in socially conscious investment solutions.

Highlight of Robo Advisors in India:

- HDFC introduced its AI banking chat bot services named Electronic Virtual Assistant-EVA, designed to provide faster services such as information about branch addresses, IFSC codes of different branches, interest rates of various loan rates based on customer questions are offered by EVA. The bot has spread across many forums, including Google Assistant and Alexa.
- In 2017, the State Bank of India (SBI) launched SBI Intelligent Assistant (SIA), an AI-based financial chatbot that can answer millions of inquiries per day about various information such as house loan, education loan, vehicle loan, and personal loans. Google answers roughly 25% of inquiries, while the SIA can process up to 10k searches per second. This chatbot is multilinguistic and can answer or text in 14 different languages.
- Yes Bank's AI based Chatbot – YES ROBOT was introduced in 2018. Customers can execute financial and non-financial needs using YES ROBOT without having to slog through numerous online pages. Further, they can manage their debit and credit cards through this AI enhanced chatbots and they can view their account summaries, pay bills, get rewards, and use their cards internationally.
- Two robots from Hang Seng Bank in Hong Kong, Haro and Dori, are able to talk in Chinese and English, comprehend Cantonese, and blend English and Chinese. They sell rapid solutions to a range of demands to consumers. Omni also engages with consumers on the bank's website, mobile app, and WhatsApp and replies to inquiries about real estate, personal loans, credit cards, health insurance, and travel insurance services. HARO is an acronym for "Help; Note; It Responds."
- Customers can find offers and restaurants with the aid of DORI ('Food; Donations; Prizes; Interactive,' available on Facebook Messenger).
- Indus Assist is an AI enabled chatbot developed by IndusInd Bank in collaboration with Amazon's Alexa, was introduced

in 2018. This enables customers to access banking services by simply speaking to Alexa. Customers can use voice-based chatbot to carry out their financial and non-financial banking tasks on various voice assistants such as Amazon Echo, Siri, and Alexa etc.

16.3.8   Points to be Consider while Selection of Robo-Advisor

The following factors need to be taken into account when an investor wishes to invest and manage their account with the aid of a robo advisor.

Goal setting: Investors should think about their goals before reviewing robo advisors. Some people may just need advice on selecting investments for a portfolio with only one goal in mind, while others may be saving for several goals. Once investors know what they want, they can decide if it's enough to own one investment model that has a set asset allocation and automatically rebalances to take advantage of portfolio efficiencies like tax-loss harvesting and automatic investment, or if they need a little more help to save for multiple goals at once.

Facilitate goal planning: Robo advisors should offer tools and advice for investors to learn about their risk tolerance and what they need to reach their short- and long-term goals. In addition to risk tolerance, investors need to take into consideration their time horizon and how long they have to reach those goals. Investors should also find out how customized the portfolio will fit their goals and time horizon.

Understand the fees and minimum investments: Robo advisory costs and minimum investment levels vary by platform and service. Some don't require a minimum amount to open an account, with annual account fees as low as 0.25%, which means $25 for every $10,000 invested annually. Those account fees are on top of the fees for the mutual funds and exchange-traded funds. Investors who don't need much human support and just want a small amount of smart portfolio management should look for the lowest management fee. People who want a mid-level service such as access to phone representatives or live chats may need to pay more for that option or have larger minimum balances.

Check the ease of access: "How well does the design appeal to you? How easy is it to use? Investors should look at what type of calculators and educational information is available. They should also see if the robo advisor offers other financial services such as savings or banking capabilities.

Make sure goals are well integrated: For people who are saving for more than one goal, make sure all those goals are integrated. Many people with long-term goals may have plans to save for their children's college education and retirement. Investors should look for a service that helps them allocate their savings across these two goals, and they should get specific dollar recommendations of how much to be saving.

Dive into the offerings: To keep expenses down, robo advisors generally offer low-cost, index-based mutual funds and ETFs. But, investors should look beyond simple portfolio construction and understand the type of mutual funds and ETFs offered. What are those investments? Are they proprietary funds? Or are they third-party funds? Some offer in-house investment funds and some offer funds from several different issuers to create their model portfolios. The platform should explain how they perform due diligence when selecting funds for their different asset allocation models.

Know when a robo advisor isn't right: Robo advisors can help people with small amounts of money automatically invest in equities or fixed income, but there could be even cheaper options available. Depending on costs or investment minimums, it may make more sense to open a diversified mutual fund when an investor only has a small dollar to invest. "Robo advisors came about to facilitate investing in small dollar amounts because the mutual fund industry didn't do a great job of accommodating that," he says. "Now that option exists in the mutual fund world." One example is Fidelity Investment's line of zero-expense mutual funds, which have no account minimums, with no account fees.

16.3.9   Benefits of Robo-Advisors

An investor can access where he is going with any device to monitor his portfolio and adjust his financial goals in the app as life gives them changes. While the idea of using an automated system to manage their investment portfolio may seem unattractive to some investors, for many it may be a good option for a few reasons.

Easy to access: The robo consultant can be accessed easily if there is an internet connection. Many robos are intended to straighten. But what makes them more affordable than the standard advisor for managing human resources is that money is low.

Neutrality: It is an AI-based consultant, which uses a mathematical algorithm for appraising an investor. This makes it impartial.

Comprehensive services: Today robo advisors offer a range of services that include services such as retirement planning, tax strategic schemes and portfolio re-evaluation. A quarter can manage a portfolio and reduce any debts in one place.

Tracking investment priorities: A quarterly advisor builds the investment goals based on investor's profile. Once a quarterly advisor account is created, it will continue to inspire responsible decision-making that is very critical in the future. For example, priorities such as life insurance are or long-term goals such as retirement planning are often overlooked by new investors. Robo Advisors like Paytm Money, Scripbox, and Indwealth have got a built-in mechanism that helps in tracking those goals with timely reminders.

Low cost: The main benefit of robo consultants is that they are cheaper option than the traditional consultants. By eliminating human performance, online forums provide equally costly services. Most quarterly advisers charge a flat annual fee of .5% per certificate compared to the standard 1% to 2% rate demanded by a personal financial adviser.

Efficiency: Efficiency is one of the key benefits that these Internet platforms have. For example, if anyone wants to do commercial work, he needs to meet a financial adviser, explain his requirements and then wait for it to do his job. Now, all that can be done by pressing a few buttons inside the comfort of your home.

Automated rebalance: The majority of robo-advisors rebalance customer portfolio automatically to prevent it from straying from their desired asset allocation. For an example, a investors desires asset allocation of 90% equities and 10% bonds. If stocks have a horrible year, investors portfolio will end the year with an allocation of 85% equities and 15% bonds. Robo-advisor adjusts their portfolio as a result, selling some bonds and buying more stocks.

Emotion free investment in decisions: Emotional investing is one reason why the average person's investments underperform the market. Instead of adopting the long perspective, they respond to recent market movements. They become more open to the concept of investing once the market has increased for a while since it appears "safe." It is frequently at that point, when it is overinflated and primed for a market correction, that it is least safe. Similar to when stocks decline, investors become fearful and sell. As a result, a vicious cycle of buying high and selling low is created, causing novice investors to lose money on stocks instead of making it. That's not what robots do. Instead of being driven by fear, greed, or hunches, they invest according to reasonable, long-term investing principles.

16.3.10 Limitations of Robo-Advisors

- One of the most important problems for robo consultants is their unequal level. While some use advanced AI and machine learning for creating portfolios of style, most robots in the market still prefer simpler methods.

- Lack of Robo advisors on human interference can also be an obstacle.
- High-value people with a large portfolios or those who want to take a large portion of their savings account find it less favourable. Such investors may seem to be convinced of people's advice, especially when markets are volatile
- They do not provide educational services and are less likely to teach the basics of investment and financial planning.

Can Robo Advisor replace Human?

It is impossible in the immediate future. The aim of the robo advisors is to provide resources to the previously neglected market segment and to increase the work for the human advisers. The main benefit of robo advisors is that businesses can now provide professional investment management services to investors at a fraction of the cost they would have previously done. Previously, investors would pay a consultant at least 1% of their total assets under management to manage their portfolio, but now, a quarterly adviser can do it for free or less than 0.25 percent each year. Because of the low cost and the opportunity to start with a small initial balance, investment opportunities are now available in a wide range of clients, allowing businesses to offer more attractive options to benefit their business. Companies can also use robo consultants to help their human counselors work more effectively. Applying artificial intelligence to automate basic management or monitoring tasks can free up time for counselors to focus on high-value work. Another advantage of using a learning machine to evaluate large amounts of financial data is that it can expose opportunities that human advisers may not have considered, especially when market conditions change rapidly.

16.4 Acceptance of Robo-Advisor

16.4.1 Theoretical Background and Research Propositions

According to relationship marketing paradigms and social exchange theory, the main elements of collaboration are trust, perceived risk, psychological response, and visual application. Particularly in the context of e-commerce, buyers and sellers. Robo-advisors eliminate the role of sellers because they are only used by clients [19]. A digital investment advising tool based on financial product preferences is what Robo Advisor is all about. The absence of direct communication between the consultant and the client is a key characteristic of Robo Consultants, it should be underlined.

Perceived Risk: It is defined as the investor's direct belief and fear of loss of the desired result. In this e-world, visual risk is considered as an important driver of consumer's intention to accept an technology [20].

Visual usage: According to the social exchange theory, "thoughtful usage" is a useful explanation for why customers choose to contact with people or stop doing so. The buyer assessed the usefulness of the transaction in comparison to a standard that indicates a person's cost-benefit ratio. The definition of "perceived gain" in the context of technology use is the belief that the application of new technology enhances or enhances performance [21]. The extent of consumer belief that employing robo-advisors enhances performance, productivity, and yields investment advice is referred to as approval in the context of robo-advisors.

Trust: "Trust is the loyalty of the trade partner" this is the definition of trust [22]. It is regarded crucial for developing a successful connection. Barter arrangements that could be more expensive than they might be worth are avoided. Due to the distance and lack of control customers frequently perceive greater risk online than in traditional shopping areas [23]. As a result, customers' initial form of e-commerce engagement is trust [24].

16.4.2 A Glimpse of Earlier Research Studies

An experimental research was conducted by Jung [25] to evaluate the needs of a robo-advisor from the viewpoint of the investors, it was discovered that the dimension of trustworthiness had a significant impact on how consumers with little experience, a tight budget, and low risk tolerance felt about the robo-advisors.

In a study conducted by a researcher [26], which considered 171 students of German University, were given the choice between four investment management services and the sum of 5000 euros; a human advisor, hybrid robo-advisor service [27], completely automated robo-advisor or a delegated human advisor. The researcher found that behavioural intention could be significantly predicted by anticipating performance and perceived risk. The employment of automated robo advisor services showed performance expectancy which ended up with rise in behavioural intention.

Through the perspective of the UTAUT acceptance model, a research was conducted by [28], which evaluated the uptake of robo-advisors. The study also showed a positive impact of social influence, perceived advantage and perceive trust on the intention to use robo advisors for investment management. Similar research was done by [29] using the extended TAM model as the foundation and familiarity and subjective norm were considered as additional variables. The result of the research proved that PE and PEOU were predictors of attitude towards customer intention to use the new technology called robo-advisor.

16.4.3   Methodology and Hypothesis

Taking into UTAUT [30] model as baseline, research was conducted to examine, the customer's behavioral intention to accept the emerging technology of robo-advisors. The UTAUT model was built around important predictors are performance expectancy of robo advisor, effort expectancy, trustworthiness, social influence, financial literacy, facilitating factors and tenancy to rely on them. A conceptual framework was developed to find out the predictors which will be influencing customers' decision to use robo-advisors.

Performance expectancy of robo advisor: It refers to the extent to which the customers believes the robo advisor's performance, hence they can extend their usage of the application. The current research, examines the willingness of the investors and intention to adopt robo advisor if it depends on the performance of robo advisors financial management [31].

H1: Performance expectancy has an impact on investors acceptance of robo advisors

Effort expectancy: The belief about the particular technology involves little to no effort is known as effort expectation [20]. The degree to which customers believe using robo-advisors is simple, easy, and pleasant may influence their behavioural intention to accept them.

H2: Effort expectancy has an impact on investors acceptance of robo advisors

Social influence: People at the time of taking decision whether to use a technology, often rely on the opinions of others. This is known as social influence [32].

H3: Social influence has an impact on investors acceptance of robo advisors

Facilitating conditions: The term "facilitating conditions" refers to perceived environmental facilitators or barriers on ease of usage or difficulty of carrying out an activity [31].

H4: Facilitating condition has an impact on investor's acceptance of robo advisors

Trust: In general, it has been demonstrated that consumer's desire to embrace modern technology, such as new payment systems, is driven by trust. Users intention to use robo advisor are trust worthy. Emotional unbiased decision by robo advisor can increase clients trust [28].

H5: Trust has an impact on investors acceptance of robo advisors

Perceived Financial Literacy: The self-assessed and perceived financial knowledge of the customer is referred to as financial knowledge [33].

H6: Perceived Financial knowledge has an impact on investors acceptance of robo advisors

Tendency to Relay on technology: A important predictor of the adoption of robo-advisors may be consumers' propensity to rely on them rather than human advisors [31].

H7: Tendency to relay has an impact on investors acceptance of robo advisors. A conceptual framework was developed to find out the intention to accept robo-advisors, and hypotheses H1 to H7 were plotted in the following Figure 16.2.

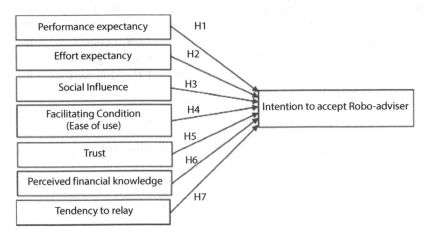

Figure 16.2 Conceptual framework & hypotheses.

16.4.4   Collection of Data

The survey data were collected from various respondents globally to measure the intention of investors towards robo advisors. In this regards, questionnaires were distributed to respondents were between the age group of 18-50 years. Further the respondents must possessed an investment portfolio. 150 respondents were considered for this study to know their intention to accept robo advisors.

16.4.5   Hypotheses Testing

SEM is used to find out how components are linked using multiple regression techniques. Multiple regression tests are a statistical method in which more than one independent variable may be analysed to predict a single dependent variable. It may also illustrate how a collection of independent factors explain a share of the variation at a significant level in a dependent variable.

The model fit indices of the proposed model are Chi-Square data is 351.045 with 154 degrees of freedom and os 2/df is 2.21 which shows an adequate fit. The GFI (Goodness of Fit Index) achieved is 0.930, while the AGFI (Goodness of Fit Adjusted Index) is 0.912, above the required 0.90. The CFI and NFI (Normal Fit index) values computed are more than 0.90, indicating that the model fits perfectly with the data. It was discovered that RMSEA is 0.038, which is lower than 0.08, and that it confirms the model fit.

SEM is used to find out how components are linked using multiple regression techniques. Multiple regression tests are a statistical method in which more than one independent variable may be analysed to predict a single dependent variable. It may also illustrate how a collection of independent factors explain a share of the variation at a significant level in a dependent variable. The Table 16.3 illustrated the different weights of regression of independent variables.

Table 16.3 Testing results - regression weights.

Hypothesis	p-value	Significance
H1	.57	.002
H2	.53	.021
H3	.28	.010
H4	.28	.022
H5	.58	.016
H6	.22	.042
H7	.36	.030

The Regression estimates and their significance for the entire path are calculated. It shows the amount of the change in dependent variable for one unit change in the independent variable. The relative contribution of each predictor variable to each dependent variable is given by the standardized estimates in the above table. The result of the model demonstrates that the behavioral desire to use financial robo-advisors is positively and significantly connected to performance expectancy. Similar to this is a favorable and statistically significant correlation between social impact and the investor's inclination to use the automated financial robo-advisors. The intention to accept the robo-advisors is correlated with investor's trust in them. Additionally, a greater correlation has been shown between perceived financial literacy/knowledge and robo-advisor usage. By implementing this advising service, investors who consider themselves to be financial literate/savvy choose to get guidance from robo-advisors. The findings also indicate that there is a behavioral desire to use financial robo-advisors that increases with the tendency to rely on this new technology based robo-advisors. The adoption of these robo-advisors are found to be affected by effort expectancy and facilitative conditions also. Investor's behavioral intention to use automated robo-advisors is significantly influenced by all the predictors.

16.5 Conclusion

Due to technological improvements in this day and age, a variety of portfolio management platforms now present the idea of the Robo-advisor as the most cutting-edge investment advisor available today. With the aid of a Robo-advisor, investors can easily manage their investment portfolio; it will help them to choose worthwhile investment possibilities depending on the risk tolerance and implementing a methodical approach.

Even though Robo-advisor will manage investor's investments and provide them with services that have risk-adjusted returns. Investors will still need to improve their financial literacy in order to understand the advice given by the Robo-advisor and in turn, make wise financial decisions.

References

1. M. Richardson and R. Clesham, "Rise of the machines? The evolving role of AI technologies in high-stakes assessment," Lond. Rev. Educ., vol. 19, no. 1, Mar. 2021, doi: 10.14324/LRE.19.1.09.
2. R. Vinuesa et al., "The role of artificial intelligence in achieving the Sustainable Development Goals," Nat. Commun., vol. 11, p. 233, Jan. 2020, doi: 10.1038/s41467-019-14108-y.
3. A. Chandani, "Robo Advisor: Emergence, Present Status, and Future," p. 7, 2022.
4. J. Trivedi, "Examining the Customer Experience of Using Banking Chatbots and Its Impact on Brand Love: The Moderating Role of Perceived Risk," J. Internet Commer., vol. 18, no. 1, pp. 91–111, Jan. 2019, doi: 10.1080/15332861.2019.1567188.
5. P. Scholz, Robo-Advisory: Investing in the Digital Age. Springer Nature, 2020.

6. J. E. Fisch, M. Labouré, and J. A. Turner, "The Emergence of the Robo-Advisor," in The Disruptive Impact of FinTech on Retirement Systems, Oxford University Press, 2019, pp. 13–37. doi: 10.1093/oso/9780198845553.003.0002.

7. Alex, "The Complete Guide To UK Robo Advisors," Smart Money Smart Living, Oct. 12, 2016. https://smartmoneysmartliving.com/2016/10/12/complete-guide-uk-robo-advisors/ (accessed Jul. 11, 2022).

8. A.-L. Kümpel, "Fintech: Bei der Geldanlage geht der Trend zum Robo Advisor," BerlinValley, Nov. 21, 2016. https://berlinvalley.com/fintech-geldanlage-trend-robo-advisor/ (accessed Jul. 11, 2022).

9. P. N. N, P, and R, "Betterment: Jon Stein," NPR, Oct. 29, 2018. Accessed: Jul. 11, 2022. [Online]. Available: https://www.npr.org/2018/10/26/661049018/betterment-jon-stein

10. "To Advise, or Not to Advise—How Robo-Advisors Evaluate the Risk Preferences of Private Investors | The Journal of Wealth Management." https://jwm.pm-research.com/content/21/2/70 (accessed Jul. 11, 2022).

11. P. A. L. de Castro and R. Annoni, "Towards autonomous investment analysts — Helping people to make good investment decisions," in 2016 Future Technologies Conference (FTC), Dec. 2016, pp. 74–80. doi: 10.1109/FTC.2016.7821592.

12. "The Use of Digital Technology and Automation in Wealth Management are creating the Growth Opportunities for the Robo Advisory Market Globally." https://www.researchdive.com/8537/robo-advisory-market (accessed Jul. 11, 2022).

13. R. Dive, "Global Robo Advisory Market Expected to Rise at a CAGR of 39.9% and Surpass $59,344.5 Million during the Forecast Period from 2021 to 2028 [228-Pages] | Confirmed by Research Dive," GlobeNewswire News Room, Mar. 23, 2022. https://www.globenewswire.com/news-release/2022/03/23/2408634/0/en/Global-Robo-Advisory-Market-Expected-to-Rise-at-a-CAGR-of-39-9-and-Surpass-59-344-5-Million-during-the-Forecast-Period-from-2021-to-2028-228-Pages-Confirmed-by-Research-Dive.html (accessed Jul. 11, 2022).

14. J. E. Fisch, M. Labouré, and J. A. Turner, "The Emergence of the Robo-Advisor," in The Disruptive Impact of FinTech on Retirement Systems, Oxford University Press, 2019, pp. 13–37. doi: 10.1093/oso/9780198845553.003.0002.

15. "All about Robo Advisory!" https://blog.finology.in/investing/robo-advisory (accessed Jul. 11, 2022).

16. "What Is A Robo-Advisor And How Does It Work? – Forbes Advisor INDIA." https://www.forbes.com/advisor/in/investing/what-is-a-robo-advisor-and-how-does-it-work/ (accessed Jul. 11, 2022).

17. "Best Robo-Advisors," Investopedia. https://www.investopedia.com/best-robo-advisors-4693125 (accessed Jul. 11, 2022).

18. B. Friedberg, "Top-10 Robo-Advisors By Assets Under Management," Forbes Advisor, Sep. 27, 2021. https://www.forbes.com/advisor/investing/top-robo-advisors-by-aum/ (accessed Jul. 11, 2022).

19. M. Bruckes, D. Westmattelmann, A. Oldeweme, and G. Schewe, "Determinants and Barriers of Adopting Robo-Advisory Services," p. 10.

20. M. Featherman, "Extending the Technology Acceptance Model by Inclusion of Perceived Risk," p. 4.

21. F. D. Davis, "Perceived Usefulness, Perceived Ease of Use, and User Acceptance of Information Technology," MIS Q., vol. 13, no. 3, pp. 319–340, 1989, doi: 10.2307/249008.

22. R. M. Morgan and S. D. Hunt, "The Commitment-Trust Theory of Relationship Marketing," J. Mark., vol. 58, no. 3, p. 20, Jul. 1994, doi: 10.2307/1252308.

23. "Toward a Generic Model of Trust for Electronic Commerce," Int. J. Electron. Commer., vol. 5, no. 2, pp. 61–74, Dec. 2000, doi: 10.1080/10864415.2000. 11044201.

24. K. Wu, Y. Zhao, Q. Zhu, X. Tan, and H. Zheng, "A meta-analysis of the impact of trust on technology acceptance model: Investigation of moderating influence of subject and context type," Int. J. Inf. Manag., vol. 31, no. 6, pp. 572–581, Dec. 2011, doi: 10.1016/j.ijinfomgt.2011.03.004.

25. D. Jung, V. Dorner, C. Weinhardt, and H. Pusmaz, "Designing a robo-advisor for risk-averse, low-budget consumers," Electron. Mark., vol. 28, no. 3, pp. 367–380, Aug. 2018, doi: 10.1007/s12525-017-0279-9.

26. A. Rühr, B. Berger, and T. Hess, "Can I Control My Robo-Advisor? Trade-Offs in Automation and User Control in (Digital) Investment Management," AMCIS 2019 Proc., Jul. 2019, [Online]. Available: https://aisel.aisnet.org/amcis2019/cognitive_in_is/cognitive_in_is/2

27. "Deloitte-Robo-safe.pdf." Accessed: Jul. 11, 2022. [Online]. Available: https://www2.deloitte.com/content/dam/Deloitte/de/Documents/financial-services/Deloitte-Robo-safe.pdf

28. P. Italia, "The role of risk and trust in the adoption of robo-advisory in Italy," p. 32.

29. D. Belanche, L. V. Casaló, and C. Flavián, "Artificial Intelligence in FinTech: understanding robo-advisors adoption among customers," Ind. Manag. Data Syst., vol. 119, no. 7, pp. 1411–1430, Aug. 2019, doi: 10.1108/IMDS-08-2018-0368.

30. "User Acceptance of Information Technology: Toward a Unified View on JSTOR." https://www.jstor.org/stable/30036540 (accessed Jul. 11, 2022).

31. L. Y. Gan, M. T. I. Khan, and T. W. Liew, "Understanding consumer's adoption of financial robo-advisors at the outbreak of the COVID-19 crisis in Malaysia," Financ. Plan. Rev., vol. 4, no. 3, p. e1127, Sep. 2021, doi: 10.1002/cfp2.1127.

32. V. Venkatesh, J. Y. L. Thong, and X. Xu, "Consumer Acceptance and Use of Information Technology: Extending the Unified Theory of Acceptance and Use of Technology," MIS Q., vol. 36, no. 1, pp. 157–178, 2012, doi: 10.2307/41410412.

33. O. Mitchell, "Older Women's Labor Market Attachment, Retirement Planning, and Household Debt," p. 38.

17

Super Apps: The Natural Progression in Fin-Tech

Kavitha D.*, Uma Maheswari B. and Sujatha R.

PSG Institute of Management, PSG College of Technology, Coimbatore, Tamil Nadu, India

Abstract

Super Apps refer to an ecosystem that includes within itself a full suite of solutions such as banking, marketplace, and lifestyle services to satisfy various needs of a user. They provide a seamless and integrated experience and save them from switching between multiple individual apps. The market space for Super Apps is highly competitive, with fin-tech giants, banking companies, and big tech rivalling each other to acquire and retain consumers. The concept of a "Super App" seems to be a natural progression from the various offerings of the fin-tech sector. This chapter provides insights into the evolution of the concept of Super Apps, the market, key players, their business models, and their role in financial inclusion. The chapter also details the risks inherent to Super Apps and the measures to mitigate the same.

Keywords: Super app, mobile application, Fin-tech, financial inclusion, consolidation, banks, financial services

17.1 Introduction

A "super app" refers to a "cluster of applications" that are contained within a single dedicated app. It refers to an ecosystem that includes a full suite of solutions such as banking, e-commerce, and lifestyle services to satisfy the various needs of a user on one single platform [8]. It serves as a one-stop solution for users and reduces the effort required to accomplish multiple tasks

---

*Corresponding author: kavitha@psgim.ac.in

Mohd Naved, V. Ajantha Devi, and Aditya Kumar Gupta (eds.) Fintech and Cryptocurrency, (383–412)

that users want to perform online [15]. They provide a seamless and integrated experience and save users from downloading and switching between multiple individual apps. Though the term "Super App" was coined by Mike Lazaridis, the founder of BlackBerry, in 2010, the increased momentum is rather recent, after the Chinese single-use app "WeChat" expanded its offering to become a "Super App". The growth of the platform-based industry has been driven largely by the rapid growth in the usage of mobile phones, more specifically smart phones, across the world. A survey by Deloitte reported that all developed countries had a mobile penetration of at least 90%, with developing countries following very closely. As in 2021, according to Statista, there were about 15 billion mobile devices used worldwide, with a smart phone penetration rate of 78% and about 6 billion smart phone subscriptions. The proliferation of mobile apps into our everyday lives has resulted in a greater need for solutions via the digital mode. This increasing reliance on digital solutions has led to the creation of numerous apps that satisfy various needs of users. From basic services such as hailing a ride to banking and payment solutions, apps seem to exist for every need of a user. Besides the applications provided by the mobile device, downloads from popular sources such as Google Play or the Apple App Store have risen to astounding levels. The onset of the pandemic has further accelerated the pace of digitization. It can be said that there is no industry now that does not have a digital presence.

Super Apps have become an indispensable part of the lives of people in most of the countries in the east, and these entities are gaining prominence as a way of life in most of the emerging economies. However, in the western world, super apps have not yet become as popular as in the east. The slow growth is attributed to the change in customer preferences during the last decade towards fragmentation and unbundling of products and services rather than bundling. The stringent data privacy policies and the cautiousness of users have also been reasons for the slow-paced growth. The concept of using a single homogenous user base to drive growth in multiple verticals is the basic ideology behind the Super App. As a business model, the Super Apps have gained popularity and have attracted huge investments from funders. Individual investors are, however, very sceptical about the business model as the long-term prospects of such investments are not very clear. The success of the early entrants into the industry has forced many players to follow suit. However, as the heterogeneity of the business model results in a defocus of businesses on their core offerings, which may disrupt strength in core verticals. In the banking and financial services industry, Super Apps have disrupted traditional banking services offered by banks and financial institutions. Though the innovative products from the fin-tech and technology giants have resulted in improving financial inclusion across the world, the flip side is, however, the creation of a monopoly due to the large user base available to the technology giants and the inherent dangers and instability that are imminent from such consolidation.

17.2   Journey from an App to a Super App

The journey to the making of a Super App requires a single-purpose app that has a strong presence and is scalable. All the major super apps in existence began their presence as single-purpose apps. This basic service offered through the app should have the potential to draw a large user base and be scalable. However, this might not be possible for all apps. In most cases, retention and revenue generation, two key factors that determine the success of an app, may not be achievable. In some cases, the user base may be present but without adequate revenue generation. In other cases, the revenue model may be clear but with a smaller user base. In such cases, there is a necessity for the app service provider to launch other apps that complement the existing service and ensure sustainability. For example, adding an e-commerce platform or payment wallet may be a natural extension for a messaging app. This imminent need to retain users and ensure adequate revenue generation has prompted several app service providers to offer solutions for multiple user needs. The next logical step would be to identify specific requirements of users and bundle existing services to create new ones or to launch new services. Initially, these extensions are restricted to the other service or product offerings of the company. Once the company has a significant user base that can be used for personalised offerings, the process then becomes a virtual loop with more user needs identified, resulting in the addition of many more apps. As many companies may not have the required competence to develop and launch apps for all the user requirements, the most feasible strategy for expansion will be through the integration of third-party apps. These third-party apps help in adding diversified services for the users. The virtual cycle then continues, resulting in the app moving from just being an app to an ecosystem of numerous mini apps to serve user needs, obtaining the status of a "Super App". Super apps are therefore a natural progression from single-solution apps (Figure 17.1).

17.3   Super App vs. A Vertically Integrated App

The key dissimilarity between a vertically integrated app and a super app is that the latter offers numerous unrelated services offered either by it or

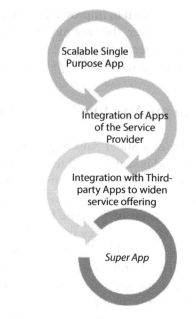

Figure 17.1 The journey from an App to a Super App.

by third-party providers. Though the services may be bundled together for better usability, they are, in most cases, diverse and unrelated. A vertically integrated app also has multiple service offerings, but all the services are related and from the same vertical. For example, Monzo offers a variety of apps for various purposes, but all of them fall into the banking/financial services sector. A Super App provides the experience of a mall, but the vertically integrated app is an easy-to-use option or as a solution for those customers who prefer a mobile app rather than internet banking. Most of the neo-banking apps also fall into this category. The basic intention is for the company to ensure that its services are available on a mobile platform. In most cases, the journey to Super App status goes through the vertically integrated app route.

17.4 Architecture and Design of Super Apps

The architecture of a Super App lays the foundation for its future developments and enhancements. It encompasses the set of techniques, patterns, and interfaces that are essential to building a fully functional system. It should be designed with a long-term perspective as it will influence the basic structure, size, and scalability of the app. The cost of operating and maintaining the Super App is also dependent on the architecture. Irrespective of the type of architecture chosen to develop the Super app, the following are some of the features that are essential for an app to be successful: testability, reliability, scalability, ease of navigation, compatibility with mobile devices, performance in the expected bandwidth and time taken for development. The mobile app architecture typically consists of three tiers: the presentation layer, the business layer, and the data layer (Figure 17.2).

Presentation Layer: This layer, also known as the user interface, is the periphery of the Super App and what is evident to the user. It consists of both the user interface (UI) and the user experience (UX). The themes to be used, fonts, colour, placement etc., form the UI. The UX determines how the user feels when interacting with the app. Hence, appropriate insights into the needs and preferences of the target user segment are essential to create a relevant UX.

Business Logic Layer: Also known as the application layer, the logic, workflow, and entities for processing client requests are encompassed in this layer. The rules for data exchange, security, data caching, authentication, exception management, and data validation are defined in this layer. The structure of this layer determines the functional efficiency and the resources required for the app. This is the most complex layer of the app.

Data Layer: This layer facilitates data transactions in the app and is crucial as it helps to meet the requirements of the app. It consists of the data utilities, access components, and service agents. The data format to be used should be carefully chosen as it determines the ease with which it can be maintained and rescaled overtime to meet changing business needs.

As Super Apps are mobile-based, the compatibility of the app with various mobile devices is crucial and should be borne in mind during the development phase. The layout of the various services provided through

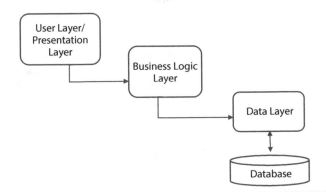

Figure 17.2 Layers in an App.

the app and the way in which they are connected, deployed, maintained, and updated is determined based on the architecture used. The following are some of the architectures adopted by leading Super Apps.

17.4.1   Monolithic Architecture

In this kind of app, the functionality is contained within a single process/container which contains several different components combined into a single process. For example, Grab follows this architecture. All the constituent modules are self-contained into one large application and are tightly coupled and interconnected with each other (Figure 17.3). The entire application functions as one large, indivisible unit. The flipside of monolithic architecture is that if there is a need to update one module, it may be difficult and resource-intensive. Also, problems in one component may cause the entire application to become dysfunctional.

17.4.2   Modular Architecture

In this type of architecture, the application is broken down into loosely coupled, smaller functional units to enable functional independence (Figure 17.4). Each module has its own process independence and performs a specific task, but can be easily linked together with other modules to form a larger application. The major advantage that this type of architecture has over a monolith is that one or more independent modules can be combined or reused to create another module based on user requirements. This helps to reduce development costs significantly, especially when

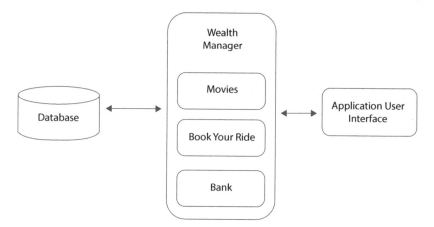

Figure 17.3 Monolithic architecture.

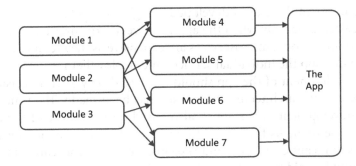

Figure 17.4 Modular architecture.

improvements are required to fulfil user expectations. Also, the modularization makes improvement and maintenance quick and less expensive.

17.4.3   Microservices Architecture

This is a service-oriented architecture in which a single application comprised of a set of small modules is developed (Figure 17.5). However, each of the constituents is a separate monolith of its own and has developed as an independent operating entity. As these modules are individual entities, they are smaller in size and easier to update based on changing user requirements. Also, updates or issues in one module will not cause problems in the remaining modules. The major benefit of the microservices architecture is that each of the modules can be developed using a different technology that will be appropriate for that particular service. This also decreases the boot-up time and memory usage of the app, making it faster.

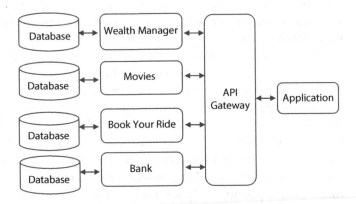

Figure 17.5 Microservices architecture.

The scalability of these apps developed using this architecture is comparatively easier, especially when the app has a very large user base. In terms of development costs, microservices are expensive as they require multiple teams to develop the individual services and deploy them.

The development of the app should be started only after a decision on the nature of the architecture to be used has been made. The time taken for the development of the app is also based on the nature of the architecture to be used. As the implications of the decision are long term and involve significant cost, time, and resources, considerable care and attention should be paid before a final decision is made.

17.5   Business Models of Super Apps

Super Apps are based on 'Digital Business Models.' A digital business model is one in which the business is characterised by digital innovation; acquisition of customers is through digital channels; payments are in the digital mode; and the digital/platform medium serves as the unique selling proposition of the Super App. There are several digital business models that are adopted by Super Apps to be profitable and to sustain profits. Some of the models that are common in the Super App space are

- Free Model: In this category, the users of the app are not charged a fee for usage. The services are offered free with the expectation of being able to monetize the user base through the introduction of one or more apps at latter stages. The revenue for such models is basically from the advertisements posted. In many super apps, a free model is used only for a few basic services, such as messaging or calling, to attract users. However, this model cannot be used for all the mini-apps within the Super App ecosystem.
- Freemium Model: In this model, the basic version of the app will be made available free of cost, but upgrades will be charged. This model is based on the expectation that users' needs will expand with continued usage of the app, and hence they will not hesitate to use a paid version of the app to avail better service offerings. On Demand/Subscription Model: In this model, the virtual services are charged based on their usage. For example, watching movies, television shows etc. This model is possible only for a few of the services within

a Super App. Essential services such as banking services, shopping, etc., cannot be offered through this model.

- Market Place Model: In this model, both the buyer and the seller use the Super App as a market place for their transaction. The revenue for the Super App company is through the transaction fees from merchants or usage charges from the customers. In some cases, there may be a fee charged for the seller to list their app on the Super App platform. This category includes the majority of ride sharing and travel booking services. Super Apps generally use a combination of the above models to attract and retain users. The success of the model depends on the extent to which the business model will be able to create and deliver value to the users.

17.6 The Super App Market Space and the Business Models

The app space is a red ocean with numerous apps for any need of a user. Not all have been able to develop into Super Apps. The following section highlights some of the key players in the segment, the services they offer and their revenue model.

17.6.1 WeChat

WeChat/Weixin, a Chinese Super App, is one of the earliest and most successful Super Apps. Popularly referred to as the 'one app that rules them all', it was developed by the Chinese technology behemoth Tencent. The journey started with WeChat messenger, an app that was initially developed by the company as a text and voice-messaging app in 2011. Within a decade of its existence, it has over a billion users and hosts numerous apps within it to serve the users' needs. The ban on several foreign websites and apps in China has been a catalyst for the astounding growth of WeChat. In 2013, the app added a payment system to enable users to transfer funds, receive money, and pay bills. As a logical extension, the addition of other services such as online booking for travel and hotels, rider sharing, investments, insurance, crowd funding, etc. has been launched. The integration of retailers into the app has resulted in the retention of a large user base. With an app for almost every need of a user, WeChat has become a Super App (Figure 17.6). Apart from the countless mini apps and innovations such as download-free apps that are lite, WeChat has been able to create a monopoly in the Chinese market. The success of the app has been attributed to its ability to imbibe the needs of Chinese users and provide services accordingly. For example, one of the most popular services of WeChat is the 'red envelope' money that the Chinese use to gift money during their new year. WeChat capitalised on this by offering a virtual 'red envelope' on its payment app, resulting in attracting users and increasing the volume of transactions.

WeChat also serves as a platform for several third-party companies and allows them to create mini-programs that can run within the app. Such mini-programs have gained popularity among users as they target specific needs and user groups. For example, Tesla's mini app helps to schedule test drives, locate the nearest charging stations, and also share their experiences. Similarly, Mobike, a bike-sharing mini-program, allows users to find bikes and use their bikes without leaving the WeChat app. Several mini-programs in the gaming domain also leverage on the user base of WeChat and have been able to become profitable in a short span of time.

Revenue Model of WeChat

Though most of the apps for individual users are free to download, WeChat also provides some of its services, such as marketing, to business clients at a cost. Revenue generation from the individual users is based on the value-added services such as stickers, games, etc. Gaming has been one major source of revenue for the firm, followed by the live streaming app. Also, due to its large user base, the app enjoys significant inflows from advertisements. The app provides bloggers the autonomy to negotiate the placement of ads within their content, which has been a key differentiator that helped the app create a loyal customer base.

As the app has made it possible for users to complete all their requirements without leaving the app, it has gained a loyal customer base. Most of the app providers, excluding key rivals of the company, have started to create a WeChat version of their app. These have also contributed to WeChat Pay being the most popular payment app among users. Though the company does not report the revenue from the app, the astounding growth of the revenue generated from the social networks has grown from 24 billion RMB in 2015 to 108 billion RMB in 2021. The fin-tech arm, which comprises the payment ecosystem, has also been a core revenue generator. As the platform has integrated its payment solutions with multiple mini apps within it, the volume of transactions has grown from 800 billion RMB in 2019 to 1.6 trillion RMB in 2020.

17.6.2   Alipay

A close competitor of WeChat, Alipay is yet another Chinese Super App. However, unlike its competitor, Alipay started off as a payment platform in 2004 for transactions done using Alibaba's e-commerce platform. The core need for a payment app emerged from the fact that some of the vendors on Alibaba's e-commerce platform failed to ship the product despite receiving the payment. As this reduced trust among the customers, Alipay, a third-party escrow payment system, was established. After the launch of the system, the seller is credited only when the product purchase is completed and verified by the buyer. The user data gathered is used to create a credit-rating for the users, which is then used by Ant Financial for its other products and services such as investments, insurance, loans, etc. The platform has evolved from a payment enabler to a digital life-service platform for the user's financial and banking needs (Figure 17.6).

Revenue Model of Alipay
As Alipay started off as an escrow account that holds the funds until the product is delivered, a large chunk of its revenue comes from the interest

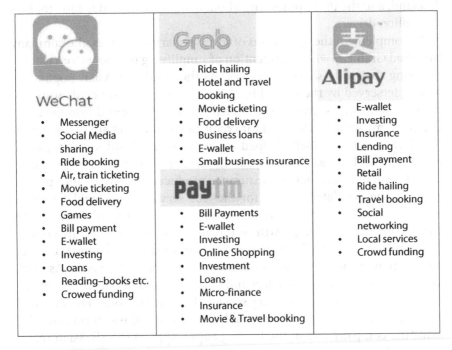

Figure 17.6 Leading super apps and their offering.

generated from the funds in the escrow account. Despite the growth of WeChat, Alipay still remains the leader in terms of transaction volume in the Chinese third-party mobile payment market. Revenue is also generated from the transaction fees that Alipay charges the merchants. Alipay also has a large credit business, "credit tech," through which loans are extended to users. The interest income, along with the partner fees and brokerage from the investment and insurance apps, yields a significant revenue. Other ancillary services such as rides, bookings, etc., and advertisements are also a source of revenue for the firm.

17.6.3   Grab

Grab, the most popular Super App in Southeast Asia, is a 2011 app launched by Singapore-based Grab Holdings Inc. The company is now worth more than $14 billion, a remarkable increase in a decade. The first app to be launched was GrabTaxi, an online ride hailing service and dispatch platform that connected provided an internet platform to connect users who were in need of a ride with those who were ready to offer one. Within a decade of its existence, Grab has grown to be one of the largest on-demand businesses. The app is extensively used in Malaysia, Singapore, Indonesia, Thailand, and the Philippines with about 6 million daily rides and employs 2.8 million drivers.

To complement the operations of its ride-sharing services, the company launched Grab Pay with the intention of simplifying payments for customers using their ride-sharing services. As the Southeast Asian population was underserved by the formal banking system and credit cards were not available to a large segment, the launch of Grab Pay tapped into the cashless economy without the need for credit cards. The 'prepaid cards' option that was launched initially helped to attract users. Besides serving as an e-wallet, Grab Pay has also forayed into the banking services by providing loans for small businesses and insurance products for drivers. The app also provides the 'pay later' option for the ride services that enables month-end accumulated payment for rides without any additional cost. Besides the organic growth, the growth of the app was propelled by the company's acquisition of Uber's business in six Southeast Asian countries, which drove it to become the largest on-demand "super app" in SE Asia. As a natural extension to leverage its fleet and to provide additional sources of revenue to the drivers, food delivery services like 'Grab Food' were launched. The addition of grocery delivery and several other fin-tech products has made the company one of the leading Super Apps in the SE Asian region (Figure 17.6).

Revenue Model of Grab

Grab's total revenue for the year 2021 was reported at $675 million, an increase of 44% from the previous year. The majority of its revenue is through the primary ride hailing services. GrabTaxi receives a portion of the revenue generated based on the per-kilometre rates that users pay for their rides. It charges between 16% (Philippines) and 25% (Malaysia) of the journey charge to use their app service. The proportion charged varies according to the area in which the ride is offered. The merchant fees and delivery charges for its food and grocery deliveries are the second largest. Though it does fin-tech solutions, the revenue from its offerings such as loans, investments, and insurance is not yet a significant contributor to its revenues. The company was able to beat many of its competitors due to its hyper-local strategy. Also, being a home-grown player has its own set of advantages, such as cultural factors that have helped Grab come up with products and solutions that ease the lives of users in the markets they serve.

17.6.4   Paytm

Paytm started off as a prepaid mobile and DTH (direct-to-home) recharge platform in 2010 and has grown to become one of the most valued fin-tech companies in the Indian subcontinent. The app has now expanded its service offering into e-commerce, travel ticket booking, movie tickets, payment for utilities etc. The Paytm Wallet is one of its primary products and has more than 450 million users. The app provides the full range of financial solutions to not just consumers but also to merchants and other online platforms. The foray into the insurance, banking, and gaming sectors has pushed the app towards becoming a Super App (Figure 17.6).

The company's mini app store has more than 1000 apps installed, making it one of the leading Super Apps in India. In its quest to increase the number of mini apps hosted, the company has made available a DIY process flow for app developers. Despite the various offerings and the increase in penetration, the company is yet to achieve profitability. It has set the pace in the Indian digital landscape.

Paytm's Revenue Model

Paytm controls approximately 14% of the digital payment market in India, with approximately USD 8 billion in transactions as of September 2021. Revenues flow from its services to individual users, business users, and through its financial services. The cloud-based and e-commerce services contribute to 25% of its revenue, while the financial services contribute the rest. The basic revenue streams in any app-based company are escrow account balances in accounts, fees on funds transfers, and user fees for their other services. The launch of 'digital gold' services and Paytm bank has accelerated the revenue generation through financial services.

17.6.5 The Latest Entrant: Tata Neu

The most recent addition to the list of Super Apps is Tata Neu. The app was launched by the conglomerate Tata Group in April 2022. The platform provides users with access to all the product and service offerings of the Tata Group. The app has started with an initial user base of 120 million users and has 2,500 offline stores enrolled. The app currently provides a wide range of customer-first services such as air ticket booking, hotel reservations, car reservations, groceries, food delivery services, and financial services such as investments, utility payments, and money transfer options. The app seeks to garner user support through its reward program, in which users can earn Neu Coins based on their transactions in the app. The app also intends to offer Neu Pass, an exclusive membership to app users that provides privileges in all Tata Brands as well as additional Neu coins for app purchases.

17.6.6 Other Players

Besides the above, there are numerous other super apps such as Go-Jek, Rappi, and Kakao that are popular in the respective countries and regions. However, the concept has yet to gain traction in western nations. Many of the players, such as Google, Apple, Square, and Paypal, are starting to expand their service offerings by developing financial service apps. Retaining giants such as Walmart and Amazon are also in the race. The huge population in China, India, and other Southeast Asian countries has been a basic factor that has led to the success of the Super Apps in those regions. The scalability of the app depends on the user base, and this could be a limiting factor for developed nations. Also, as data protection regulations are more stringent in many developed nations, this could be a deterrent to app developers. The success of WeChat in China has also been attributed mainly to the country's restrictions on other apps such as Google, Facebook, Whatsapp, etc. As such regulations do not exist in many other nations, it still remains to be seen if the other competitors are able to reach the scale and size of WeChat or Alipay.

17.7   Factors Contributing to the Success of Super Apps

The success of a Super App depends on the number of solutions that are provided and the revenue generation capability of the entire bundle of solutions provided. However, there are certain key characteristics that are worth mentioning. This section elaborates on some of the key factors that determine the success of the Super Apps.

Hardware Agnostic

Though the concept of "Super App" as given by the founder of Blackberry relied on specific hardware requirements, the developments in the industry have been to create apps that are compatible with any device irrespective of hardware specifications. For example, all leading super apps such as WeChat, Grab, Paytm, etc., are available for both Android and iOS platforms with the same functionalities.

Optimization with Mobile Device

Super Apps target mobile users and, hence, it is essential to ensure that the user experience of the app is not hindered by the capability and performance of the mobile device. As users might possess a variety of devices, it is essential for the providers to consider the entire spectrum of users and the devices that they may use. Compatibility with various screen sizes and memory capacity are two features that require the attention of app developers. The wide range of choices available to users and the compulsion to seek services through other apps lead to a stiff battle for the limited storage of mobile devices. Consequently, only the apps that are able to provide apps that are optimized for the capability of the device will survive.

User-Friendliness

User experience is crucial for the success of any app. The app should be designed so that users can comprehend and learn its usage with ease. If users must spend a large amount of time learning how to use a product before they can benefit from it, they will reject it. Even if the app can provide immediate value to users, the propensity to abandon the app is greater if the user experience is not delightful. The responsiveness of the app is one basic feature that augments the other features and enhances the user-friendliness of the app. Additionally, giving users a customised, sophisticated visual design and making the app simple to use will leave a lasting impression on their minds, encouraging them to look forward to using it rather than viewing it as a chore.

Ease of Downloading & On-boarding

This is one of the basic features of any app that requires the attention of the app developer. From a user perspective, the download size of the app is very crucial. As the mobile devices of the users are already cluttered with numerous other apps, the Super App should have an optimum size. Larger apps receive fewer downloads. The app should also facilitate easy on boarding for both the users and the vendors. If not, app fatigue will set in and users may not download the app. The sign-in process should be effortless, and the app should be able to sync the data with all its offerings. Simple and easy shopping and payment processes are also vital. For vendors, the platform should allow for simple on boarding with minimal effort and by leveraging the company's APIs.

Data Security and Privacy

Data is the foundation on which the success of a Super App rests. Super Apps rely on volumes of personal data to create unique user experiences that are personalized. These are possible only with large volumes of data collection about users. Increasing awareness among users about data privacy and infringement is forcing app providers to improve their data security systems. Though data collection and transfer laws have become more stringent than before, Super Apps in one sense reduce the amount of data collected by third-party tools that increase the risk of data piracy. The data gathered by the Super App provider creates only a closed data ecosystem, and the analysis of such first-party data to provide a personalised user experience in many countries is not classified as data tracking. However, when a super app is integrating several third-party apps within its ecosystem, it is essential to ensure the users that the data gathered will remain safe and will not be shared. Since most of the firms providing the Super Apps are large, it is essential to invest in high-security, single-tenancy data storage. Greater responsibility by the providers of super apps in such systems will instil confidence among the users and protect them from fraud and cyber-attacks.

Ability to cater to diverse users (heterogeneous market) - Inclusivity

The concept of a "Super App" seems to be an oxymoron in today's marketplace that is keen on providing personalised solutions to users. Attempt to provide a unified solution to a diverse market by integrating multiple apps. The success of WeChat can be attributed to the homogeneity of the Chinese market. However, if the market is heterogeneous, the customer acquisition costs will increase due to adaptions for multiple languages, cultures, and customer expectations. Apps such as WeChat, Grab, Alipay, and Go-Jek focus on the Asian/SE Asian/Chinese market, which is considered to be relatively more homogeneous than the western world. One reason for the slow growth of such Super Apps in the developed world is heterogeneity. Success will be guaranteed only when the app provider is able to integrate the diverse expectations.

Customer loyalty

Customer loyalty is a prime factor that ensures customer retention in the increasingly competitive app space. The success of the Super App is a logical extension of a single-purpose app. The customer loyalty of the single-use app is the primary factor that guarantees the success of the Super App. Gaining customer insights and CRM are key to acquiring a loyal customer base. In the digital landscape, creating trust amongst the users is a prime factor in retaining them. Most users may download not just one but multiple Super Apps for the sake of comparing experiences, ease of use, pricing, offers, and loyalty benefits. The key to success is to generate repetitive usage of the app without shifting to competitors. The experience provided by the Super App also helps to shift loyalty from the underlying single-use app to the Super App. Creating such loyal customers will go a long way in getting customers to use various other apps within the Super App. For example, when a customer uses a banking app within a super app and has positive experiences, the loyalty of the customer will shift from the financial services provider to the super app.

Speed of Navigation/Response

Users lose attention if the app takes longer to respond and navigate. Irrespective of the number of apps that are embedded within, the Super App should be able to provide fast navigation and response.

Tough to crack/Safe

The app should be designed with adequate safety protocols that make it tough to hack. As Super Apps gather and store vast amounts of data, ensuring that the app is built using an appropriate architecture is key to protecting the app from cyber-attacks. The design should be such that replicating the features to create a phishing attack is difficult.

Offline Mode/features
Though most of the transactions can be completed only when there is access to the internet, some basic features must be made available in the offline mode as well. This has become one of the most sought after features in many developing and underdeveloped nations where data availability is restricted. For people residing in remote regions, the availability of key services such as ride booking or banking will be an added advantage.

Integration with social media
A Super App that only offers serious apps is unlikely to succeed in the present scenario. It is necessary for the apps to provide integration with a social media platform so as to attract customers. Some of the most successful super apps, such as WeChat, started their journey by being a single-purpose app, more specifically a messaging app. The app leveraged its customer base from such social apps and hence was able to retain customers. As a result, social media apps have the highest usage of any app, and embedding one within the Super App will help improve usage and retention.

Bundling of products and pricing
An efficient bundling of the functionalities that most users might want and offering them as a service guarantees success for the Super Apps. Such an offering will become more attractive if a lower price is offered than when the individual services are available. Such deals will serve as a point of attraction for other users and stimulate demand. Bundling of services that complement each other or with a service that is in high demand can help to create demand for services that do not have a high market share. For example, offering insurance products at a discounted price for users of banking services or booking a ride when a user books a ticket for a movie, etc. are commonly bundled services.

17.8   Super Apps in Fin-Tech and their Role in the Financial Services Segment

The Ernst and Young Global Fin-tech Adoption Index (2019) showed the adoption rate stood at 64%, a huge leap from the 20165 levels of 16% [11]. Fin-Tech was initially used to refer to the firms that provided integration of technology in the financial services sector to enhance or automate the process. In some cases, fin-tech has also led to disruptive innovations in the segment. These include applications for both mobiles and computers. China and India are the leaders in the segment and have been home to several cutting-edge fin-tech firms and solutions. Though the initial years of the fin-tech revolution were contributed by start-ups, the latter years saw increasing participation from large technology players, called the Big Techs. The segment is today populated with small payers, big techs, and banks, all vying for a share in the same digital financial market-space.

The Super Apps have emerged as a significant player in the fin-tech arena with their widespread offerings (Figure 17.7). As financial applications and services draw a large number of users into the Super App platform, they have become one of the most common offerings in Super Apps. Alongside the increased usage of smartphones and the need for digital products, the large segment of the unbanked population across the world has provided a tremendous opportunity for players seeking to venture into the digital financial services segment. The digitization of the services and the possibility to provide mobile-first versions has led to a vast product and service offering in the segment. The old players in the financial services sector, such as banks and financial institutions, have also realised the opportunity. Several fin-tech firms, realising the sweet spot in the digital payment sector, have also capitalised on the opportunity. For example, paytm, which was a payment enabler, has expanded its offering in the financial services vertical. Several fin-tech companies have expanded their services beyond basic services to include more advanced technology-based products such as crypto and blockchain, as well as additional verticals such as insurance, investment, and wealth management. The financial services offered by the leading technology giants and the Super Apps are presented in Table 17.1.

Besides the large user databases that these companies possess, the transactional data available to these firms offers them a competitive advantage over the traditional banks. Using targeted marketing strategies, such firms are able to gain a greater market penetration than traditional banks. The

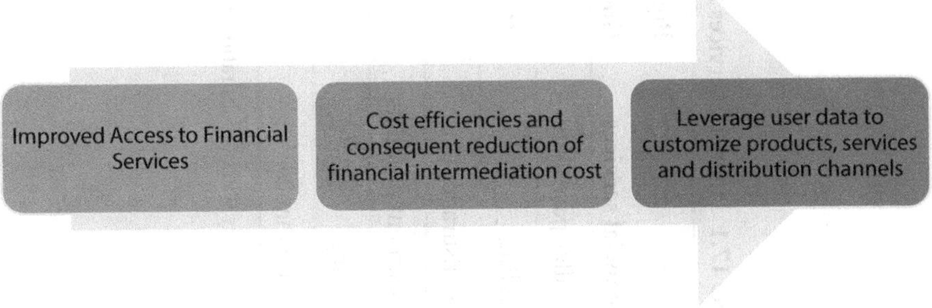

| Improved Access to Financial Services | Cost efficiencies and consequent reduction of financial intermediation cost | Leverage user data to customize products, services and distribution channels |

Figure 17.7 Potential of super apps in financial service offerings.

Table 17.1 Financial services by super apps.

| Financial services | Big Tech/Super Apps | | | | | | | |
	Google	Facebook	Amazon	Tencent (WeChat)	Ant group (Alipay)	Paytm	Tata Neu
e-wallet/payments	✓	✓	✓	✓	✓	✓	✓
Lending	✓*	✓*	✓*	✓	✓	✓	
Life Insurance			✓	✓	✓	✓	✓
Investment products				✓	✓	✓	✓
Banking	✓*			✓	✓	✓%	
Micro Finance				✓	✓	✓	

✓* Indirectly with collaborations; ✓ - Directly; ✓% - Limited operations alternative data that is possessed by fin-tech firms has been found to have better predictive ability in determining financial needs, credit scores, and repayment patterns [7]. Fraud detection and income-estimation models have also been found to work better with additional behavioural and transactional data generated from Super Apps [3, 5].

17.9   Role of Super Apps in Financial Inclusion

The number of unbanked adults across the globe is about 1.7 billion, indicating the high opportunity available for banks and financial service providers. Financial inclusion is not a factor just in developing and underdeveloped nations. For example, the survey by the Federal Deposit Insurance Corporation (FDIC) in the US in 2019 reported that 7.1 million households in the country were unbanked. About 50% of these cited minimum-balance requirements of banks as a barrier to accessing a formal bank. Despite the attention of policymakers and governments, inclusion still remains a challenge, especially in the developing and underdeveloped regions. The inclusion of this underserved category into the banking ambit will aid in creating a social transformation and also improve the economic well-being of those segments. The impact is not just in the individual segment but also on the business segment as well. Many of the small businesses that are not able to access a formal financial service provider will be better off due to the innovative product offerings of the fin-tech sector [9]. The fact that 79% of adults in developing economies own a phone has made financial inclusion a possibility. Technology-driven financial innovations have the potential to further financial inclusion as they can by-pass the current infrastructural barriers in the traditional banking sector [12].

For example, in India, Paytm has helped numerous small and micro businesses jump into digitised payments. Paytm karo', meaning do paytm transfer, has become almost synonymous with any payment. Because the business model does not charge merchants a commission, adoption has been extremely high. This has led to the creation of an entire ecosystem of services that are required by these small merchants, such as loans, insurance, etc. The inclusion of services for the unorganised and informal sector has led to the rapid growth of Paytm in India.

Similarly, on the African continent, super apps such as Jumia Pay, Haabari, M_Pesa, Whatsapp, and Facebook have gained prominence. As Super Apps are not data-heavy, the user base has increased substantially. Large numbers of citizens do not have access to the system or are not integrated into the formal banking system. The financial services provided through the Super Apps, due to their low level of complexity and ease of use, have gained acceptance across the continent.

As financial inclusion drives economic growth [1], governments are viewing mobile-first services as a means to achieve their inclusion objectives. The incumbents in the industry are also gearing up to match the Super App revolution. For example, DBS bank has been fast in the process of jumping into the platform-based bandwagon. DigiBank, its platform-based operations, provides all banking operations on the smart phone in India and Indonesia. Besides the traditional banking services, the bank has also provided a platform for buying and selling used cars, for travel and real estate. State Bank of India (SBI) has launched its digital platform Yono in India, which gives users access to a variety of financial and allied services such as travel bookings, online shopping, bill payments, and so on.

The regulatory norms that bind the traditional banks and their traditional ways of operations act as a limiting factor in creating solutions that enable people with lower education levels and weaker economic backgrounds. Most of the app-based financial service products from players in the non-banking arena have captured users only based on their user-friendly features. Solutions targeting the unbanked population use several key elements such as local language options, simple financial terminologies, graphical user interfaces, and simple authentication processes, etc. Some of the Super Apps also heavily leverage on the cultural aspects that affect the savings and payment patterns of users in a particular region or country.

Though the traditional financial service sector operators are bound to adhere to more stringent regulatory norms, the shift in customer requirements from an offline to an online array of services has forced them to either provide digital solutions on their own or partner with leading platforms to offer Banking as a service (Baas). In these kinds of offerings, incumbent banks integrate their services or products with a third party. This has been possible with open banking and API integration. For example, the Apple Credit Card is backed by Goldman Sachs Bank. Numerous point-of-sale loans disbursed by the Super Apps are an example of Baas. The rise of open banking, a phenomenon in which Super Apps collect financial data from multiple sources in order to identify financial needs and target customers, also helps to serve the excluded segments of the population. The increasing trend of offering banking-as-a-service on apps has also resulted in greater financial inclusion, which is expected to grow in the future.

17.10   Benefits of Super Apps in the Financial Services Sector

The Super Apps provide numerous benefits to the banking and financial services sector (Figure 17.8) in comparison to the traditional banks and financial institutions. Some of them are

17.10.1   Economies of Scale & Cost of Financial Intermediation

The traditional banking sector, despite its large customer base, is facing a risk due to its inability to reduce the cost of financial intermediation. The cost is as high as what it was in the 1900s. The various technological advancements have failed to help the banks reduce this. Fin-tech is a way in which this is made possible, specifically those in the Super App category. The large number of users and the huge volumes of user data generated make it possible for the app to offer financial services based on user need. Also, the reduction in human intervention required to take the service [3] to the customer helps to reduce the cost significantly. Contradictory to this, in a traditional banking environment, the presence of a branch with staff would be necessary, adding to the cost of intermediation. In contrast, the large and growing user base of the Super Apps has made the platform-based financial services more scalable. Also, new products rely on technological advancements and have very low fixed cost structures [6].

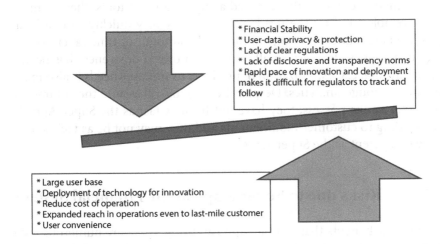

Figure 17.8 Benefits and risks.

By attracting more users, the cost per user goes down significantly for these operators, which in turn helps them offer them at more competitive terms for the unserved category.

17.10.2 Size & Speed of Product and Service Offerings

Most of the Super Apps have been able to create products and services that cater to even the smallest requirements of their users. With access to high volumes of user data, the Super Apps are able to make very quick decisions on whether a customer is eligible for a product or not. For example, Alipay takes only three minutes to validate the customer and approve a loan. As most of these small customers will not be able to fulfil the requirements of a traditional bank, the Super Apps have been able to capture that market share. Also, as the processing costs would be higher in many cases than the financial needs of small users, they are excluded from the formal banking system. Sometimes, processes such as filling out forms, providing the required documents, and the waiting period of incumbent banks intimidate users. As they are technically reduced in a digital world, Super Apps have been able to bring numerous such users into the formal banking ambit.

17.10.3 The Power of Data and the Speed of Responsiveness

As indicated earlier, the live user data that Super Apps own has been the key to their success. With advanced analytics and AI tools, these companies are able to sense the needs of their users very quickly. Similarly, as products are launched in digital mode, the amount of time taken to create such apps is also very small. This speed of responsiveness has been a great advantage. Customization of products to suit user needs is also made possible through analytics. Despite the large user base and the volumes of data that banks possess, they have not been as fast as the Super Apps in responding to customer requirements and they may not be as technologically competent as the Super Apps.

17.11 Risks due to Super Apps in the Financial System

Despite the benefits that a Super App can bring, there are numerous risks that arise due to such technology-based operations (Figure 17.8). Some of them are as follows.

17.11.1   Financial Stability

The entry of the Super Aps into the financial services arena has been regulated by strict policies to ensure financial stability within the financial system. As their services rely on innovations through technology developments, some of the traditional regulations such as liquidity and solvency requirements cannot be enforced on them, increasing the risk for the customers. However, some of the Super Apps such as Paytm have been able to gain an entry into the banking segment in India through the 'payments bank' licence obtained in 2017. Though credit cards cannot be issued and loans cannot be advanced, the payment bank has made banking services possible for numerous small businesses. The bank, in its short span of existence, has about 300 million wallets and 60 million bank accounts, giving a big push to financial inclusion in India.

Tencent, the company offering WeChat, has been able to obtain permission from the regulators for micro financing, insurance, and mutual fund investments on its messenger platform. Even in developed nations, there is a gradual shift in the financial services offerings, with Facebook and Apple leveraging their payment platforms for payment applications. Sector specific risks that undermine financial stability can be overcome by framing regulations for the platform operators. The flipside of this is that innovation may be curtailed. Also, as competition is very high, the platform-based models may seek to increase their revenues without verifying if the customer is credit-worthy or not. The increased revenue generated by the user experience on the platform's other apps will serve as an incentive for such actions. If left unregulated, this will result in increased operational risks and will be a huge threat to the financial system.

17.11.2   Market Concentration

The rapid expansion of Super Apps creates a systemic risk [14] in the financial system. The risk is high in the Asian countries where Super Apps are more prominent and have a large user base. A significant threat emerges due to the market concentration that is possible due to the Super Apps. Concentration risk arises from not just the users enrolled in the app but also because the big techs are the cloud service providers for the incumbent banks as well. The vulnerabilities from such high dependence create a potential threat to the system. The data possessed by the Super Apps will by itself result in a huge data asymmetry, leading to concentration and dominance in the market. In China, the high degree of concentration is observed using measures of HHI (Herfindahl–Hirschman Index), a measure of market concentration [2].

17.11.3   Dis-Intermediation of Banks from Customer

The ease of use of platform-based apps, as well as their rapid adoption results in significant disintermediation of banks from customers. Fin-tech innovations have led to the removal of multiple layers that existed in the payment system. The dependence on the platforms for payment systems leads to further disintermediation. As more layers are added between the bank and the customer, a shift in customer loyalty from the bank to the Super App will happen. Customer relationships will, in such cases, move away from the bank to the app provider.

17.12   Regulatory Measures to Mitigate the Risks

As the above risks are imminent and the fact that Super Apps and their dominance cannot be ignored, countries have geared up by formulating regulations to mitigate the risks [4]. Some countries have very stringent regulatory mechanisms in place, while a few others have a "let things happen" approach. Not all the regulations have a curtailing effect on the system. For example, in India, the launch of the UPI has been a catalyst for the digital economy while at the same time increasing the power of the Reserve Bank of India. As data privacy and the concentration of the market pose imminent risks, several countries have formulated new or amended old regulations accordingly. Some of the prominent regulations are presented in Table 17.2.

17.13   The Future of Super Apps

Despite the fact that Super Apps seem to be a logical extension to single-purpose apps and that they have been successful in some countries, there are several challenges. In the West and in more developed economies, the adoption of Super Apps cannot be expected to be as fast or large as that in China and India. Consumers in the developed nations are more mature and are already using well established traditional financial products, which reduces the need for Super Apps. Though digital versions of traditional products will be a necessity, they may rely on the bank for such services [13]. The legacy industry has well established and developed

Table 17.2 Key regulatory initiatives.

Name of the initiative	Details	Countries where applicable
Unified Payments Interface (UPI)	An instant real-time payment system that can be accessed by all payment service providers, UPI helps to link more than one bank account into a single mobile application for transfer of funds	India
Regulation on Non-banking Payment Agencies by PBOC	Regulations for setting up and operation of non-banking payment agencies	China
Know Your Customer (KYC)	Collection and periodic updation of details of customers as done by a traditional bank	Many Countries
Measures for Protection of Financial Consumer Rights and Interests, 2020	Incorporation of appropriate measures to protect rights and interests of financial consumers through corporate governance and internal control systems	China
General Data Protection Regulation (GDPR)	Implemented in 2018, laid rules with regard to the processing of personal data. It made obtaining customer consent necessary before information can be shared.	European Union
Data Privacy Regulation	Available in most countries with varying levels of intensity to protect valuable customer data.	Few best include California, Australia, Singapore, China, Switzerland, India

products that fit the needs of the users in these nations. Also, the usage of computers is high in developed nations, and hence a smart phone-based application may not be a real need. Also, developed nations have a well-established internet economy, which has also been cited as a reason for the slow-growth of Super Apps [10]. In developed countries, trust in Super Apps for data protection is also low, posing a challenge to the growth of such apps in the financial services sector.

The growth of the Super Apps in China was also largely due to the ban imposed by the Chinese government on the Big Techs such as Google, Twitter, Facebook etc. This is not the case in the developed nations, where the technology giants have a significant user base. The dominance of the Super Apps in the SE Asian region and Africa in the payment sector relies on creating a cashless economy. However, in the West, cashless may not fit the bill due to the high dependence on credit-based patterns. For example, in the US, credit cards occupy a large market share and it may be difficult to move such customers to a cashless option that requires a cash balance in the account. The need to conquer the emerging user base in the developed nations requires technology giants and traditional banks to forge partnerships so as to create innovative solutions to tap the users.

17.14   Conclusion

Super Apps have disrupted the operations of not just the traditional financial services sector but also the fin-tech industry. The ease with which the Super Apps customise service offerings for their large user base. The immense value that such services have created for their users has fuelled their success. The deregulation of Super Apps and the adoption of an open banking architecture in many countries are sure to increase the markets for Super Apps. The increasing prominence also leads to an increase in the regulatory landscape, creating more challenges. Data privacy laws, competition laws, and consumer protection laws will determine the pace of growth of the Super Apps. The key feature of personalization may also not remain if such stringent rules come into force. Though numerous competitors may exist in the initial phases, not all players will be able to grow and sustain. This will create a lop-sided market resulting in a monopoly or monopolistic market, leading to more monitoring and operating regulations, which in turn lead to numerous legal battles. But, until then, all seems rosy for the Super Apps.

References

1. A. Barajas, T. Beck, M. Belhaj, S. B. Naceur, V. Cerra, and M. S. Qureshi, Financial inclusion: what have we learned so far? What do we have to learn? *IMF Working Papers*, 2020. doi: 10.5089/9781513553009.001

2. Financial Stability Board, FinTech and market structure in financial services: Market developments and potential financial stability implications. *Financial Innovation Network, Financial Stability Board, Basel, Switzerland, 2019.*

3. G. Suarez, J. Raful, M. A. Luque, C. F. Valencia, and A. Correa-Bahnsen, Enhancing User's Income Estimation with Super-App Alternative Data. *arXiv preprint arXiv:2104.05831,* 2021. doi; 10.48550/arXiv.2104.05831

4. J. C. Crisanto, J. Ehrentraud, and M. Fabian, Big techs in finance: regulatory approaches and policy options. *FSI Briefs*, Vol.12, pp. 1-15, 2021.

5. J. D. Acevedo-Viloria, S. S. Pérez, J. Solano, , D. Zarruk-Valencia, , F. G. Paulin, and A. Correa-Bahnsen, Feature-Level Fusion of Super-App and Telecommunication Alternative Data Sources for Credit Card Fraud Detection. *2021 IEEE International Conference on Intelligence and Security Informatics (ISI)*. pp. 1-6, 2021. doi: 10.1109/ISI53945.2021.9624796

6. K. Croxson, J. Frost, L. Gambacorta, and T. Valletti, Platform-based business models and financial inclusion. *BIS Papers*, 2022.

7. L. Roa, A. Correa-Bahnsen, G. Suarez, F. Cortés-Tejada, M. A. Luque, and C. Bravo, Super-app behavioral patterns in credit risk models: Financial, statistical and regulatory implications. *Expert Systems with Applications*, Vol.169, pp.114486, 2021. doi: 10.1016/j.eswa.2020.114486

8. M. Steinberg, LINE as super app: Platformization in East Asia. *Social Media+ Society*, Vol.6, No.2, 2020. 2056305120933285.

9. P. K. Ozili. Financial inclusion research around the world: A review. *Forum for social economics*. Vol.50, No.4, pp. 457-479, 2021. doi:10.1080/07360932. 2020.1715238

10. R. Rodenbaugh, A deep dive into super apps and why they're booming in the East and not the West. Tech in Asia. Available at: https://www.techinasia. com/deep-dive-super-appbooming-east-not-west, 2020.

11. S. Walden, What is fintech and how does it affect how I bank. *Forbes Advisor,* 2020.

12. T. Chinoda, and F. Kwenda, Do mobile phones, economic growth, bank competition and stability matter for financial inclusion in Africa?. *Cogent Economics & Finance*. Vol. 7, No.1, pp.1622180, 2019. doi: 10.1080/23322039.2019.1622180

13. V. Murinde, E. Rizopoulos, and M. Zachariadis The impact of the Fin Tech revolution on the future of banking: Opportunities and risks. *International Review of Financial Analysis*, Vol.81, p.102103, 2022. doi: 10.1016/j.irfa. 2022.102103

14. X. Vives Digital disruption in banking. *Annual Review of Financial Economics*, Vol.11, pp.243-272, 2019.

15. Y. Zhang-Zhang, S. Rohlfer, and J. Rajasekera, An eco-systematic view of cross-sector FinTech: The case of Alibaba and Tencent. *Sustainability*, Vol.1 2, No.21, pp.8907, 2020. doi:10.3390/su12218907
16. https://global.alipay.com
17. https://grab.com
18. https://paytm.com
19. https://www.statista.com/statistics/245501/multiple-mobile-device-ownership-worldwide/#:~:text=In%202021%2C%20the%20number%20of,devices%20 compared%20to%202020%20levels
20. https://www.statista.com/statistics/203734/global-smartphone-penetration-per-capita-since-2005/
21. https://www.tata.com/tatadigital
22. https://www.wechat.com

Index

Page numbers followed by f and t indicate figures and tables, respectively.

Also of Interest

Check out these other Related Titles

VALUE FOR MONEY: How to Show the Value for Money for All Types of Projects and Programs in Governments, Non-Governmental Organizations, Nonprofits, and Businesses, By Patricia Pulliam Phillips, Jack J. Phillips, Gina Paone, and Cyndi Huff Gaudet, ISBN: 9781119322658. The most thorough, comprehensive, and detailed explanation of showing the value for money in the public sector.

THE VALUE OF INNOVATION: Knowing, Proving, and Showing the Value of Innovation and Creativity, By Jack J. Phillips and Patricia Pulliam Phillips, ISBN: 9781119242376. Written by some of the most well-known authors in the world for using ROI (Return On Investment) strategies and processes, this groundbreaking new volume provides practical, easy-to-implement methodologies for measuring the impact and ROI for any creativity or innovation program.

ENRON ASCENDING: The Forgotten Years, 1984â€"1996, By Robert L. Bradley Jr Series: Political Capitalism (A Tetralogy), ISBN: 9781118549575. *Enron Ascending: The Forgotten Years* is the third installment of Bradleyâ€™s tetralogy on political capitalism, inspired by the rise and fall of Enron.

EDISON TO ENRON: ENERGY MARKETS AND POLITICAL STRATEGIES: Book 2 in a Tetralogy on Political Capitalism, By Robert L. Bradley Jr., ISBN: 9780470917367. While explaining the connections between Enron and Edison, the book takes the reader through the flamboyant history of the American energy industry and sets the stage for Ken Lay's entry on the energy stage.

CAPITALISM AT WORK: Business, Government and Energy, By Robert L. Bradley Jr., ISBN: 9780976404170. Provides a penetrating and multidisciplinary explanation of the demise of Enron and breaks new ground regarding public policies toward business.

FACTORIES OF THE FUTURE: Technological Advances in the Manufacturing Industry, Edited by Chandan Deep Singh and Harleen Kaur, ISBN: 9781119864943. The book provides insight into various technologies adopted and to be adopted in the future by industries and measures the impact of these technologies on manufacturing performance and their sustainability.

ARTIFICIAL INTELLIGENCE AND DATA MINING IN SECURITY FRAMEWORKS, Edited by Neeraj Bhargava, Ritu Bhargava, Pramod Singh Rathore, and Rashmi Agrawal, ISBN 9781119760405. Written and edited by a team of experts in the field, this outstanding new volume offers solutions to the problems of security, outlining the concepts behind allowing computers to learn from experience and understand the world in terms of a hierarchy of concepts.

MACHINE LEARNING AND DATA SCIENCE: Fundamentals and Applications, Edited by Prateek Agrawal, Charu Gupta, Anand Sharma, Vishu Madaan, and Nisheeth Joshi, ISBN: 9781119775614. Written and edited by a team of experts in the field, this collection of papers reflects the most up-to-date and comprehensive current state of machine learning and data science for industry, government, and academia.

SECURITY ISSUES AND PRIVACY CONCERNS IN INDUSTRY 4.0 APPLICATIONS, Edited by Shibin David, R. S. Anand, V. Jeyakrishnan, and M. Niranjanamurthy, ISBN: 9781119775621. Written and edited by a team of international experts, this is the most comprehensive and up-to-date coverage of the security and privacy issues surrounding Industry 4.0 applications, a must-have for any library.

CYBER SECURITY AND DIGITAL FORENSICS: Challenges and Future Trends, Edited by Mangesh M. Ghonge, Sabyasachi Pramanik, Ramchandra Mangrulkar, and Dac-Nhuong Le, ISBN: 9781119795636. Written and edited by a team of world renowned experts in the field, this groundbreaking new volume covers key technical topics and gives readers a comprehensive understanding of the latest research findings in cyber security and digital forensics.

DEEP LEARNING APPROACHES TO CLOUD SECURITY, edited by Pramod Singh Rathore, Vishal Dutt, Rashmi Agrawal, Satya Murthy Sasubilli, and Srinivasa Rao Swarna, ISBN 9781119760528. Covering one of the most important subjects to our society today, this editorial team delves into solutions taken from evolving deep learning approaches, solutions allow computers to learn from experience and understand the world in terms of a hierarchy of concepts.

MACHINE LEARNING TECHNIQUES AND ANALYTICS FOR CLOUD SECURITY, Edited by Rajdeep Chakraborty, Anupam Ghosh and Jyotsna Kumar Mandal, ISBN: 9781119762256. This book covers new methods, surveys, case studies, and policy with almost all machine learning techniques and analytics for cloud security solutions.

SECURITY DESIGNS FOR THE CLOUD, IOT AND SOCIAL NETWORKING, Edited by Dac-Nhuong Le, Chintin Bhatt and Mani Madhukar, ISBN: 9781119592266. The book provides cutting-edge research that delivers insights into the tools, opportunities, novel strategies, techniques, and challenges for handling security issues in cloud computing, Internet of Things and social networking.

DESIGN AND ANALYSIS OF SECURITY PROTOCOLS FOR COMMUNICATION, Edited by Dinesh Goyal, S. Balamurugan, Sheng-Lung Peng and O.P. Verma, ISBN: 9781119555643. The book combines analysis and comparison of various security protocols such as HTTP, SMTP, RTP, RTCP, FTP, UDP for mobile or multimedia streaming security protocol.

Printed in the USA/Agawam, MA
May 21, 2024

866493.001